"Florian Schmidlechner's *Animation in Austria* takes readers on a captivating journey through the Austrian animation scene, offering valuable insights into both the artistry and technology behind it, making it a must-read for enthusiasts and professionals alike."

Virgil Widrich, *Oscar-nominated and award-winning Austrian director, screenwriter, and multimedia artist, acclaimed for his groundbreaking contributions to film and digital art.*

"The emergence of the new Austrian animated film is presented in an exemplary manner. The texts are authentic, factually accurate, and meticulously researched – highly recommended."

Hubert Sielecki, *father of the Studio for Experimental Animated Film at the University of Applied Arts Vienna, founder of ASIFA Austria, artist, and animated filmmaker.*

Animation in Austria

This book provides a comprehensive account of Austrian animation history, as well as an analysis of the current state of the industry in competition with American and cheaper international products in the face of dwindling budgets.

The book outlines the history of the Austrian animated film from the actual beginnings at the time of the First World War. It looks at the reconstruction of the animation industry during the 1950s and 1960s and covers experimental animation from the 1970s onward. The final part of the book explores modern Austrian animation and looks ahead to the future of animation production within the country.

This book will be of great interest to academics, students, and professionals working and researching in the field of animation.

Florian Schmidlechner has been researching animation history at the University of Vienna's Institute of Contemporary History since 2007. Alongside his publishing and lecturing, he has contributed to international projects such as the US DVD *More Cartoons for Victory!* (2012) and a 2015 documentary for German television. Recently, he co-authored a chapter on the history of the Austrian animated film for *The Encyclopedia of Animation Studies*, published by Bloomsbury.

European Animation Series

Series Editor:

Rolf Giesen, a German film historian, screenwriter, lecturer, and collector who specialized in VFX and animation, Germany.

European Animation explores the current state of animation production in various European countries derived from a social, historic, political, economic, and artistic background. The series tells what made animated movies possible in Europe and is a prognosis foreseeing a change in future animation production.

Animation in Croatia: Zagreb School and Beyond
Midhat Ajanovic

Animation in Germany
Rolf Giesen

Animation in Austria: An Almost Invisible Art
Florian Schmidlechner

For more information about this series, please visit http://www.routledge.com/European-Animation/book-series/EUANIM

Animation in Austria
An Almost Invisible Art

Florian Schmidlechner

CRC Press
Taylor & Francis Group
Boca Raton London New York

CRC Press is an imprint of the
Taylor & Francis Group, an **informa** business

Designed cover image: Benjamin Swiczinsky

First edition published 2025
by CRC Press
2385 NW Executive Center Drive, Suite 320, Boca Raton FL 33431

and by CRC Press
4 Park Square, Milton Park, Abingdon, Oxon, OX14 4RN

CRC Press is an imprint of Taylor & Francis Group, LLC

ISBN: 978-1-032-54148-8 (hbk)
ISBN: 978-1-032-54164-8 (pbk)
ISBN: 978-1-003-41544-2 (ebk)

DOI: 10.1201/9781003415442

Typeset in Times
by codeMantra

To my father, Josef (1945–2024), whose almost invisible struggle mirrored Clark Kent's unseen strength before he dons the Superman cape. Fly in Peace.

Contents

Acknowledgments

I want to express my deepest gratitude to everyone who has supported and inspired me throughout the journey of creating this book:

Josef Aichholzer, Dirk Alt, Sandra Annett, Thomas Ballhausen, Paul Barritt, Jerry Beck, Laraine Bennett, Dunja Bernatzky, Dieter Bernauer-Schilcher, Franz Blaas, Thomas Bogner, Sarah Braid, Ulu Braun, Paolo Caneppele, Rastko Ćirić, Joanna Crowley, Johannes Ecker, Corinna Eigner, Michael Enter, Michael Epstein, Richard Fehsl, Wolfgang Georgsdorf, Felix Geremus, Susanne Gierczynski, Rolf Giesen, Gottfried Gusenbauer, Jürgen Hagler, Bettina Haintz, Vivien Halas, Peter Hathorn, Bernhard Hemetsberger, Peter Höhsl, Lars Jakobsen, Nikolaus Jantsch, Eszter Kondor, Renate Kordon, Ilse Kovacevic, Gerald Kreisel, Marcello La Speranza, Silvia Lang, Norbert Lechner, Susanne Lindtberg, Inge Link, Matthias Markl, Robert Mastny, Ulrike Messer-Krol, Karin Moser, Andreas Munck, Isabell Munck, Márton Orosz, René Perraudin, Franziska Proksa (née Bruckner), Axel Puluj, Christian Puluj, Peter Putz, Wolfgang Reinisch, Thomas Renoldner, Florian Satzinger, Joachim Schätz, Bernd Scheithauer, Thomas Schleischitz, Kristina Schmiedl, Birgit Scholin, Sebastian Claudius Semler, Hubert Sielecki, Christoph Staber, Thomas Steiner, Claudius Stemmler, J.P. Storm, Stefan Stratil, Rolf Stumm, Daniel Šuljić, Benjamin Swiczinsky, Gerd Titelbach, Peter Tscherkassky, Leah Vrecer, Marianne Weichberger, Paul Wenninger, Virgil Widrich, Alexander Wieser, Anne Zwiener, and Walter Zwiener.

The author conducted interviews with:

Josef Aichholzer	June 20, 2023, in Vienna
Paul Barritt	June 8, 2023, in Graz
Richard Fehsl and Ilse Kovacevic	February 17, 2024, in Vienna
Nikolaus Jantsch and Praved Krishnapilla (in collaboration with Franziska Proksa)	April 10, 2024, in Vienna
Florian Satzinger	June 9, 2023, in Graz
Birgit Scholin (as an online conference, in collaboration with Franziska Proksa)	May 28, 2024, in Vienna
Stefan Stratil	February 9, 2024, in Vienna
Benjamin Swiczinsky	July 5, 2023, in Vienna
Anne and Walter Zwiener (as an online conference)	September 26, 2023, in Vienna and Dornbirn

All interviewees provided their consent to be quoted.

The author conducted telephone conversations with:

Michael Enter	October 20, 2023
Michael Epstein	November 27, 2023

Richard Fehsl	June 28, 2023
Florian Julino	June 22, 2023
Rüdiger Morawetz	October 2, 2023
Marianne Weichberger	March 24, June 23, and September 24, 2024

The following archives, libraries, and institutions have generously provided information and documents in support of this work:

Archiv der Akademie der Künste, Berlin/Archives of the Akademie der Künste (Academy Archives), Berlin (thanks to Susan Todd)

Archiv des Künstlerhauses, Wien/Vienna Künstlerhaus Archives (thanks to Nikolaus Domes)

Archiv Institut Kadotheum Wien/Archive Institute Kadotheum Vienna (thanks to Robert Kaldy-Karo)

Archiv Maria Lassnig Stiftung, Wien/Archive of the Maria Lassnig Foundation, Vienna (thanks to Johanna Ortner)

ASIFA Austria, Wien/ASIFA Austria, Vienna (thanks to Thomas Renoldner, Stefan Stratil, and Daniel Šuljić)

Bibliothek und Sammlungen der Höheren Graphischen Bundes-Lehr- und Versuchsanstalt Wien/Library and Collections of the Federal Training and Research Institute for Graphic Arts and Media Vienna (thanks to Klaus Walder)

Bundesarchiv (BArch), Berlin/German Federal Archives, Berlin (thanks to Jonas Nordheim)

Bürgerservice Gemeinde Kreuttal/Citizen Service Office of the Municipality of Kreuttal (thanks to Elisabeth Essl)

Das Ewige Archiv, ewigesarchiv.at/The Eternal Archives, ewigesarchiv.at (thanks to Peter Putz)

Graz Museum (thanks to Katharina Mraček-Gabalier)

HTL Spengergasse, Abteilung Design, Wien/HTL Spengergasse, Department of Design, Vienna (thanks to Karin Gibley and Werner Pramel)

Karikaturmuseum Krems, Kunstmeile Krems Betriebs GmbH/Caricature Museum Krems, Art Mile Krems (thanks to Daniela Bernhard and Gottfried Gusenbauer)

Kunsthandel Hitzenberger, Wien/Art Trade Hitzenberger, Vienna (thanks to Michaela Hitzenberger)

Kunstsammlung und Archiv, Universität für angewandte Kunst Wien/Collection and Archive, University of Applied Arts Vienna (thanks to Nathalie Feitsch)

Ludwig Boltzmann Institute for Digital History (LBIDH), Vienna (thanks to Vrääth Öhner)

Magistrat der Stadt Wiener Neustadt/Municipality of the City of Wiener Neustadt (thanks to Matthias Kasteiner)

Marktgemeinde Bad Deutsch-Altenburg/Market Town Bad Deutsch-Altenburg (thanks to Brigitte Hofer-Siller)

Österreichische Akademie der Wissenschaften (ÖAW), Wien/Austrian Academy of Sciences, Vienna (thanks to Irene Nawrocka)

Österreichische Mediathek, Technisches Museum Wien/Austrian Mediathek, Vienna Technical Museum

Österreichisches Staatsarchiv (ÖStA), Wien/Austrian State Archives, Vienna (thanks to Dieter Lautner and Hana Keller)
Otto and Marie Neurath Isotype Collection, University of Reading (thanks to Emma Minns)
Sternwarte Kremsmünster/Observatory of Kremsmünster (thanks to P. Amand Kraml)
Svenska Filminstitutet, Bildarkivet/Swedish Film Institute, Stills Archive, Stockholm, Sweden (thanks to Krister Collin and Julia Mettenleiter)
Toonder Compagnie BV, Amsterdam (thanks to Willem Feltkamp)
Tricky Women/Tricky Realities, Culture2Culture, Vienna (thanks to Waltraud Grausgruber and Tanja Putzer)
Universitätsarchiv der Akademie der bildenden Künste Wien/Academy of Fine Arts Vienna, University Archives (thanks to Ulrike Hirhager)
Universitätsbibliothek der Universität Wien (UB Wien)/University Library of Vienna (thanks to Louise Hartmann)
Verband Österreichischer Film-Autoren (VÖFA), Neunkirchen/Association of Austrian Film Authors, Neunkirchen (thanks to Peter Glatzl and Egon Stoiber)
Verstorbenensuche Friedhöfe Wien/Deceased Search Vienna Cemeteries (thanks to Gerald Bartosch)
VIENNALE Office Management, Vienna (thanks to Hellmut Goebl)
Wiener Stadt- und Landesarchiv, Wien/Municipal and Provincial Archives of Vienna (thanks to Michaela Laichmann)

Film Archives

AV-Medienstelle der Diözese Innsbruck/AV Media Service of the Diocese of Innsbruck (thanks to Bernhard Lammer)
CLAAS KGaA mbH, Group History (Archive), Harsewinkel
Deutsches Landwirtschaftsmuseum (DLM), Stuttgart-Hohenheim/German Agricultural Museum, Stuttgart-Hohenheim (thanks to Frank Emmerich)
Education Group GmbH, Linz (thanks to Peter Eiselmair and Gerhard Kaiserseder)
Fachbereichsbibliothek Biologie der Universität Wien/Biology Library of the University of Vienna (thanks to Eva-Maria Mikschi-Marischler)
Filmarchiv Austria, Vienna (thanks to Aldijana Bećirović, Jona Haidenthaler, Kristina Höch, Armin Loacker, Magomed Lulaew, Susanne Rocca, Nikolaus Wostry, and Florian Wrobel)
Filmoteka Narodowa – Instytut Audiowizualny, Warszawa/Polish National Film Archive – Audiovisual Institute, Warsaw (thanks to Adrian Smykowski)
Fondazione Cineteca di Bologna, Archivio Film (thanks to Andrea Meneghelli)
Institut für Film und Bild in Wissenschaft und Unterricht (FWU), München/Institute for Film and Pictures in Science and Education, Munich (thanks to Andrea Löhr)
Merck KGaA, Corporate History, Darmstadt (thanks to Christian Fenselau)
Národní filmový archiv (NFA), Praha/Czech Film Archive, Prague (thanks to Jan Křipač, Jaroslav Lopour, Michaela Mertová, and Lucia Petříková)
ORF-Archiv, Wien/ORF Archive, Vienna
Österreichisches Filmmuseum, Wien/Austrian Film Museum, Vienna (thanks to Paolo Caneppele, Kevin Lutz, Elisabeth Streit, Tom Waibel, and Stefanie Zingl)

Pädagogische Hochschule Steiermark/University College of Teacher Education, Graz (thanks to Constanza Furtlehner-Schlacher and Philip Rauter)
United States Holocaust Memorial Museum (USHMM), Washington, D.C. (thanks to Bruce Levy)
Videothek des Instituts für Theater-, Film- und Medienwissenschaft, Universität Wien/Video Library of the Institute for Theater, Film and Media Studies, University of Vienna (thanks to Anton Fuxjäger and Kateryna Pokydina)
WaRis Tiroler Filmarchiv/WaRis Tyrolean Film Archive, Bad Reichenhall & Innsbruck (thanks to Christian Riml and Helma Türk)
Zentrum für Kunst und Medien Karlsruhe (ZKM); Sammlung, Archive & Forschung/ Center for Art and Media Karlsruhe; Collections, Archives & Research (thanks to Felix Mittelberger)

Film Production Companies

Aichholzer Filmproduktion GmbH, Wien/Aichholzer Film Production, Vienna (thanks to Josef Aichholzer and Sabine Hein)
arx anima animation studio GmbH, Vienna (thanks to Dunja Bernatzky and Kris Staber)
Deutsche Bibelgesellschaft, Stuttgart/German Bible Society, Stuttgart (thanks to Elvira Jaiser and Mathias Jeschke)
Forlaget Fabel, Skanderborg, Denmark (thanks to Lars Jakobsen)
Kaiserlicht OG, Vienna (thanks to Felix Geremus)
STUMM-FILM Dr. Rolf Stumm Medien GmbH, Ludwigsburg (thanks to Rolf Stumm and Nikolaus Weißenhorn)
SWICZ Animation e.U., Vienna (thanks to Benjamin Swiczinsky)
Virgil Widrich Film- und Multimediaproduktions GmbH, Wien/Virgil Widrich Film and Multimedia Productions GmbH, Vienna (thanks to Virgil Widrich)
wega Filmproduktionsges.m.b.h, Wien/wega film vienna (thanks to Christian Bachmann and Melisa Krasniqi)
Zakka Films, Hamden, CT, USA (thanks to Ono Seiko)

Newspaper and Magazine Archives

Die ganze WOCHE GmbH (thanks to Barbara Falk)
"Die Presse" Verlags-Gesellschaft m.b.H. & Co KG (thanks to Michael M. Boschner)
Kleine Zeitung GmbH & Co KG (thanks to Hartwig Sauer)
Krone-Verlag Gesellschaft m.b.H. & Co. KG. (thanks to Martin Kriegel)
Manstein Zeitschriftenverlagsgesellschaft m.b.H. (thanks to Xhuljeta Jonuzi)
ORF Marketing & Creation GmbH & Co KG (thanks to Karin Schuster)
Österreichische Nationalbibliothek (ÖNB), Wien/Austrian National Library, Vienna
Russmedia Digital GmbH, Schwarzach (thanks to Matthias Rauch)
Salzburger Nachrichten Medien GmbH & Co. KG (thanks to Aloisia Eibl)
tele-Zeitschriftenverlagsges.mbH & Co KG (thanks to Martin Haiden-Klee)
vormagazin GmbH (thanks to Sebastian Höllmüller)
Wienbibliothek im Rathaus, Wien/Vienna City Library

Prologue: A Nation of Animation without Animation

In spring 2023, the first teaser for the HBO miniseries *The Regime* (2024), starring Kate Winslet (b. 1975), showcased Vienna's Schönbrunn Palace against the city's skyline. However, by the time the series was released in 2024, the scene had been digitally altered: the palace was enhanced with additional floors, and the surrounding Vienna cityscape was replaced by an anonymous town set against a mountainous backdrop. "A standard effect in VFX terms," explained Christoph Staber (b. 1979), co-founder of the Austrian animation studio *arx anima* (as cited in Priesching 2024: 18). Vienna became virtually invisible in the series – mirroring the often-overlooked status of Austrian animated film.

"Austria is a nation of animation films without animation films," observed Stefan Stratil (b. 1963), animator and co-founder of *ASIFA Austria*, in his evaluation of the country's animation landscape (as cited in Pavido 2019: para. 1). Although Austria may not be widely recognized as an animation hub, its contributions to the field date back to the pre-cinema era. Some historians even regard Simon Stampfer (1790–1864), with his 1832 invention of the 'stroboscopic discs,' as the world's first animator. Early experiments in Austrian animated film are believed to have occurred as early as 1906, just months after *Humorous Phases of Funny Faces* (1906), the first animated film captured on standard picture film. Despite this rich history, by 2024, Austria had been involved in fewer than ten animated feature film projects, while Luxembourg – a country nearly 30 times smaller – had contributed to over 40. "When I need animation specialists in Vienna, whether for stop-motion, claymation, or other specialized techniques, I bring in staff from Luxembourg," remarked Luxembourgish-Austrian animator Bady Minck (b. 1956) in 2006 (as cited in Mattuschka and Groschup 2010: 355).

The reasons for this imbalance are varied. One persistent issue has been film financing, as in most European countries, producing commercially viable films is the exception rather than the rule. When Austria introduced the so-called 'Kulturgroschen' (cultural penny) in 1949, this levy on each cinema ticket sold was not initially meant for film funding. It was only through the efforts of Dr. J.P. Haustein (1888–1973), the film advisor for the Federal Ministry of Education, that part of this tax was eventually allocated to cultural film production. Austria was the last country in Western Europe to pass a proper film funding law in late 1980, enabling film projects to receive government support starting in 1981. Despite this, filmmakers continued to face financial struggles. By 1985, Nobel Prize laureate Elfriede Jelinek (b. 1946) succinctly observed: "Eighty percent of filmmaking is about securing funding" (as cited in Trenczak and Kehldorfer 1985: 13).

The struggle for funding persisted well into the 21st century. By 2011, one of Austria's film funding bodies "had concluded that animation was not considered film and therefore no longer eligible for film funding" (Thomas Bogner, email to the author, dated January 22, 2024). This decision played a pivotal role in the downfall of *CINE Cartoon*, Austria's leading animation studio at the beginning of the millennium. When Walter Zwiener (b. 1953) began work on his animated feature film *Noron: Der Kampf um Ampoa* (Noron: The Battle for Ampoa, 2015), his application for film funding was unsuccessful. Ultimately, he received only €3,000 from the province of Vorarlberg, which didn't even cover the cost of the film's score.

Josef Aichholzer (b. 1950), producer of the animated feature film *Rotzbub* (Snotty Boy, 2021), echoed these challenges: "Back then, there wasn't even a dedicated application form for animation projects" (interview with the author on June 20, 2023). According to him, there were internal debates within the funding bodies about whether such a large-scale project should be supported. In the end, Aichholzer, as Austria's first Oscar-winning producer, benefited from a certain level of trust. The film's eventual success as Austria's highest-grossing film of 2022 helped pave the way for future endeavors.

However, the battle for animation funding continues. In 2017, Studio *NÖT* launched a petition urging the Austrian *Verwertungsgesellschaft der Filmschaffenden* (VdFS, Collecting Society of Audiovisual Authors) to include animated films in royalty payments. Yet, as of 2023, the VdFS Distribution Rules still exclude "Animation/animated and live-action cartoons, puppetry" (VdFS Distribution Rules 2023: 5). As recently as 2024, an animation filmmaker, speaking off the record, claimed that Austria likely has the most inadequate animation film funding in Europe.

Austria was also a latecomer in the field of animation education. It wasn't until 1982 that the University of Applied Arts Vienna established a studio dedicated to experimental animated film. Two years later, the University of Educational Sciences in Klagenfurt (Carinthia) followed suit with a similar initiative. Some of the newly established universities of applied sciences, founded from 1994 onward, gradually began incorporating animation into their curricula beginning in 1996. For example, the University of Applied Sciences Hagenberg in Upper Austria integrated animation into its Media Technology and Design program, while the University of Applied Sciences Salzburg did the same in its MultiMediaArt program. Despite these advances, animation filmmaker Benjamin Swiczinsky (b. 1982) remained critical of Austria's educational landscape for animation as late as 2012, emphasizing the persistent gaps in the field:

"While the University of Applied Arts offers an animation class focused on experimental film, the training there is purely artistic and lacks a holistic approach – unlike Ludwigsburg [Germany], where artistic elements are woven into a broader, comprehensive framework. On the other hand, Austrian universities of applied sciences teach technical skills, but they don't cover essential aspects like directing, film editing, or storytelling" (Benjamin Swiczinsky, as cited in Eigner 2013: 44).

Austria now offers a broader range of educational programs beyond traditional universities. These include the animation course at HTL Spengergasse in Vienna and the diploma program in Animation & Experimental Film at the Vienna Art School.

The reluctance toward animation in Austria remains a subject of speculation. Historically, American animated films were highly popular in Austria well into the 1930s. While the Nazis in Germany were already condemning Mickey Mouse, the Austrian press was still poking fun at such reactions. According to Benjamin

Swiczinsky, the hesitancy may be rooted in Austria's wartime and post-war history, during which American comics were seen as "enemy culture" and dismissed as "pulp fiction." Furthermore, a persistent divide between entertainment and high culture remains, with classical music and theater holding special esteem in Austria. Animation, often relegated to children's entertainment, "isn't seen as culture and isn't taken seriously" (Benjamin Swiczinsky, interview with the author on July 5, 2023). Even the avant-garde, which provided a niche for Austrian animation for many years, faced significant hostility from the press as early as the 1920s – possibly hindering the full development of animation as an art form in the country.

Stefan Stratil's description of Austria as a "nation of animation films without animation films" (as cited in Pavido 2019: para. 1) can be interpreted to highlight how Austrian animation remained largely invisible to the general public for decades. Even as late as 2019, film critic Marina Pavido referred to Austrian animation as "the invisible art" (Pavido 2019). For many years, animation also held a marginal place in Austria's film festival landscape. The *Vienna Shorts Festival* (VIS) – Austria's only *Academy Awards Short Films Qualifying Festival* as of 2023 – did not introduce a dedicated animation competition until 2010, despite the festival being established in 2004. The invisibility of animation in Austria was so pervasive that a 2011 symposium on the medium was aptly titled *UNDER the RADAR*, underscoring animation's overlooked status.

Even in Austrian film historiography, animation has long been overlooked. Esteemed animation filmmaker and historian Thomas Renoldner (b. 1960) made significant strides in addressing this with his work *Animated Films in Austria 1920–1970* (1998). In his contribution to the anthology *Die Kunst des Einzelbilds: Animation in Österreich – 1832 bis heute* (The Art of Single Frame: Animation in Austria – 1832 to the Present, 2010), Renoldner presented the first comprehensive history of the Austrian animation. Nevertheless, many aspects and animators from Austria's animation history have remained obscure until now. For instance, Paul Ludwig Winter (1885–1954) directed *Seipel's Sanierung* (Seipel's Economic Recovery, 1922/1923), a film previously considered anonymous. The influential contributions of Friedrich Kuplent (1905–1985), an amateur animation filmmaker active in the late 1920s, have largely gone unnoticed for a long time. Similarly, Max Vrecer (1951–2010), one of the few filmmakers to venture into narrative cartoons during the 1970s, has also been overlooked for many years.

Several Austrian animators remain barely known within their home country. Otto Waffenschmied (1901–1971) and Richard Dillenz (1892–1959), for example, were commissioned during World War II to produce films aimed at competing with *Disney* for the German market. Similarly, George Hoellering (1897–1980) directed propaganda trailers for the British *Ministry of Information* (MoI) during the same period. Another figure more recognized internationally than in Austria is Otto Neurath (1882–1945), whose visual language, Isotype, had a significant influence on animation worldwide. When the theater group *1927* incorporated Neurath-inspired animations into their stage play *Mehr als alles auf der Welt* (Please Right Back, 2022) and presented it in Austria, the tribute went unnoticed by the local audience.

Austria's contributions to international productions have often gone unnoticed as well. For example, the TV series *Talis und die tausend Aufgaben*

(Talis and the Thousand Tasks, 2000–2001) is frequently labeled as a French-German co-production, despite the crucial role played by the Austrian studio *CINE Cartoon* in its development. Similarly, the intricately crafted animated intro sequence by the Austrian studio *NÖT* for *A Hologram for the King* (2016), starring Tom Hanks (b. 1956), was reduced to just a few seconds in the final cut. *NÖT*'s involvement in storyboarding and set design for the animated feature *Fritzi: Eine Wendewundergeschichte* (Fritzi: A Revolutionary Tale, 2019) was also largely overlooked, with the film being credited as a German-Luxembourgish-Belgian-Czech co-production.

For Benjamin Swiczinsky, "the best animation is often the one you don't see" ('2 Days Animation Festival' 2017, 00:02:32). While he was referring to digital effects in live-action films, his statement also captures the essence of Austrian animation: the finest work often goes unseen. Despite this limited visibility, chronic underfunding, and stiff competition, animators like Birgit Scholin (b. 1984) remain steadfast in their dedication: "I'm captivated by animation, and I simply can't give it up. If I did, I'd have to sacrifice so much of myself that I wouldn't be happy anymore" (interview with the author in collaboration with Franziska Proksa on May 28, 2024). Austrian animation may be almost invisible, but the passion behind it shines through in every frame.

Part 1

From Flickers to Frames

Animation through the Lens of Innovation and War

1 Turning the Wheel
Pre-Cinema Animation

"Es ist Mein Wille" ("It is my will") was proclaimed by the Austrian Emperor Franz Joseph I (1830–1916) on December 20, 1857, regarding the urban restructuring of Vienna.[1] The capital of the Habsburg Empire was going to receive an aesthetic upgrade inspired by the Parisian model. The former city wall was turned into the 'Ringstraße' (Vienna Ring Road), a boulevard lined with the magnificent buildings that still define the city today.[2] During the construction phase, which lasted until the 1910s, there were a significant architectural transformation and a flourishing of Austrian art and culture. Architects like Theophil Hansen (1813–1891) and Otto Wagner (1841–1918) influenced the city's appearance, and the composer Johann Strauss II (1825–1899) became known as the 'waltz king' for his musical compositions. Additionally, Sigmund Freud (1856–1939) established modern psychoanalysis, Gustav Klimt (1862–1918) and Egon Schiele (1890–1918) contributed to *Wiener Moderne* (Viennese Modernism) through their paintings, and literary figures such as Karl Kraus (1874–1936) and Arthur Schnitzler (1862–1931) engaged in debates in Viennese coffee houses. Vienna's population almost tripled from over 600,000 in 1857 to nearly 1.8 million in 1900, transforming the city into a melting pot of Central European cultures around 1900.[3] This golden era of art and culture also witnessed the emergence of film as the so-called seventh art. Austrians played a significant role in further developing the illusion of movement, known since prehistoric times, into film projection.[4]

THE FIRST ANIMATOR IN THE WORLD?

Austria is not typically considered a major film-producing country in the traditional sense. Nevertheless, Austrian scholars and inventors provided crucial contributions, particularly in the early days of cinematography. The mathematician Joseph Petzval (1807–1891) and the optician Friedrich Voigtländer (1812–1878) developed the first portrait lens, known as the 'Petzval lens,' in Vienna in 1840. This lens was later also used for film projectors. Ernst Mach (1838–1916), who taught in Prague (then Austria-Hungary) and gave his name to the 'Mach number,' is considered the first to formulate the principle of time-lapse in 1888. The Viennese Theodor Reich (1861–1939), alongside the French Lumière brothers, constructed a motion picture camera, a creation that is now solely attributed to the Lumières. The priest and physicist August Musger (1868–1929) patented an apparatus for producing slow-motion pictures in September 1904. He is thus considered the inventor of this process. For animator and historian Thomas Renoldner (b. 1960), the 'wheel of life' developed by Simon von Stampfer (1790–1864),[5] Professor of Practical Geometry in Vienna, was one of Austria's most important contributions to the development of cinematography

DOI: 10.1201/9781003415442-2

(cf. Renoldner 2010: 42). This device, also called a stroboscope, was utilized to animate individual images into motion sequences.

In an article in the *Zeitschrift für Physik und Mathematik* (Journal of Physics and Mathematics), the experiments of British physicist Michael Faraday (1791–1867) on optical motion illusions were discussed. Simon Stampfer developed his 'stroboscopic discs' (also called 'optical magic discs') at the end of 1832, inspired by Faraday's work. These were cardboard discs with depictions of moving figures or shapes. When you looked through a slit on the edge of the disc and turned it in front of a mirror, it created the illusion of seeing moving figures or shapes in the reflection. After producing the first six discs, Stampfer offered his invention to the Viennese publisher *Trentsensky & Vieweg*, who marketed it commercially. The high demand for this 'optical toy,' for which Stampfer applied for a patent in April 1833, led to a second expanded edition in July of the same year.

Thomas Renoldner suggests that the images, which are partially abstract and partially figurative, can be seen as the "primal cell of animation" (Renoldner 2010: 44) in Austria and already indicate the different directions in which it would develop. For example, discs like *Hämmernde Schmiede* (Hammering Smiths) or *Mädchen am Ziehbrunnen* (Girl at the Drawing Well) portrayed almost documentary-like work processes. Meanwhile, *Velocipede* demonstrated the proper use of a running wheel, akin to an educational film. Another disc featured a boy juggling four balls while spinning around his axis in a jump, which showcased an almost unbelievable feat. Renoldner points out that "Animation here uses its potential to make the 'impossible possible,' the film trick is invented" (Renoldner 2010: 47).

The artwork *Köpfe nach Höhe und Breite sich verzerrend* (Heads Distorting by Height and Width) moved toward surrealist film and foreshadowed the morphing effect known today. Meanwhile, discs featuring geometric figures were reminiscent of experimental animated films, and those with geometric constructions like gears or hammer works anticipated metaphorical animated films. Lastly, there was a disc that appeared to only display abstract graphic elements at first but then, through movement, formed the word 'Optik' (Optics), reminiscent of avant-garde film (Figure 1.1). Additionally, discs that combined naturalistic representations on the edges with abstract movements in the center have also been preserved.

Some film historians consider Simon Stampfer to be the world's first animator, "having drawn jumping and dancing cartoon characters almost 100 years before Walt Disney" (Floimair 1998: 5). In fact, Stampfer described all the technical basics of animated film in his patent, except for projection. Another Austrian, army lieutenant Franz von Uchatius (1811–1881), addressed this 'gap' in animated film technology about ten years later. Inspired by his superior, Franz von Hauslab (1798–1883), Uchatius utilized Stampfer's stroboscopic disc principle to project moving images onto a wall. Uchatius, one of the leading inventors and constructors in the Austro-Hungarian army, developed a cinematographic projection apparatus in 1845. This invention made it possible for the first time to project transparent images on rotating glass panes, creating animation: "It was not yet photographs that Uchatius projected, but rather drawn sequences of movement; thus, it was the birth of the animated film" (Zglinicki 1979: 132). Uchatius is, therefore, considered the father of the 'moving picture.'[6] By 1853, he had improved his invention,

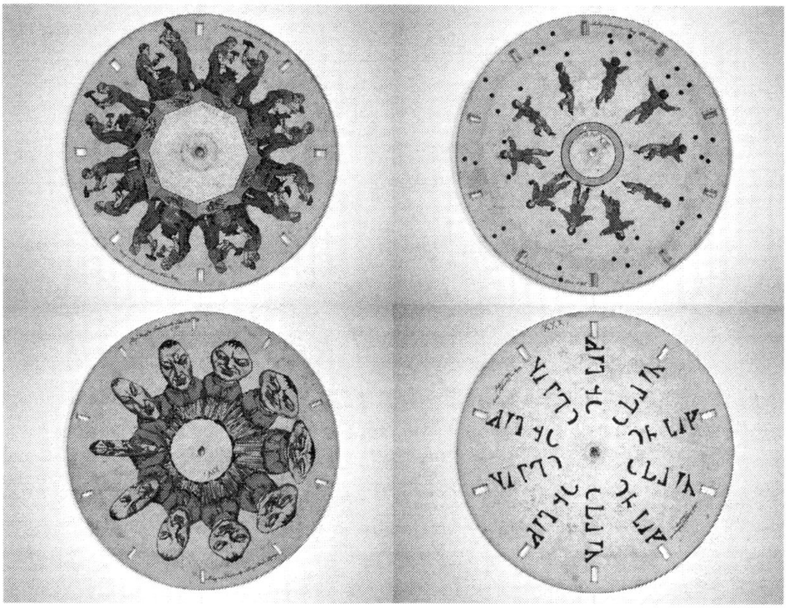

FIGURE 1.1 Four stroboscopic discs by Simon Stampfer, distributed by the Viennese publisher *Trentsensky & Vieweg* in 1833. (Courtesy of Observatory of Kremsmünster (P. Amand Kraml).)

which was used to demonstrate physical and ballistic motion processes at the Vienna Military School (Figure 1.2).

Another pioneer of cinematography from Austria was Ludwig Döbler (1801–1864), a Viennese showman and magician who patented a projecting phenakistiscope called *Phantaskop* (Phantascope) in 1847. It improved Franz Uchatius' initial projection device, which could only project tiny images (6 inches in diameter).[7] For the projection, he used the Austrian invention of the 'Petzval lens.' Döbler showcased his invention at the *Theater an der Josefstadt* in Vienna in the spring of 1847, introducing large projections of moving images for the first time. His audience included the Austrian Emperor Ferdinand I (1793–1875). Simon Stampfer's stroboscopic discs partly inspired Döbler's series of pictures. They were given titles such as *Der türkische Gaukler* (The Turkish Conjuror), *Der Reifspringer* (The Ring Jumper), *Die kleine Cavalcade* (Small Parade), *Der Holzschneider* (The Woodcutter), *Der chinesische Gaukler* (The Chinese Conjuror), *Der Stelzentänzer* (The Strutting Dancer), *Der Seiltänzer* (The Tightrope Walker), and *Die Duellanten* (The Duellists). Döbler traveled with his 'traveling cinema' throughout half of Europe, and his performances are considered today as the first successful public screenings of stroboscopic animation.

Joseph Plateau (1801–1883), a Belgian physicist, independently developed the phenakistiscope around the same time as Simon Stampfer. He created a series of 16 individual images depicting a dancer on a spinning disc. Stampfer's invention became more widespread due to patent protection and early commercial exploitation. Stampfer's 'stroboscopic discs' also contributed to naming the 'stroboscopic

FIGURE 1.2 This watercolor by Georg Dill, depicting a demonstration by Franz Uchatius in 1854, is the only known contemporary image of a phenakistiscope in use. (Courtesy of Archive of the Institute Kadotheum, Vienna (Robert Kaldy-Karo).)

effect' outside Austria. Surprisingly, Stampfer was largely forgotten by historians, with Plateau often credited as the father of cinema instead.[8] Austria's contribution to the history of animated film remained almost invisible. Even in Austria, Stampfer's contribution to film history was nearly forgotten for a long time. Since 2012, the city of Salzburg has biennially awarded a young filmmaker's prize. In 2014, the prize was named *Simon S.* in honor of Stampfer. That same year, an animated film titled *Kangaroos Can't Jump Backwards* (directed by Rafael Mayrhofer), which critically addressed the question of unlimited growth, also received an award.

GYRO GEARLOOSE AND HIS LITTLE HELPER FROM AUSTRIA

Austrian inventiveness and technical expertise also played a significant role in advancing animated film beyond Austria. The Fleischer brothers, Walt Disney's (1901–1966) biggest competitors in the 1930s, made pioneering contributions to animated film and had Austrian roots. Max Fleischer (1883–1972) was born in Krakow, then part of the Austro-Hungarian province of Galicia (present-day Poland). At that time, Krakow was considered one of the centers of Jewish life in the Habsburg Monarchy. In the 19th century, there was a gradual legal equalization of the Jewish population, culminating in the Austro-Hungarian Compromise of 1867. Many Jews then felt connected to the Austrian imperial house and 'assimilated.' The Fleischer family was also among the 'assimilated Jews' who spoke German and adopted

German names – Aaron and Malka, the Fleischer brothers' parents, became Wilhelm and Amalia Fleischer. However, due to increasing anti-Semitism and poverty, the family immigrated to New York (USA) in 1887. Even though the family quickly integrated – Wilhelm became William, and English was the only language spoken in the Fleischer household – they remained attached to their Austrian roots. When Max Fleischer underwent a security check at *Paramount* after the outbreak of World War II, he claimed Vienna as his birthplace and kept his Austrian citizenship "until it became necessary to become American in 1942 to keep his job" (Ulrich 2004: 133).

Max Fleischer, along with his American-born brother David 'Dave' Fleischer (1894–1979), became enthusiastic about animated films. Between 1914 and 1916, he invented the technique of rotoscoping. This involved projecting individual film frames onto a glass panel, allowing a drafter to trace them onto paper – similar to tracing. With this technique, for which he received a patent in 1917, he created realistic human motion sequences for the first time. For example, the Fleischer brothers used rotoscoping to animate Gulliver in *Gulliver's Travels* (1939) and the characters in their *Superman* series (from 1941). *Disney* also used this technique to give Snow White in *Snow White and the Seven Dwarfs* (1937) a more human appearance. The method spread worldwide and influenced the work of numerous animation pioneers. In Egypt, for example, the Frenkel brothers used the process in the 1930s to animate contemporary singers and belly dancers alongside their animated hero, Mish-Mish Effendi. *Soyuzmultfilm*, the Soviet Union's primary animation studio, used the process starting in 1938 to create Soviet hero characters. In China, the Wan brothers employed the process to produce Asia's first animated feature film, *Tiě shàn gōngzhǔ* (Princess Iron Fan, 1941).

The Fleischer brothers were also pioneers in creating animated sound films. In 1924, they collaborated with inventor Lee de Forest (1873–1961) to release the first animated films with synchronized sound. Two years later, they released *My Old Kentucky Home* (1926), the first animated film with lip-synchronized sound. This was years ahead of their competitor, Walt Disney, who released his first animated film with synchronized sound, *Steamboat Willie*, in 1928.

Technical expertise from Austria was sought after in another part of the world to help set up an animated film industry. Henryk Henenfeld, born in 1910 in Skole (then Austria-Hungary, now Ukraine), completed his technical studies in Vienna and then worked as a mechanical engineer for *Westinghouse* distributors in Austria, Switzerland, and Turkey. In 1941, he joined *Asea Electric*, the Indian distributor of *Westinghouse*. Henenfeld contributed to the war effort by installing air-conditioning, refrigeration, and ventilation systems in war-related facilities and military buildings. When the *Information Films of India*, under the Ministry of Information, constructed a new studio with a *Cartoon Film Unit* in Bombay in 1944, Henenfeld played a crucial role in installing air-conditioning and refrigeration systems. This project was one of the largest of its kind in India at that time. In February 1946, the *Administrative Officer of Information Films of India* concluded: "I have no doubt that Mr. Henenfeld's special qualifications and experience connected with the processing of films – for which refrigeration and air-conditioning is essential – will be of great value to us in future" (*Application from Mr Henryk Henenfeld for Nationalization*, 1946: [18]).

Although Henenfeld's contribution to the *Cartoon Film Unit* was described as "most essential" (*Application from Mr Henryk Henenfeld for Nationalization*, 1946: [18]), his impact on animation history remained almost invisible.

NOTES

1 The decree, penned on December 20, 1857, was published on the front page of the *Wiener Zeitung* (Viennese Newspaper) on December 25, 1857.
2 Buildings erected during this era included the Main Building of the University, City Hall, Parliament, Neue Burg (part of the Hofburg), State Opera, Burgtheater, Votivkirche, Stock Exchange, Museum of Art History, and Museum of Natural History.
3 *Wien 1900* (Vienna 1900) is still synonymous with the beginning of Viennese modernism.
4 Based on Rolf Giesen's (b. 1953) definition, animation is "a sequence of individual images which, seen together, convey the impression of a sequence of movements" (Giesen 2003: 7). As a result, some historians argue that a clay cup dating back to the Bronze Age may be the earliest example of animation. The 5,200-year-old cup, originally from what is now Iran, depicted a series of images showing a goat jumping onto a tree and eating its leaves when the cup was turned. This sequence of images also served as the basis for the Austrian animated film *Cornucopia* (2022, directed by Ani Antonova and Dimiter Ovtcharov), which was screened in Vienna in the spring of 2023 at the *Tricky Women/Tricky Realities Animation Festival.*
5 Simon Stampfer stated his year of birth as 1792, but current research, based on the birth register of his home parish, confirms the year as 1790 (cf. Strasser 1998: 12–13).
6 The Englishman T.W. Naylor conceived the idea for a projector as early as 1842. His description, along with a drawing, was published in 1843 and translated into German in 1844. However, it seems that Naylor never actually implemented his idea.
7 Since the 1920s, there has been a persistent legend that Franz Uchatius saw no practical use in his machine and sold it to Ludwig Döbler for a ridiculous price. However, there are no primary sources to substantiate this story. Surprisingly, as of 2023, it can even be found on a website of the Austrian Federal Ministry of Defense: https://www.denkmal-heer.at/wissenswertes/lager-uchatius-lager-kaisersteinbruch
8 Thomas Renoldner notes that even in an exhibition on film history in Annecy, France – the location of the world's oldest animation festival – Simon Stampfer's discs were displayed without his name being mentioned (Renoldner 2010: 43).

2 The Emperor's New Films
Animation's Emergence during WWI

When the 'moving pictures' were invented, Austria was a vast empire – the Austro-Hungarian Dual Monarchy covered an area of over 676,000 km^2 in 1908, approximately the size of Texas (USA). Its territory included present-day Austria, Hungary, the Czech Republic, Slovakia, Slovenia, Croatia, Bosnia-Herzegovina, and parts of Italy, Serbia, Montenegro, Romania, Poland, and Ukraine. To address the escalating nationality conflicts that threatened the Habsburg Empire's unity, political strategists even proposed the formation of the *Vereinigte Staaten von Groß-Österreich* (United States of Greater Austria) modeled after the USA. However, this plan did not materialize. After the assassination of the Austrian heir to the throne, Archduke Franz Ferdinand (1863–1914), in Sarajevo (now part of Bosnia-Herzegovina) on June 28, 1914, Austria-Hungary declared war on the Kingdom of Serbia a month later due to suspicions of Serbian support for the separatist responsible for the assassination. The chain reaction created by the constellation of alliances eventually led to the First World War.

Following the defeat in World War I, the Austro-Hungarian Empire disintegrated, leading to significant geopolitical changes. All that remained of the vast multiethnic state was a significantly smaller region, often referred to as 'Restösterreich' (the rest of Austria). This new state measured just under 84,000 km^2, comparable to the size of South Carolina (USA). Consequently, the population plummeted from nearly 53 million in 1914 to 6.4 million in 1919.[1] As a result, Austria lost significant potential. The visionary power of animated film in the former crown lands is evidenced by the *Zagreb School of Animated Films* and the Czech puppet animation films from Zlín. It wasn't until the 1960s that Austria began to catch up in animated film.

AN IDEAL FILMMAKING: AUSTRIA'S FIRST ANIMATED FILMS

Since March 1896, there has been documented evidence of public-commercial film screenings in Austria. Right from the start, the so-called 'Trickfilme' (trick films) gained considerable popularity. Initially, this category encompassed not only 'Zeichenfilme' (animated cartoons) but also all films employing film tricks like stop-motion or time-lapse techniques.[2] Notably, Segundo de Chomón (1871–1929), described as "[o]ne of the finest artists of early animation" (Bendazzi (ed.) 2016a: 70), created the 'Illusionsfilm' (illusion film) *La gallina de los huevos de oro* (The Hen that Laid the Golden Eggs, 1905) for *Pathé Frères* in Spain. Its Austrian release in 1906 as *Die Henne mit den goldenen Eiern* (The Hen with the Golden Eggs) sparked a significant surge in interest:

DOI: 10.1201/9781003415442-3

"This film found such lively appeal among cinema owners and the public that it generated an enormous number of orders by the standards of the time. Despite the limited number of cinemas in existence, no fewer than 96 orders for the film were placed with Pathé, [...]" (Kinematographische Rundschau, December 31, 1911: 5).

The first animated film on standard picture film is considered to be *Humorous Phases of Funny Faces* by J. Stuart Blackton (1875–1941), released in April 1906 in the USA. It showcased the hand of a rapid sketch artist whose drawings magically came to life. Just months later, Austrian Josef Halbritter (1890–1978) reportedly had a similar idea. Upon receiving a camera as a Christmas present in 1906,[3] he utilized it to capture street scenes and a rapid sketch artist performing in a vaudeville act. Unable to capture the chalk marks on film, he invited the artist to a private demonstration in his parents' villa garden. Although he achieved successful footage of the artist's rapid sketches, Halbritter was frustrated that the artist kept covering his work. He then proposed having the cartoonist step out of the picture after each stroke. Thrilled by this groundbreaking achievement – Austria's first animated film – Halbritter decided to dedicate himself to animation. He explored the idea of constructing an animation stand with a technician friend and initiated discussions with illustrators, cartoonists, and graphic artists. However, as a wave of technically superior animated films flooded Austria from abroad, Halbritter abandoned his animation ambitions and focused on cultural, industrial, and short feature films instead.

When commercial films were first produced in Vienna in 1906, they primarily consisted of erotic content aimed at the so-called 'Herrenabende' (gentlemen's evenings). Also known as 'Pariser Abende' (Parisian evenings) owing to their origins, these screenings occurred around eight o'clock in the evening, following the afternoon show, and showcased brief, disjointed erotic films. *Saturn-Film*, responsible for these productions, was not only considered the first Austrian film production company but, "for a short time, even became synonymous with film production under the [Austro-Hungarian] double-headed eagle" (Kieninger 1999: 7). There is speculation by animator and historian Thomas Renoldner (b. 1960) that some of these films may have been animated (cf. Renoldner and Frischengruber 1998: 5).[4] Although the police eventually intervened to stop these activities, the church criticized cinemas for focusing too much on entertainment. In April 1910, a representative of the Protestant Church penned an article titled *Der Kinematograph und seine Auswüchse* (The Cinematograph and Its Excesses), expressing concerns about the situation: "It is a pity that bad things have to attach themselves to good things. [...] Unfortunately, even the cinematograph, which could have had such a great influence on the education and ennoblement of our people, has quickly fallen onto a slippery slope" (Salzburger Volksblatt, April 16, 1910: 17). In supporting his argument, the writer cited examples from a current cinema program booklet, including an animated film called *Verhexte Streichhölzer* (Enchanted Matches), which was likely a stop-motion film. The author concluded, "So everything serves to excite the laughing muscles, stimulate the imagination, and heighten the excitement to its peak" (Salzburger Volksblatt, April 16, 1910: 17).

It's difficult to pinpoint precisely when the first Austrian animated film was created, apart from amateur and unofficial films. However, by the early 1910s, there was a noticeable uptick in interest in the technology behind 'Trickfilme' (trick films). In October 1910, the contemporary press mentioned, "The trick film

'Die geheimnisvollen Künste' (The Mysterious Arts) is sure to pique curiosity about the process behind such films" (Linzer Tages-Post, October 9, 1910: 6). A few months later, the audience's curiosity was satisfied when the article *Die 'Wunder' der Kinoschauspiele* (The 'Wonders' of Cinematic Performances) was published in a Viennese newspaper. The article delved into the question, "How are cinematographic tricks recorded?" and provided insights into "[t]he creation of magic pictures" (Neues Wiener Tagblatt, February 12, 1911: 13). In late 1911 and early 1912, Dr. Hans Lehmann (1875–1917) published an essay titled *Kinematographische Tricks* (Cinematographic Tricks) in various newspapers nationwide.[5] One of the topics covered in the essay was the detailed explanation of how stop-motion films were produced (cf. Lehmann 1911: 1–2). Notably, the earliest known and surviving Austrian animated film, *Ideale Filmerzeugung* (Ideal Filmmaking, 1913/1914), was created using stop-motion animation (Figure 2.1).

FIGURE 2.1 Filmstrip from *Ideale Filmerzeugung* (Ideal Filmmaking, 1914), the oldest surviving animated film from Austria. (Courtesy of Filmarchiv Austria, Vienna.)

Serving as a sort of 'image film,' *Ideale Filmerzeugung* (Ideal Filmmaking) aimed to showcase the accomplishments of the *Sascha-Filmfabrik*. The film studio had relocated from Pfraumberg (now Přimda in the Czech Republic) to Vienna in 1912. The film highlighted the entire production process, from the perforation of raw film to its development and duplication. To provide an unobstructed view of the machinery and processes involved in film production, cinematographer Ludwig Schaschek (1888–1948) utilized object animation. The pioneering approach of *Ideale Filmerzeugung* (Ideal Filmmaking) placed film itself as the central figure, cementing its status as "the earliest source in which filmmaking technology was documented" (Der Standard, January 17, 2003a: para. 2). Coincidentally, it inadvertently became Austria's first science fiction film, in which machines gained independence from humans: "Without human assistance and with virtually no human roles, this short film reflects on film production processes and celebrates, as if only by accident, the dominance of machines over these men of yore" (Ballhausen 2015: 250).

The film's release in January 1914 sparked a resurgence of interest in cinematic trickery. In March of the same year, a Viennese newspaper published an article titled *Wirklichkeit und Trick im Kino* (Reality and Trick in Cinema; cf. Neue Freie Presse, March 8, 1914: 28) delving into the mystery of stop-motion film, among other things. On April 16, 1914, Alfred Deutsch-German (1870–1943), a screenwriter who worked on animated films during the First World War,[6] delivered a lecture on *Kunst im Kino* (Art in Cinema), also exploring the concept of 'Trickfilm' (trick film).[7]

ANIMATION INDUSTRY AS WAR INDUSTRY

In 1914, as World War I began, the first studio operator established continuous animation film production in Austria. Robert Müller (1877–1942), a producer and film distributor working for *Pathé Frères* since 1903, played a crucial role in building branches and a cinema network for the company in Austria-Hungary. Taking over the Vienna *Pathé* branch in mid-1914, he renamed it *Robert Müller-Film*. The outbreak of war led to a shortage of foreign animated films in the market,[8] prompting Müller to address this gap by hiring cartoonist Theodor 'Theo' Zasche (1862–1922) to create a series of propaganda cartoon films.[9] These films, released under the title *Österreichische Kriegskarikaturen* (Austrian War Caricatures), were distributed weekly from November 1914 onward:

"Then came 'Als der Russe vor Przemysl stand' (As the Russian Stood Before Przemysl), 'a drawn heroic epic.' The second film, 'Das neue Dreigestirn' (The Three New Stars), dealt with the axis Moscow, Paris, London, with hateful caricatures of the relevant statesmen. The third film of the series [Wie der Schani und seine kleine Schwester die Kriegsanleihe zeichnen wollen (How Schani and His Little Sister Want to Subscribe to the War Loan)] is the story of a small boy and his sister who hope to draw a war loan, only to find out that, for this, one needs money. And then the fourth film of the series, 'Der Zar und seine lieben Juden' (The Tsar and His Dear Jews), in which, of all people, Tsar Nikolaus [Nikolai II] is shown in the time-honored manner as a friend and protector of Jews. But here, Zasche went over the top, and for the individual Jewish types, turned out a row of smear campaign characters" (Peter A. Schauer, as translated in Renoldner and Frischengruber 1998: 5).[10]

Some films were so controversial that even the censors objected to them. For instance, a censorship decision regarding *Das neue Dreigestirn* (The Three New Stars, 1914) was published in the press, stating: "The inscription 'Lausland' (louse land) above the [Russian] bear is to be omitted" (Kinematographische Rundschau, November 22, 1914: 58).

Following those, there were endurance cartoons titled *Der Traum des Reservisten* (The Reservist's Dream, 1914) and *Das Kriegs-A.B.C.* (The War ABC, 1915). From 1915 onward, *Oppenheimer & Reiter*, a film distributor, also introduced 'topical cartoons' that were displayed alongside war newsreels.[11] Among these cartoons was *Streichhölzchen* (Little Matchsticks, 1915), where matches formed various caricatures: "In the end, they culminate in a modern apotheosis, with the emperors of Austria and Germany at the center" (Kinematographische Rundschau, January 3, 1915b: 40). Additionally, press artist and film poster painter Theo Matejko (né Matejka, 1893–1946) created an animated cartoon named *Zeit-Karikaturen* (Current Caricatures, 1915) at his film studio.

After creating its film *Ideale Filmerzeugung* (Ideal Filmmaking, 1913/1914), *Sascha-Film* initially focused on using the stop-motion technique. In 1915, an intriguing "animated film featuring shoes" (Kinematographische Rundschau, October 31, 1915a: 59) known as *Fräulein Wildleders Liebesroman* (Miss Suede's Romance Novel) was released. The film depicted the shoes of a man and a woman coming to life and giving birth to children's shoes.[12] This unique concept was praised as a revival of the essence of cinematography, with the observation that "film is once again, and finally, working with the elements intrinsic to cinematography, and where this is the case, the effect is uninhibited by anything" (Wiener Allgemeine Zeitung, December 1, 1915: 3). As the leading film producer of the silent era, *Sascha-Film* also aimed to partake in the triumph of animated cartoons. To achieve this, it employed the services of poster painter Rob (né Karl Robitsek, 1891–died after 1952), who had previously created film posters for propaganda feature films and the studio's newsreels. Rob, who had been running his own publishing house since 1916, produced promotional films for the Sixth War Loan in 1917, with titles such as *Der sichere Weg zum Frieden* (The Sure Path to Peace), *Die feldgraue Krone* (The Gray Crown), and *Wir und die Anderen* (We and the Others). However, by the late stage of the war, enthusiasm for these propaganda animated films had waned, and screening them became a 'patriotic duty.' As a result, the films were made available to cinemas free of charge. In 1920, animator Peter Eng (1892–1939) mockingly remarked about Rob's animated films, saying that Austria owed them "a four-week postponement of the end of the war" (Eng 1920: 7).

During the war weariness of 1917, a noteworthy shift occurred as poster artist Otto Dely (né Otto Luis Erdélyi, 1884–1935) began creating animated films unrelated to the ongoing war. A native of Vienna, Otto Dely is recognized as one of the trailblazers of Austrian and German animated film.[13] His notable works included the animated series *Neue Lichtspielereien* (New Light Games, starting from 1915)[14] for the German *Union-Vitascope*, as well as war-themed animated cartoons titled

Delys lebende Karikaturen (Dely's Living Caricatures, 1916) for the *National-Film* in Berlin.[15] Upon returning to Vienna, he crafted the animated film *Die drei Mäderln* (The Three Girls, 1916/1917) at *Sascha-Film*. This film was described as a "parodic caricature" (Kinematographische Rundschau, November 12, 1916: 13) of the operetta *Das Dreimäderlhaus* (The House of the Three Girls), which had premiered in 1916. Continuing his work, he produced *Der unterbrochene Ringkampf* (The Interrupted Wrestling Match, 1917), depicting a fight between an East African and a Viennese boxer. Additionally, Dely is credited with *Jückijoli* (alternatively *Yückijoli*, 1917), a somewhat macabre film portraying a cuckolded Chinese man nailing his wife and her lover to a tree with a dagger before hanging himself. Dely's apolitical films acted as a contrasting counterpart to the inflammatory films produced by others during the same period. Nevertheless, even Dely was not spared from Austrian wartime propaganda. In 1918, he created two anti-British propaganda animated films, *Der Popanz* (The Bogeyman) and *Das Meerestier* (The Sea Creature), for the Army High Command's Enemy Counterintelligence Unit. These films were used to bolster troop morale. In February 1918, he released the animated cartoon *Etwas wissenschaftliches vom Wetter* (Something Scientific About the Weather) as a continuation of his series *Neue Lichtspielereien* (New Light Games), illustrating his growing despair over the ongoing war:

"In this film, made during the last and coldest winter of the war, he showed the pains and pleasures of man throughout the four seasons. The, in this context, defeatist end of the film is an illustration of the meaning of 'winter.' First, one saw how nice and warm people were before the war, from cavemen right up to the crackling flames of an open fireplace, whilst during the war, there is no heat. In February 1918, one could not be more explicit…" (Peter A. Schauer, as translated in Renoldner and Frischengruber 1998: 5).[16]

INK AND CELLULOID TRIUMPH

When the war ended in November 1918, Austria found itself on the losing side, yet the Austrian animated film industry emerged as a clear winner. The widespread appeal of the 'Karikaturenfilme' (caricature films) solidified their place as an essential component of the *Sascha-Journal* newsreel. Renowned caricaturists like Karl Robitsek and Theo Matejko created drawings of prominent figures featured in these films. However, *Sascha-Film* faced new competition as another significant studio, *Astoria-Filmfabrik*, established its own animation film department immediately after the war. Not only did *Astoria-Film* rise to become the country's second-largest film producer, but it also became one of the most modern studios in Europe. Additionally, *Filmag Filmindustrie*, founded in 1917, also shifted its focus to animated films and became the third-largest producer in the post-war years. The animated film *Gretls Filmtraum* (Gretl's Film Dream, 1918) depicted a woman yearning for a career as a film diva, seeing her idols parade through her dream. The press praised it, stating, "It is remarkable how closely the drawn caricatures resemble well-known film stars and vividly bring them to life on the screen with just a few strokes. This new technique is making significant progress and is on the verge of becoming its own genre of art" (Neue Kino-Rundschau, November 23, 1918: 10). Another film, *Wien zur Kriegs- und Friedenszeit* (Vienna in Times of War and Peace, 1919), caricatured one of the 'Wiener Typen' (Viennese characters), the Viennese janitor.

The anonymous film could be one of the earliest animated films created by Peter Eng in Austria. He "was considered the most Viennese of all Viennese animators" (Schauer 1997: 41) and expressed "the Viennese way of mocking with grotesque humor in animated film" (Die Stunde, April 25, 1923: 5). Following the completion of the animated film *Die Entfettungskur* (The Slimming Cure) for a South German studio in the spring of 1919, Eng worked on an animated series called *Mausi und Lausi* (Mousi and Lausi) for the Viennese *Sascha-Film*. By the fall of 1919, two films had been produced, one of which featured the titular boys traveling to America.[17] Eng's prominence grew as he emerged as the leading figure in Austrian animated filmmaking during the 1920s.

Today, the exact number of animated films produced in Austria by 1920 cannot be determined. Fewer than 40 films can be accounted for, and only one has survived.[18] However, in 1920, Peter Eng claimed to have already produced over 80 animated films for *Sascha-Film*, *Filmag*, and *Astoria-Film* (cf. Renoldner and Frischengruber 1998: 9). This discrepancy renders the first chapter of Austrian animation history almost invisible.

NOTES

1 The population decline resulting from the war is vividly illustrated by the example of Vienna. The city reached a population of 2 million in 1910, temporarily increasing to 2.35 million due to the influx of refugees during the First World War. Subsequently, there was a continuous population decrease until the 1980s, reaching 1.5 million by 1981. It wasn't until late 2023 that the city's population again surpassed the 2 million mark after more than a century.

2 As late as 1916, the press, in an article titled *Der Trickfilm* (The Trick Film), remained steadfast in its belief: "With the current development of the film industry, almost every major film is, in a sense, a trick film, as the effects have increasingly been enhanced by technical tricks" (Reichspost, March 25, 1916: 22).

3 There is no contemporary evidence to support this legend. The only available sources are two typescripts: one by Peter A. Schauer (1930–2018) and another by an anonymous author, possibly Schauer as well. The latter dated the story back to 1908 (cf. *Die ersten 50 Jahre des österreichischen Zeichentrickfilms* 1987: 5).

4 This implies that these movies would have been created in Austria a full 20 years before the release of the first US erotic animated film, *Eveready Harton in Buried Treasure* (1928 or 1929). Thomas Renoldner referenced the anonymous erotic animated film *Schöpfungsgeschichte* (Creation Story), produced around 1920, to suggest the existence of such films (cf. Renoldner and Frischengruber 1998: 5). This film depicted God creating Adam and Eve purely for his voyeuristic pleasure.

5 After facing financial difficulties, the Austrian August Musger (1868–1929) had to relinquish his 1904 patent for a slow-motion shot device in 1912. Subsequently, in 1914, Dr. Hans Lehmann developed his own apparatus in Germany, which was then publicly introduced in 1916. Despite maintaining a prolonged correspondence with Musger and the obvious basis of his invention on Musger's work, Dr. Lehmann did not credit Musger in any way.

6 One of his accomplishments was writing the script for the animated film *Der Traum des Reservisten* (The Reservist's Dream, 1914), directed by Theo Zasche (1862–1922).
7 The lecture was covered in various newspapers, including Neues Wiener Tagblatt, April 16 (1914: 14).
8 The impact was mainly on French films, whereas animated films from neutral Sweden were still being imported. Before the USA entered the war in 1917, Austrian cinemas also featured North American films, including the famous cartoons of Charlie Chaplin (1889–1977). Interestingly, even 'patriotic' animated films from Germany, despite containing anti-Semitic elements, were brought into the country by Jewish film distributors like the *Hugo Engel-Film*, sparking a significant trend of imitation.
9 Fritz Schönpflug (1873–1951), the Viennese illustrator, was also approached, but he was unavailable as he was busy creating posters and postcards.
10 Given the films' status as lost and the absence of contemporary synopses, it remains unclear which sources Peter A. Schauer used for these content descriptions. Therefore, it's important to approach them with due caution.
11 According to Peter A. Schauer, certain films portrayed anti-Semitic themes (cf. Schauer 1997: 17).
12 Before making this film, *Sascha-Film* apparently created numerous 'trick films' that have been forgotten over time: "The Sascha-Filmfabrik has rightfully earned acclaim for its series of truly excellent trick films" (Kinematographische Rundschau, October 31, 1915a: 59).
13 At this point, it's worth mentioning Walter Trier (1890–1951), who hailed from Prague (then Austria-Hungary). Coming from a German-speaking family, the cartoonist created six animated films in Germany between 1919 and 1921.
14 The press described the first part as "a kind of Wilhelm Busch on film" (Kinematographische Rundschau, February 28, 1915c: 63). The second episode, *Der Frosch* (The Frog, 1915), followed, and *Naturgeschichte des Hundes* (Natural History of the Dog) was released in 1916.
15 The German press spoke of "brilliantly sketched caricatured asides on contemporary history by Dely" (as cited in Giesen and Goergen n.d.). It's almost ironic that *Polo-Filmvertrieb*, established by the British Josef Powell before the war, introduced these films to Austria under the series title *Kriegskarikaturen von Dely* (War Caricatures by Dely).
16 Given the lack of primary sources, it's advisable to take Peter A. Schauer's description of the contents with a grain of salt (see footnote 10).
17 The exact number of episodes produced for this series remains a mystery. The IMDb includes a third film titled *Mausi und Lausi wählen* (Mousi and Lausi Vote, 1920), attributed to *Astoria-Film*. It is plausible that Peter Eng created additional episodes until the conclusion of his career as an animator in the late 1920s. This is suggested by the mention of "Mousi and Lausi, the naughty children" in the article *Die tanzenden Männchen* (The Dancing Little Men) about the production of animated films (Porges 1930: 12).
18 According to *Filmarchiv Austria*, only a tiny fraction of Austrian silent films, estimated to be less than 10%, have been preserved (cf. Kieninger 1999: 7).

3 Imperial Frames

Austria's Animation Legacy in Habsburg Successor States

Austrian history is intricately intertwined with the prestigious dynasty of the Habsburgs. Since the late 13th century, the Habsburg Monarchy, a diverse and complex entity, took shape from the Duchy of Austria. Its boundaries constantly shifted due to inheritance and conquest, eventually evolving into a multinational state. The Habsburgs governed Austria for nearly 650 years, almost 3 times as long as the existence of the United States. At various points, the Habsburgs held sway over territories that now comprise Switzerland (the Habsburgs' ancestral homeland), Germany, Spain, Portugal, France, the Netherlands, Belgium, Luxembourg, and San Marino. Additionally, they briefly established a presence in Liechtenstein and deployed their forces into Kosovo and northern Macedonia while combating the Ottomans. The Spanish Habsburgs also briefly oversaw Monaco as a protectorate. Furthermore, Bulgaria had strong connections to the ruling dynasty, culminating in the election of Ferdinand I (1861–1948) – a native of Vienna and an Austro-Hungarian officer at the time – as king in 1887.

When the first films were produced in Austria, the Habsburg Monarchy ranked as the second-largest country in Europe by area, trailing only the Russian Empire, and the third largest by population, following the Russian and German Empires. Its vast territory extended from Lake Constance in the west to the Carpathian Mountains in the east, covering Prague in the north and much of the Balkans in the south and reaching as far as Lake Garda in present-day Italy. However, while some viewed the Danube monarchy as a 'Völkerfamilie' (family of nations), others perceived it as a 'Völkerkerker' (dungeon of nations). Publicist Kersten Knipp (b. 1966) noted: "The Habsburg Empire was a highly complex political construct, composed of peoples and states that would hardly have united on their own, connected by little more than the fact that they were all ruled from Vienna" (as cited in Röder et al. 2018: para. 5).

The German-speaking community identified mainly with the monarchy in Vienna, even though they were mostly in the minority outside of present-day Austria. It would, therefore, be presumptuous to assert that all animated filmmakers born in the former crown lands before 1918 were Austrians. This would imply that Jiří Trnka (1912–1969) and Hermína Týrlová (1900–1993), who were born in today's Czech Republic, were as much Austrians as George Pal (né György Pál Marczincsak, 1908–1980) or John Halas (né János Halász, 1912–1995), who were born in today's Hungary. Conversely, it would be equally incorrect to label Johann Weichberger (1910–1992, b. in Trieste, now Italy) as Italian or Peter Eng (1892–1939, b. in Olomouc, now the Czech Republic) as Czech.[1]

DOI: 10.1201/9781003415442-4

The animated film production developed simultaneously in at least two crown lands alongside Vienna. In Budapest, István Kató-Kiszly (1895–1963) created the cut-out animation film *Zsirb Ödön* around 1914. Meanwhile, in Krakow (today's Poland), the first animated films were produced from 1917. The independent nature of these productions in Vienna, Budapest, and Krakow raises the question of "[w]hether an Austrian animated film even existed as a unifying, state-bound form" (Winkelmayer 2004: 104). Despite this, Austria made an almost invisible contribution to developing animated film in some of the former crown lands.

ANIMATION AS THE HIGHEST FILM ART: POLAND

Before the First World War outbreak, the present-day Poland region was partitioned among the dominant forces of Germany, Russia, and Austria. Krakow, known as the 'Polish center' within the Danube Monarchy, was under Austrian influence and continues to reflect this heritage today. Many architects from Krakow received their education in Vienna, and the traditional Viennese coffee house culture has become a permanent fixture in the city. Additionally, Krakow served as a significant artistic hub where Austrian and Polish cultures intertwined. Notably, it was in Krakow, during the period of Austria-Hungary rule in 1916 or 1917, that the first animated films on the territory of present-day Poland were produced.

The early pioneers of Polish animated film included film critic Karol Irzykowski (1873–1944), journalist Feliks Kuczkowski (1884–1970), and painter Lucjan Kobierski (1889–1943). Irzykowski delved into the theoretical aspects of animated film in his writings from 1913, while Kuczkowski, an amateur filmmaker, took a practical approach from 1916 onward. Kuczkowski's first avant-garde animated film, *Flirt krzesełek* (Flirting Chairs, 1916 or 1917), based on 38 drawings by Kobierski, was shot in Vienna due to infrastructure limitations. Unfortunately, the film is lost, with only a few stills remaining (Figure 3.1). Kuczkowski and Kobierski were creatively inspired by the same artistic influences as the avant-garde movement *Formizm* (Formism), which emerged in Krakow in 1917: Expressionism and Futurism. They were also impacted by international artists like Léopold Survage (1879–1968), a French painter, and Oskar Fischinger (1900–1967), a German-American filmmaker known for his contributions to abstract film. Kuczkowski further explored his idea of a 'synthetic-visionary' film with his second animated film, *Luneta ma dwa końce* (A Telescope Has Two Ends), created in 1916 or 1917.[2]

In 1924, Karol Irzykowski published the first comprehensive film study in Polish, titled *Dziesiąta Muza: Zagadnienia Estetyczne Kina* (The Tenth Muse: The Aesthetic Aspects of Cinema). In this work, he dedicated a separate chapter to the animated film. Irzykowski regarded Feliks Kuczkowski as "a true innovator of Polish cinema" and praised his films as "cinema of pure movement" (translated into English in Kuc 2016: 55). However, Irzykowski's theoretical treatise was shaped not just by Kuczkowski, with whom he frequently visited the cinemas and analyzed the films they watched, but also by the Austrian psychologist and philosopher Rudolf Maria Holzapfel (1874–1930). Holzapfel originated from Krakow but departed the city during his teenage years following his father's untimely passing. He then became a globetrotter, spending numerous years in Austria before the commencement of the First

FIGURE 3.1 One of the few surviving frames from *Flirt krzesełek* (Flirting Chairs, 1916 or 1917), Poland's first animated film, shot in Vienna. (Courtesy of Filmoteka Narodowa, Warsaw.)

World War. Irzykowski, who had studied German, directly referenced Holzapfel's major work *Panidealische Psychologie der sozialen Gefühle* (Panidealist Philosophy of Social Emotions), published in German in 1901: "The cinema is certainly not a pure and emphatic art – as is painting – and can only be ascribed to what Holzapfal terms the 'inauthentic' arts, i.e., those which work with the given materials of nature (gardening, the art of the actor, pedagogy) and which can, in his opinion, scale even greater heights than 'the arts proper'" (translated into English in Irzykowski and Coates 1987: 116). Irzykowski believed that true art draws inspiration from itself rather than simply depicting nature, and he applied this thesis of Holzapfel to film. He firmly believed that "the *traditional film is merely a temporary substitute for the animated film.* [...] Indeed, *only the potential of this particular genre validates the artistic nature of cinema*" (translated into German in Irzykowski and Helbig-Mischewski 2013: 56–57). Karol Irzykowski's groundbreaking ideas greatly influenced the work of Polish avant-garde artist Jan Lenica (1928–2001), whom the German press referred to as "arguably the most important artist ever to engage with animated film" (as cited in Der Spiegel, December 22, 1968: 151). Additionally, Stefan Themerson (1910–1988), a prominent figure in Polish avant-garde film of the 1930s, also incorporated Irzykowski's theses into his writings. Despite this, Irzykowski's work remains relatively unknown outside of Poland and has only been published in excerpts in English and German. At a lecture in September 1947, an Austrian church representative concluded similarly to Irzykowski without knowing the book: "Father Diego Götz concludes with an original theory that animated film has a great future ahead. He predicts it will surpass live-action film in public favor, just as film once replaced theater" (Welt am Abend, October 2, 1947: 3). Without a doubt, modern blockbuster movies heavily rely on digital effects. For instance, director James Cameron (b. 1954) referred to his 2009 film *Avatar* as a fusion of live-action and computer-generated animation.

"AUSTRIA AS A BRIDGE BETWEEN EAST AND WEST": CZECH REPUBLIC

Although Berthold Bartosch (1893–1968) didn't create any films in his birthplace of northern Bohemia, which was part of Austria-Hungary and is now part of the Czech Republic, he remains a significant figure in Czech animation history. Coming from a German-speaking family, he was initially drawn to the capital of the Danube monarchy. In 1911, he embarked on a 2-year internship as a draftsman with a Viennese architect. Subsequently, from 1913 to 1917, he pursued his studies in architecture and art at the Academy of Fine Arts Vienna. When Bartosch became interested in film, he crossed paths with the leftist social scientist Dr. Erwin Hanslik (1880–1940). In 1915, under the impact of the First World War and with a vision of fostering international understanding, Hanslik established the *Institut für Kulturforschung* (Institute for Cultural Research):

"According to Dr. Hanslik, Vienna should become a center of human culture, a place of education for humanity, in which all peoples have a shared interest. The planned cultural and humanistic awakening, which the world urgently needs today, should take root in Central Europe, particularly in Vienna. The small circle formed during the war for this purpose, independent of all statehood and open to all peoples and parties, aims to contribute to this through the work of humanity…" (as cited in Neue Kino-Rundschau, August 9, 1919: 4).

Based on Erwin Hanslik's suggestion, Berthold Bartosch founded an animation film studio in 1918, bringing together graduates of the *Kunstgewerbeschule* (School of Applied Arts, now University of Applied Arts) and artists from the Klimt Group. Under the series title *Die deutschösterreichische und tschechoslowakische Republik* (The German Austrian and Czechoslovak Republics), Bartosch created six cartographic, geological, and geographical films from 1918 to 1919. In these films, he also explored the social and political ideas of the philosopher and Czechoslovak state founder Tomáš Masaryk (1850–1937).[3] On May 20, 1919, the series was showcased as a compilation film titled *Menschheit* (Humanity) or *Neue Menschheit* (New Humanity),[4] with the attendance of US diplomat Archibald Cary Coolidge (1866–1928). The Austrian press dubbed it "the strangest film screening ever shown: the animated film as a scientific and popular educational tool!" (Der neue Tag, May 22, 1919: 6). A journal described the content of the film *Das Werden des tschechoslowakischen Staates* (The Emergence of the Czechoslovak State) in the following manner:

"On the screen, the outlines of the Czechoslovak linguistic territory emerge. One then sees the Czech flood pouring over the borders, conquering the German-speaking areas, occupying German Bohemia, advancing to the demarcation line in Hungary, moving towards Bratislava, and attempting to form a corridor to Southern Slavia. Everything is shown schematically, eye-catching, and understandable for everyone" (Neues Wiener Journal, May 28, 1919: 6).

In the period leading up to 1919, three additional films were produced before Berthold Bartosch departed from Vienna. These films were *Der Raum Österreich als Brücke zwischen Ost und West* (The Austrian Region as a Bridge Between East and West), *Die Menschheit ohne Staatennetz* (Humanity Without a Network of States), and *Das Problem der Mitte* (The Problem of the Center). In the summer of 1919, Erwin Hanslik and Bartosch made their way to Berlin, intending to establish a German branch of the Cultural Research Institute. Noteworthy founding members on the German side included art historian Carl Koch (1892–1963) and Dr. Hans Cürlis (1889–1982), who played a crucial role in its expansion and eventually became its director. According to Cürlis, Bartosch was "one of the true pioneers of the artistic style in cartographic-statistical film" (Cürlis 1924: 211). Through Paul Wegener's (1874–1948) introduction, Lotte Reiniger (1899–1981) became part of the Institute, where she produced her first silhouette film, *Das Ornament des verliebten Herzens* (The Ornament of the Lovestruck Heart, 1919), in collaboration with Berthold Bartosch and her future husband, Carl Koch. Additionally, Bartosch was involved in Germany's first animated feature film, Lotte Reiniger's *Die Abenteuer des Prinzen Achmed* (The Adventures of Prince Achmed, 1923–1926).

Berthold Bartosch, a committed pacifist, relocated to Paris in 1930 due to the rise of National Socialism. There, he brought to life his most ambitious project, *L'Idée* (The Idea), which he worked on until 1932. According to film historian William Moritz (1941–2004), this is "the first animation film created as an art-work with serious, even tragic, social and philosophical themes" (Moritz 1997: 93). Unfortunately, Bartosch's other political works, including the anti-war animated film *Saint-François, ou Cauchemars et rêves* (St. Francis, or Nightmares and Dreams, 1939) and an animated satire of Adolf Hitler (1889–1945) that he began in 1938, were destroyed during the Nazi occupation of France (1940–1944). Additionally, Bartosch's animated advertising films from the pre- and post-war period, along with the preliminary work for the animated feature film *Cosmos*, to which Bartosch devoted at least a decade, have been lost. This means that Bartosch's animation work is almost entirely invisible.

"FAR-REACHING AND INSPIRING": HUNGARY

Following the collapse of Austria-Hungary, the aftermath of the First World War resulted in former crown lands battling over territories in a series of military conflicts. By mid-1919, tensions between Hungary and Romania reached a boiling point. As the conflict unfolded, Romanian forces successfully seized control of the Hungarian capital city of Budapest. This event not only led to the downfall of the short-lived Hungarian Soviet Republic but also prompted 'purges' driven partly by anti-Semitic motives. Subsequently, this fraught political atmosphere resulted in an exodus of Hungarian artists.

Many of them sought refuge in Vienna, which briefly blossomed as a hub for the avant-garde in the early 1920s. Notable among these emigrants was László Moholy-Nagy (né Weisz, 1895–1946), who later moved to Germany. Beginning in 1929, he created multiple films in Germany, one of which was his sole abstract film titled *Ein Lichtspiel Schwarz-Weiss-Grau* (A Lightplay Black White Gray, 1932), widely regarded as the cornerstone of his artistic creations. While no animated films from the avant-garde movement were created in Vienna, the city's status as the hub of the art movement directly influenced the development of the first Hungarian avant-garde film.

In 1924, György Gerő (1905–died after 1935), known as "the father of Hungarian Dadaism" (Orosz 2014: 4), released a film script titled *Béla*. He aimed to produce a movie that didn't involve actors, focusing on "an art form that underscores the coherence of visual representation" (Orosz 2014: 3). When the *Internationale Ausstellung neuer Theatertechnik* (International Exhibition of New Theatrical Techniques), curated by Friedrich Kiesler (later Frederick Kiesler, 1890–1965), took place in the fall of 1924 as part of the Music and Theater Festival of the City of Vienna, it became a gathering point for the avant-garde art scene. This unconventional exhibition, blurring the lines between theater and cinema, featured the premiere of the French avant-garde film *Ballet Mécanique* (Mechanical Ballet, 1924), which debuted in Germany in 1925 and France in 1926. It is evident that this Dadaist film had a significant impact on Gerő's film project. When he released some frames of his completed (and now lost) film in January 1927, they bore a closer resemblance to *Ballet Mécanique* (Mechanical Ballet, 1924) than to his original script.[5] Unfortunately, Vienna also marked the end of Gerő's hopeful career. In 1935, he was labeled as neurotic in a political trial and was confined to a private clinic in Vienna, where all trace of him was lost. In 2010, US media artist Bruce Checefsky (b. 1957) created a reinterpretation of *Béla* based on the original film music, bringing the invisible to light more than 80 years after the original.

Another significant figure in Hungarian animation with solid ties to Vienna was John Halas. Born in Budapest (then Austria-Hungary, now Hungary) on April 16, 1912, he was the youngest of 7 children. His mother, Berta Singer, hailed from Vienna. Halas' childhood was characterized by hardship. At the age of 3, his mother took him to Vienna to visit his grandmother, the family matriarch. With the assistance of the Red Cross, his grandmother arranged for John and his brother Antal to stay with their aunt in Switzerland after the First World War ended. Although facing food shortages amid warring states, Switzerland, as a neutral country, had a much better food supply than the former Dual Monarchy. After about 6 months, John Halas returned to Budapest via Vienna. Years later, he vividly recounted his passage through a revolutionary-stricken Austria:

"Fighting flared up between the Austro-Hungarians and the anti-Habsburg Communists. As we traveled through Austria, we were in the center of a battle. For days, the train was decked with Red Cross flags and signs, and we were told to hide under our seats since some of the passengers were military Communists. At some points of the journey we could hear gunfire, terrible things were happening around us, but to me as a small child, it looked more like a chaotic circus act" (John Halas, as cited in Halas 2006: 79).

John Halas, who honed his skills in animated film under George Pal, co-founded *Coloriton* in 1932 with Gyula Macskássy (1912–1971) and Félix Kassowitz (1907–1983), establishing one of Hungary's earliest studios dedicated to animated film.[6] While in Vienna, he gained valuable experiences that shaped his career in the animated film industry:

"It was during 1934 when, with my colleague … I took a round trip to attend the European premiere of Charlie Chaplin's *Modern Times* with the Disney cartoon *How to Play Polo*, with Goofy, in Vienna. We loved the films … The experience of seeing the work of Chaplin and Disney was far-reaching and inspired us for a long time" (John Halas, as cited in Coulter-Smith 2005: 92).

John Halas' film endeavors captured the spotlight in Great Britain. In late 1936, he arrived in London and crossed paths with his future wife, Joy Batchelor (1914–1991), in 1937. Together, they established *Halas & Batchelor* in 1940, which became the leading animation film studio in Great Britain for an extensive period. The studio's productions also reached Austria, notably with the 1950 release of *Der Schuhmacher und der Hutmacher* (The Shoemaker and the Hater), which advocated for the US economic reconstruction program in Europe, popularly known as the Marshall Plan. Furthermore, in 1965, *The Symphony Orchestra* received an award in Vienna. In 1984, John Halas significantly impacted Austrian animated film during the *Annecy International Animation Film Festival.* Hubert Sielecki (b. 1946), the director of Austria's first university animation film studio, was further inspired to establish an Austrian branch of the international animation umbrella organization *Association Internationale du Film d'Animation* (ASIFA) after a conversation with Halas, who was the president of ASIFA at that time.

FROM COLLAPSE TO OPPORTUNITY: FORMER YUGOSLAVIA

The collapse of the multiethnic Austro-Hungarian state significantly impacted the Austrian film industry. Vienna, which previously held a sizable market share, lost its influence. *Sascha-Filmindustrie*, the largest Austrian film production company during the silent and early sound film era, leveraged its extensive network to establish branches in various Eastern European capitals of former crown lands. Notably, one of these branches was *Bosna-Film* in Zagreb, the capital of the Kingdom of Yugoslavia.[7] This studio played a pivotal role in the country's early animation history.

Sergije Tagatz (1898–1973) is widely regarded as the trailblazer of Yugoslavian animated film. He arrived in 1922 from Yalta (Crimea Peninsula), which was then part of the Soviet Union, where he initially experimented with animated films at producer Joseph N. Ermolieff's (1889–1962) studio.[8] Initially, Tagatz sustained himself by creating short advertisements featuring animated logos for products like shoe polish and tea. Subsequently, *Bosna-Film* recruited him, and he animated the company logo for the opening credits of their films, employing a captivating unfolding spiral effect with the company's name. Following this, he also created an animated film trailer for the 1923 US feature film *The Kid* (1921), which had been imported to Yugoslavia. In this project, he skillfully drew and animated the head of the American child star Jackie Coogan (1914–1984). Despite impressing the studio head, who was thoroughly convinced by the results, no further projects of this nature were pursued. Nevertheless, Tagatz was appointed as the company's laboratory director. Although he did not create any more animated films during his lifetime, he made significant contributions to Yugoslavian cinema as a cameraman, technician, and theoretician.

NOTES

1 Indeed, John Halas was categorized as a "Monarchie-Österreicher" (Monarchy-Austrian) in the register of *Österreichische Flüchtlinge in Großbritannien* (Austrian Refugees in Great Britain), documented as part of the research project *Österreichische Literatur im Exil seit 1933* (Austrian Literature in Exile Since 1933) at the University of Salzburg

(cf. Müller 2002: 1 & 9). According to a commonly used definition, individuals born into German-speaking families in Austria-Hungary are considered Austrians. Following this distinction, Max Fleischer (1883–1972), Peter Eng (1892–1939), Johann Weichberger (1910–1992), and Berthold Bartosch (1893–1968) would be categorized as Austrians, while John Halas (1912–1995) and George Pal (1908–1980) would be classified as Hungarians. Jiří Trnka (1912–1969) and Hermína Týrlová (1900–1993) would be viewed as Czechs and so on.

2 The shooting location of this second film is listed as either Vienna or Warsaw, depending on the source.

3 The films included are as follows: *Das Werden des tschechoslowakischen Staates* (The Emergence of the Czechoslovak State, 100 m), *Das Werden des polnischen Staates* (The Emergence of the Polish State, 100 m), *Das Werden des südslawischen Staates* (The Emergence of the South Slavic State, 100 m), *Das Werden des deutschen Staates* (The Emergence of the German State, 200 m), *West und Ost* (West and East, 200 m), and *Der tschechoslowakische Staat* (The Czechoslovak State, 200 m).

4 The film cycle called *Menschheit* (Humanity) showcased Berthold Bartosch's initial four films encapsulated as *Staatenschau* (National Exhibition) and his two other films as *Völkerschau* (Ethnographic Exhibition), which were interrupted by a lecture. Plans were underway to expand the series to include *Wirtschaftsschau* (Economic Exhibition), *Gesellschaftsschau* (Social Exhibition), and *Weltschau* (World Exhibition, consisting of three film parts) in May 1919 (cf. Erde, May 20, 1919: 2). However, Bartosch's emigration to Germany seems to have prevented the completion of these additions.

5 It's believed that György Gerő most likely learned about the film from fellow artists residing in Vienna (cf. Orosz 2014: 3). In any case, he maintained close ties with the Hungarian artistic community in Vienna – partly due to his writings in various Viennese newspapers and magazines, such as the *Bécsi Magyar Újság* (Viennese Hungarian Daily) and the magazine *MA* (short for *Magyar Aktivizmus*, meaning Hungarian Activism), which had been in circulation in Vienna since 1920 as an exile publication.

6 *Coloriton*, established in 1932, has long been regarded as Hungary's first animation studio. However, research shows that as early as 1929/1930, an animation studio named *Pantofilm* produced two animated films (cf. Orosz 2011: 4).

7 Similar to Austria-Hungary, Yugoslavia was a multiethnic state that included the regions of the current nations of Croatia, Slovenia, Serbia, Montenegro, North Macedonia, Kosovo, and Bosnia and Herzegovina.

8 Following the Russian Revolution in 1917, prominent film producers like Joseph N. Ermolieff and Aleksandr Khanzhonkov (1877–1945) decided to move to the Crimean Peninsula to continue their film production away from the ongoing armed conflict. After they departed from the country in the early 1920s, their film studios were eventually combined to create what would later be known as *Mosfilm*, the most well-known film company in the Soviet Union.

4 Twenties Turnaround
The Rise and Fall of Animation

At the start of the 1920s, an effort was made to create educational animated films, even though animation had primarily served as entertainment up to that point.[1] In May 1920, the *Neue Kino-Rundschau* (New Cinema Review) published an article titled *Das Arbeitsfeld des Lehrfilms* (The Work Field of the Educational Film), which discussed the use of schematic animated films in areas such as 'Rassenkunde' ('racial science') in Germany.[2] In Austria, an educational animated film aimed to explain the consequences of the dissolution of Austria-Hungary. The press, under the title *Der Film im Dienste des politischen Lebens* (The Film in the Service of Political Life), explained the aim:

"To show laymen and those indifferent to the fragmentation of the homeland the damage it causes to everyone, an animated film illustrates these losses. It depicts what is lost in terms of coal and the personal damage incurred. Informative tables, presented in an engaging and effective manner, illustrate mine production, the amount consumed by industry, the railroads, and the required delivery quantities. The film is intended to enlighten both domestic and foreign audiences" (Tages-Post, October 2, 1920: 8).

Austria experienced significant political and cinematic upheaval during the early 1920s. The Austrian film industry, along with animated film production, appeared to be entering a prosperous period. Despite the decline of film production in other parts of Europe, Austria saw the establishment of numerous film companies. Consequently, the annual film output increased from about 40 films in 1912 to over a hundred in the early 1920s. Due to high inflation, film production in Austria became more cost-effective than in neighboring Germany, resulting in a significant inflow of foreign currency. Vienna's central geographic location in the heart of Europe further contributed to its advantageous position in the evolving film landscape: "Austria, the land with a centuries-old culture, architectural monuments, and magnificent landscapes that could be reached within a few hours of the studio, was apparently the future of the European film industry" (Walter Fritz, as translated in Renoldner and Frischengruber 1998: 6). For a brief period, Vienna served as the focal point of Central European film production.

In 1922, Austria successfully stabilized its currency with assistance from a League of Nations bond, while Germany faced hyperinflation in 1923. Around the same time, the Berlin film producer *Ufa* constructed modern studios in Babelsberg and Berlin-Tempelhof. This led to a flourishing German film industry, triggering an outflow of talent from Austria. As a result, Austria underwent a significant

DOI: 10.1201/9781003415442-5

transformation: the number of film producers dwindled from over 20 to just three. In contrast, the number of film distributors surged to over 70 (cf. Renoldner and Frischengruber 1998: 12). These distributors massively imported foreign live-action and animated films, particularly from the USA.[3] From the mid-1920s onward, only the niche of advertising films remained for Austrian animated films, with a few exceptions. The introduction of sound film in Austrian cinemas in the early 1930s brought about another significant change for film producers: "All film directors of that era were once again newcomers, pioneers in the field of sound film" (Gesek 1987: 1). The shift to sound film instigated a complete generational turnover in Austrian animated film, with none of the animators from the 1920s still active in the 1930s. When Mickey Mouse first gained popularity on Austrian screens in 1930, it prompted a trend of *Disney* imitation films that continued to influence the industry even after World War II (1939–1945).

FIRST FRAMES FROM THE FIRST STUDIO

According to the British film critic L'Estrange Fawcett (1894–1961), there were just two animators in Austria in 1928: "In Ladislaus Tuszynski and Peter Eng, Austria possesses two innovative artists" (L'Estrange Fawcett, as translated in Renoldner and Frischengruber 1998: 6). Ladislaus Tuszyński (1876–1943) was born in Lemberg (now Lviv in Ukraine, then Austria-Hungary) and moved to Vienna with his mother after losing his father in 1886. His career as an illustrator took off in the late 1890s, contributing to various magazines and newspapers. Notably, he spent nearly 40 years working for the *Kronen Zeitung*, which began publication in 1900. Tuszyński's interest in film blossomed during World War I (1914–1918), and in 1918, his screenplay *Das andere Ich* (The Other I) was filmed by *Sascha-Film*. When *Astoria-Film* was established right after the war, Tuszyński took on the role of artistic advisor and head of equipment for the film company. He was involved in virtually every aspect of filmmaking, whether directing, acting, writing scripts, designing sets, or working as a dramaturge: "Thus, there is no aspect of cinema that is foreign to the artist, and this is also – combined with his eminent talent for drawing – the secret of his success as an animator" (Peter Eng, as translated in Renoldner and Frischengruber 1998: 7).

In February 1920, Robert Reich (1882–1944) took on the director role at *Astoria-Film*. Reich pioneered using film for advertising purposes following the conclusion of the First World War. He began to focus increasingly on animated films, which he released collectively under the title *Das lachende Plakat* (The Laughing Poster). His aim now was not only to bolster promotional efforts but also to enhance narrative animated film: "As the first in Austria, the Astoria Film Company sets itself the task of bringing animation as a specific film genre to the international market, and it is hoped that these efforts will be appreciated by the public" (Peter Eng, as translated in Renoldner and Frischengruber 1998: 6).

In June 1920, another management reorganization at *Astoria-Film* promoted Ladislaus Tuszyński to head of the animation department (Figure 4.1). This was the first department of its kind in Austria. Alongside Heinz Hanus (1882–1972), the studio's artistic director, Tuszyński created intricate live-action feature films incorporating animated elements. The inaugural film in the series *Deutsche Sagen und*

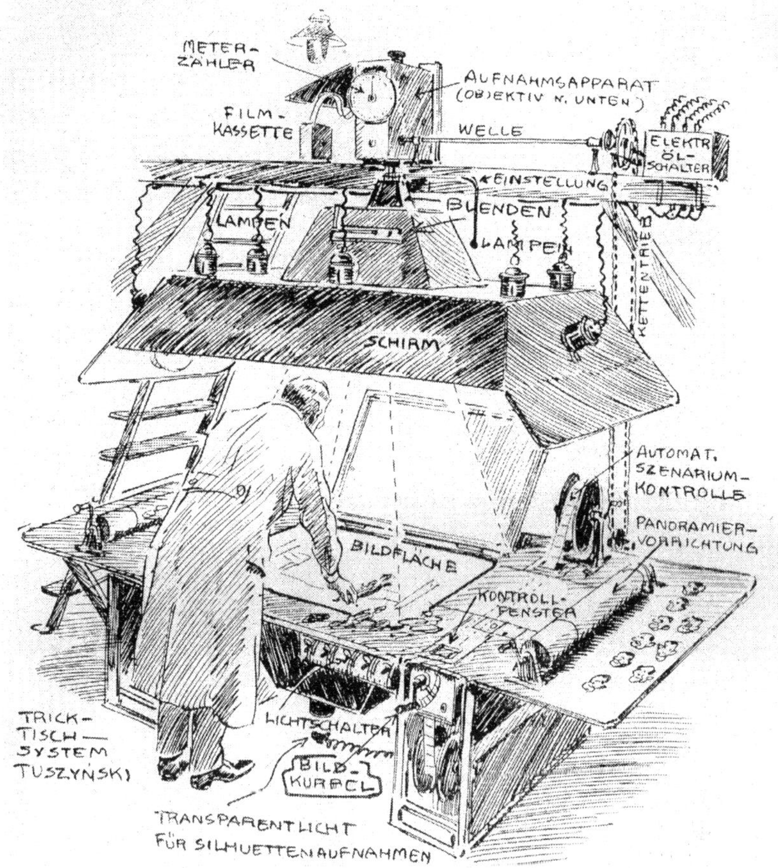

FIGURE 4.1 Animation stand system designed by Ladislaus Tuszyński. (Source: L'Estrange Fawcett.)

Märchen (German Legends and Fairy Tales), *Zwerg Nase* (Dwarf Nose), hit theaters just in time for Christmas in 1920. Initially targeted at youth audiences, its exceptional artistic quality quickly led to its repositioning as a film for adults.[4] The film gained international acclaim, being released in Germany and exported to Sweden under the title *Dvärgen Långnäsa*. Tuszyński went on to collaborate on other feature films, including *Das Weib des Irren* (The Wife of the Madman, 1921) and *Die Legende vom Gevatter Tod* (The Legend of the Grim Reaper, 1921). A fragment of the feature film *Kalif Storch* (Caliph Stork, 1922) has survived, showcasing Tuszyński's impressive skills. He used hand puppets for the transformation sequence of the main characters into storks and combined them with drawn animation sequences, as well as photo cutouts for floating objects: "The achievements of trick drawing are cleverly and imaginatively integrated with regular film shots, leaving the baffled viewer initially confronted with a seemingly insoluble riddle" (Der Filmbote, June 3, 1922: 19).

Ladislaus Tuszyński also created animated films using the pseudonym Strix (Figure 4.2). In late 1920, a film titled *Die Jagd nach dem Kopfe* (The Hunt for

FIGURE 4.2 Storyboard page created by Ladislaus Tuszyński. (Source: L'Estrange Fawcett.)

the Lost Head) was released as an introduction to the series *Aus den Memoiren des berühmten Detektivs Harry Packs* (The Adventures of the Famous Detective Harry Packs). Starting in 1919, Tuszyński spent a year and a half working on the film, which, at a length of 500 m, was considered the longest animated film in Austria at the time. This record remained unbroken for decades. The press reported on it on July 3, 1920:

"Tuszynski's images reveal, through the execution of the figures, in the treatment of the backgrounds, and in the perception of the villain, a subtle execution that sometimes leads to a complete illusion of reality. His 'decorations,' if one may call them such, are of overflowing richness, the movements of his 'actors' so masterfully transposed from real life. In this, Tuszynski is inexhaustible in devising original movements and plots and shows himself as master of this new drawing technique" (*Neue Kino-Rundschau*, as translated in Renoldner and Frischengruber 1998: 8).

The now-lost film told the peculiar story of a professor who misplaced his head in a moment of forgetfulness and continued to lecture without it. A burglar then stole the head but ended up losing it while fleeing and eventually hanged himself. The surviving sequel, *Amaranta* (1921), presents an equally bizarre story set in an amusement park, where an African banjo player falls in love with a woman with no lower half, an attraction of the showman. After kidnapping her, they encounter various complications as they run away. Ultimately, they reach a deserted island and start a family with two dark-skinned children's heads planted in pots. Although the press stated in 1920 that *Astoria-Film* expressed a "particular interest in the genre of animated film" (Der Filmbote No. 27, July 3, 1920: 15), it turned out to be Tuszyński's final venture into animation. He shifted his attention to feature films until 1924 before fully committing to his work as a newspaper illustrator.

Unlike his colleague, Peter Eng's (né Peter Anton Engelmann, 1892–1939) animation career outlasted the production crisis. He was undoubtedly one of the most prominent figures in Austrian silent-era animated film, yet his enigmatic biography remains a speculation subject and has required multiple revisions.[5] During his teenage years, he journeyed to the USA and reportedly began his career as a street sketch artist on Broadway in New York. Following this, he found employment as a newspaper cartoonist in New York and Philadelphia (PA).[6] Moreover, it is said that he also gained experience in creating comics, working in advertising, painting portraits, and designing exhibitions. "At any rate, Peter Eng was in the US and must have come into contact with animated films there, learning the current techniques of animation" (Schneider 2011: 122). Eng returned to Europe during World War I and lived in Vienna starting from July 1918, possibly becoming an Austrian citizen. From 1918, he claimed to be employed as an animator for the Viennese *Sascha-Film*. However, his first confirmed animated film, *Die Entfettungskur* (The Slimming Cure), was produced for a film studio in Munich, southern Germany, and presented to film censors in March 1919. In 1919, at least two installments of the film series *Mausi und Lausi* (Mousi and Lausi) were created for the Vienna-based *Sascha-Film*. These films featured the eponymous characters traveling to America and various other locations.[7] Working at *Sascha-Film*, Eng appreciated the working conditions and the creative freedom given to him by film entrepreneur Sascha Kolowrat-Krakowsky (1886–1927), which was quite different from the way Walt Disney (1901–1966) operated:

"One of the most ideal animated film entrepreneurs was Count Kolowrat. He possessed a quality that I never, ever found again in a film industrialist. He was content to provide the materials to the draftsman and never had any 'funny ideas.' He gave me an operator, a draftsman, and a camera, and came to the screening. That was all" (Eng 1936: 2).

Following the reorganization of *Astoria-Film* in 1920, Peter Eng took charge of the animation department at the company in collaboration with Ladislaus Tuszyński. It appears that he continued to work on his animated series *Mausi und Lausi* (Mousi and Lausi) during that time, but apart from this, there is no verified information available regarding his film production at *Astoria-Film*.[8] In September 1921, Eng gained attention at the *Wiener Kino-Messe* (Vienna Cinema Exhibition), a part of the first *Wiener Internationale Messe* (WIM, Vienna International Exhibition). The exhibition aimed to reestablish Vienna as an international cultural center following the monarchy's collapse and alleviate its economic isolation. One of the highlights of the *Kino-Messe* (Cinema Exhibition) was "the animation pavilion, in which Mr. Peter Eng makes caricatures of some of the visitors and then, in front of their eyes, changes the drawings into an animation, which the viewer can see the next day projected in the pavilion" (*Die Filmwelt*, as translated in Renoldner and Frischengruber 1998: 10). Eng originally intended to develop and copy the films in his pavilion for same-day viewing, but this plan proved technically unfeasible. Using cutout figures, Eng adorned the main wall of his pavilion with images of his film characters at different points of motion. Two years later, Eng created a promotional trailer for the WIM titled *Die Entdeckung Wiens am Nordpol* (The Discovery of Vienna at the North Pole, 1923).[9] It featured whimsical animation sequences depicting life at the North

Pole, including making ice cream and lubricating the Earth's axis with reindeer fat daily. The trailer also showcased the screening of a Viennese exhibition film in the polar cinema, illustrating the titular discovery of Vienna by the North Pole inhabitants, with one of them embarking on a live-action sequence.

Peter Eng was also tasked by the *Staatliche Filmhauptstelle* (FHS, State Film Headquarters) to create the promotional film *Der geistige Arbeiter* (The Intellectual Worker, 1921/1922), which aimed to promote the welfare kitchens established by Eugenie Schwarzwald (née Nußbaum, 1872–1940) during World War I. After this project, it seems that he focused on creating advertising animations. To facilitate this, he rented the animation studio of *Astoria-Film* as needed. In April of 1923, it was reported by the media:

"Peter Eng […] has been one of the outstanding cartoonists for New York newspapers, with which he still collaborates today. His page-long, drawn episodes from everyday American life featuring recurring characters are now revived and, with grotesque humor, poke fun at the Viennese way in animated films. In just a minute, he knows how to create comical, grotesque, and effective advertising. One forgets the purpose, overlooking the fact that they have become the victim of an advertisement while admiring his nimble pencil and the technical art of animation" (Die Stunde, April 25, 1923: 5).

Amid the production crisis, commercials were also affected. In June 1923, Peter Eng released a bitterly ironic report detailing the production of an advertising film for a shoe dealer: "With literary escapades reminiscent of Dadaism, Peter Eng essentially expresses his despair at his profession, which was earning him less and less money in light of the cinema crisis" (Renoldner 2010: 74). Eng's desperation seemed to be so intense that he attempted, unsuccessfully, to seek fortune in Berlin, Germany.[10] In 1928, Eng stated that despite producing a film for the tax authority,[11] he had "not received a single governmental or municipal commission" (Peter Eng, as cited in Moser 2019: 219). However, during the latter half of the 1920s, he produced several animated advertising films for municipal institutions and organizations. This included *Ja, warum fahrns denn net?* (Well, Why Aren't You Driving?, 1924/1925) for the *Wiener Verkehrsbetriebe* (Vienna Public Transport Company). Additionally, he produced the animated film *Lerne schwimmen!* (Learn to Swim!, 1926) and the live-action film *Schillers Räuber* (Schiller's Robbers, 1926) for the *Amalienbad*, which was one of the most modern public indoor swimming pools in Europe when it opened in 1926.

In the few advertising films preserved by Peter Eng, he preferred to work with the cutout animation technique (a kind of stop motion with drawn, cutout figures), which he combined with live-action film sequences. Clearly passionate about blending animation and live-action film, Eng ventured into uncharted territory in 1927 by producing 26 episodes of the *Spieltricks* (Trick Plays) series.[12] These episodes were marketed as 'living trick films' featuring a 'living trick figure.' The description reads:

"In these films, the leading lady [Louise Wilhelm] is 'moved' by the director's hand, requiring her to act in a trick-like manner to achieve effects similar to those of a drawn paper figure. This serves as a touchstone for true film aptitude in acting. For months, Peter Eng experimented with drawing, photography, and lighting" (Mein Film (58), 1927: 7).

In the spring of 1929, Peter Eng's last film produced in Austria hit the screens: *Ihm geht's an den Kragen. Ein Tanzfilm von Peter Eng* (He's in Trouble. A Dance Film by Peter Eng).[13] It is unclear why Eng did not continue making films in Austria after this. According to legend, he depicted a high-ranking politician from the city government disparagingly on one of his advertising posters for the *Wiener Verkehrsbetriebe* (Vienna Public Transport Company) in 1929. As a result, all the posters were taken down overnight, and public contracts ceased following this scandal.[14] This incident could also clarify his relocation to Berlin, where he created his last known animated film, *Mathé-Revue* (1929), for Berlin's *Terra-Film*. This sound film served as a notable representation of Austrian art:

"This animated film features topical satirical content and clever lyrics by the esteemed Viennese satirist Theodor Waldau (Wauwau). The music is composed by H. E. Heller [Hans Ewald Heller (1894–1966), an Austrian composer]. The film achieved the remarkable feat of fully resolving the issue of organically connecting image, word, and sound through non-mechanical means. Its Berlin screening generated considerable excitement among interested audiences. Rose Mathé, renowned for her performances at the Vienna State Opera, was enlisted to perform the challenging vocal parts" (Mein Film (162), 1929: B).

During the 1930s, Peter Eng's favored cutout animation technique fell out of favor, with critics stating that "an animated film made this way does not evoke pleasure; everything appears angular, awkward, and unnaturally jerky" (Die Wiener Bühne, July 1938: 29). This shift could have also played a part in bringing an end to Eng's career as an animator. How many films he created during his roughly ten-year stint as an active animator is uncertain. While some sources indicate 600 animated films (cf. Havas 2012: 33), others, such as the contemporary press in 1928, claimed "38 live-action commercials and over 900 advertising cartoons" (as cited in Moser 2019: 220).[15] Both figures may be exaggerated due to Eng's skill in self-promotion, but they highlight his significant influence on the early history of Austrian animation.[16]

MORE THAN TWO BRUSHES BEHIND THE FRAMES

Even though Ladislaus Tuszyński and Peter Eng were undeniably the leading figures in Austrian animated film during the 1920s, it's essential to acknowledge that other exceptionally talented individuals also contributed significantly to the industry. One such individual was Michael Maibaum (1876–1942?), originally from Warsaw, Poland, who later became an Austrian citizen after settling in Vienna in 1904. In his primary occupation as an architect, he made significant contributions, including his involvement in the design of the Vienna Concert Hall. During the early 1920s, he developed a keen interest in the art of filmmaking and animation. In 1921, he participated in director Hans Steinhoff's (né Johannes Reiter, 1882–1945) first feature film, *Kleider machen Leute* (Clothes Make the Man, 1921), creating a cinematic special effect for the fragmentarily preserved movie. This effect made houses appear to sway, as seen by drunken tavern-goers. He also produced an intricately animated dream sequence using the cutout animation technique, a method also employed by Peter Eng. Shortly after, he started working for Karl Köfinger (1879–1938), who had been creating short films since 1923 and eventually became the leading producer of short films and commercials in the 1920s. Using the cutout animation technique again, Maibaum created the advertising cartoon *Der Stiefelputzer als Liebesamor* (The Bootblack as Love Cupid, 1923/1924) for *Cavalier* shoe polish.[17] The film portrays a bootblack with skin as black as the advertised shoe polish. Through his exceptional shoeshine services, one of his customers impresses his beloved with his freshly polished shoes. Maibaum drew inspiration from cinematic models like Ladislaus Tuszyński's *Amaranta* (1921), using a racist portrayal of the shoeshine boy and a subtle erotic undertone.[18] Maibaum's involvement in another film project is documented in press accounts. In March 1924, there was coverage of the production of the feature film *Gullivers Reisen* (Gulliver's Travels) by the recently established *Renaissance-Kunstfilm*. It was reported that Maibaum was responsible for creating the animated drawings for the film and that "The screening of the film, which deserves the greatest interest in every respect and is guaranteed to be a sure success from the outset, is scheduled for early April" (Der Filmbote, March 1, 1924: 15). Despite this initial confidence, the film's production was halted. Fear of US competition may have played a role in this decision, as shortly afterward, the press announced *Universal*'s plans for a film adaptation of the classic story. It seems that Maibaum's career in filmmaking ended with the production crisis in the mid-1920s, as there are no further references to his cinematic works after 1924.[19]

The German Louis Seel (also known as Luis or Ludwig, 1889–?) is frequently mentioned in connection with the Austrian animated film of the 1920s. Like Peter Eng, who worked in Germany (Munich, Berlin), the USA (New York, Philadelphia), and Denmark (Copenhagen), Seel is known as a globetrotter. He learned the craft of animation in the USA around 1916 by assisting in the production of the animated series *Mutt and Jeff,* based on the comic by Bud Fisher (1885–1954). Then, from 1918, he created his own series called *Screen Novelties.* In 1919, upon his return to Germany, he became one of the pioneers of German animated film. From 1921 to 1926, he created the animated series *Münchner Bilderbogen* (Picture Sheets from Munich),[20] which gained international popularity in around 40 countries. During this period, he also worked in New York (1924) and Great Britain (1925). His series was so well-received in Austria that he traveled to Vienna in 1925 to produce the pilot for a spin-off series titled *Wiener Bilderbogen* (Viennese Picture Book). In May 1925, the media covered the creator of *Münchner Bilderbogen* (Picture Sheets from Munich) and his intentions for Vienna: "The creator of the above, Louis Seel, has recently moved his activities to Vienna. [...] It is hoped that the artist will remain in our city for a long time, [as his] films have been running so successfully in Viennese cinemas" (*Der Filmbote*, as translated in Renoldner and Frischengruber 1998: 11).

In the context of the *Brooklyn Radio Exposition* in 1925 in New York (USA), Louis Seel envisioned the future potential of radio transmissions in *Wiener Bilderbogen Nr. 1* (Viennese Picture Book No. 1, 1925), depicting innovative inventions for the Viennese woman of tomorrow. These included taking a radio-magnetic bath in the morning, receiving warm air radio-thermally from the Sahara in winter, and utilizing radio-magnetic clothing. In his futuristic film, Seel even foresaw technological advancements, like the wife communicating with her friend wirelessly, using radio-optical technology to observe her husband, transmitting a slap to a rival through a data glove, and the husband using a flat-screen television for cinematic purposes.

In the film's final scene, the wife departs "with her lover beyond the treacherous ether waves" and travels to New York. Indeed, Seel played a significant role in bridging the gap between the continents. For instance, he introduced the rotoscoping process, initially developed in the USA by Austrian-born Max Fleischer (1883–1972), to Europe.

ALMOST INVISIBLE ANIMATION PIONEERS

An unsung pioneer of animated filmmaking emerged in the early 1920s: Paul Ludwig Winter (1885–1954).[21] His journey began with a live-action short film at *Reform-Film* in Vienna in 1919. He then ventured into the production of the feature film *Vergeltung* (Odplata in Czech, Retaliation in English) for *Urania-Film Prag* in Czechoslovakia in 1920. Upon returning to Vienna, he completed the animated film *Das ideale Auto* (The Ideal Car) in 1921 for *Sascha-Film*, representing the first installment in his series *Der Trick im Trickfilm* (The Trick in the Trick Film). In doing so, Winter employed experimental techniques otherwise only associated with international luminaries such as Norman McLaren (1914–1987) and Len Lye (1901–1980): "Paul Winter, leveraging his extensive technical expertise, has developed a new chemical and copying process, along with a unique filming technique. For now, he handles everything on his own without any outside assistance: drawing, photographing, copying, retouching, and introducing an entirely new element to film – etching" (Die Filmwelt (6), 1921a: 13). The series, later named *Autoserie* (Car Series), continued with *500 Dollar Prämie* (500 Dollar Reward, 1921), *Popo als Chauffeur* (Popo as Chauffeur, 1921), and *Popo und der Grand Prix* (Popo and the Grand Prix, 1921). The press was highly enthusiastic about the announcement of these films, stating, "From all this, it is clear that the program of Sascha Film A.-G. is exceptionally rich in every respect and that the company stands at the forefront of the Austrian film industry, successfully securing a leading position in the world market" (Die Filmwelt (11), 1921b: 6).

In 1922, the animator ventured into business on his own with *Winter-Film* and created animated films such as *Berühmte Köpfe* (Famous Heads, 1922) and *Launen der Mode* (Fancies of Fashion, 1922).[22] Additionally, he made an unspecified "Siedlungsfilm" (Settlement Film) using the stop-motion process: "For the settlement film, many hands were needed to create the house cubes that seemingly roll up on their own and assemble into a block of houses. The cubes were pushed into the recording room piece by piece, a task that took many hours" (Der Tag, October 19, 1923: 8). Due to the hot lamplight, a few cardboard cubes became misshapen and needed meticulous regluing. Furthermore, Paul Ludwig Winter created trick shots for educational scientific films like *Hygiene der Ehe* (Marital Hygiene, 1922), which was even exported to the USA.

Paul Ludwig Winter's most notable accomplishment was *Winter-Woche* (Winter-Week), starting in 1923. Unlike the *Sascha-Journal* newsreel, which only included animated films as separate features, *Winter-Woche* (Winter-Week) was a fully animated newsreel (Figure 4.3). The fifth edition demonstrates the extensive variety of subjects covered. It commences with scientific content on X-rays, leads into coverage of a soccer match between Germany and Austria, touches on fashion themes such as hat and shoe trends, and concludes with political commentary:

FIGURE 4.3 The global success of the *Winter-Woche* (Winter-Week), spotlighted in a newspaper ad in 1923. (Source: Die Filmwelt (No. 3/1923).)

"Then Mr. Winter turns to political satire, and we can admire Minister [Benito] Mussolini as he, while fighting everything red, hunts the fox – the social democrat of the animal world – thus never abandoning fascism, even in sports." Jackie Coogan (1914–1984), the US child star, is also depicted "comically as the 48th star of the American flag" (Die Filmwelt (5), 1923a: 6).

Special editions like *Mondaine Mode* (High-Fashion, 1923), *Aktuelles von Sport und Mode* (News from Sports and Fashion, 1923), *Aus Sowjetrussland* (From Soviet Russia, 1923), or *Um die sich der Film dreht* (Around Whom the Film Revolves, 1923) were published irregularly in addition to the regular issue. These special editions featured caricatures of actors ranging from Mary Pickford (née Gladys Louise Smith, 1892–1979) to Charlie Chaplin (1889–1977). It seems that Paul Ludwig Winter dabbled in various animation techniques. While a full-page comic ad (!) in March 1923 still displayed a drawing hand on the screen, the special edition *Meister der Tonkunst* (Masters of Musical Art, 1923), published in September, featured silhouettes of famous composers in silhouette cutouts. This innovative concept brought Winter international recognition:

"The 'Winterwoche' (Winter Week) is beginning to gain significance for the film industry far beyond Austria's borders, as it will now be regularly shown in England, Sweden, and Czechoslovakia. As a result, future editions of 'Winterwoche' will be more expansive, becoming more international and attracting greater interest here [in Austria] as well" (Die Filmwelt (7), 1923c: 14).

According to censorship reports, Paul Ludwig Winter was also the creator of the political animated film *Seipel's Sanierung* (Seipel's Economic Recovery, 1922/1923), which had not been attributed until now:[23] Amid the ongoing economic crisis, Austrian politicians in late 1922 sought to prevent national bankruptcy by securing a League of Nations loan. The loan came with strict austerity measures, including layoffs in the civil service and increased taxes. Criticism of Christian-Social Chancellor Ignaz Seipel (1876–1932) peaked with this election advertisement cartoon by the *Sozialdemokratische Arbeiterpartei* (Social Democratic Workers' Party) during the National Council election in the autumn of 1923: "The film's highlight is its self-reflexive animation; notably, even the left-wing election campaign doesn't shy away from playing the antisemitism card through the caricature of a 'Geldjude' (moneyed Jew)" (Michael Loebenstein, as cited in Dewald et al. 2007: 287). In early October 1923, a public screening became a major event when "Das Kino der Zehntausend" (The Cinema of Ten Thousand) was set up on a vacant lot in the city center (Arbeiter-Zeitung, October 5, 1923: 8). The screening featured the film alongside a second election advertising cartoon titled *Der arme Hausherr oder: Der Mieterschutz in Gefahr* (The Poor Landlord, or: Tenant Protection in Danger, 1923)[24] and a Charlie Chaplin film. According to the *Arbeiter-Zeitung* (Workers' Newspaper, a paper of the labor movement), the two animated films prompted as much laughter as the Chaplin flick. However, the success of *Winter-Film* was short-lived as it soon faced a decline, likely due to the production crisis, with no issues of *Winter-Woche* (Winter-Week) traceable after February 1924.[25]

Peer Andersen, whose real name was Georg Rakoczy, is another overlooked animator from the 1920s. Before venturing into the film world, he created advertising graphics and caricatures for various newspapers. While working for the film studio *Ing. Alfred v. Barris*, he produced a series of animated films that gained popularity beyond Vienna despite focusing on local themes. One of his notable works, *Stern des Südens* (Southern Star), was released in the fall of 1920 and described as "a well-drawn animated film with doggerel verses that aroused general merriment" (Neue Kino-Rundschau, November 6, 1920b: 19). Upon arriving in Vienna in December 1922, Siegmund Breitbart (1893–1925), a renowned wrestler and performer known as the strongest man in the world, quickly gained popularity among the Viennese public.[26] In conjunction with the release of his film *Der Eisenkönig* (The Iron King, 1923), the magazine *Die Filmwelt* (The Film World) dedicated a special issue to Breitbart: "Vienna has chosen a new favorite, and the way it has embraced Breitbart, who has become one of us in the two months since his arrival, reflects the true essence of genuine Viennese character – one that even the hardships of the toughest times have neither weakened nor destroyed" (Lauterstein 1923: 2). Alfred von Barris was eager to capitalize on this success and requested Breitbart's permission to feature him and some of his rivals in an animated film. Initially doubtful, Breitbart's skepticism transformed into excitement. In early March, the animated film spoof *Breitbart und die Konkurrenz* (Breitbart and the Competition, 1923) was released, "which, according to experts, ranks among the best in this film genre" (Das Kino-Journal, March 10, 1923: 3). In December of that same year, Andersen became a shareholder of *'Vox' Reklame und Film Gesellschaft m. b. H.*, a company specialized in creating advertising posters and films. Quite openly, Andersen 'poached' from his most famous colleagues – when he illustrated the article *Abenteuer mit dem Autobus* (Adventures with the Bus) in April 1925 with caricatures, his drawings were so similar to those of Peter Eng that the newspaper noted: "Not drawings by Eng, but by Peer Andersen" (Mailler 1925: 7). Two years later, he created an election ad animation for the Austrian Unity List – a coalition of anti-Marxist parties – which he named *Wiener Bilderbogen* (Viennese Picture Book, 1927), freely after Louis Seel.[27]

THE MAX FLEISCHER OF AMATEUR FILM

Ever since the dawn of cinematography, people have wanted to recreate the cinema experience in their own homes. While various forms of 'home cinema' were already present in the early 1900s, it wasn't until the mid-1920s that the widespread availability of narrow film formats (9.5 and 16 mm), corresponding projectors, and portable film cameras fueled the growth of an amateur film movement.

Established in Vienna in 1927, the *Klub der Kinoamateure Österreichs* (KdKÖ, Austrian Film Amateurs Club) holds the esteemed title of being the oldest active amateur film club globally. One of Austria's most important amateur film pioneers and a club member was Friedrich Kuplent (1905–1985), also known as Frikup. His experimental short film *Prater* (1929) is widely regarded as a groundbreaking piece of work in the Austrian film avant-garde. This movement only emerged in non-amateur film circles following World War II. The film, which could also be interpreted as a 'Stadtsinfonie' (city symphony), employed a variety of film tricks. It has been overlooked until now that Kuplent also played a significant role in animated film.

Starting in the spring of 1928, Friedrich Kuplent repeatedly garnered attention in amateur film circles. His regular lecture series featured topics such as *Expressionismus im Film* (Expressionism in Film) and *Der Zeichenfilm für den Kino-Amateur* (The Animated Cartoon for the Cinema Amateur). From the summer of 1928, he created title drawings for KdKÖ members free of charge. Later that fall, he achieved third place in the film prize competition of the amateur film magazine *Photo-Sport*. His animated film *Die Rivalen* (The Rivals, 1928) was likened to Max Fleischer's *Out of the Inkwell* (1918–1929):

"An exemplary solution for the animated film, punctuated by lively scenes where the animated character interacts with the real world. Like Max Fleischmann [sic!], Kuplent presents a character that begins on paper and then suddenly comes to life, running through the room, hiding in the inkwell, and more. We commend the author for this outstanding work" (Photo-Sport, November 1928: 4).

From 1929 onward, Friedrich Kuplent regularly contributed as a guest writer to *Photo-Sport*. This included an article in October 1930 about the potential of the copying trick titled *Tricks mit verkehrter Kamera* (Tricks with Upside Down Camera) and an article in December 1930 called *Hinter den Kulissen des Amateurtrickfilmers* (Behind the Scenes of the Amateur Animator). In the January 1934 issue, he even suggested that amateur filmmakers engage in animated cartoons as "a way to spend the long winter evenings" (Kuplent 1934: 15). Furthermore, he conducted classes where he taught aspiring filmmakers the techniques of trick filming and creating animated films. In addition to his film work, he also wrote guidebooks published in Germany. For example, the cover of *Der Amateur-Tonfilm* (The Amateur Sound Film, 1931) showcased a banjo-playing Mickey Mouse, adding a touch of whimsy to the subject matter. In another publication, *Zauberbuch des Kino-Amateurs: Tricks über Tricks* (Magic Book of the Cinema Amateur: Tricks Upon Tricks, 1936), he explored 'Zeichentrickfilme' (animated cartoons) and 'Kombinationszeichentrickfilme' (live-action/traditionally animated hybrid films) alongside film tricks. In his own live-action/animation hybrids, the unmistakable influence of Max Fleischer remained evident – the animated character in *Dummy lebt* (Dummy is Alive) and *Dummy lebt wieder* (Dummy is Alive Again, 1934/1935) bore a strong resemblance to Koko the Clown.

Like the Fleischer brothers, Friedrich Kuplent was also a pioneer of sound film. In his animated film *Parade der Zinnsoldaten* (Parade of the Tin Soldiers, 1930), he showcased paper-cut soldier figures marching to the sounds of a record. The contemporary press hailed this as the "first amateur sound film" (Fränkel 1930: 586). With his films, Kuplent not only bridged to the Viennese post-war avant-garde but also paved the way for amateur filmmakers like Hans O. Sindelar (1921–2014) and Rudolf Enter (1927–2017). From the 1960s onward, they could turn their hobby into a (second) profession.

NOTES

1 In October 1920, Helene Littmann (1866–1945), an official of the association *Jugend-Bildung* (Youth Education), reported that the association had been organizing cinema screenings for schoolchildren for 3 years. They also relied on animated films to make the events more engaging: "Our program primarily featured educational films, with a short comedy or animated film serving as the finale" (Littmann 1920: 6).
2 Cf. Neue Kino-Rundschau, May 1, 1920d: 12.
3 As early as 1917, American animated films such as the *Mutt & Jeff* series or the *Charlie Chaplin* cartoons were occasionally imported to Austria.
4 This probably had economic reasons as well. A review of the film noted "that the production costs are so high that the rental fee for children's screenings is nearly unaffordable" (Neue Kino-Rundschau, November 20, 1920c: 21)
5 In 1998, it was still assumed that Peter Eng had successfully emigrated to the USA in 1938 (cf. Renoldner and Frischengruber 1998: 18). Today, it seems certain that Peter Eng and his wife took their own lives in Olmütz (now Olomouc, Czech Republic) in March 1939 (cf. Schneider 2011: 132).
6 His work for the *Philadelphia Evening Telegraph* and *The Saturday Evening Post* (both in Philadelphia, PA) is confirmed. It is also speculated that he contributed to the *New York Evening Telegram* (cf. Havas 2012: 30).
7 According to his statements, Peter Eng also worked for Viennese *Filmag*. It is possible that he authored the animated films *Gretls Filmtraum* (Gretl's Film Dream, 1918) and *Wien zur Kriegs- und Friedenszeit* (Vienna in Times of War and Peace, 1919) that were produced there.
8 The IMDb lists a film called *Mausi und Lausi wählen* (Mousi and Lausi Vote, 1920). The literature (cf. Schneider 2011: 140) also mentions the film titles *Die Frau und die Mode* (The Woman and Fashion), *Kinotypen* (Cinematic Types), and *Aus der Werkstatt des Films* (From the Workshop of Film). However, no documents from contemporary sources could be found for any of these titles.

9 The film is often said to have been made in 1921 or 1922. Still, it was first mentioned in the press in 1923 as a "new animated film" (Die Filmwelt (6), 1923b: 14). It was previously believed that Ladislaus Tuszyński collaborated on the film, but this is no longer assumed. In 1926, the film was re-issued.

10 At least, that's what Peter Eng claimed in the article *Trickfilmkarriere* (Animation Career). The text was one of Eng's satirical pieces, and its level of truth was likely not very high. He claimed that his career as an animator began with a commission to portray the general director of a film company. Since the director constantly talked and gestured, Eng "drew 3,081 frames of his hand movements, cut them out at home, spread them on the floor, and photographed them in 9×12. I glued the pictures together and sold the whole thing to Urania under the title *Gestikulationsarten eines Tobsüchtigen. Lehrfilm von Peter Eng* (Gesticulation Types of a Frenzied Person. Educational Film by Peter Eng)" (Eng 1925: 44).

11 This could refer to the approximately half-hour-long live-action film *Wo sich das Rathaus die Steuern holt* (Where the City Hall Collects Taxes, 1923), which contained several animated sequences.

12 This is likely a blend of the German terms 'Spielfilm' (live-action film) and 'Trickfilm' (trick film).

13 Since the film is considered lost, it's uncertain if it was an animated film. However, Peter Eng had already produced a "Trickfilmtanz" (Trick Film Dance) in 1920 (Wiener Allgemeine Zeitung, February 6, 1920: 2).

14 In fact, Peter Eng faced intense criticism in the press in 1929: "But why did he choose such unattractive models as the archetypes for his Viennese passengers, leading every foreigner to believe that the ugliest people are native to Vienna" (Neuigkeits-Welt-Blatt No. 148, June 28, 1929: 5). Additionally, his posters in the trams, intended to educate passengers about discipline, were considered bothersome. The behavioral guidelines were regarded as "a matter of upbringing and personal tact; the relevant image is unlikely to leave much of an impression on young people" (Freiheit!, May 17, 1929: 4).

15 Only seven of Peter Eng's advertising films have survived. They are *Der geistige Arbeiter* (The Intellectual Worker, 1921/1922), *Die Entdeckung Wiens am Nordpol* (The Discovery of Vienna at the North Pole, 1923), *Ja, warum fahrns denn net?* (Well, Why Aren't You Driving?, 1924/1925), *Lerne schwimmen*! (Learn to Swim!, 1926), *Schillers Räuber* (Schiller's Robbers, 1926), and the two undated animated films *Ferrowatt Wunderfilm* (Ferrowatt Wonder Film) and *Die beste Metalldrahtlampe* (The Best Metal Wire Lamp) for Ferrowatt. The surviving advertisement film *Wo sich das Rathaus die Steuern holt* (Where the City Hall Collects Taxes, 1923) is also likely attributed to Eng. The loss of Eng's films may be connected to "the common practice at the time of reusing film reels" (Zan 2012: [2]).

16 Peter Eng also played a vital role in a closely related art form to animation. As a caricaturist, he is credited with introducing the speech balloon comic to the German-speaking world in the early 1920s after encountering it in America (cf. Havas 2012: 28–35).

17 An article in the May 1930 issue of the magazine *Österreichische Reklame* (Austrian Advertising) demonstrates the extensive effort required for creating cutout animated films: "According to a report from an animation workshop, an artist was tasked with creating 141 pairs of cutout hands to accurately depict the action of opening a shoe polish tin" (as cited in Moser 2019: 216).

18 Louis Seel's animated film *Wiener Bilderbogen Nr. 1* (Viennese Picture Book No. 1, 1925), which will be discussed further, also intertwined themes of eroticism and racism. Additionally, two anonymously preserved animated films titled *Blühender Unsinn* (Flourishing Nonsense, 1929) and *Schöpfungsgeschichte* (Creation Story, c. 1920) contained elements of erotic content.

19 A censorship list dated March 17, 1923, also includes the film title *Der Lausbub* (The Rascal). Apart from Michael Maibaum's name, the entry contains no further information (facsimile in Caneppele (ed.) 2002: 47). Another censorship list dated March 25, 1936, includes a lottery advertisement film titled *Kultur ins Volk* (Culture to the People), attributed to an architect named Michael Maybaum (facsimile in Ballhausen and Caneppele (eds.) 2009: 189). However, it remains unclear whether this refers to Maibaum or if the film is animated.

20 The series was also known as *Münchner Filmbilderbogen* (Film Picture Sheets from Munich) and later as *Louis Seel Filmbilderbogen* (Film Picture Sheets from Louis Seel).

21 As of August 2023, the Czech film archive NFA listed the life dates of 1879–1934 in its biographical database. In response to a reference to Paul L. Winter's application for admission to the *Reichsfachschaft Film*, which indicated the year of birth as 1885, Jaroslav Lopour replied: "unfortunately, the date of birth and death were entered in the 1990s by a former employee with the note that the dates are not certain/verified. The year 1885 will be correct" (email to the author, dated August 31, 2023). The exact year of death couldn't be confirmed, but according to records from the Vienna cemeteries, a person named Paul Ludwig Winter was cremated in 1954. Gerald Bartosch (in an email to the author dated October 2, 2023) confirmed that this individual was born in 1885.

22 This was likely the film *Frühlingserwachen in der Mode* (Spring Awakening in Fashion), announced as early as 1921.

23 Facsimile in Caneppele (ed.) 2002: 102.

24 Based on the existing censorship record, which indicates that it was created by *Engfilm*, the producer of this second political animated film was probably Peter Eng (cf. Caneppele (ed.) 2002: 102).

25 Paul L. Winter apparently wanted to return to filmmaking in the early 1930s, applying for admission to the *Reichsfachschaft Film*, but no films by him from that period are known to exist.

26 Siegmund Breitbart later found success in the USA as well. For instance, on November 27, 1923, he used only his teeth to pull a carriage carrying 50 passengers through the streets of Washington, DC.

27 The film was shown as a supporting program for the social drama *Von 1923 bis 1927* (From 1923 to 1927, 1927), also produced by Peer Andersen.

5 It's a Mouse!
Disney Copycats in the 1930s

In the early 1930s, foreign animated film productions, notably *Disney*'s Mickey Mouse and *Silly Symphonies*, took over Austrian movie screens. While the National Socialists in Germany were already vehemently opposing "the dirty and filthy vermin," the Austrian press was mocking this cultural conflict:

"The Nazis have identified a new enemy. In addition to the French, Poles, Jews, Freemasons, and Jesuits, there is yet another menace gnawing at the very marrow of the German people: Mickey Mouse. [...] The German-nationalist ideal beast wants nothing to do with you; it dons its swastika and grunts at you with hostility" (Arbeiter-Zeitung, June 26, 1931: 4).

Initially, Austrian filmmakers did not compete with *Disney*, reportedly because the Austrian audience was "oversaturated" and "the genre of animated sound films in Vienna has not had as many fans in recent months as it once did"[1] (as cited in Laqua 1992: 120). Despite the alleged oversaturation, Mickey Mouse's popularity peaked in Austria in the mid-1930s. The *Illustrierter Film-Kurier* (Illustrated Film Courier) dedicated a lavishly illustrated issue (No. 1273, 1935) titled *Micky spielt auf* (Mickey Strikes Up) exclusively to *Disney*'s current distribution program. Robert Reich (1882–1944) also desired to partake in this success, expressing his intention to "produce domestic 'Sillies' and 'Mickeys'" (Der Morgen, March 23, 1936: 10) through his newly established *S.S.S. Trickfilm-Gesellschaft* (S.S.S. Animation Company). For this purpose, he enlisted his former employee Peter Eng (1892–1939) and the composer Hans Ewald Heller (1894–1966), who had collaborated on a sound animated film together in 1929. However, by March 1936, it was reported that "these projects have become very quiet" (Der Morgen, March 23, 1936: 10). In that same year, Eng, who had joined *Sascha-Film* in 1918, commemorated *18 Jahre Trickfilm* (18 Years of Animation) and adorned the article of the same title with a character sketch and a background drawing, likely produced during this project (cf. Eng 1936: 1) (Figure 5.1).

Bruno Wozak (1903–1944), the most significant animator of the 1930s, had a distinctive style that differed significantly from the animated films of the 1920s. Undoubtedly influenced by *Disney*'s model, he described character design as follows:

"Crucial, yet challenging, is the artistic design of the characters. It often takes multiple attempts, experimenting with different poses, to find the perfect one. Animated films demand simplicity combined with witty, grotesque exaggeration in both form and movement. This is the core principle of animation. Naturalistic designs tend to be less effective, and realistic movements lack the liveliness required; they become dull and unengaging. For this reason, animated characters typically have round heads, with hands and feet simplified into round shapes, and their movements are exaggerated for greater impact" (Bruno Wozak, as cited in Mittagausgabe, June 28, 1937: 2).

DOI: 10.1201/9781003415442-6

FIGURE 5.1 Figure design by Peter Eng from around 1936 on a celluloid strip with a space for the soundtrack. (Source: Tonfilm Theater Tanz (No. 5/1936).)

In his film's musical design, Bruno Wozak employed two approaches. In some films, he synchronized the movements of his characters with pre-existing music. In contrast, in others, he arranged the music to match the visual recording – a technique pioneered by *Disney* and recognized globally as 'Mickey Mousing.'

A LION'S LEAP INTO PROMOTIONAL ANIMATION

The only known animated films from the 1930s originate from the environment of the *Wozak/Thomas* studio, the most important animation studio of the interwar period. The friends Bruno Wozak and Johann 'Hans' Thomas (1903–1980)[2] studied together for one semester in 1918/1919 at the *Kunstgewerbeschule Wien* (Vienna School of Arts and Crafts, now University of Applied Arts Vienna). After that, they pursued further studies in sculpture, graphics, and painting.[3] After gaining experience as a poster designer in an advertising agency from 1930 onward, Thomas ventured into the field of animated film together with his partner. They established their collaborative studio in Vienna's Neubaugasse in 1934. The studio's primary creative force was unquestionably Wozak, as highlighted in a press article titled *Ein Löwensprung = 24 Kunstwerke* (A Lion's Leap = 24 Artworks): "A film studio like this isn't large. It consists of a camera room with equipment and two rooms with drawing tables – that's it" (Die Wiener Bühne (475), July 1938: 29). Regarding animation, the article further stated, "one needs only a pencil and patience. Everyone has a pencil, only a few have the patience, but only the select have the talent to unite both – the Viennese Bruno Wozak being one of them" (as translated in Renoldner and Frischengruber 1998: 13).

Initially, the studio worked for the advertising film service of Hans Ludwig Böhm (1890–1950), which had existed since 1934. The 'Gewerbesperre' (trade ban) almost prevented Böhm from obtaining a trade license. This measure was introduced to control the growing number of self-employed tradespeople during a period of increasing unemployment. However, there was optimism that Böhm, one of the co-founders of the *Tobis* film group in Germany, would create top-notch films. He consistently turned to animation – all surviving films employed animation techniques, such as bringing product packaging to life through stop motion.

The oldest known advertising cartoon created by the *Wozak/Thomas* studio for Hans Ludwig Böhm is *Die Sphinx bei der Morgentoilette* (The Sphinx at the Morning Toilet, 1934/1935).[4] In this cartoon, a sphinx laments its black teeth, but a monkey arrives with the toothpaste promoted to help. Another cartoon, *Morgenstunde* (Morning Hour, 1935), produced anonymously, may also have originated from *Wozak/Thomas*. This commercial, which promotes tube shampoo and is made in Gasparcolor, represents the first use of color film in advertising animation in Austria. In *Der Radio-Automat* (The Radio Automat, 1936), brownies construct and operate a radio to demonstrate its workings. Several storyboard drafts exist for the undated *Das Waschmonster* (The Washing Monster), another advertisement film of that era (Figure 5.2).

However, there was also an attempt in the studio's environment to establish Austrian animated films internationally beyond advertising films. In pursuit of this goal, the *Colibrifilm Vienna* studio, based in Neubaugasse as well, was tasked with creating a collection of opera parodies using the Gasparcolor process titled *Crazy Parody* for the global market. Financed by a wealthy entrepreneur,[5] the first animated film produced was *Carmen* (1935), which condensed the 3-hour opera of the same name into approximately 10 minutes. In this animated version, José and Escamillo compete for Carmen's affection, but in the end, she leaves with El Toro, the bull.

FIGURE 5.2 Storyboard designs for the *Wozak/Thomas* commercial *Das Waschmonster* (The Washing Monster, n.d.). (Courtesy of Graz Museum.)

While an advertising film in 1937 could be produced with three or four assistants in 5–6 weeks, this film took at least 3 months to complete.[6] The team was expanded to ten members to meet the demands of the project's scale. Stefan Wessely (1888–1935) and his wife,[7] who also wrote the screenplay, were mainly responsible for the project. In the early 1920s, Wessely, a film architect and draftsman, was involved in producing epic films like *Sodom und Gomorrha* (Sodom and Gomorrah, 1922). He also participated in the incomplete film *Gullivers Reisen* (Gulliver's Travels, 1924), with animated drawings provided by Michael Maibaum (1876–1942?). For the opera parody, Wessely was responsible for crafting the characters. In addition to assistants such as Wilhelm 'Willy' Jaruska (1916–2008),[8] who also worked for *Wozak/Thomas*, several students from the *Kunstgewerbeschule Wien* (Vienna School of Arts and Crafts, now University of Applied Arts Vienna) were recruited. This included Wilhelm 'Bil' Spira (1913–1999),[9] Richard Erdoes (or Erdös in German, 1912–2008), and Susi Weigel (1914–1990). After *Carmen* had been completed, the opera *Aida* was also set to be parodied. However, although the animated film was convincing in its design, the second project was abandoned, and the team was disbanded.[10] "The failure was – oh, the irony! – due to the music, which is a paradox for an opera parody" (Spira 1997: 30). To include as many of the opera's melodies as possible in the short film, composers Marjan Rawicz (1898–1970) and Walter Landauer (1910–1983) had to condense them accordingly: "Whenever the ear recognized the opening notes of an aria, they were abruptly interrupted by fragments of a different theme, followed by a third and fourth melody. This constant disruption made it an example of how not to handle such transitions" (Spira 1997: 30).

Subsequently, *Wozak/Thomas* focused on creating animated commercials. Upon Hans Ludwig Böhm's emigration to London (Great Britain) in the autumn of 1936, the studio initially secured an advertising project for the state: *Reise durch Österreich* (A Journey Through Austria, 1937), an advertising film promoting the investment loan to expand the country's railway and road infrastructure. After that, the studio focused on handling advertising projects for *Mayer's Filmbüro* (renamed *Adi Mayer's Filmbüro*, or *AMF*, in 1938). Several advertising films were created for different companies, including *Ein orientalisches Wunder* (An Oriental Wonder, 1937), which promoted the Oriental blend of *Falk Kalif* cigarettes. In this commercial, a snake charmer plays his flute to make a rope ascend to his lover's balcony, and together, they disappear on a flying carpet while smoking a cigarette. In the fall of 1937, the promotional film *Das Hammer Schlaraffenland* (The Hammer Wonderland), 800-m long (equivalent to about 30 minutes), was launched to promote the *Hammerbrot* (Hammerbread) industrial bakery. Amid two lengthy film scenes, a delightful approximately 5-minute animated sequence emerges. In the first scene, a child falls asleep while reading an advertising booklet called *Das Hammerbrot-Schlaraffenland* (The Hammerbread Wonderland), published from 1937 onward. In the dream sequence, the inhabitants of the land of milk and honey are portrayed as hand-drawn animated characters busily crafting an assortment of baked goods. For instance, fruits fall directly from the trees onto flying dough sheets.

A film similar to that was *Strom für Alles* (Electricity for Everything, 1938), created for the *Wiener Elektrizitätswerke* (Vienna Electricity Company). It showcased the generation and diverse uses of electricity. The approximately 20-minute "model advertising film" showcased "cheerful animated illustrations" featuring a little electron character that guided viewers through the presentation: "The effort to present the workings of electricity in the form of a cultural film, while making the somewhat dry subject engaging in a distinctively Viennese way, has been highly successful" (Kleine Volks-Zeitung, November 5, 1938: 5). Other advertising animations included *Der Stern der Zeit* (The Star of Time, 1937), *Mädchen für alles* (Girl for Everything, 1938),[11] and *Aufstehen!* (Stand Up!, 1938) for *Junghans* watches; *Nur die Ruhe…* (Only the Peace…, 1938) for the *Falk* cigarette, *Die Arche Noah* (Noah's Ark, 1938) for *Bally Shoes* (Figure 5.3), and the color animation *Ihr Geheimnis* (Her Secret, 1938) for *Brauns* fabric dyes. Some of the animated commercials drew inspiration from Oskar Fischinger (1900–1967), a pioneer of abstract film. For instance, a cigarette film featured cigarette tubes attached to the ground with pins, dancing in a manner reminiscent of Fischinger's *Muratti greift ein* (Muratti Gets in the Act, 1934). Similarly, *Laßt Farben sprechen* (Let Colors Speak, 1938) evokes Fischinger's legendary abstract advertising film *Alle Kreise erfaßt Tolirag* (All Circles Captured by Tolirag, 1933/1934):

"A color advertisement for cigarette tubes, where the colors red, yellow, and green dissolve into the final blue through a mix of ornamental and figurative movements. From this blue, the packaging appears, containing the double-filter Olleschau tubes" (*Zulassungskarte Prüf-Nr. 49012 der Film-Prüfstelle Berlin*, August 31, 1938: [1]–[2])[12].

The studio peaked between 1936 and 1938, partly driven by political factors. During the mid-1930s, Austria, with the support of the Austrofascist Ministry of Trade, witnessed the professionalization of the advertising and short film production industry. By the spring of 1936, "the profession of producer of short films changed

FIGURE 5.3 Concept drawing for the *Wozak/Thomas* advertising film *Die Arche Noah* (Noah's Ark, 1938) for *Bally Shoes*. (Photographer: Michaela Hitzenberger. Courtesy of Kunsthandel Hitzenberger, Vienna.)

to a protected profession requiring a license, thus shielding the market from new competitors" (Schätz 2016: 259). This led to a ban on foreign-made ads for domestic businesses, causing the number of Austrian advertising films to increase from 21 in 1932 to 61 in 1936. This also benefited *Wozak/Thomas*, as most of the studio's advertising films can be traced back to 1937 and 1938 (Figure 5.4). During this productive phase, an attempt was made to establish an international presence in the advertising field. Hungarian Desider Gross (né Dezső Grósz, 1902–1962) played a vital role in this effort. He was responsible for the foreign business of the *Gasparcolor* company, which produced color film materials, and managed a Europe-wide advertising film network from Prague. On behalf of Gross, *Wozak/Thomas* created the advertising animation *Tider Krever* (Time Requires, 1936) using the *Gasparcolor* technique for the Norwegian *Tiedmanns Tobaksfabrik*.

After the *'Anschluss' Österreichs* (annexation of Austria) into Nazi Germany in March 1938, the advertising film industry experienced a decline: "The decrease in competition was in no small part due to National Socialist persecution, which led, for instance, to the deportation and eventual death of influential Austrian advertising film producer Robert Reich" (Schätz 2016: 259). Consequently, advertising film production significantly dropped, with *AMF* emerging as one of the few remaining producers. Despite the challenging circumstances, *Wozak/Thomas* continued to create advertising cartoons until the autumn of 1939, including works such as *Die größte Sensation* (The Greatest Sensation, 1939), which promoted a new gas tariff, and *Die Geburt der ELIX-Lampe* (The Birth of the ELIX Lamp, 1939), which showcased lamps manufactured by the *ELIN* company.[13]

Considering the challenging economic circumstances following the onset of World War II (1939–1945), *AMF* needed to broaden its scope of work. As a result, it undertook commissioned projects for *Wien-Film*'s cultural film department, which was established in 1938. Adi Mayer (1908–1960) directed the first cultural film,

FIGURE 5.4 Color design for an undated Viking advertising film by *Wozak/Thomas*. (Photographer: Michaela Hitzenberger. Courtesy of Kunsthandel Hitzenberger, Vienna.)

Von Ohr zu Ohr (From Ear to Ear, 1939). Commissioned by the German Reichspost, it also featured animated sequences by Bruno Wozak: "In animated cartoon sequences, viewers learn how a telephone works – just like the human ear. In the animated scenes, sound waves take the form of little flying figures entering the ear canal" (Baumann and Gold (eds.) 2007: 142). Due to the wartime advertising decline, Bruno Wozak began directing cultural films at *AMF* in 1940. These films include *Flößer* (Raftsmen, 1940/1941) and *Augen* (Eyes, 1941), the latter featuring animations. Additionally, Wozak was involved in the special effects for the cultural film *Dein besseres Ich* (Your Better Self, 1941/1942).[14]

After Bruno Wozak and Hans Thomas were drafted in 1941, their film careers ended abruptly. Despite this setback, *AMF* continued producing cultural films until 1943, with their final wartime production being the commissioned work *Der 100kV-Ölkabelring der Wiener E-Werke* (The 100kV Oil Cable Ring of the Vienna Electric Works, 1943). This production also featured trick shots by A. Ziegler.[15] Following this, film operations were suspended until September 1945 due to the war, resulting in a significant break in Austrian animated film production.

TAKEN THE BRUSH FROM THE GIFTED HANDS

"Who has a sense of humor? It's the person who toils for 10 years, 10 hours a day, trying to lift the spirits of a depressed city with essays, caricatures, and posters, receives not a single commission from the state or city, doesn't even have a studio, and eventually realizes the only authority interested in his work is the tax office – yet still doesn't commit suicide. That person has a sense of humor" (Peter Eng, as cited in Moser 2019: 219).

In a letter from Vienna printed in 1928, Peter Eng expressed these defeatist sentiments. Humor died a decade later when Eng took his own life to escape the terror of the Nazi regime. Following Austria's annexation into Nazi Germany in March 1938, many others faced a similar fate, including film producer Robert Reich, composer Hans Ewald Heller, and animators Michael Maibaum and Bruno Wozak, who either emigrated or perished between 1939 and 1944.

Peter Eng, hailing from a Jewish family, was the most captivating personality in Austrian animated films during the 1920s and resided in Berlin from 1929 until the Nazi regime came to power in 1933. He returned to Vienna through his hometown of Olmütz (formerly Austria-Hungary, now Olomouc in the Czech Republic). The Austrian press somewhat euphemistically stated, "Peter Eng, the popular Viennese illustrator, has returned to Vienna from an extended trip" (Die Stunde, October 4, 1934: 2). His efforts to reenter the field of animated film proved unsuccessful. Instead, Eng returned to working as a caricaturist and commercial artist and pursued activities as a songwriter and composer of chansons. One of his final public appearances in this capacity was mentioned in the March 1938 edition of the publication *Tonfilm Theater Tanz* (Sound-film Theater Dance) – featured alongside a photograph of the later Nazi director Leni Riefenstahl (1902–2003) promoting one of her movies (cf. Tonfilm Theater Tanz, 6 (3), March 1938: 8). Following the annexation of Austria and the accompanying anti-Semitic terror, Peter Eng and his wife Anna Eng (née Pölz, 1886–1939)[16] returned to Olmütz and made efforts to relocate to the United States. Upon the

German troops' occupation of Czechoslovakia in March 1939, the couple ended their own lives – just a few days before the awaited departure documents arrived.

Robert Reich, a Jewish film producer, endeavored to create Austrian animated films similar to *Disney*'s during the mid-1930s along with Peter Eng. He also fell victim to National Socialism. After being imprisoned multiple times, he was deported to the Theresienstadt Ghetto in the Czech Republic in January 1943. Later, in May 1944, he was transferred to the Auschwitz concentration camp in Poland, where it is believed that he was gassed. Hans Ewald Heller, the composer who collaborated with Peter Eng on a sound cartoon in 1929 and was also supposed to work on the *Disney*-rivaling films, successfully immigrated to the USA via France in March 1939. There, he focused on arranging film music.

Following his cinema career, Ladislaus Tuszyński (1876–1943), who co-headed the animation department at *Astoria-Film* with Peter Eng in the early 1920s, continued to illustrate newspapers. Upon the annexation of Austria, he responded to the prevailing zeitgeist by "creating his final large-scale illustrations for the Kronen Zeitung entirely in the style of blatant Nazi propaganda" (Renoldner 2010: 76). He also did not survive the war, although the reasons for his death were different, as stated in the obituary in the *Kronen Zeitung*: "A severe heart condition had soured his final years until death finally took the brush and pen from his gifted hands" (Wiener Kronen Zeitung, September 29, 1943: 4).

In the mid-1920s, Michael Maibaum, originally from Warsaw (now Poland, then Austria-Hungary), created at least one advertising animation film and animated sequences for two feature films in Austria. Even as late as March 1937, Maibaum secured a trade license "for the production of short films" (Moser 2019: 167).[17] However, due to the annexation of Austria, he was compelled to immigrate to Warsaw in May 1938 because of his Jewish heritage. Following the invasion of Poland by the Third Reich in September 1939, which initiated World War II, the authorities established the Warsaw Ghetto in mid-1940, where the Jewish community was forced to live in deplorable conditions. When the ghetto was disbanded in the summer of 1942, Maibaum was deported to the Białystok Ghetto in Poland. All signs of him vanished after his final letter on December 3, 1942. In the summer of 1947, his wife had him legally declared dead.

Film producer Robert Müller (1877–1942) faced a similar fate. During World War I, Müller was among the first to commission the creation of propaganda animated films. Some of these films conveyed anti-Semitic messages despite Müller being of Jewish heritage. His film career ended following the annexation of Austria. In April 1942, he was deported to the Włodawa Ghetto (Poland) and perished there or in the Sobibor extermination camp (Poland).

Austria's only successful studio specializing in animated film up to that time was established by Bruno Wozak and Hans Thomas in 1934. However, their venture was interrupted in 1941 when both were enlisted. Thomas served as a cartographic draftsman in the Wehrmacht (armed forces of Nazi Germany), while Wozak tragically lost his life in a partisan attack in Montenegro on September 25, 1944. "After the war, Thomas and Jaruschka [sic!] continued with their artistic activities, but without the enthusiasm for animation of Bruno Wozak, the drive was no longer there, and a continuation of the animation studio was not to be contemplated" (Renoldner and Frischengruber 1998: 14).

As late as 1935, Vienna-born composer Norbert Gingold (1903–1996) recruited Bil Spira and Richard Erdoes to embark on an animated film project in Paris, France. Following the completion of *Der falsche Mustapha* (The False Mustapha, 1935/1936), Gingold sold the film to the Austrian *Tobis-Sascha*, excluding the credits of the two artists.[18] Austria's annexation marked the beginning of a difficult journey for both artists – Erdoes, forced to flee due to his Jewish heritage, eventually made his way to the USA via Belgium, France, and Great Britain in 1940. In the USA, he pursued a career as a graphic artist, contributing illustrations to various works, including a children's book by Dr. Seuss (né Theodor Seuss Geisel, 1904–1991). Spira was repeatedly interned by the Nazis. In France, he used his talent to forge identity papers until an informer betrayed him. He survived the concentration camps and settled in Paris after the war, where he resumed his work as an illustrator. After the outbreak of war, Susi Weigel was the sole remaining animator from the previous group who continued working in Germany, effectively guiding Austrian animation into exile.

NOTES

1 The absence of competition might have been due to cost concerns. Despite claims in the media that animated films were cheaper to produce than live-action films, the Film Department of the Ministry of Education found this to be the opposite in 1932. Based on their analysis, the costs of producing animated films were at least three times higher than those of live-action films (cf. Moser 2019: 216).

2 All literature regarding the *Wozak/Thomas* studio refers to Karl Thomas. However, according to contemporary press, Bruno Wozak's partner was the "painter and graphic artist Hans Thomas" (Mittagausgabe, June 28, 1937: 2). Upon review, no sources were found for individuals named Karl or Hans Thomas with the specified birthdate of June 14, 1903 (for the birthdate cf. Renoldner 2010: 84). Nonetheless, archives at the University of Applied Arts Vienna contain records of Bruno Wozak and Johann Thomas engaging in joint studies. Johann Thomas's birthdate in these records aligns with the provided date of June 14, 1903 (*Nationale Bruno Wozak* 1918 and *Nationale Johann Thomas* 1918, respectively; Collection and Archive, University of Applied Arts Vienna; thanks to Nathalie Feitsch). It seems that Johann began calling himself Hans after completing his studies. This is supported by the biographical details of the artist Hans Thomas, which align with key aspects such as date of birth, education, and military service. The confusion between Hans and Karl could stem from errors in transcribing the Kurrent script, where the visual similarities of the two names can lead to misidentification.

3 Between 1919 and 1922, Bruno Wozak pursued sculpture studies at the *Kunstgewerbeschule Wien* (Vienna School of Arts and Crafts, now University of Applied Arts Vienna). Subsequently, he spent a year at the *Kunstgewerbeschule München* (Munich School of Arts and Crafts) and continued his sculpture studies at the Academy of Fine Arts Vienna from 1924 to 1929. Although a biography indicates that Hans Thomas also studied at the Academy of Fine Arts Vienna from 1925 to 1928, there are no records of Karl, Johann, or Hans Thomas in the university archives (thanks to Ulrike Hirhager).

4 The film underwent censorship in late December 1934 and was released for screening in 1935.

5 The entrepreneur's name appears inconsistently in the literature – sometimes referred to as Arthur Werther (cf. Frischengruber and Renoldner 1998: 14) and other times as Arthur Werner (cf. Renoldner 2010: 88).

6 Thomas Renoldner (b. 1960) notes that the production "took at least a year" (Renoldner 2010: 89). However, a press report from March 1935 cites 2 months for the drawing process and a total production time of 3 months, excluding the musical soundtrack, which had been created in advance (cf. Moderne Welt, 16 (6): 10, 39).

7 The literature refers to Stefan Wessely's wife as Hatvani or Etvani. However, his obituary, published in January 1936, states that he was married to the screenwriter Rosa Wachtel (cf. Mein Film (523), January 1936: I). A press article from August 1935 references a male animator named Etvanik (cf. Die Stunde, August 8, 1935: 9).

8 Wilhelm Jaruska's responsibilities included tasks such as mixing colors and handling sheets of cellophane. According to Bil Spira, he encouraged Jaruska to pursue drawing (cf. Spira 1997: 32), which Jaruska wholeheartedly embraced by attending the *Kunstgewerbeschule Wien* (Vienna School of Arts and Crafts, now University of Applied Arts Vienna) from 1935 to 1937.

9 According to Bil Spira's autobiography, he advanced within the project to become the head animator, which didn't sit well with Stefan Wessely and his wife (cf. Spira 1997: 29–30).

10 At least, that's the information provided by Bil Spira in his biography (cf. Spira 1997: 30). However, Stefan Wessely's obituary hints that he may have begun work on *Aida*: "Stefan Wessely [...] turned to animation in his later years and had recently completed a charming short film, a parody of the opera 'Carmen.' Unfortunately, death claimed him unexpectedly while he was working on a new project" (Mein Film (523), January 1936: I).

11 This is not to be confused with the 1937 German feature film with the same title.

12 The author would like to thank Karin Moser (b. 1974) for providing a copy of the censorship card.

13 Bruno Wozak reportedly contributed to the creation of various animated commercials produced by German companies in 1938/39: *Alarm* (Commerz Film, 1938), *Die Geisterstunde* (The Witching Hour, Ufa, 1938), and *Adi, der Waschbär* (Adi the Raccoon, Tiller-Film, 1939).

14 Edith Matzalik (1903–1968), an architect and graphic designer, collaborated with Bruno Wozak on the animations and effects for *Augen* (Eyes, 1941) and *Dein besseres Ich* (Your Better Self, 1941/1942).

15 A. Ziegler may refer to either August Friedrich Ziegler (1903–?), who attended the special youth art course at the *Kunstgewerbeschule Wien* (Vienna School of Arts and Crafts, now University of Applied Arts Vienna) from 1914 to 1916, or Andreas Anton Ziegler (1894–1974), a commercial graphic artist who, after training at the Academy of Fine Arts Vienna, became one of the most prolific film poster painters in Vienna during the 1920s and 1930s.

16 Anna Pölz, also known as Anna Engländer-Pölz, is believed to have received her training as an illustrator in New York (USA). It is unclear whether Peter Eng encountered her there or met her later at *Die Muskete* (The Musket) magazine, where they both worked as draftspersons from 1919 onward.

17 No film projects by Michael Maibaum from this period are known. A censorship list dated March 25, 1936, includes a lottery advertisement film titled *Kultur ins Volk* (Culture to the People), attributed to an architect named Michael Maybaum (facsimile in Ballhausen and Caneppele (eds.) 2009: 189). However, it remains unclear whether this refers to Maibaum or if the film is animated.

18 After Bil Spira lodged a complaint with *Tobis-Sascha*, the company proposed altering the opening credits, but he would have been responsible for covering the associated costs. The dispute eventually escalated to the Commercial Court (cf. Der Wiener Tag, March 26, 1937: 9). In the end, Spira won the case, with *Tobis-Sascha* being ordered to alter the credits and pay damages (cf. Spira 1997: 44).

6 An Austrian Superman
Austria's Heroes in the World of Animation

Even before the Austrian animators migrated to Germany during World War II (1939–1945), significant filmmakers had already emigrated to English-speaking nations. Max Fleischer (1883–1972) departed Austria-Hungary with his family as early as 1887. Alongside his US-born brother Dave Fleischer (1894–1979), he became one of the most prominent and globally influential animators of the 1920s and 1930s, on par with Walt Disney (1901–1966). Besides pioneering the rotoscoping process, animated characters like Koko the Clown, Betty Boop, Popeye, and Superman gained worldwide acclaim, inspiring animators across all continents.

The Austrian sociologist and national economist Otto Karl Wilhelm Neurath (1882–1945) developed a picture language starting in the mid-1920s. He initially named it the *Wiener Methode der Bildstatistik* (Vienna Method of Pictorial Statistics) and renamed it Isotype (International System of Typographic Picture Education) in 1934. This precursor to modern pictograms was created to make statistical information understandable to people who were illiterate or lacked formal education, aiming to democratize knowledge: "his idea was about transparency of information rather than an objectification of information" (Paul Barritt in an interview with the author on June 8, 2023). Due to political reasons, Neurath fled to The Hague (Netherlands) in 1934 and later sought refuge in London (Great Britain) in 1940. By then, his innovative visual language had already captured attention and was being utilized in animated films. Neurath further advanced his work by establishing the *Isotype Institute* in Oxford (Great Britain) in 1942, where he personally contributed to the production of several films. However, his visual language had already become well known in animated films in the United States and Canada.

Film director George Hoellering (né Georg Michael Höllering, 1897–1980) was born near Vienna in Baden. He fled to Great Britain due to political and family reasons, as his wife was Jewish. In Germany, he managed the production of the proletarian film *Kuhle Wampe* (Whither Germany?, 1931/1932). In 1932, facing the Nazi threat, he returned to Vienna. Following the Austrian Civil War in February 1934, Hoellering left the country, first for Hungary and then in 1936 for Great Britain, where he initially found work in a cinema. In 1940, he was interned for a few months as an 'enemy alien' on the Isle of Man, where he struck up a friendship with Peter Strausfeld (1910–1980), a German graphic artist who was also interned. As the managing director of *Film Traders*, Hoellering produced propaganda films for the *Ministry of Information* (MoI) starting in 1942. During the war, the MoI recognized the potential of using short, animated films as an effective propaganda tool. Therefore, beginning in 1943, Hoellering created about half a dozen propaganda animations for

DOI: 10.1201/9781003415442-7

the MoI. Working with Strausfeld as his chief cartoonist, they produced amusing and innovative animated films that diverged from the prevalent *Disney* style in Britain. For instance, *TIM Marches Back* (1944)[1] aimed to illustrate the necessity of free telephone lines during the war through a couple dancing on the lines: "The loosely sketched lines and shapes offer fleeting moments of abstraction that hint at other possibilities for the form" (Stewart 2021: 68). The studio's most famous animated film is *Skeleton in the Cupboard* (1943). The film follows George, a skeleton, who sees a MoI trailer in the cinema and then enters a bone-collecting container to track down Adolf Hitler (1889–1945) as part of a bomb. Following World War II, when the MoI reduced the production of such *Public Information Films* (PIFs), Hoellering and Strausfeld shifted away from animated films. Instead, Hoellering worked on several short films and the drama *Murder in the Cathedral* (1951), for which Strausfeld won an award for production design at the 12th *Venice International Film Festival* in Italy. Being disappointed with the film posters provided by the studios, Hoellering took matters into his own hands by asking his friend Strausfeld to design advertising posters. These posters significantly impacted the London cityscape until Hoellering died in early 1980.

The influence of Austrians on international animated film extended beyond scientific and cinematographic expertise to also encompass music. In 1930, German filmmaker Lotte Reiniger (1899–1981) began creating productions inspired by the music of her favorite composer, Austrian Wolfgang Amadeus Mozart (1756–1791). Similarly, George Pal (1908–1980), a native of Austria-Hungary, brought the character Mr. Strauss to life in his puppet films starting in 1934. He drew inspiration from the Austrian composer Johann Strauss II (1825–1899) and used him as a powerful symbol of resistance during World War II. In 1939, musicologist Anneliese Landau (1903–1991), a German-American with Austrian heritage, portrayed composer Franz Schubert (1797–1828) as an outsider. She suggested that through Schubert, the lime tree "became a symbol of protection against a hurting outside world" (Anneliese Landau, as cited in Hirsch 2007: 487). According to her, "Schubert is beauty that never can be destroyed" (Anneliese Landau, as cited in Hirsch 2007: 487). The music of Schubert served as a point of connection for Jewish and Austrian communities who had escaped from Nazi Germany. This connection was also reflected in British and American animated films, demonstrating the impact of Schubert's music across different cultures and art forms.

BETTY BOOP: AN AUSTRIAN "CARTOON AMBASSADOR"?

Max Fleischer, described as a "Monarchy Austrian,"[2] was born in Krakau (Krakow), then part of Austria-Hungary and now Poland. Although his family relocated to the USA in 1887, Fleischer maintained a strong connection with Austria. This connection was apparent not only in Max Fleischer's personal history, such as identifying Vienna as his birthplace during a security check at *Paramount* in World War II and retaining his Austrian citizenship until 1942, but also in the filmmaking endeavors of the brothers Max and Dave Fleischer.[3] Although films like *Gulliver's Travels* (1939) and *Ants in the Plants* (1940) were clearly intended as political allegories, *Fleischer Studios* maintained a relatively cautious stance toward Nazi Germany (to which Austria had been annexed in 1938). This was particularly evident in comparison to other animation studios. Even after the departure of the Fleischer brothers at the end of 1941,[4] this cautious approach persisted until the studio was rebranded as *Famous Studios* in mid-1942. In contrast, Walt Disney's *The New Spirit* was already taking a stand against Nazi Germany in January 1942 and George Pal's *Tulips Shall Grow* in June 1942.

After conscription was introduced in the USA in 1940, "both features and shorts used that as subject matter, promoting patriotism without focusing on an enemy" (Mayerson 1997: [2]). The portrayal of military conflict and the subsequent battle against Nazi Germany was not unique to the Fleischer brothers but was particularly noticeable in their films. In *Fightin' Pals* (1940), Popeye travels to Africa to find his friend Bluto. During his journey, as he sails past a map of Europe, the continent is labeled "THEM," contrasting with "US" for the USA. In this scene, clouds of smoke and sounds of gunfire depict the atmosphere in Europe. Nearly a month before the US entered the war, Popeye made his first appearance as a Marine in *The Mighty NaVy* (1941).[5] While stationed on an aircraft carrier, he is unexpectedly attacked by an enemy convoy of ships. Although the enemy planes bear an emblem strongly reminiscent of the swastika, the ships sail under a flag with the inscription "Enemy (name your own)." Following the attack on Pearl Harbor on December 7, 1941, the Popeye cartoons took on a much sharper tone, mainly directed against the Japanese until mid-1942.[6] The last cartoon from *Fleischer Studios* featuring Popeye, *Baby Wants a Bottleship* (released on July 3, 1942), contained at least a subtle dig at Adolf Hitler.[7] The studio exercised even more remarkable restraint with its *Superman* series, which had been in production since the latter part of 1941. Until mid-1942, the series maintained a sci-fi adventure theme, with only one fleeting reference to war when Lois and Clark pass by a war bonds advertising poster in *The Bulleteers* (1942).[8] It was not until the studio became *Famous Studios* that Superman's character underwent a political transformation, requiring him to engage in active combat against the Japanese and Nazis in five out of the remaining eight episodes to be produced.

The Fleischer brothers' personal background was also evident in their characters, including Superman. The creators of Superman, Jerry Siegel (1914–1996) and Joe Shuster (1914–1992) hailed from Jewish immigrant families, much like the Fleischer brothers themselves: "The story of Superman is also a classic immigrant narrative, reflecting the challenges of assimilating into American society. Superman even carries the Hebrew birth name 'Kal-El' ('voice of God'), symbolizing Jewish immigrants" (Schmidlechner 2011: 305).

The significant role played by the Fleischer brothers in bringing the character to the big screen emphasizes its biographical aspect. Additionally, their influence directly impacted the character: "[B]ecause covering long distances by jumping, as had been common in the comics until then, would have looked ridiculous on screen, the Fleischer brothers taught Superman how to fly" (Schmidlechner 2011: 306). The character Betty Boop was even more closely linked to the biography of the Fleischer brothers. *Minnie the Moocher* (1932) showcases Betty Boop's parents, unmistakably portraying them as Jewish immigrants from Austria, reflecting the brothers' own heritage – for example, when the father "rants in an Austrian Jewish dialect (there is more Germanic than Russian Yiddish in the accents)" (Klein 1993: 63).

The influence of the Fleischer brothers' experience of emigration and a sense of displacement is most evident in *Betty Boop's Ups and Downs* (1932), where Betty expresses her feeling of not having a true home with the lyrics, "There's no place upon this earth that's home sweet home to me."

"When she sings at the end of the film 'Any old place upon this earth is home sweet home to me!,' it resonates not only with Jewish emigrants around the world but also with animation itself, which by then had found a home worldwide – thanks in no small part to the global success of the Fleischer brothers' animated films" (Schmidlechner 2011: 314).

The impact of the Fleischer brothers' films and characters reached across the globe, leaving a lasting influence in various regions. For instance, in Europe, Austrian Friedrich Kuplent (1905–1985) fashioned a character inspired by Koko the Clown in the 1920s and was subsequently likened to Max Fleischer in the Austrian media (cf. the chapter on the 1920s). Furthermore, in France, Paul Grimault (1905–1994) established his studio *Les Gémeaux* (The Gemini) in 1936 with the ambitious aim "to make shorts to compete with Hollywood imports, especially Betty Boop" (Neupert 2014: 100). During the same year, the Frenkel brothers, known as pioneers of North African animation, released *Mafish Fayda* (It's Useless *aka* Nothing to Do, 1936) in Egypt, featuring an "Egyptian Betty Boop" (Frenkel 2005: [5]) alongside the protagonist Mish-Mish Effendi. Notably, the influence of the Fleischer brothers was especially significant in Asia.

Filipino filmmaker and film historian Nick Deocampo (b. 1959) stated that the animated film *Bloto* was created in the Philippines during the 1930s. This film was said to be "inspired by the arch-rival of the American *Popeye*" (Tolentino 2001: 180) and would have marked the Philippines' first venture into animated filmmaking. Deocampo mentioned that the information "came from an obscure source" and added that he "hardly [can] find a trace regarding the claim" (social media message to the author, October 3, 2022). The first Korean animated film production was reported by *The Chosun Ilbo* (Daily News from Korea) on November 25, 1936: "While the names of Mickey Mouse and Betty Boop are known throughout the world, there has not yet been an animated character created in Chosun [Korea]. Now, due to Kim Yong-woon and Im Seok-gi, in association with Jeongrim Movie Company, the production of *Gaeggum* has begun" (as translated in Annett 2014: 144). When the Wan brothers produced *Tiě shàn gōngzhǔ* (Princess Iron Fan, 1941) in China, it marked Asia's first animated feature. In this film, certain characters bore similarities to American models: "Fox Spirit is a Chinese version of Betty Boop" (Du 2019: 48).

In Japan, the character of Betty Boop was incredibly beloved, frequently making cameo appearances in numerous films. For instance, in the live-action feature *Tonari no Yae-chan* (Our Neighbor, Miss Yae; 1934), the main characters attend a screening of the Betty Boop film *Ha! Ha! Ha!* (1934). Furthermore, in the animated film *Mori no Yakyu-dan* (Baseball in the Forest, 1934), Betty Boop chauffeurs the film hero's girlfriend to a sports stadium. In another animated film, *Tengu Taiji* (Heavenly Dog Extermination, 1934), a samurai resembles a male Betty Boop clone: "It plays on, or rather plays *against*, her canonical appearances as an American film star by situating her in a markedly 'Japanese' setting" (Annett 2014: 46). Upon discovering Betty Boop's popularity in Japan, the Fleischer brothers responded by creating the cartoon

A Language All My Own (1935) specifically for the Japanese audience. In this cartoon, Betty Boop travels to Japan and sings on stage, first in English while wearing her iconic short dress and then in Japanese while dressed in a kimono. To ensure that Betty Boop's actions were culturally appropriate and wouldn't offend Japanese audiences, head animator Myron Waldman (1908–2006) sought the feedback of Japanese exchange students by showing them the scenes: "This carefully crafted love letter to the Japanese people solidified Betty's already growing popularity in Japan, a popularity that exists to this day" (*Betty Boop in Japan* n.d.: para. 1). The moment when Betty Boop adjusted her dress to transform it into a kimono was a significant turning point in her character design. The enactment of the Hays Code in 1934, a self-censorship regulation by the American film industry, ended Betty Boop's portrayal as a sex symbol. Despite this, the character remained popular in Japan. For instance, in *Mabō no Tōkyō Olympic Taikai* (Mabō's Tokyo Olympics, 1936),[9] Betty was showcased as a spectator at the Olympic Games, originally scheduled in Japan in 1940.[10] Even in the films of the *Omochabako Series* (Toybox Series, 1934), Mickey Mouse was already depicted as a 'Western villain.' However, the characters created by the Fleischer brothers were largely spared from this portrayal, even during the Pacific War between Japan and the United States (1941–1945).[11] For instance, in *Momotarō no Umiwashi* (Momotarō's Sea Eagles, 1943), the American enemy is represented solely by Bluto, Popeye's evil counterpart.[12] The presence of Popeye and Betty Boop on the film poster "suggests that the Fleischers' star characters still worked as a box-office draw" (Annett 2014: 69). Some film scholars consider Betty Boop's appearance to have had the most significant influence on modern Japanese anime: "One should not forget those big eyes in Asian cartoons. They are not part of an inferiority complex but were introduced by Osamu Tezuka who liked Betty Boop so much that he copied her big eyes that became a trademark of Japanese and later Asian animation" (Giesen and Khan 2018: 187). Osamu Tezuka (1928–1989), also known as 'The Father of Manga and Anime' and 'The Walt Disney of Japan,' set an example that nearly all Japanese animators have followed since.[13] According to Sandra Annett, Betty Boop served as a "cartoon ambassador" (Annett 2014: 19). Because of her Austrian heritage, she uniquely represented both the USA and Austria.[14]

ISOTYPE IN MOTION: OTTO NEURATH'S ANIMATED LANGUAGE

In 1925, Otto Neurath began developing the *Wiener Methode der Bildstatistik* (Vienna Method of Pictorial Statistics). Neurath expressed his desire for "diagrams that move" (Neurath 1946: para. 5) quite early in his work. Initial experiments with film were underway by 1927, and they subsequently made their way to the USA by 1930.[15] Following her husband's passing, Marie Neurath (né Reidemeister, 1898–1986) paid tribute to his film-related endeavors in a memorial penned a few weeks after his death:

"The housing achievements were shown on a map: one after the other the big buildings appeared, and the garden cities too, and then, to compare the area built upon with the central district, they moved together and covered just that district. Charts that show the development of membership of some organizations seemed to lend themselves to filmic representation. One member waved to a group, and after

FIGURE 6.1 Gerd Arntz (1900–1988) while drawing the pictogram for 'Unemployed' at the *Gesellschafts- und Wirtschaftsmuseum*, Vienna (c. 1932). (Courtesy of Otto and Marie Neurath Isotype Collection, University of Reading.)

the other they moved along, lining up at the side of the first. Another little film is still vivid in my memory, it was about school feeding, the children holding their little plates, and the 'knoedel' (balls) flying from a big pot through the air on the plates. These were modest first attempts, but it was fun to look at them, and they were a kind of success even in the United States" (Neurath 1946: para. 5).

Otto Neurath's visual language system attracted attention in London, Great Britain, during the early 1930s (Figure 6.1). An exhibition in the spring of 1933 showcased the system, and in the fall of the same year, the *British Film Institute* (BFI) arranged a lecture by Neurath. Mary Field (1896–1968) was a trailblazer in the British documentary film movement and a pivotal figure in British children's cinema. Subsequently, she and her colleagues produced the animated films *The Expansion of Germany 1870–1914* (1936) and *The Development of English Railways* (1936). These films "successfully and delightfully made their subjects palatable with an adaptation of the system, with such devices as little trains chugging along the railway map" (Low 1979: 29). Mary Field and her team were also involved in a significant film project helmed by Michael Polanyi (né Mihály Polányi, 1891–1876), a Hungarian who migrated to Britain in 1933. The versatile scholar, previously active in Germany, left the country due to the escalating anti-Semitism. Like his brother Karl Polanyi (1886–1964), an economic historian and social anthropologist born in Vienna, he shared an interest "in the connection between the economic and the social" (Festré 2020: 23). Strongly inspired by the writings of the *Österreichische Schule* (Austrian School) and the 1936 groundbreaking work of British economist John Maynard Keynes (1883–1946) on the relationship between money and unemployment, Michael Polanyi aimed "to represent economic ideas by moving diagrams, that is by film, and to use this representation for teaching in schools and adult classes" (Polanyi 1940: 1). His resulting 25-minute animated film, *An Outline of the Working of Money* (often called *Money*), was presented to the *Manchester Statistical Society* in March 1938.

In 1939, Michael Polanyi intended to create a sequel to the film titled *Population and Economic Life*. However, he decided to use the feedback from the screenings to develop an expanded version of the original film. This second iteration was produced again in collaboration with Mary Field and her team, with financial backing from the *Rockefeller Foundation*, based in New York (USA).[16] *Unemployment and Money*, completed in April 1940, was nearly the UK's first animated feature film.[17] According to the BFI, it was "[r]eportedly the first animated diagrammatic film" (*BFI Collections Search* n.d., Synopsis). While Polanyi didn't explicitly mention Otto Neurath and his visual language Isotype in his writings, it's evident that he was influenced by it: "Otto Neurath's Isotype was both a source of inspiration and a threat to Polanyi's own endeavors" (Bíró 2020: 337).

Shortly after, Otto Neurath could apply his visual language in a British animated film for the first time. Just before the German invasion of the Netherlands in May 1940, Neurath and his illustrator Marie Reidemeister escaped to Great Britain. Upon their arrival, they were detained as 'enemy aliens' on the Isle of Man. After 8 months, the pair were finally released in February 1941, thanks to the many declarations of support from Albert Einstein (1879–1955) and others. Following their marriage, the couple established the *Isotype Institute* in Oxford.[18] On April 7, 1941, they received a request from documentary film producer Paul Rotha (né Thompson, 1907–1984) to incorporate Neurath's visual language into his films. Rotha first learned about Neurath when he came across his book *Modern Man in the Making* (1939). This book, published by *Alfred A. Knopf, Inc.* in the United States, used a picture-text format to explore the history of human civilization. It sparked significant interest in the English-speaking world. As for Neurath, the collaboration in a film with Rotha proved to be intriguing for several reasons:

"Firstly, it allowed for the systematic development of a new application for their visual language. While films had previously been used sporadically in Vienna, the collaboration with Rotha elevated this work to a far more professional standard, promising a significantly broader audience. Secondly, this work was explicitly aimed against National Socialism, a point Otto Neurath emphasized repeatedly. Lastly, the financial aspect should not be overlooked, as the film work was well-paid and provided the institute with a steady stream of lucrative commissions" (Sandner 2019: 230).

On October 20, 1941, the film *A Few Ounces a Day* was released. It highlighted the critical need to gather raw materials to compensate for the supply ships destroyed by the Nazis. This film marked not only the debut of the *Isotype Institute*'s participation in an animated production but also the first commissioned animated propaganda film by the MoI. Following its release, contemporary critics expressed great enthusiasm for the film:

"The manner of presentation is unique. The statistics are brought to life through animated unit symbols called isotypes. These have hitherto only been used in graphic form, i.e. statically. [...] Possibly the most effective short film the M.O.I. has commissioned. It has information and instruction on a vital issue and is an effective call to us all to take action" (Documentary News Letter, 2 (11) 1941: 207).

The film was incredibly successful. Starting in 1942, it was used in cinemas, factories, and canteens and also gained popularity in the USA. Its impact was so profound that it inspired *Halas & Batchelor* in their initial project for the MoI: "*Filling the Gap*, released in April 1942, was something of a hybrid, mixing Isotype-style graphics of milk and wheat sacks with a doe-eyed prize cow and anthropomorphized vegetables marching off to dig their own way to victory" (Stewart 2021: 67).[19] The *Isotype Institute* created animated sequences for several short documentaries, including *Defeat Diphtheria* (1941), *Blood Transfusion* (1941/1942), and *Total War in Britain* (1945). Additionally, it contributed to longer documentaries such as *World of Plenty* (1943) and *Land of Promise* (1945/1946). In 1945, Otto Neurath and Paul Rotha established *Unifilm Ltd.* with the vision: "To make complete films in the Isotype method, like 'A Few Ounces a Day,' of which a medical subject '*Endocrinology of the Menstrual Cycle*' in color is the first" (Documentary News Letter, 5 (50) 1945: 100). Unfortunately, Neurath passed away in 1946 before the completion of the film.

In the United States, the Isotype visual language gained increased recognition in the 1930s, primarily due to the efforts of Rudolf Modley (1906–1976) from Vienna. Modley, who had previously assisted Otto Neurath in Vienna during the 1920s, relocated to the USA in the early 1930s. Upon arriving in New York, he established *Pictorial Statistics, Inc.* in 1934, employing a visual language akin to Isotype. Modley's book *How to Use Pictorial Statistics* (1937) was praised as an "effective job of Americanization" (Evart G. Routzahn, as cited in Sandner 2021: 33) of Neurath's picture language. That same year, Modley also conducted experiments with pictograph animation before ultimately concentrating on creating pictorial diagrams for print media. Among the numerous imitators of Neurath's picture language in the US, Philip E. Ragan (1909–1989), a Philadelphia (Pennsylvania) resident, distinguished himself through his distinctive pictogram design influenced by the Art Deco style. In 1934, he led *Sociographics Philadelphia*, an organization that visually represented statistical data in the Isotype style: "In the late 1930s, Sociographics became known as a US leader in the use of the Isotype technique" (Ihara 2022: 2855).

Philip Ragan may have interacted with Rudolf Modley and Otto Neurath, who traveled to the US for half a year in September 1936. Concurrently, Ragan initiated his work on films for the *Works Progress Administration* (WPA).[20] The anonymous diagrammatic film *Is Work Relief Better Than the Dole?* (1936), which utilized limited animation, is speculated to be among his initial experiments. It is possible that Ragan also incorporated pictograms in the WPA film *Shock Troops of Disaster* (1939), which depicted the agency's relief efforts following hurricane devastation in the eastern United States. However, Ragan's animation career truly began with John Grierson (1898–1972), often referred to as "the father of the documentary film movement in the English-speaking world" (Barsam 1992: 77). In 1939, Grierson spearheaded the establishment of the *National Film Board of Canada* (NFB) on behalf of the Canadian government. His prior collaborations with renowned international animation artists like Len Lye (1901–1980, New Zealand), Lotte Reiniger (Germany), and Norman McLaren (1914–1987, Scotland) during his work in Great Britain laid the foundation for his ambition to include an animation department from the board's inception. However, his focus on producing the documentary series *Canada Carries On* (1940–1959) and *The World in Action* (1941–1945) postponed the realization of this goal. Instead, Grierson recruited Philip Ragan to create the animated film *Controls for Victory* (1940). This animated debut film was so persuasive that Grierson not only commissioned multiple films from Walt Disney but also from Philip Ragan, who was described by the press in 1949 as the "Disney of the Scientists" (McIlvaine 1949: 6). This was to fulfill the film quota assigned to Grierson by the *National War Finance Committee. Philip Ragan Associates, Inc.* produced approximately 40 animated films between 1941 and 1945. These films explained the war's economic impact and outlined guidelines for the war effort to the Canadian public. In 1944, *The Educational Screen* described these films:

"Ragan's films are unique in several ways. First of all, they deal exclusively with ideas or statistics which are pictured by animated geometric graphic symbols and are presented through an animated silhouette technique. This silhouette technique is not limited to black and white but combines shades of gray with them. Ragan maintains that his technique is different from Disney's and that Disney makes pictures that imitate reality, while he deals exclusively in symbols" (Dugan 1944: 350).

While innovative, the films' lack of color gives off a cold and somewhat gloomy vibe, especially compared to the NFB's other vibrant films: "Seldom have economic principles been so brilliantly schematized; but seldom has the screen been put to so lifeless and impersonal a use" (Spottiswoode 1951: 23). For instructional films, Ragan introduced the silhouette of a worker known as Plugger, who "became as familiar to Canadians as Walt Disney characters" (Scott 1947: 14). Additionally, Ragan's films gained attention in the United States as well. The *U.S. News Review, Issue No. 5* (1942), published by the *Office of War Information*, featured Ragan's film *Unmanned Machines Mean Unarmed Men* (1942). The film explained the impact of the factory worker shortage on the military.

Post war, Philip Ragan produced the political animated film *One World or None* (1946),[21] recognized as "the first 'atomic scare' film" (Schwartz 2021: 10). This film was specifically designed for the US market and created within nine months on behalf of *The National Committee on Atomic Information*.[22] In an animated format, the film portrays the remarkable scientific accomplishments in nuclear research. This includes the work of Lise Meitner (1878–1968), an Austrian scientist, and her theoretical explanation of nuclear fission. It then illustrates the catastrophic impact of an atomic bomb being dropped on American cities like New York, Chicago, and San Francisco. The central theme of the film emphasizes the necessity of international collaboration in controlling nuclear weapons, especially in the aftermath of the near-global devastation experienced during World War II. When the film premiered at the *Institute for Advanced Study* (IAS) in Princeton, New Jersey, Albert Einstein, who had contributed to the book of the same name, reportedly conveyed to Ragan: "Your film is a great achievement, and, too, it is an artistic success" (Albert Einstein, as cited in McIlvaine 1949: 7).

Otto Neurath's visual language, Isotype, gained global recognition through animated films, yet he remains relatively unknown in Austria compared to his international fame. In early December 1945, the Austrian press reported Otto Neurath as *Ein Wiedergefundener* (Someone Rediscovered) after his speech in a British radio broadcast for Austria. Neurath was an Austrian exile who had worked abroad and "remained Austrian," as the newspaper wrote (Arbeiter-Zeitung, December 1, 1945: 3). Despite the expressed hope for Neurath's return to Vienna "to assist in the reconstruction of Austria" (Arbeiter-Zeitung, December 1, 1945: 3), his untimely death on December 22, 1945, shattered these aspirations. Not until 2022 did the British theater group *1927* introduce animation sequences inspired by Neurath to the Viennese theater stage. Interestingly, the Austrian audience did not perceive Neurath's visionary visual language as such, resulting in its almost invisible presence to the spectators.

STRIKING A CHORD: AUSTRIAN MUSIC AGAINST THE NAZIS

Throughout her career, Lotte Reiniger, the German silhouette animator, maintained strong connections to Austria and Austrian music. During the First World War (1914–1918), Reiniger was responsible for designing the title sequences of several feature films. It wasn't until 1919 that she crafted her first independent silhouette film, titled *Das Ornament des verliebten Herzens* (The Ornament of the Lovestruck Heart), at the Berlin *Institut für Kulturforschung* (Institute for Cultural Research). This institute, established in 1919 by Berthold Bartosch (1893–1968) and Dr. Erwin Hanslik (1880–1940) from Vienna, served as a counterpart to the Viennese institute of the same name and was headed by Hans Cürlis (1889–1982). Bartosch, born in 1893 in Polaun (now Kořenov, Czech Republic), then part of Austria-Hungary, became a close collaborator of Reiniger. He worked on several of her films, including the internationally acclaimed animated feature *Die Abenteuer des Prinzen Achmed* (The Adventures of Prince Achmed, 1926). Reiniger utilized the music of her favorite Austrian composer, Wolfgang Amadeus Mozart, for her first sound film, *Zehn Minuten Mozart* (Ten Minutes of Mozart, 1930), specifically *Eine kleine Nachtmusik* (A Little Night Music, 1787) and *Così fan tutte* (1789/1790). Additionally, she was commissioned by Austrian composer Fritz Kreisler (1875–1962) to create the silhouette film *Sissi* (1932) as an entr'acte for the operetta *Sissy* (1932), while Kreisler was residing in Berlin. The operetta, which debuted in Vienna just before Christmas 1932, featured Austrian actress Hedy Lamarr (née Hedwig Eva Maria Kiesler, 1914–2000) in the leading role of Empress Elisabeth of Austria (1837–1898). Subsequently, Lamarr pursued a career in Hollywood. After Hollywood purchased the film rights, it produced *The King Steps Out* (1936). However, following the *'Anschluss' Österreichs* (annexation of Austria) into Nazi Germany in March 1938, the operetta became prohibited from being performed. This was due to composer Fritz Kreisler's Jewish heritage, prompting his emigration to the USA in 1939.

In the mid-1930s, Lotte Reiniger departed from Nazi Germany. Before leaving, she created *Papageno* (1935), a film inspired by Mozart's *Die Zauberflöte* (The Magic Flute, 1791). That same year, she relocated to London with her husband, Carl Koch (1892–1963). Her musical films were seen by German refugees in London as "a wonderfully comforting symbol [...] of freedom and courage to face life" (as cited in Happ 2004: 51–52). Reiniger's adoration for Mozart, which she referred to as "Mozartfimmel (Mozart mania)" (Lotte Reiniger, as cited in Heller 1986: para. 1), remained evident in her works. In Great Britain, she crafted *A Night in a Harem* (1958), based on his opera *Die Entführung aus dem Serail* (The Abduction from the Seraglio, 1782). In 1971, Reiniger created approximately 140 silhouettes depicting the four Mozart operas *Figaros Hochzeit* (The Marriage of Figaro, 1786), *Don Giovanni* (1787), *Così fan tutte* (1789/1790), and *Die Zauberflöte* (The Magic Flute, 1791). These were later compiled into a book titled *Mozart: Die großen Opern in*

Scherenschnitten von Lotte Reiniger (Mozart: The Great Operas in Silhouettes by Lotte Reiniger), published in 1987.

George Pal, the acclaimed animation filmmaker, also deeply admired Austrian music. He was born György Pál Marczincsak in 1908 in Cegléd (known as Zieglet in German), a Hungarian town that was part of Austria-Hungary at the time. After completing his studies at the Hungarian University of Fine Arts, he began working at *Hunnia Film Studio* in 1928, where he learned animation fundamentals from Hollywood-trained George Feld. In the early 1930s, he relocated to Berlin, where he became a prominent figure in the early days of German animation. The rise of the Nazis in 1933 prompted him to emigrate. After passing through Prague and Paris, he eventually settled in Eindhoven (Netherlands) in 1934. While in Eindhoven, he focused on creating stop-motion advertisements for the *Philips* corporation and the British client *Horlicks Malted Milk*. His advertising film *The Ship of the Ether* (1934) for *Philips Radio* featured musicians from various European cities, including Rome (Italy), Paris (France), Munich (Germany), and Hilversum (Netherlands). Pal demonstrated his connection to Austrian culture by featuring a café violinist from Vienna and a prototype of the character Mr. Strauss, modeled after Austrian composer Johann Strauss II, performing one of his waltzes for an extended time.

Following the outbreak of World War II, George Pal departed from Europe just a few months before the German Wehrmacht occupied the Netherlands: "One step ahead of the Nazis, George Pal fled the Netherlands for Hollywood, where he now ridicules Hitler's hordes" (Taylor 1943: 15). During his time at *Paramount*, he created his famous animated puppet films known as *Puppetoons*, earning an honorary Oscar in 1943 for their development. In January 1942, he released one of his most well-known *Puppetoons*, the Oscar-nominated *Tulips Shall Grow*. The film portrays the invasion of the Netherlands by a mechanical army called "The Screwballs," which ultimately starts to rust and fall apart due to a thunderstorm. The character of composer Johann Strauss II, further developed by George Pal, also battles against this army of machines: "With the war raging overseas, George created the mythical Mr. Strauss as a symbol of the will of the people of Europe to resist and defeat those who would be their masters" (*The Fantasy Film Worlds of George Pal* 1985, 00:13:45). In *Mr. Strauss Takes a Walk* (1942), the Austrian composer finds inspiration from the beautiful flora and fauna of the Vienna Woods, leading to the creation of his globally renowned compositions. Subsequently, in *Bravo, Mr. Strauss* (1943), Vienna comes under attack by the mechanical army.[23] The statue of Strauss, located in Vienna's 'Stadtpark' (City Park), witnesses the destruction of its beloved city and abruptly springs to life (Figure 6.2). Drawing parallels to the famous tale of *The Pied Piper of Hamelin*, Strauss entices the army into the Danube, where it meets its ultimate demise in the water. Furthermore, the character reappears in *The Little Broadcast* (1943), portraying the role of a conductor.

George Pal's films featuring Mr. Strauss seamlessly blended into a series of American movies that portrayed Austria in a positive light. The 1938 live-action feature film *The Great Waltz*, released just before Austria's annexation into Nazi Germany, used nostalgia and classical music by Johann Strauss II to create a distance between the country and its saber-rattling German neighbor. Additionally, the film portrayed Austria's purported democratic endeavors as drawing it closer to the

FIGURE 6.2 George Pal with his Puppetoon figure Mr. Strauss in 1943. (Source: Collier's Magazine, January 16, 1943.)

United States than to the German Reich. In 1939, Hugh Harman (1903–1982) produced several peace-themed animated films, including the Oscar-nominated *Peace on Earth* (1939). Interestingly, he was mistakenly credited with a Nobel Peace Prize nomination for this work.[24] Shortly after the start of World War II, he released *The Blue Danube* (1939), an animated adaptation of Johann Strauss II's waltz of the same name. This film, incorporating lively colors and picturesque landscapes, can be interpreted as a portrayal of the yearning for a world at peace. The live-action feature film *Florian* (1940) draws comparisons between the Austro-Hungarian multiethnic state and the United States, "while the fate of the aristocracy and patriotic Austrians during the short-lived revolution after World War I echoes the events of March 1938" (Vansant 2019: 94). This image cultivation also encompassed Austrian composer Franz Schubert: "In the 1941 film *New Wine*, Schubert's struggles are conveyed in his music and serve as comfort and inspiration in troubled times. Moreover, the repressive regime of Schubert's time was designed to parallel the contemporary situation in Austria" (Vansant 2019: 94).

During the 1930s and early 1940s, Franz Schubert became a prominent identification figure for Jewish and Austrian communities. For instance, the *Kulturbund Deutscher Juden* (Culture League of German Jews), a self-support organization sanctioned by the Nazis to oversee and segregate Jewish artists affected by the work ban, regularly arranged classical music concerts. Schubert was the second most frequently performed composer, just behind Felix Mendelssohn Bartholdy (1809–1847). This was partly because of his association with the Jewish community in Vienna. In 1828, Schubert composed a musical setting for a psalm at the request of cantor Salomon Sulzer (1804–1890), making him the "only great composer before the twentieth century to compose a setting in Hebrew of the liturgy for the synagogue" (Jacobson 1997: 9). Moreover, Schubert was perceived as an outsider with whom the Jewish community could relate during its oppression. But there were also pragmatic motives for this. While Jewish artists were swiftly prohibited from performing works by German composers, Schubert himself was not considered a 'German' composer until the annexation of Austria into Nazi Germany in 1938.

Following the annexation of Austria, it became crucial for German propagandists to 'Aryanize' artists such as Franz Schubert to establish a unified cultural identity accepted by both Germans and Austrians. However, this endeavor faced challenges as the Nazis viewed Schubert as "one of the most complicated problems of German music" (Karl Hasse, as translated in Hirsch 2007: 490). Schubert's music was perceived as gentler and more feminine in contrast to that of Ludwig van Beethoven (1770–1827), a favored composer of the Nazis and a significant figure in their cultural propaganda. Notably, Schubert's contemporary, Robert Schumann (1810–1856), had already remarked on this issue:

"Schubert appears almost girlish compared to Beethoven – far more talkative, softer, and expansive; beside him, he seems like a child playing carelessly among giants. This is how his symphonic movements relate to Beethoven's: in their intimacy, they can only be attributed to Schubert. Certainly, Schubert has his powerful moments and grand works, but his relationship to Beethoven is like that of woman to man – where the latter commands, the former pleads and persuades" (Schumann 1838: 238).

In his book *Musik und Rasse* (Music and Race, 1937), music writer and SS member Richard Eichenauer (1893–1956) suggested that Franz Schubert's "softer" nature stemmed from his "Eastern-Nordic" heritage, based solely on preserved paintings of Schubert (Eichenauer 1937: 232–233).[25] Additionally, Schubert was deeply connected to the Austrian soul, as noted by US writer Thomas Wolfe (1900–1938) during the 1928 celebrations of Schubert's 100th death anniversary in Vienna: "I think Schubert has become a great symbol to these people, standing for all that was best and greatest in 'the good old time'. He is Vienna incarnate … and he is rooted in their hearts forever" (Thomas Wolfe, as cited in Hirsch 2007: 491).

Even after Austria's annexation into Nazi Germany, Jewish and Austrian emigrants continued to identify with Franz Schubert. The British animated film *The Grenade* (1944) vividly depicted the contrast between Ludwig van Beethoven and Schubert, highlighting Schubert's portrayal as an outsider. The film was part of the newsreel *Worker and War-Front* (1942–1946), specifically tailored for the British working class and screened in armaments factories. The plot revolves around a small tea kettle that Boy Scouts discover and transport to an armaments factory, where it is transformed into a small hand grenade. The grenade feels insignificant amid the massive war machinery and embodies the role of an outsider. When it befriends an English soldier, they journey to the front lines together, where the grenade is used to attack a German position. In an unexpected turn of events, the grenade not only obliterates the German position but also vanquishes Hermann Göring (1893–1946), Joseph Goebbels (1897–1945), and Adolf Hitler. It then confronts the German 'Reichsadler' (Reich's Eagle) in the ultimate showdown, which amusingly ends with the eagle turning into a roast chicken. The use of music plays a crucial role in these events. During poignant moments in the film, such as when the tea kettle is sent to the factory as waste or when it befriends the soldier, the audience hears Schubert's *Symphony No. 8* (published posthumously in 1839). During tense situations, such as when the soldier and the grenade show their strength or when the grenade is hurled at a German gun position, Beethoven's *Symphony No. 5* (1807/1808) is played.

When *Fantasia* (1940) premiered in the USA on November 13, 1940, it concluded with the haunting *Night on Bald Mountain* (1867) by Modest Mussorgsky (1839–1881), followed by a fresh interpretation of Schubert's *Ellens dritter Gesang* (Ellen's Third Song, 1825), also known as *Ave Maria*. According to accounts from a story conference, Walt Disney recognized Franz Schubert's music as a source of hope: "The forces of good on one side and of evil on the other is what I'm trying to see in this thing" (Walt Disney, as cited in Culhane 1983: 203). The segment, for which a distinct companion book was released in the USA and Great Britain, was described as:

"One of the greatest pieces of devotional music ever composed, Schubert's *Ave Maria* has been inspiring singers, orchestras, and music lovers for more than a hundred years. When it was selected as a concluding number in the first Walt Disney Concert Feature, *Fantasia*, it offered an exciting challenge to the finest creative minds of the Disney organization. Hundreds of paintings and sketches were prepared in an endeavor to explore various ways of visualizing that glorious music – of translating its spirit and meaning from sound to sight" (Field 1940: [3]).

Indeed, the movie's final scene marked a significant moment in animation history. Consisting of 217 feet of film, it is recognized as the "longest [continuous] scene in an animated film up to that time" (Culhane 1983: 203).[26] During its production, renowned US writer Rachel Field (1894–1942) visited the studio and was struck by the mystical quality of the images. Field was scheduled to create a contemporary adaptation of the text, but only one of her verses made it into the final version of the movie:

> "Ave Maria, Heaven's bride, the bells ring out in solemn praise
> For you the anguish and the pride, the living glory of our nights and days.
> The Prince of Peace your arms embrace while hosts of darkness fade and cower.
> Oh, save us, Mother full of grace, in life, and in our dying hour. Hail Mary!"

In the movie, the narrator, composer Deems Taylor (1885–1966), characterizes *Ave Maria* as a "message of the triumph of hope and life over the powers of despair and death." The scene shows a procession of lights "until we reach the end and emerge in a blaze of morning light. Once again, the powers of life and hope have triumphed over the hosts of death and despair" (Deems Taylor, as cited in Culhane 1983: 203). Interestingly, the day after the movie's premiere, the German Luftwaffe (air force) launched its most intense attack to that date on an English city during the 'Battle of Britain' (1940–1941). This attack on Coventry, aimed at undermining British morale, sparked a renewed will to resist, marking a pivotal moment in the war effort. It's difficult not to see *Disney*'s portrayal of the struggle between good and evil as an allegory for the horrors of World War II and the aspiration to overcome Nazi Germany. Similarly, *Warner Bros.*' animated film *A Corny Concerto* (1943), crafted as a satire of *Disney*'s *Fantasia* (1940), also reflects references to the wartime era.[27] Notably, this cartoon features two waltzes not included in *Fantasia* (1940): *Tales from the Vienna Woods* (1868) and *The Blue Danube* (1866) by Austrian composer Johann Strauss II. In parallel, George Pal depicted Strauss as a resistance fighter against the Nazis in *Bravo, Mr. Strauss* (1943). When *Fantasia* (1940) arrived in Austria in the 1950s, its final scene was surprisingly met with a negative review: "We are less fond [...] of the interpretations of Mussorgsky's 'Night on Bald Mountain' [...] and Schubert's 'Ave Maria,' as they deviate from traditional conceptions" (Paimann's Filmlisten, January 28, 1959: 10).

However, just as Ludwig van Beethoven was used for both National Socialist and Allied propaganda,[28] Franz Schubert also became part of fascist propaganda. In the 1934 Japanese anime *Ponsuke no Haru* (Spring Comes to Ponsuke) by Ikuo Ōishi (1901–1944), often referred to as the "Japanese Disney" (Kato 2017: para. 7), the main character Ponsuke shoots a bird from the sky and plucks it. Despite being thought dead, the bird rises, reassembles its plumage, and marches away with a shouldered feather to the tune of Schubert's *Militärmarsch* (March Militaire, 1826). This film was created at a time when Japan often portrayed itself in anime as a militarily inferior underdog yet superior to any opponent due to its determination. As a result, in 1934, the same year that Betty Boop was featured as a Japanese character in *Tengu Taiji* (Heavenly Dog Extermination), Schubert's portrayal as an outsider was also integrated into Japanese military propaganda.[29]

NOTES

1 The abbreviation TIM stands for 'time-in-minutes' and was frequently used as a nickname for time announcements in the UK.
2 The term 'Monarchie-Österreicher' (Monarchy Austrians) commonly refers to individuals born into German-speaking families within the crown lands of the Danube Monarchy. These German-speaking families typically harbored a strong sense of attachment to the Crown in Vienna.
3 See the first chapter of this book for additional information on Max Fleischer's biography.
4 *Paramount* assumed control of *Fleischer Studios* in the spring of 1941 due to the Fleischer brothers' inability to settle their debts. Following Dave Fleischer's departure from the studio, Max Fleischer was also required to resign. He complied with this demand in December 1941. For contractual reasons, the studio operated as *Fleischer Studios* until the summer of 1942, after which it transitioned to *Famous Studios*. This new venture was overseen by Max Fleischer's son-in-law Seymour Kneitel (1908–1964) and others.
5 The film's title intentionally capitalizes the 'V' in 'Navy' to reference the Victory sign.
6 One instance of this is the film *Blunder Below* (1942), which faced censorship in certain TV broadcasts due to its racist portrayal of the Japanese.
7 After getting struck by an anchor, Popeye exclaims: "It should happen to Hitler."
8 In certain film versions, the poster was black colored, making it difficult to spot. However, a restored version has been available since 2006, in which the poster is clearly discernible.

9 The film also has a more well-known abbreviated version titled *Mabō no Dai Kyōsō* (Mabō's Big Race, 1936).

10 Due to the ongoing Second Sino-Japanese War since 1937, Japan relinquished its opportunity to host the 1940 Summer Olympics to the *International Olympic Committee* (IOC) in July 1938, as the country needed to allocate its resources to the war effort.

11 One rare instance of a Fleischer character representing the American adversary was seen in *Sora no Arawashi* (Sky Eagles, 1938). In the film, Japanese animal aviators aim at a cloud resembling Popeye.

12 In the Vichy France propaganda animation film *Nimbus Libéré* (Nimbus Released, 1944), the scenario was altered, showing Popeye as the pilot of an American bomber, accompanied by Mickey Mouse and Donald Duck. Ironically, German Luftwaffe pilots also adorned their aircraft with American cartoon characters like Mickey Mouse and Betty Boop as insignia.

13 Characters in anime, such as those in the series *Dr. Slump: Arale-chan* (Dr. Slump Show, 1981–1986) or the 2007 music video *Love to Live By* (m-flo loves Chara), drew inspiration from Betty Boop. Betty Boop's influence can also be seen in the anime series *Urusei Yatsura* (1981–1986) and *Mahō no Tenshi Kurīmī Mami* (Creamy Mami, the Magic Angel; 1983–1984), as well as in the anime feature film *Kurenai no Buta* (Porco Rosso, 1992).

14 Max Fleischer's Austrian heritage may not be widely recognized in Austria, but the Fleischer brothers' characters are well known here as well. At the *Narzissenfest* (Daffodil Festival) in Bad Aussee (Styria), Austria's largest flower festival, a Popeye flower figurine won first place in two categories in June 2023. This impressive figure was crafted by 45 individuals who invested 650 hours in processing 90,000 daffodils.

15 Otto Neurath identified 1927 as the commencement of his film work in his autobiography, *From Hieroglyphics to Isotype* (1946). In her obituary, *Isotype in Films* (1946), his widow, Marie Neurath, mentioned that the initial experiments were conducted in 1927 or 1928.

16 His brother Karl Polanyi, born in Austria, also secured a 2-year grant from the *Rockefeller Foundation*. This grant assisted him in finishing his book *The Great Transformation* (1944) while he was in the United States.

17 According to Michael Polanyi, the 35-mm film version ran for 4,000 feet or 45 minutes (cf. Polanyi 1940: 1). In contrast, the 16 mm film version stored in the BFI runs for 1,400 feet or 39 minutes (cf. *BFI Collections Search* n.d., Collections). Consequently, the film falls just short of the 40-minute limit set by the *Academy of Motion Picture Arts and Sciences*, which awards the Oscars.

18 The establishment of the Institute was made official in early 1942, yet it had already been acknowledged in the credits of *A Few Ounces a Day* (1941).

19 While the combination of diagrams and anthropomorphizing received positive feedback from the press, the film faced criticism for its overall presentation: "By adopting the cartoon's flexibility and some hint of its inconsequential gaiety in their diagram sequences, and by retaining something of the diagram's essential simplicity in their pure cartoon sequences, the makers have achieved a lively and entertaining film. In details, however, it falls below the high standard it sets itself" (Documentary News Letter, 3 (4), 1942: 55).

20 The press explained Philip Ragan's fascination with animated film as follows: "Not being satisfied with static presentations, he turned to film animations of pictorial graphs and charts" (Business Screen Magazine, 8 (8), 1947: 34).

21 The film was originally envisioned as the introductory part of a series called *Problems of Peace*, which was set to cover topics such as *World Government*, *World Trade*, and *Race*. Another planned series was titled *The Nations* and would feature films on the USSR, USA, Britain, China, India, France, and the Nations of the Middle East. The

films *Mutual Aid* (1944) and *Money, Goods and Prices* (1945), created for Canada, were intended as prototypes for *World Trade*. "However, the evaluating committee felt that the film [One World or None] did not do a clear and thorough job" (Starr (ed.) 1951: 217).

22 Philip Ragan also incorporated the film into his 1950 campaign for the American Congressional election.

23 In March 1938, Austria was annexed into Nazi Germany without any military resistance, leading the Allies to consider it the first victim of the Nazis. This perspective was also depicted in *The Nazis Strike* (1943), a film from the *Why We Fight* (1942–1945) series, where a *Disney*-produced map animation symbolically shows ink dripping from a swastika onto Austrian territory. The Moscow Declarations of November 1943 consequently stated that the annexation of Austria was deemed invalid.

24 The myth, which was still being shared as recently as 2020 in the comprehensive book *Historical Dictionary of Animation and Cartoons* (Dobson 2020: 119), seems to have originated from a newspaper obituary: "Mr. Harman was also nominated for the Nobel Peace Prize for his 1939 antiwar feature, 'Peace on Earth'" (New York Times, November 30, 1982: 12). In truth, the Nobel Peace Prize was not awarded from 1939 to 1943, and there is no evidence of a nomination on the official website *nobelprize.org* (as of 2023).

25 In a review of the book *Musik und Rasse* (Music and Race, 1932), Paul Bekker (1882–1937), while living in exile in France, assessed the author, Richard Eichenauer: "With naive obstinacy, he exposes the consequences of racial theory, even penetrating deeply into the realm of purely German music. In doing so, he inevitably becomes an unwitting comedian – stupidity and ignorance are always the prerequisites for the racial theorist" (Bekker 1934: 4).

26 Inspired by this, Klaus Werner Voß (1953–2022) produced an acclaimed new version of *Ave Maria* (2013), which received multiple awards. German Oscar winner Thomas Stellmach (b. 1965) shared his thoughts on the reinterpretation: "I have just received your remake of AVE MARIA to view. I have never seen such a clean restoration. ;-)) Disney fingers would lick if all your movies would you prepare for today's youth in Flash" (Thomas Stellmach, as translated in Voß 2014: para. 1).

27 A baby black swan faces rejection from its family and even a predatory buzzard, which brands it with a sign reading "Rejected 4F," a classification used for unsuitable individuals in the US *Selective Service System*. Ultimately, it morphs into a type of fighter plane and comes to the rescue of its siblings, who then embrace it as one of their own.

28 The head motif of Ludwig van Beethoven's *Symphony No. 5* ("Ta Ta Ta Taaa") resembles the Morse code for the letter V, which is three short signals followed by one long signal. Because of this resemblance, the 'fate motif' became the acoustic signal for the BBC's 'V for Victory' campaign. Beginning in July of 1941, Winston Churchill (1874–1965) popularized the V-shaped gesture in Britain as a symbol of confidence for victory. Eventually, the V symbol and its associated acoustic signal were also embraced in US propaganda efforts.

29 Modern Japanese anime also shows a clear preference for classical Austrian music, as Monika Nguyen's 2010 research report on *Viennese Classicism in Japanese Animation* demonstrated when submitted as the final report for a research grant.

Part 2

From War Rooms to Animation Studios

Austria's Journey into the Digital Age

7 Animated Exile
Austrian Creators during WWII

When Leni Riefenstahl (1902–2003) approached Hollywood in late 1938, after gaining notoriety as Adolf Hitler's (1889–1945) favored director for her Reich Party Rally (1933–1935) and *Olympia* films (1936–1938), she found most doors closed. However, Walt Disney (1901–1966) was among the few who welcomed her on December 8. While Riefenstahl aimed to establish herself in Hollywood, Disney was still seeking to sell his movie *Snow White and the Seven Dwarfs* (1937) to the German Reich, which now included Austria following its annexation in March 1938. Before this, Austria had been Disney's key German-speaking market, as his distributor, *RKO Radio Pictures,* had shut down its German branch in 1935 due to foreign exchange export restrictions. In early 1938, Austrian newspapers were still announcing the planned Vienna premiere of *Snow White* for the spring of that year (cf. Österr. Film-Zeitung, January 7, 1938: 2). Subsequently, a German version for the German-speaking audience was created in May 1938 (cf. Garncarz 2015: 233). However, due to the *'Anschluss' Österreichs* (annexation of Austria), Switzerland was the only country to screen the German-language version of the movie.[1]

The previous belief that the German dubbing was completed in Austria has been disproven, as it is now confirmed that the film was dubbed in the Netherlands, where some of the involved actors had sought refuge from the German Reich. Additionally, it has been clarified that the assumption about Austrian actress Paula Wessely (1907–2000) providing the voice for Snow White is incorrect. However, many of the staff had strong connections to Austria. For example, Snow White's voice actress, Hortense Raky (1918–2006), was born in Berlin (Germany) but received her acting training in Vienna, where she began her career in theater and cinema. Due to her opposition to the Nazi regime and her relationship with the Jewish actor Willy Stettner (1895–1961), she faced obstacles in achieving a breakthrough in Germany. Following the annexation of Austria, she relocated to Switzerland. Stettner, the voice actor for the prince in the German version of *Snow White*, also sought to escape to Switzerland. He arrived in Austria from Germany through the Netherlands following the Nazi takeover and eventually escaped to England. Otto Wallburg (né Otto Maximilian Wasserzug, 1889–1944), who voiced the dwarf Doc, was also of Jewish origin. He relocated to Austria following the Nazi takeover of Germany but fled to the Netherlands after the annexation of Austria. In the Netherlands, he was apprehended by the Nazis in 1940 and later perished in the gas chambers of the Auschwitz concentration camp in Poland in 1944. The Jewish filmmaker Kurt Gerron (né Gerson, 1897–1944) directed the dubbing and provided voices for several supporting roles. He briefly sought refuge in Austria while fleeing from the regime. Subsequently,

DOI: 10.1201/9781003415442-9

he was arrested in the Netherlands and later died in the Auschwitz concentration camp in 1944.

After unsuccessful negotiations with *RKO Radio Pictures*, the German dubbed version of the film was archived at the Reichsfilmarchiv in 1939. Despite this, *Snow White* made its way into the German market with the help of an Austrian children's newspaper. Hans Steinsberg, who began producing children's newspapers in Vienna in 1926, also distributed them in the German Reich. When several cartoonists left Austria following its annexation, Steinsberg started printing *Disney* comics. For instance, the newspaper *Schmetterling* (Butterfly) featured Enterich Emmerich, better known as Donald Duck, from 1938. Between 1938 and 1939, *Disney*'s *Snow White* was serialized in comic form in the children's newspaper *Kiebitz* (Lapwing). In the German-language edition, the prince was depicted with blond hair instead of dark, aligning with the ideal image of the 'blond Teuton'.

AUSTRIA'S ROLE IN GERMANY'S DISNEY QUEST

In the mid-1930s, there was an effort in the German Reich to shift animated films from primarily being used for commercials to establishing a competitive production to *Disney*'s *Silly Symphonies*. An Austrian cartoonist played a significant role in this endeavor. *Ufa*, the largest German film company, decided in August 1934 to create a pilot film to launch commercial-free animated film production. They enlisted the services of Otto Waffenschmied (né Wawrzyckek, 1901–1971), a native of Vienna, for this task. Waffenschmied was known as the most prolific comic artist in the German-speaking region during the interwar period. After finishing his studies at the *Kunstgewerbeschule Wien* (Vienna School of Arts and Crafts, now University of Applied Arts Vienna) in 1919, he came to Germany via Denmark. From 1929 to 1941, he published the comic magazine *Dideldum* (Diddle-Boom). For *Ufa*, Waffenschmied planned a series around the character *Tilo Voss*, described by the media as "a cinematic heir to the traditional trickster figures of German folklore." They further remarked, "Tilo Voss may live in the forest, but as a child of the 20th century, he is well-versed in every modern technological advancement. His mischief unfolds in the wide space between the rustling of the trees and the roar of airplane engines" (Völkischer Beobachter, June 22, 1935: 6). On November 30, 1934, Waffenschmied successfully demonstrated a test strip, but it was not completely convincing. During a meeting on December 7, 1934, the *Ufa* board decided to start with the production of just one film, even though producing three films would have decreased the cost per film from 20,000 to 17,000 Reichsmarks (cf. Giesen and Storm 2012: 9–10). Simultaneously, Bernhard Huth (1905–?) and Egon von Tresckow (1907–1952) were reassigned from the advertising film department to assist with the production. The team's task was to create the "first German animated color film" (Völkischer Beobachter, June 22, 1935: 6) with a length of approximately 250 m for the 1935/1936 distribution program. However, the production encountered challenges, including increasing costs and artistic disagreements, resulting in repeated delays. For instance, a report from May 7, 1935, mentioned "that Waffenschmied's first draft did not have enough gags. For this reason, the manuscript had to be changed to American slapstick. In the new version, it is suitable" (as translated in Giesen and Storm 2012: 10). Despite this modification, discrepancies persisted, and during an *Ufa* board meeting on September 6, 1935, it was stated: "According to the present suggestions made by Waffenschmied, who contractually has to be involved in production, the film would be twice as long and cost three to four times above the approved budget" (as translated in Giesen and Storm 2012: 10–11). After the project was terminated, Waffenschmied was invoiced for the expenses totaling 14,000 Reichsmark. This setback significantly dampened *Ufa*'s aspirations. Even in 1937, when negotiating with an animation film producer, a report advised against making hasty commitments "in light of the bad experiences with the Waffenschmied color films" (as cited in Alt 2013: 195).

Nevertheless, another effort to rival *Disney* emerged with assistance from an Austrian. Right after the occupation of Czechoslovakia in March 1939, Berlin expressed interest in the Prague film studios. These studios boasted modern equipment, relatively lower wages, and proximity to Berlin compared to studios such as the *Bavaria Film* studios near Munich. *A-B Aktien-Filmfabriken* (A-B Filmové továrny) was taken over and eventually became *Prag-Film AG*, specializing in feature film production. Furthermore, *Ateliér filmových triků* (AFIT, Studio for Film Tricks), founded in Prague in 1935, was acquired in 1940 and rebranded as *AFIT-Zeichenfilmproduktion* (AFIT Animated Film Production). With only a handful of animators, the studio – previously known for creating title cards, subtitles, and special effects for movies – aimed to compete with *Disney* by making an animated feature film. Josef H. Pfister (1903-?) was named trustee on October 1, 1940, and Austrian Richard Dillenz (1892–1959)[2] was appointed artistic director.

Richard Dillenz, a native of Vienna, took a circuitous route to the world of animated film. Starting in 1909, he pursued a painting education at the Academy of Fine Arts in Munich. Upon returning to Austria during the war, he shifted his focus to architecture and studied at the *Kunstgewerbeschule Wien* (now University of Applied Arts Vienna) from 1915 to 1919. It was during this time that his exceptional talent for painting was discovered.[3] In April 1918, he co-founded the artist group *Bewegung* (Movement). Subsequently, he saw several of his paintings published and debuted in exhibitions. In February 1925, he ventured into entrepreneurship, founding a lingerie store in Vienna, only to close it a year later. He then opened a ladies' fashion store in Berlin. In 1930, he served as the head of the fashion school at the *Höhere Fachschule für Textil- und Bekleidungsindustrie* (Technical School for the Textile and Clothing Industries) in Berlin. During that period, he crossed paths with Josef Pfister, the manager of a fashion salon. Together, they not only authored the theoretical treatise *Deutsche Mode?* (German Fashion?, 1931) but also established the *Modeschule Berlin* (Berlin Fashion School) in 1932 at the private art school *Sturm* (Storm). Dillenz assumed leadership of the school, later renamed *Modeschule Dillenz* (Fashion School Dillenz), while Pfister took on the role of lecturer for culture and art education. In 1933, Dillenz joined the board of a new institution, which led to his initial involvement with the film craft:

"With the intention of politically regulating clothing, the 'German Fashion Office' (renamed the 'German Fashion Institute' in October 1933) was established in Berlin in June 1933, three months before the founding of the Reich Chamber of Culture, under the honorary chairmanship of Magda Goebbels. Costume designers for entertainment films, among others, were expected to seek guidance from this institution" (Bertschik 2005: 283).

"At the urging of the National Socialists" (Gierczynski 2005: 24), the fashion school was closed in 1938. Following this, Richard Dillenz and Josef Pfister transitioned to the film industry; Pfister assumed the role of a production group head at *Tobis Filmkunst* and later became the film company's press spokesman, while Dillenz pursued a career as a film fashion designer.[4] The reason behind the appointment of the inexperienced Dillenz as artistic director of the Prague animation studio in October 1940 remains unclear. However, "female fashion illustrators and designers were sought after by the animation film industry" (Giesen 2023: 272). According to an inventory of the *AFIT* estate, the Czech Film Archive (NFA) speculates that Dillenz might have misrepresented himself as an expert (cf. NFA (ed.) 2010: III).

Although Richard Dillenz lacked experience in creating animation, he had a precise vision for the kind of film he wanted to bring to life: an animated feature based on the opera *Orfeo ed Euridice* (Orpheus and Eurydice), which originally premiered at Vienna's Burgtheater in 1762. The drawing team, consisting of approximately 100 members, was largely composed of recent secondary school graduates and art students from shuttered universities. Among them was Jiří Brdečka (1917–1982), who gained acclaim as the 'Master of Czech Animation' post war. He later reflected on this period, stating: "Back then, I did not consider my new job of major significance to my life. For me, as for the other Czechs involved, it was mostly a way to survive the war in a relatively pleasant environment – in a word, to avoid the dismal factories of the occupier" (Brdečka 2015: 109).

Understanding Richard Dillenz's character proved challenging for his colleagues. In a guest article for the press, he openly advocated for National Socialist ideologies, drawing parallels between the French Revolution of 1789 and the National Socialists' rise to power, labeling it the "German Revolution":

"The German Revolution of 1933 seeks to fundamentally redefine clothing, transforming it into a unique expression of the National Socialist spirit and the new era it heralds. The objectives, methods, and potential of this National Socialist, and therefore distinctly German, fashion are inherently and inevitably tied to the organic development of the NSDAP's [Nationalsozialistische Deutsche Arbeiterpartei, English: National Socialist German Workers' Party] program" (Sport im Bild, 40 (6), March 20, 1934: 258).

On August 12, 1933, Thea Sternheim (née Olga Maria Theresia Gustava Bauer, 1883–1971), a German writer, made a note about Richard Dillenz and his wife:

"At the forefront of fashion in the new Germany is the Dillenz couple, that […] embarrassingly cloying petty bourgeois duo who had already made me uncomfortable at the fashion school they founded. […] So, this is what they look like – the unseen standard-bearers of the new regime, sycophants of heavy industry and the bloody camarilla" (Thea Sternheim, as cited in Ehrsam and Wyss (eds.) 2002: 265).

Jiří Brdečka, however, recalled it differently: "This likable gray-haired man of fifty or so, with the looks and manners of a German intellectual, discreetly hinted at his anti-Nazism before us Czechs, but greeted German visits wearing the NSDAP party badge; this much was understandable" (Brdečka 2015: 111). Uncertain of

Richard Dillenz's provenance, Czech cartoonists speculated that an American financier was behind his expensive suits – possibly even Walt Disney himself.

In Berlin, there was a desire to review the outcomes of the nearly one million Reichsmarks project.[5] However, the existing material was not sufficiently prepared for screening. Consequently, the team created a short film titled *Der Zauberlehrling* (The Sorcerer's Apprentice, 1943), which ran for about 11 minutes and shifted the setting to medieval Prague. Following a test screening in Berlin, the film was deemed unsatisfactory. Shortly after, the team received an unauthorized black-and-white copy of Disney's movie *Fantasia* (1940), featuring Mickey Mouse as the Sorcerer's Apprentice: "Apparently, our German bread givers preferred the work of the enemy to that of their fellow man and occasional NSDAP member" (Brdečka 2015: 114). The project for the animated feature film *Orpheus in der Unterwelt* (Orpheus in the Underworld) was halted, and Richard Dillenz was removed from his role as artistic director. On June 23, 1943, the *AFIT* studio and its staff became part of *Prag-Film AG* and started operating under the name *Zeichenfilmabteilung der Prag-Film AG* (Animation Department of Prag-Film AG). In a later interview, Horst von Möllendorf (1906–1992), who assumed the artistic direction, recollected these events:

"I didn't even know they had a copy [of *Fantasia*] here at that time. I didn't see it back then either, but of course, the Disney story was so captivating. I saw a few completed drawings [of the Dillenz version] in Prague; they weren't even humorous characters, but rather realistic depictions, and I vividly remember the water Dillenz had drawn at Prag-Film, dripping sadly down the walls somehow. Goebbels had surely seen a copy of the Disney version. So, making that comparison, one could roughly assume that nothing would come of it" (Horst von Möllendorf, as cited in Giesen 2020: 129).

Despite the setback, Horst von Möllendorf graciously acknowledged Richard Dillenz's accomplishment in establishing the studio. Essentially, Möllendorf acquired an animation studio with advanced technology, and the employees had accumulated several years of experience (Figure 7.1). Following the war, a few staff members joined the *Brothers in Trick* collective, bringing a fresh artistic perspective and unique poetic style to post-war Czechoslovak animated films.

After Josef Pfister's discharge from military service due to health reasons, he and Richard Dillenz began discussing the return of film material, some staff, and studio equipment in the spring of 1944. These negotiations continued until mid-1944, culminating in an agreement on May 20.[6] The formal revival of *AFIT*, privately managed by the two, took place on July 22. Initially, Dillenz and Pfister aimed to produce commercials inspired by the American Popeye model, but eventually shifted to working on Wehrmacht commissions, particularly for the Luftwaffe. Ultimately, the studio had to cease operations in the fall of 1944 due to the ongoing war.

Following his unsuccessful attempt at animated filmmaking in Czechoslovakia, Richard Dillenz returned to Austria and established *Dillenz Zeichenfilm GmbH* in 1946. However, due to its lack of success in producing animated films, the company rebranded as *Dillenz-Film-Produktion* in 1951, focusing on creating 'Heimatfilme' (sentimental films with regional background) and cultural films. Meanwhile, Josef Pfister, who had been involved in pedagogical methods during the establishment of the fashion

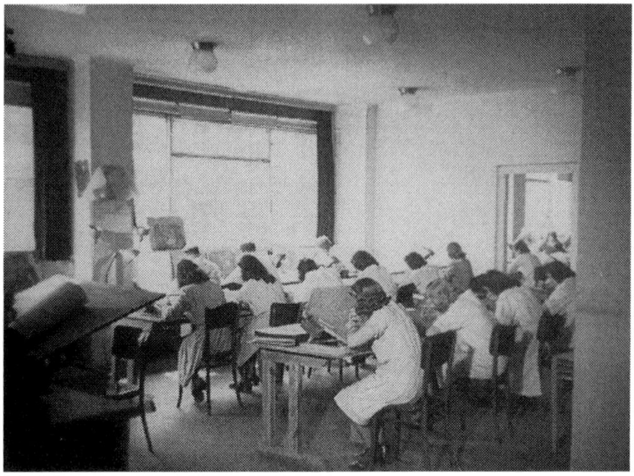

FIGURE 7.1 The *AFIT* studio, after being incorporated into *Prag-Film AG* in 1943. (Courtesy of Národní filmový archiv, Prague.)

school, began contributing to the formation of the German Bundeswehr in 1952, where he played a key role in developing and implementing educational principles.

TWO AGAINST THE TIDE: WEICHBERGER & WEIGEL

Johann Weichberger (1910–1992) and Susanne 'Susi' Weigel (1914–1990) stand out as the sole Austrian animators who successfully executed their own film projects during World War II. Johann Weichberger, born in Trieste (formerly Austria-Hungary, now Italy), studied at the *Kunstgewerbeschule Wien* (now University of Applied Arts Vienna) before relocating to Bern, Switzerland, in 1933. There, he spent 2 years learning the art of animation from film pioneer Julius Pinschewer (1883–1961).[7] Upon returning to Vienna, Weichberger began his career in the advertising film industry.[8] Following Austria's annexation in 1938, he moved to Berlin, the new center for German-language animation. Initially, he worked for *Döring-Film*, *Ufa*, and *Commerz-Film*, creating animated commercials. Notable projects from this period include *Gartenzauber* (Garden Magic, 1939) for *Hero-Helvetia*'s vegetable and fruit juices, and *Goldregen* (Golden Rain, 1939) for the *Sparkasse* bank.

Since 1940, Johann Weichberger was employed by *Degeto-Kulturfilm*, a subsidiary of *Tobis Filmkunst*, where he created entertaining short cartoons for the *Degeto-Schmalfilm-Schrank* home cinema program. He received a monthly salary of 1,500 Reichsmark for his work. The series titled *Fritz und Fratz* (Fritz and Fratz) recounts the escapades of identical twin brothers. In *Die blinden Passagiere* (The Blind Passengers), they secretly board a ship to join their uncle's trip around the world. The second story, *Der Spuk an Bord* (Spook Aboard), involves a stowaway pickpocket commencing his misdeeds. The ship's cook suspects the twins, leading to *Die wilde Jagd* (The Wild Hunt). However, *Die kleinen Helden* (The Little Heroes) ultimately catch the real thief and are honored by the whole crew (Figure 7.2).

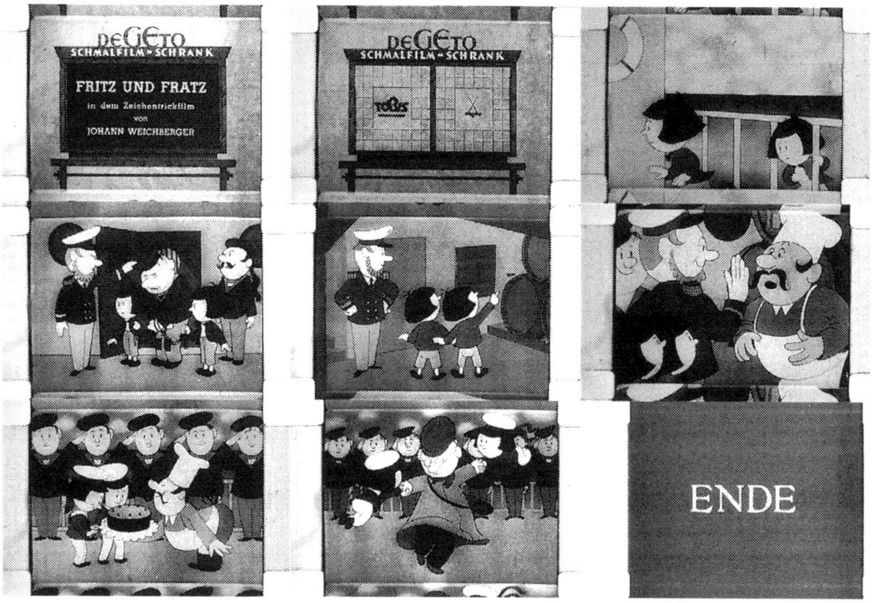

FIGURE 7.2 Filmstrips from *Die kleinen Helden* (The Little Heroes) by Johann Weichberger. (Source: Private collection (Permission by Marianne Weichberger).)

FIGURE 7.3 Rare photo of a Danish inbetweener with a cel from the *Fritz & Fratz* series. (Courtesy of Forlaget Fabel (Lars Jakobsen).)

In previous German and English literature, it was believed that Johann Weichberger designed all 12 parts of the series. In fact, parts five to eight were produced in Denmark (Figure 7.3), likely due to Weichberger being drafted into the Wehrmacht in October 1941. This can be confirmed both stylistically and in terms of content. In the Danish promotional cartoon *Kokkens Fidus* (Chef's Trick, 1939), designed by the same team, a ship's captain is saved from a cannibal cooking pot by being exchanged for the advertised sausages by the ship's cook. Similarly, *Onkel bei den Menschenfressern* (Uncle with the Man-Eaters) and *Dem Tod entronnen* (Escaping Death) share a nearly identical story, where the twins rescue their uncle Steffen from the cooking pot:

"Most of the Danish animators did not approve the occupation of Nazi Germany in 1943, and they made the cannibals walk like German soldiers – and take a civilian like Uncle Steffen – Fritz and Fratz as the freedom fighters who saved Uncle Steffen from the cruel Cannibals/Nazis… Nobody saw that hidden story or between-the-lines story – but for Danish eyes at that time, it was quite obvious, and even better to know it was sold in Germany…" (Lars Jakobsen, email to the author, dated June 21, 2010).

However, the episodes created by Johann Weichberger only tangentially touched on the war by portraying the absence of parents and the familiar escapism seen in German films of that time. This escapism was evident in the last four episodes, set in India and produced after Weichberger's release from the Wehrmacht between 1943 and 1944. In *Jumbo als Retter* (Jumbo as Savior), the twins assist a professor's India expedition by inflating a balloon with the help of an elephant reminiscent of *Disney*'s *Dumbo* (1941). *Die Landung im Wunderland* (The Landing in Wonderland) is accomplished using a fakir's rope. In *Der geheimnisvolle Tempel* (The Mysterious Temple), they ride on a sacred cow, and in the final episode, they aid a maharajah *Auf Tigerjagd* (On Tiger Hunt). In May 1943, Weichberger was hired by *Ufa Sonderproduktion*. As a result, he was excused from military service at their request to develop the animated film *Knax, das törichte Zwerglein* (Knax, the Stupid Little Dwarf).

The Weichberger family narrowly survived the Allied air attacks on Berlin in November 1943. While his wife took the children back to Vienna, Johann Weichberger was relocated to Zlín in Czechoslovakia. There, Hermína Týrlová (1900–1993) created the animated film *Der brave Slim* (The Good Slim, based on Ferdy the Ant) for *Degeto-Kulturfilm*. Likely, not only the final two parts of the *Fritz und Fratz* (Fritz and Fratz) series were produced in Zlín, but also military animations for *Mars Film*,[9] a company known for its Wehrmacht instructional films: "At any rate, his wife Else mentioned that he was engaged in professional work in the film industry, about which he was not permitted to share further details" (Renoldner 2010: 92).

Susi Weigel, a draftswoman, was employed by *Degeto-Kulturfilm* from 1940 to 1942. Born in Proßnitz (formerly Austria-Hungary, now Prostějov in the Czech Republic), she later moved to Vienna, where she attended the *Kunstgewerbeschule Wien* (now University of Applied Arts Vienna) from 1929 to 1934. During her student years, she collaborated with fellow students Wilhelm 'Bil' Spira (1913–1999) and Richard Erdoes (1912–2008) on the opera cartoon *Carmen* (1935). Around 1937, she relocated to Berlin for 11 years, initially working as a graphic artist. Presumably, she worked on Johann Weichberger's *Fritz und Fratz* (Fritz and Fratz) series before taking on the role of the main inbetweener for the *Peterle* project in April 1941. Weichberger was drafted into the Wehrmacht because he refused to create propaganda animated films, which resulted in negotiations with Weigel at the end of 1941.[10] Weigel officially took over his duties in 1942. Under her production management, the four-part animated film series *Peterle's Abenteuer* (Peterle's Adventures, 1941–1942) was brought to life.

When the series was being produced, Johann Weichberger was allowed to continue working on it in his spare time. Despite playing a secondary role, he was still credited first, as was customary. After the war, Johannes Eckardt (1887–1966), the managing director of *Degeto-Kulturfilm* and also from Austria, acknowledged Susi Weigel as the main force behind the series:

"I am pleased to confirm that from 1940 to 1942, you created animated films for the substandard film series of Degeto, a subsidiary of Tobis-Filmkunst GmbH. Notably, you brought to life the successful series 'Peterles Abenteuer' (Peterle's Adventures)" (Johannes Eckardt, as cited in Blumesberger 2008: 8).

The series – featuring *Die beiden Ausreisser* (The Two Runaways), *Peterle im Zirkus* (Peterle in the Circus), *Der kleine Jäger* (The Little Hunter), and *Ein guter Fang* (A Good Catch) – shares a familiar plot with *Fritz und Fratz* (Fritz and Fratz). The storyline revolves around a boy who avoids doing homework, runs away from home with his dog, and sneaks into a circus. Once there, he gets discovered and chased by the director before eventually making it back home. The last two parts of the series show Peterle chasing a wild boar, which recalls Fritz and Fratz's tiger hunt.

Under the leadership of Austrian Johannes Eckardt, Dutch cartoonist Marten Toonder (1912–2005) was brought on board to create an animated series for *Degeto-Schmalfilm-Schrank*. Considered the "European Walt Disney" (Bendazzi (ed.) 2016a: 148), Toonder found a mentor in Austrian Friedrich Oskar 'Fritz' Gottesmann (1899–1945), who played a pivotal role in shaping his career. Born into a Jewish family, Gottesmann left Austria for Amsterdam (the Netherlands) in April 1938 following Austria's annexation. In Amsterdam, he focused on syndicating comics domestically and internationally with his publishing house, *Diana Edition International Press Service*. Toonder's early career as a comic book artist and illustrator saw modest success from 1933 until he finally made a significant breakthrough at *Diana Editions*, following his employment by Gottesmann in the summer of 1939. At *Diana Editions*, Toonder created his most famous comic character, the anthropomorphic tomcat Tom Poes (known as Tom Puss in German). Initially, this character was published only in foreign markets. During World War II, when the newspaper *De Telegraaf* faced a shortage of US Mickey Mouse comic strips, Toonder seized the opportunity to introduce his white cat in the Netherlands in March 1941. During the German occupation of the Netherlands (1940–1945), Gottesmann took steps to prevent the *Nationaal-Socialistische Beweging* (NSB, National Socialist Movement in the Netherlands) from imposing an administrator during the 'Aryanization' period. He first made Toonder his business partner in late July 1940 and then completely transferred the publishing house to him in September 1941.[11] This event is widely recognized as the establishment of Marten Toonder's animation film studio, as he had expressed his desire to create his own animated films in an interview with *De Telegraaf* in October 1941. *Polygoon*, a production company specializing in newsreels, generously supplied Toonder with production material and Mickey Mouse films from its archives for study purposes. Subsequently, several test films and commercials were created, but the production of commercial-free films was reserved for *Nederland Film*, controlled by the NSB, for which Toonder did not want to work. Toonder connected with Eduard Pelster (1892–1947) through Gottesmann. Pelster managed a cultural film distribution company and oversaw *Degeto*'s distribution in the Netherlands.

This connection led to a meeting between Marten Toonder and Johannes Eckardt in Germany, where they signed a contract on January 28, 1943, to produce a series titled *Tom Puss und das Geheimnis der Grotte* (Tom Poes and the Secret of the Grotto).[12] With Eckardt, who wasn't a committed National Socialist, Toonder "couldn't have asked for a better patron" (Hazeu 2012: 97). The production target for September 1943 was to create four parts totaling 320m. Each meter was priced at 200 guilders, equivalent to about €1,220 today. The total cost of the project was 64,000 guilders, approximately €400,000 in today's currency, with a quarter paid in advance. *Degeto* also supplied the costly cels required for the project (Figure 7.4).

It is unclear today whether all four planned series episodes were created. Only two parts, *Der Zauberer* (The Wizard) and *Der Raub im Schloss* (The Robbery in the Castle), have been preserved. Much like the *Fritz und Fratz* (Fritz and Fratz) films produced in Denmark, Marten Toonder, a staunch anti-fascist, seized the opportunity to make subversive animated films.[13] The series is based on his comic strip *Tom Poes ontdekt het geheim der blauwe aarde* (Tom Poes Discovers the Secret of the Blue Earth), which was serialized in *De Telegraaf* starting on March 16, 1941. It narrates the tale of Tom Poes, who encounters the magical dwarf Pikkin in a cave. Using a magical wand, the dwarf summons water vapor to create an army of evil giants. These menacing giants, wearing boots, march in unison toward a castle to plunder its treasures for their master. Postcards have been circulated in Germany depicting the rest of the story. In the illustration, Tom Poes stealthily enters the wizard's cave under cover of night and removes the sleeping giants' boots, causing them to vanish

FIGURE 7.4 Marten Toonder in his studio next to cels of Tom Poes, 1943. (Courtesy of Toonder Compagnie BV, Amsterdam (Willem Feltkamp).)

in a puff of smoke. Subsequently, he restrains the wizard and summons a group of friendly giants with the assistance of traditional Dutch 'Klompen' (wooden shoes), who help him carry back the stolen goods. Toonder pointed out that the resemblance between the evil giants and the German Wehrmacht soldiers in combat boots is not coincidental. The inspiration for the comic strip and subsequent film series stemmed from a story recounted by his father. Upon his return from a visit to Germany just after the Nazis ascended to power in 1933, Toonder's father commented that if you were to plant a boot in Germany, a soldier would sprout from it.[14] In the film adaptation of the comic, Toonder incorporated an idea proposed by his collaborator Henk Kabos (1912–1984). As a reference to the Austrian Arthur Seyß-Inquart (1892–1946), the Reich commissioner for the German-occupied Netherlands, and to the German Reich Minister of Propaganda Joseph Goebbels (1897–1945), Toonder and his team designed the dwarf to limp. It's quite ironic that films promoting anti-fascism were created for the German market with German funding, all thanks to the assistance of Austrian Johannes Eckardt.

The partnership between Susi Weigel and Johann Weichberger, however, was short lived. After the war, Weichberger established *Herold Zeichenfilm GmbH* in late 1948, where Weigel briefly worked. Due to a lack of orders, the studio was renamed *Herold Film GmbH* in 1952 to produce "films of all kinds" (entry in the commercial register; *Zentralblatt Handelsregister*, 51 (20), May 14, 1952: 241). That same year, Susi Weigel relocated to Bludenz (Vorarlberg, western Austria) and pursued a career as a children's book illustrator.[15] Nonetheless, this short period of collaboration holds historical significance: "Susi Weigel is thus the first known Austrian woman in the field of animation who not only worked as an employee, such as in animation or character and background design, but also created animated films as an author" (Renoldner 2010: 95). Weichberger, on the other hand, was truly a visionary ahead of his time. In the spring of 1944, the Nazi film leadership envisioned a *Europäischer Zeichenfilm Ring* (Animation Film Circle Throughout Europe), uniting the major studios in the territories occupied by the German Reich.[16] Meanwhile, the multinational animation series *Fritz und Fratz* (Fritz and Fratz) was brought to life under the guidance of Austrians Johann Weichberger and Johannes Eckardt, spanning across Germany, Denmark, and Czechoslovakia.

HOW *DEUTSCHE ZEICHENFILM* BECAME AUSTRIAN

In the summer of 1941, *Deutsche Zeichenfilm GmbH* (DZF) was established in Berlin to rival the globally influential *Disney* corporation with a German competitor. Despite receiving substantial state support, the studio, a pet project of German propaganda minister Joseph Goebbels, only completed one film. *Armer Hansi* (Poor Hansi, 1943) depicts the story of a canary who flees his golden cage but struggles to adapt to freedom and ultimately returns remorseful. Another project, *Schnuff, der Nieser* (Schnuff the Sneezer, 1944/1945), was almost completed during the war and was finished as an 'Überläufer' (defector)[17] after the war. This film narrates the story of a puppy whose sneeze propels him out of his living room, requiring rescue by his mother. Following the war, it was renamed *Purzelbaum ins Leben* (Somersault into Life, 1946).[18]

The multinational *DZF* team consisted of Germans, Dutch, French, Hungarians, exiled Russians, and Austrians. Viennese Erhard Amadeus-Dier (1893–1969) and Tyrolean Karl Julino (1904–1989) collaborated on the creation of *Armer Hansi* (Poor Hansi, 1943). Amadeus-Dier pursued studies in architecture at the *Staatsgewerbeschule Wien* (State Trade School Vienna) for 2 years and furthered his education at the Academy of Fine Arts from 1910 to 1913. Following this, he focused on music for four semesters. By 1921, he had become a member of the *Künstlerhaus Wien* (Art House Vienna). He relocated to Germany in 1938 and worked as the chief designer at the Rosenthal porcelain factory (Berlin and Selb) from 1939 to 1942. Subsequently, he joined *DZF* as a picture dramaturge and contributed as a background artist on *Armer Hansi* (Poor Hansi, 1943). When the production team moved to Vienna, he was brought back to Austria, where he designed the Austrian Schilling banknotes from 1949 to 1954. However, Amadeus-Dier's passion for film persisted. In the early 1960s, he dedicated years to creating a color marionette feature film based on the fairy tale *Vom Fischer und seiner Frau* (The Fisherman and His Wife) by the Brothers Grimm.

Karl Julino, a native of Innsbruck (Tyrol), apparently also played a role in the creation of *Armer Hansi* (Poor Hansi, 1943). Just before his passing, his son Florian Julino (1939–2023) recalled that his father had contributed to motion studies of a canary.[19] Following the disbandment of the *DZF*, Karl Julino worked on military training films. Post war, he held a senior position at a Munich advertising agency, where he produced animated films. Additionally, he worked as a set designer on the Austrian feature film *Der Teufel führt Regie* (The Devil Directs, 1951). Between scenes, Julino enjoyed sketching caricatures of the lead actor Paul Hörbiger (1894–1981). Florian Julino inherited Karl Julino's artistic talent but chose a different career path. Instead of following in his father's footsteps in animation, Florian became a renowned comic artist. He is particularly celebrated for his contributions to the iconic German comic series *Fix und Foxi* (Fix and Foxi), where he introduced the character Diabolino in 1964.

In November 1943, the British *Royal Air Force* (RAF) initiated the 'Battle of Berlin.' While Berlin experienced extensive area bombing, Vienna was primarily targeted by the *United States Army Air Forces* (USAAF). The US air war strategy focused on specific military targets rather than 'terror bombing.' Due to the escalating bombing raids in Berlin, the *DZF* was divided into five teams in November 1943. Vienna and Dachau, near Munich, became alternate locations. The groups led by Heinz Wolfgang Tischmeyer (1913–?) and Johann Antonius 'Jan' Coolen (1909–?) relocated to Vienna and settled in the neo-baroque Palais Lanckoroński.[20]

In Vienna, the *DZF* followed a similar approach to that in Berlin by recruiting almost anyone capable of wielding a pen. They specifically enlisted graduates of the *Graphische Lehr- und Versuchsanstalt* (Graphic Arts School), including individuals such as Charlotte König (née Rieder, 1927–2017)[21] and Kurt Traum (1923–?),[22] who co-founded *Traum & Maier*, a major Austrian animation studio in the post-war era. Despite receiving raw film, colors, and cellophane due to its special status, the production faced challenging conditions. The Palais was damaged by aerial bombing in 1944 due to its proximity to 'Südbahnhof' (Southern Station), and artists were frequently called up for war service.[23] The two Viennese teams failed to bring any of their projects to fruition, but they continued to cherish the vision of establishing a German animated film production. As late as 1944, the *DZF* still trained draftspersons in Vienna.[24]

The project centered on the puppy Schnuff had raised high expectations in Berlin. Originally envisioned as a feature film, it became apparent that such an extensive endeavor was no longer feasible in 1943. Instead, the project was reimagined as a series. Gerhard Fieber (1916–2013) and his team started working on the first part, *Schnuff, der Nieser* (Schnuff the Sneezer, 1944/1945), near the concentration camp in Dachau in 1944. By this time, several sequel scripts already existed and are now held in the estate of Austrian Erhard Amadeus-Dier. Accompanying an anonymous scene plan labeled *Schnuffs Drachenkampf* (Schnuff's Dragon Fight),[25] dated December 30, 1943, is a script penned by screenwriter Christian Bock (1906–1975) for another tale involving the puppy, entitled *Frühlingsanfang* (Arrival of Spring). Amadeus-Dier's shorter script was intended to streamline the story, focusing on the animals' struggle, led by a bear, against winter, without featuring the character Schnuff. Despite this, some of the team involved in the project, now titled *Frühlingslied* (Spring Song), still believed it to be a feature film. Teje Etchemendy (née Sablatnig, 1921–2013), who worked as a draftswoman at *DZF*, remained convinced until her passing that Germany's first hand-drawn feature film was being developed in Vienna.[26]

In a television interview, Rolf Giesen (b. 1953) discussed the German animated film *Der Schneemann* (The Snowman, 1943/1944). In the film, a snowman seeks to experience a singular summer, which turns out to be his final summer, by hiding in an icebox during winter. Giesen remarked: "This is downfall… It is tied to death. It's not just a melancholic film, but one that unmistakably leads to destruction. It portrays a situation that many Germans, of course, experienced during the bombing war at the time" (Rolf Giesen in 'Krieg der Zeichner' 2015, 00:25:55). Similarly, this can be linked to *Frühlingslied* (Spring Song): the animals endure the cold and hardship of winter, with only the raven finding happiness. He kisses the snowman's cheek and begins to sing to him. However, his song is interrupted by the bear's loud snoring as he hibernates in a hollow. Woken up by the raven's agitation, the bear starts to stretch and yawn, causing the snow around him to melt. The animals cheer as the bear breathes away more and more snow, revealing flowers and prompting the sun to emerge in response to the waltzlike spring song. Finally, to the raven's delight, the snowman threatens the animals with his broom. But things take a turn when he loses his balance and tumbles with a splutter into the hollow. As a result, the bear falls back asleep, leaving the animals unable to combat the snow without his assistance. Taunted by the raven, the animals begin to weep, and soon the sky joins in with its tears. Thanks to the rain, the snow melts away, and the animals sing their spring song again, while the raven flies away sulkily. This film can easily be seen as a metaphor for the German people, the Wehrmacht's defeat at Stalingrad, and the imperative for unified resistance against the regime – especially considering Erhard Amadeus-Dier's involvement in the Austrian resistance movement.

In June 1944, Joseph Goebbels, the Reich Minister of Propaganda, received a hopeful report about the production progress of the *DZF*: "Atelier Tischmeyer is preparing a film about inn signs coming to life (e.g., 'White Stag,' 'To the Sun,' 'To the Red Ox,' etc.). Completion is expected by the end of the year. Atelier Coolen is preparing a film centered on the charming character of a little bear. Completion is expected early next year" (Karl Neumann, as cited in Forster et al. n.d., under '4. August 1944. Stilllegung der Deutsche Zeichenfilm GmbH'). Charlotte König, who worked at the *DZF* in Vienna from 1944 as an inbetweener, recounted in a contemporary witness report from 2000 the creation of a film she referred to as *Der Kanarienvogel* (The Canary), which was reportedly shown at the Non-Stop Cinema on Mariahilferstraße. The completion of a film without being reported to Berlin appears improbable. It is likely that the 'redrawing' of the film *Armer Hansi* (Poor Hansi), already finished by the *DZF* in 1943, was part of the drawing training. Film director René Perraudin (b. 1947), whose parents Wilfrid (1912–2006) and Hildegard Perraudin (née Wiehl, 1912–1991)[27] were relocated from *Tobis Filmkunst* to *DZF* in Vienna in 1944, remembered his parents' descriptions of this period: "My mother became the head of the color department, while my father oversaw designing and executing the decorations. To my knowledge, the plan was not for a purely animated film but rather a blend of drawn and cutout animation combined with real objects, which would account for the inclusion of decorations (likely serving as background images). However, the project never advanced beyond the planning and preparation stages" (René Perraudin, email to the author, dated July 22, 2013).

The dream ended in September 1944 when *DZF* production was halted, prompting Heinz Tischmeyer's return to Berlin.[28] The *DZF* employees were absorbed by *Luftfahrtforschung Wien* (Aeronautics Research Vienna):[29] "Everyone was expected to transition to technical drawing and convert the presented sketches and tables into detailed final drawings" (Perraudin n.d.: para. 7). Starting in October, they began working on the Lippisch P.13a, one of the much-anticipated 'wonder weapons' intended to shift the course of the war, for Alexander Martin Lippisch's (1894–1976) design office: "This delta-wing aircraft, powered by rocket propulsion, was intended to be the first supersonic plane. However, the project did not advance beyond the development phase (it was later revisited in the USA, still under the leadership of Dr. Lippisch)" (Perraudin n.d.: para. 7). The inbetweener Charlotte König recalled:

"We had to use a crank-operated machine to calculate curves for warplanes based on lists and tables provided for the technicians. In a spacious hall with two open staircases, a ten-meter-long drawing table was set up, where we meticulously calculated and created the scale model of a spaceplane… We worked with triangular reduction rulers and a calculating machine. […] Everything was classified. Our chief draftsman produced his technical sketches in a separate room. One day, I accidentally glimpsed the drawn object on an easel, and it reminded me of disaster images from the relevant magazines…" (Charlotte König, as cited in La Speranza 2003: 116–117).

Following the Red Army's advance, the 'Battle of Vienna' in April 1945 resulted in a hush-hush operation to evacuate personnel and equipment to the airfield. They flew to Prien am Chiemsee in Bavaria, Germany, where development work was underway on the prototype of the delta flying wing, designated DM-1. The evacuation proved fortunate for the Americans, who later took control of the area, as Alexander Lippisch – later brought to the USA – is considered one of the early developers of rocket aircraft.

A pile of rubble was all that remained. After the war, Charlotte König visited the Palais Lanckoroński, where the shelves holding the cels were still abandoned in the cellar, despite the damage caused by aerial bombing. Allegedly, looters started a fire shortly afterward. Until its demolition in 1960, the Palais was known as an 'enchanted castle.' There are no surviving remnants of the Viennese production, rendering it almost invisible.

NOTES

1 For instance, the *Bieler Tagblatt* (October 12, 1938: [2]) covered the screening of the German-dubbed version in Switzerland.
2 Vital records received from Irene Nawrocka (email to the author, dated October 30, 2017) from the *Österreichische Akademie der Wissenschaften* (ÖAW, Austrian Academy of Sciences) and from Brigitte Hofer-Siller (email to the author, dated November 14, 2017) from the Market Town Bad Deutsch-Altenburg.
3 Overall rating on the leaving certificate of Richard Dillenz (cf. *Abgangszeugnis Richard Dillenz* 1919: [3]; Art Collection and Archive, University of Applied Arts Vienna; thanks to Nathalie Feitsch).
4 The two collaborated on the 1940 feature film *Das himmelblaue Abendkleid* (The Sky-Blue Evening Dress). Josef Pfister was the production manager for this project, and Richard Dillenz designed the titular dress.
5 The high expenses were likely a result of employing the Kinox process. This method evolved from the American rotoscoping technique, where actors' performances were filmed and projected onto a frosted-glass screen for tracing. Kinox projectors utilized a cold light source, enabling the extended projection of a static image without the risk of the film igniting.
6 Email from Michaela Mertová (NFA) to the author, dated October 12, 2023.
7 Based on Peter A. Schauer (1930–2018), Johann Weichberger reportedly participated in the *Filmbund*, an Austrian filmmakers' interest group, in 1932 (cf. Schauer 1999: 23). Schauer claims that Weichberger met Ladislaus Tuszyński (1876–1943) at the *Filmbund*, who then introduced him to Julius Pinschewer (cf. Schauer 1999: 27–29). Pinschewer had operated his own distribution office in Vienna since the mid-1920s (cf. Amsler 1997: 23) and reportedly considered relocating to Austria after Adolf Hitler's rise to power (cf. Schauer 1999: 28).
8 The details about Johann Weichberger's employer are conflicting. According to Peter A. Schauer, he was employed by Robert Reich (1882–1944), whom he reportedly met at the *Filmbund* (cf. Schauer 1999: 39). On the other hand, Thomas Renoldner (b. 1960) indicates that it was Robert Müller (1877–1942) (cf. Renoldner 2010: 92).
9 According to his daughter Marianne Weichberger (b. 1942), these were probably animated flight simulations (telephone conversation with the author on March 24, 2024).
10 According to Peter A. Schauer, Johann Weichberger was a candidate for the director position of a proposed Dutch division of *Deutsche Zeichenfilm GmbH*. However, the Ministry of Propaganda allegedly rejected this proposal (cf. Schauer 1999: 49). One potential reason for this decision could have been Weichberger's refusal to produce animated propaganda films.
11 Fritz Gottesmann and Marten Toonder had agreed to transfer the publishing house back after the war. However, this plan did not come to fruition. In 1942, Gottesmann had to go into hiding and was eventually discovered on August 14, 1944. On August 17, he was transported to the transit camp Westerbork. From there, like Anne Frank (1929–1945) and her family, he was sent to Auschwitz (Poland) on September 3 as part of the last transport. In January 1945, he was listed as a "stateless Jewish prisoner" in the Mauthausen concentration camp (Austria), where he passed away on February 25.

12 Shortly after, Marten Toonder and his temporary collaborator Joop Geesink (1913–1984) took over the project *Das musikalische Auto* (The Musical Car, 1943/1944) for *Ufa*. However, Geesink later withdrew from the project and created animated puppet films instead.
13 Marten Toonder utilized his drawing skills to aid the resistance movement during the German occupation of the Netherlands (1940–1945). He played a crucial role in forging various papers. In recognition of his efforts, he was honored with the *Verzetsherdenkingskruis* (Resistance Memorial Cross) in 1982.
14 In his biography *Marten Toonder* (2012), Wim Hazeu (b. 1940) emphasizes that the story was primarily inspired by the comic *Thijs IJs bestrijdt de reuzen van Pakkijs* (Thijs IJs Fights the Giants of Pakkijs), which was authored by Marten Toonder's brother Jan Gerhard Toonder (1914–1992) and illustrated by Marten Toonder in 1934.
15 Susi Weigel, in addition to other accomplishments, provided illustrations for the book *Das kleine Ich-bin-ich* (Little I-Am-Me), which was published in 1972 and co-written with Mira Lobe (née Hilde Mirjam Rosenthal, 1913–1995). Cf. the post-war chapter.
16 Cf. Giesen and Storm 2012: 126–135.
17 The term 'Überläufer' (defector) in German refers to a movie made during the time of the Third Reich that was completed or shown for the first time after the war had ended.
18 For more details about the history of *Deutsche Zeichenfilm GmbH,* cf. Giesen and Storm 2012: 74–109.
19 Telephone conversation with the author on June 22, 2023.
20 The available literature presents conflicting information about the two teams: some sources claim that Heinz Tischmeyer arrived in Vienna with 12 employees, whereas Jan Coolen arrived with 10 (cf. Agde 1998: 41). However, alternative accounts suggest that Tischmeyer came to Vienna via Dachau with 10 employees, while Coolen remained in Dachau with nine (cf. Giesen and Storm 2012: 104). According to the historical registration records of the *Wiener Stadt- und Landesarchiv* (Municipal and Provincial Archives of Vienna), Coolen was listed at Jacquingasse 18 (the address of Palais Lanckoroński) from January 7 to September 13, 1944, while Tischmeyer was registered at Hummelgasse 2 from July 15 to September 1, 1944 (email information to the author, dated March 22, 2011).
21 Charlotte Rieder, later known as König, pursued studies in commercial art from 1941 to 1944 at the *Höhere Graphische Bundes-Lehr- und Versuchsanstalt* (Federal Training and Research Institute for Graphic Arts and Media) in Vienna, as mentioned in the student directories (thanks to Klaus Walder). Silvia Lang communicated the year of her passing (email to the author, dated July 28, 2017).
22 Kurt Traum pursued studies in commercial art from 1939 to 1942 at the *Höhere Graphische Bundes-Lehr- und Versuchsanstalt* (Federal Training and Research Institute for Graphic Arts and Media) in Vienna, as confirmed by student directories (thanks to Klaus Walder).
23 The details regarding Heinz Tischmeyer's draft status are conflicting. Some sources suggest that he was indeed drafted (cf. Agde 1998: 41), while others claim: "Poor health prevented him from being drafted" (Giesen and Storm 2012: 170).
24 The memoirs of Charlotte König and an entry in a finding aid of the *Österreichisches Staatsarchiv* (Austrian State Archives) indicate this. An email from the archives to the author, dated April 28, 2011, stated that the related files were likely destroyed as early as the 1960s.
25 A cel from this project has survived (cf. Giesen 2020: 93).

26 This information was provided in an email from her daughter, Laraine Bennett (b. 1954), to the author, dated July 31, 2013. After the war, Teje Etchemendy worked at the radio station *Rot-Weiß-Rot* (RWR, Red-White-Red), which was under the supervision of the American occupation authorities. Later, she served as a secretary for the American military, where she met her future husband. After immigrating to the USA, she pursued a career as an illustrator and author.

27 René Perraudin provided the life data in an email to the author, dated October 21, 2023.

28 Jan Coolen, however, stayed in Vienna according to the historical registration records and only updated his address in September 1944. It is believed that he returned to the Netherlands after the war (cf. Agde 1998: 41).

29 According to the records in the workbook of inbetweener Herta Cmyral (1923–?), she was employed at the *DZF* until August 31, 1944, and subsequently joined *Luftfahrtforschung Wien* (Aeronautics Research Vienna) on September 4 (*Arbeitsbuch Herta Cmyral*, 1940–1945, currently held by private collector Matthias Markl).

8 Animating the Boom
How Economic Growth Rebuilt the Industry

Austrian film faced a reset immediately after the end of World War II (1939–1945), leading to the decade between 1945 and 1955 being known as 'Stunde Null' (Zero Hour). The destruction of infrastructure and material shortages were significant challenges, but there was also a lack of financial support due to the absence of state backing. After the *'Anschluss' Österreichs* (annexation of Austria) into the German Reich in 1938, the state had exerted excessive influence over the industry. Following the proclamation of the Second Republic in 1945, film production was initially left to fend for itself. Consequently, films produced by the Allied occupiers became the dominant feature in cinemas during this period.

Under the presence of US-American military forces, Austrian cinemas welcomed the return of long-awaited *Disney* films. Additionally, in 1948, US Secretary of State George C. Marshall (1880–1959) initiated the *European Recovery Program* (ERP), more commonly known as the Marshall Plan. By 1953, Austria had received $962 million, primarily in goods deliveries, equivalent to about $9.5 billion in today's economy (cf. U.S. Mission Austria (ed.) 2022, under 'The Marshall Plan in numbers'): "Austria receives the highest per capita support from the Marshall Plan of any European country, serving as a frontline state in the USA's battle against communism" ('Österreich in Farbe: Die Besatzungszeit' 2015, 00:19:08). This financial aid spurred what became known as the 'red-white-red economic miracle,' resulting in Austria's gross domestic product (GDP) surpassing its 1937 levels (the last year before Austria's annexation into the German Reich) by 1949. That same year also saw the implementation of the 'Kulturgroschen' (cultural penny), a tax on every cinema ticket to support the cultural sector. This initiative also benefited animated filmmakers, although many had already transitioned to commercial film production.

WEST MEETS EAST: CURTAIN UP FOR ANIMATION

After World War II, Austria was divided into four occupation zones, each controlled by one of the Allies: the USA, USSR, France, and Great Britain. Like Berlin, Vienna, the capital, became a divided city until the signing of the State Treaty in 1955. The confrontation between Western and Eastern powers in the four-sector city extended to the cinema. For example, *Disney*'s *Snow White and the Seven Dwarfs* (1937) premiered in Austria years before it did in Germany,[1] while animated films from the opposite side of the Iron Curtain were shown in the Soviet-occupied districts of Vienna.[2] This collision of Eastern and Western animated films reflected the different political and artistic currents of the time.

 DOI: 10.1201/9781003415442-10

Following the war, Austria saw the revival of 'non-stop cinemas' that featured continuous movie programs from morning until night, including newsreels and entertainment films. Animated films gained popularity among children and young people, with American animated films being screened just 3 months after the Allies liberated Vienna in April 1945. The 'non-stop cinemas' provided a daily escape from the war-torn world and a popular refuge during periods of limited heating fuel, allowing people to stay without limitations after paying a small admission fee.[3] However, animated films from the United States were not the only ones brought to Austria. In late September 1945, during French cultural events in the French sector of Vienna, several movies were showcased, including Paul Grimault's (1905–1994) animated film *L'Épouvantail* (The Scarecrow, 1943). Furthermore, the British animated film *Der Schuhmacher und der Hutmacher* (The Shoemaker and the Hatter, 1950) made its way to Austria in the German-dubbed version through the *Österreichisches Produktivitäts-Zentrum* (ÖPZ, Austrian Productivity Center).[4] This Marshall Plan film, produced by the renowned British animation studio *Halas & Batchelor*, aimed to provide propaganda support for the USA's economic reconstruction program initiated for Europe.[5]

In November 1946, the *Gesellschaft der Filmfreunde Österreichs* (Society for Friends of Film in Austria) organized an event called *Trickfilm gestern und heute oder: Vom Kater Felix bis zur Micky-Maus* (Animated Film Yesterday and Today or From Felix the Cat to Mickey Mouse) in Vienna. It was a huge success, with tickets being sold out multiple times, showcasing the strong interest in animated films during that time. The event featured a lecture by film collector Hermann Bieber,[6] who presented film examples and discussed the history of American animated films. He also highlighted its ties to Austrian animated film through figures like Ladislaus Tuszyński (1876–1943) and Peter Eng (1892–1939): "In this context, it is undoubtedly interesting that Walt Disney also tried, albeit unsuccessfully, to engage the Viennese production of the time with his ideas" (Mein Film, 16 (51–52), 1946: [14]).

Almost a decade after it was originally supposed to debut in Austrian cinemas, the US-American occupiers finally brought the highly anticipated *Disney* animated feature *Snow White and the Seven Dwarfs* (1937) to Austria.[7] The first documented public screening in Austria took an unexpected turn: on December 22, 1946, the film was screened for the first time in Vienna as part of Christmas festivities arranged by the US-American armed forces. The screening nearly failed because a film reel went missing during transport from Salzburg to Linz (Upper Austria). It wasn't until January 1947 that a worker, while fishing, discovered the lost reel in the Traun, a tributary of the Danube.

The presentation of their animated films and the attempt to convey their culture and values were not exclusive to the Western powers. In Vienna's Soviet sector, the *Tabor-Kino* (formerly *Zentralkino*) screened the Soviet animated film *Was werde ich sein, wenn ich groß bin?* (What Will I Be When I Grow Up?) in July 1950: "This educational cultural film demonstrates [...] that in a nation of triumphant socialism, all career paths are accessible to young people, aligned with their interests and abilities" (Österreichische Zeitung, July 30, 1950: 7). A short while later, following the screening of a Soviet animated film in the Soviet sector of the also divided city of Linz, the media remarked: "The entire production is charmingly executed, not in the exaggerated grotesque style typical of American animated films, but with delicate, fairy-tale-like finesse. The film's unobtrusive moral educates more effectively than a heavy cudgel" (Neue Zeit, December 19, 1950: 3).

In late 1950, the *Tabor-Kino* in Vienna hosted a *Tschechoslowakische Filmwoche* (Czechoslovak Film Week),[8] showcasing two propaganda animated films. *Brigade* told "the experiences of voluntary helpers who, through diligence and improved working methods, work their way into a land of milk and honey, return home heavily laden with good things, and thus recruit new helpers" (Österreichische Volksstimme No. 261, November 10, 1950: 6). With the film *Atom am Scheideweg* (Atom at a Crossroads, 1947), "it is exemplarily demonstrated that animated films, through popular and progressive treatment of a problem that concerns all of humanity today, can fight for world peace" (Österreichische Volksstimme No. 261, November 10, 1950: 6). Despite its screening in Vienna, the film faced a ban on importation into West Germany (cf. Buchloh 2002: 225).

GOVERNING THE FRAMES: STATE-COMMISSIONED ANIMATION

Apart from the occupying forces, the Austrian state also utilized animated film to communicate its value system. Although Dr. Alto Arche (1854–1940) created what may have been the world's first educational films in Austria in 1907 with government backing,[9] and films had been used in education since the early 1920s, it wasn't until after World War II that Austria developed an educational film system comparable to Germany's. In 1945, the *Staatliche Hauptstelle für Lichtbild und Bildungsfilm* (SHB, Federal Main Office for Slides and Educational Films) was established in Vienna and incorporated animated films from the outset. During the summer of 1946, the SHB organized a film program featuring international cultural films, which included the East Asian animated film *Die Rache des Drachen* (The Revenge of the Dragon). Subsequently, the SHB began producing its own animated films, such as *Zementproduktion* (Cement Production, circa 1955). Notably, the puppet animation film *Schneeweißchen und Rosenrot* (Snow-White and Rose-Red, 1949), created by painter Karl Langer (1902–died after 1952), even received a *Menzione* (honorary diploma) at the Venice Biennale (Italy) in 1950. Dr. Adolf Hübl (1895–1966), director of the SHB, emphasized the suitability of puppet-animated films for educational purposes:

"People appear kitschy in fairy tale films; they are too realistic to effectively convey the magical elements. If a dwarf is devoured in a fairy tale, it would be repulsive if portrayed by humans. Using puppets emphasizes the playful, fantastical, and surreal aspects of the story – the imaginative play that is inherent to fairy tales. The children, who can understand the plot of the fairy tale from the images alone, should remain aware that they are watching puppets" (Adolf Hübl, as cited in Filmkunst, (5), 1950: 256).

Despite its modest size, SHB's film production remained consistent. For instance, in 1966, it produced ten films, such as the puppet animation film *Rotkäppchen* (Little Red Riding Hood) and the documentary *Zwei auf der Terrasse* (Two on the Terrace), which depicted the production process of a puppet animation film.

PIONEERS UNITE: FROM SOLITARY CREATORS...

After the Second World War, Austrian film faced a significant turning point: "What was initially too much state influence became too little, as the state no longer cared about production at all. It was, so to speak, a return to the early days when individual men, whose capital was barely sufficient to produce even a single film, sometimes managed to secure financing in adventurous ways" (Oertel 1955: 21).

The challenges of creating animated films during and after World War II can be demonstrated through the experience of Gustav 'Gustl' Peuker (1913–1988).[10] In 1947, he successfully unveiled an animated puppet film, featuring a ladybug named Siebenpunkt (Sevenpointer), to the press:

"When I was about to receive a scholarship for the Film Academy, the war broke out. Just when I finally had legitimate hope of connecting with Wien-Film, the end of the war approached, leading to the cessation of Austrian film production. But I didn't give up. [...] In my spare time [...] I dedicated all those years to tackling the challenges of animated film. My dream would be to create a color puppet animation series featuring Siebenpunkt" (Gustav Peuker, as cited in Füringk 1947: [6]).

Gustav Peuker had already written multiple scripts for the proposed series, but he had to halt his work due to a shortage of material.[11] Although he remained active in film and television productions until 1980, there are no records of any other animated films he was involved in.

Another puppet animation film project faced misfortune. In July 1947, media coverage reported on the filming of the Franz Schubert (1797–1828) feature *Seine einzige Liebe* (His Only Love, 1947) at the short-lived *Royal-Film* studio. Simultaneously, in the studio's basement, Egon Walter was working on the puppet animation film *Fahrt ins Märchenland* (Trip to Fairyland): "in the middle of a green meadow stands a charming chimney sweep and a very agile puppet. A turtle approaches him, and a curious cricket peeks into the flower world" (Österreichische Zeitung, July 25, 1947: 5). It is unclear whether this project, initially intended to support the Schubert movie, was ever completed, as the press focused on criticizing the poorly made low-budget feature. Nevertheless, while the puppet film was in production, the press expressed optimism about the project: "The animation production is noteworthy; it could compete with rigid cartoon films, as it involves puppets or animals whose movements are painstakingly captured on film and then synchronized" (Österreichische Zeitung, July 25, 1947: 5).

During the post-war era, animated film production encountered various challenges, as illustrated by a collaborative project between cartoonists Franz Bresnikar (1908–1996) and Kurt Traum (1923–?), along with inbetweeners Erna Lerner and Gerti Tremmel. The team was completed by newsreel cameraman Walter Maier (b. 1927); public relations specialist Karl Hans Koizar; and technician Franz Harrer, who later joined the group and modified the hand-crank camera into an electric one. Against considerable odds, they successfully created a 12-minute silent animation film called *Archibald auf Gruselstein* (Archibald on Scary Stone) in 1947. Walter Maier later reminisced about this challenging experience:

"This project faced challenges from the start: there was no negative material, no cels, and no colors available through official channels – everything had to be sourced 'through connections' on the black market. Everyone pitched in as much as they could – names and addresses were exchanged, and identities were even changed just to secure the necessary materials. The presence of the occupying forces added many new difficulties. [...] Frequent power fluctuations at that time caused many shots to fail, necessitating repeated takes or switching to night work" (Maier 1993: 26).

An American officer facilitated the sale of the film to the USA, but it did not generate any financial gain. Subsequently, the team disbanded, with Franz Bresnikar parting ways with the duo Kurt Traum and Walter Maier, who went on to establish rival commercial film studios shortly after.

...TO ANIMATION COLLABORATORS

Right after World War II, *Wiener Zeichenfilm GmbH* was established as the first Austrian animation studio in the post-war era.[12] Due to severe material shortages, advertisements were placed in September 1945 seeking paper, cels, paints, and other drawing materials. The studio's name was inspired by *Deutsche Zeichenfilm GmbH*, the legendary German animated film production company associated with Joseph Goebbels (1897–1945), which also had a branch in Vienna toward the end of the war. Similar to the strategy of its namesake, *Wiener Zeichenfilm* produced animated films without dialogue for easier international distribution.[13] Johann Weichberger (1910–1992), who had produced animated films for the German *Degeto Film* during the war, was one of the managing directors until October 1946 before establishing his own studio. It wasn't until April 1947, when Leo Milde was appointed managing director, that *Wiener Zeichenfilm* commenced animated film production. By the summer of 1947, the first film was in production, with four more in preparation, including two intended as preludes to series with recurring characters. Leo Milde assumed the role of artistic director, with Kurt Köllner as the scriptwriter and Tilly Köllner as the composer. Nevertheless, the production turned out to be quite a challenge. With no color film material available in Austria, the short supporting films had to be made in black and white. Additionally, since no animation stand was available, Milde and Köllner took it upon themselves to swiftly build their own. As a result of these challenges, production was delayed. While the completion of the first two films was initially anticipated in 1947, the first part of the series *Wumpi* was finished as late as 1949. The film *Campanula*, a love story between two bellflowers, was almost completed in July 1949. Additionally, the studio accepted commissions from SHB to produce cultural and educational films for school instruction: "A film is currently in production that aims to showcase the scenic beauties of Austria within the framework of an animated story" (Österreichische Volksstimme, July 11, 1947: 3). Around 1951, the distributor *Apollo-Film* released another film titled *Kleine Nachtmusik* (Little Night Music). However, by the spring of 1953, *Wiener Zeichenfilm* encountered financial difficulties and was subsequently dissolved.[14]

Another post-war start-up experienced a similar downfall. Richard Dillenz (1892–1959) was tasked by Germany to set up a competing animation studio to *Disney* in German-occupied Czechoslovakia during the war. Back in Austria, Dillenz founded

Dillenz Zeichenfilm GmbH in September 1946.[15] However, the studio struggled to compete and shifted its focus away from animated films. Eventually, on September 13, 1951, the company was renamed *Dillenz-Film-Produktion.* The new direction led to the production of the two feature films *Frühlingsstimmen* (Voices of Spring, 1951/1952)[16] and *Der Verschwender* (The Spendthrift, 1952/1953). Additionally, the company produced cultural films like *Der alten Kaiser größter Schatz* (The Ancient Emperors' Greatest Treasure, 1951) and *C. L. Hollitzer, ein Künstlerleben* (C. L. Hollitzer, an Artist's Life, 1955).[17] The short-lived film company was dissolved in March 1958.[18]

Johann Weichberger, mentioned earlier, gained recognition as "the only Austrian expert in animated color films" following the war. As a result, *Wien-Film* assigned him "to establish a homegrown animation production."[19] When *Wien-Film*'s productions were increasingly handed over to *Sascha-Film*, which was re-founded at the end of 1946, Johann Weichberger set up an independent animation studio called *Herold Zeichenfilm GmbH.*[20] Alongside his wife Else Weichberger (neé Knoll, 1909–2003)[21] and his longtime companion Susi Weigel (1914–1990), his team of draftswomen included Helene 'Hella' Schiefer (later Soyka, 1924–2005).[22] Handling the camera were Ernst Papp and Eva Papp, who also served as the director of photography. This small 'film manufactory' specialized in animated cartoons and object animation.[23] Among other things, the team produced opening titles for feature films and Austrian post-war newsreels, such as *Weltjournal* (World Magazine) and *Austria Wochenschau* (Austrian Weekly Review).[24] However, the order situation was poor: "If there was an order, the small team worked several days and nights straight to meet the deadline" (Renoldner 2010: 96). Weichberger's advertising cartoon *Österreichs beste Mannschaft* (Austria's Best Team, 1949) was entirely in the spirit of reconstruction. Depicting the effects of the black market on the national economy, it used a soccer match format to showcase the harm caused by illicit cigarettes within the tobacco industry.[25] This subject was turned into an animated film form for a practical reason:

"Through its playful and symbolic representation, the animated film allows for open criticism of the 'foreign,' not 'Austrian' cigarettes brought into the country by the Allies. If real actors had been used, the physical attacks, combined with the moderator's combative rhetoric (depicting Austria fighting against notorious foreign smuggling gangs), would have been perceived as overly aggressive" (Moser 2020: 116).

In the early 1950s, Johann Weichberger faced challenges in attracting enough orders for animated films to sustain his studio economically. As a result, in April 1952, he rebranded his studio as *Herold Film GmbH* and began producing "films of all kinds" (*Zentralblatt Handelsregister*, 51 (20), May 14, 1952: 241), primarily for advertising purposes (Figure 8.1).[26] During the same year, Susi Weigel departed from the studio and, following her marriage in the autumn of 1952, relocated with her husband to the westernmost Austrian state of Vorarlberg. There, she contributed illustrations to timeless Austrian children's book classics by Mira Lobe (1913–1995).[27] Her iconic children's book illustrations, notably for *Das kleine Ich-bin-ich* (Little I-Am-Me, 1972), co-published with Mira Lobe, left a mark on the childhood of entire generations.[28]

FIGURE 8.1 Promotional brochure from *Herold Film GmbH* featuring stills from various films, including some animated works, alongside title cards highlighting the studio's diverse productions. (Courtesy of Marianne Weichberger.)

CARTOONS TO CASH: FROM ECONOMIC GLOOM TO ADVERTISING BLOOM

Johann Weichberger's *Herold Film GmbH* was not the only film production company creating animated commercials. In the early 1950s, Austria had around ten advertising film producers, three of which were engaged in animated film production. By the 1960s, the number of film studios in the country with a concession for advertising film production had grown to 90, though only 55 were actively creating advertising films. Notably, Vienna alone housed 40 of these studios, with six equipped for animated film production. While live-action films cost a maximum of 600 schillings per meter (around €400 today, adjusted for inflation), animated films could cost up to 1,100 schillings (around €700 today). Nevertheless, according to a trade journal from 1959, animated advertising films were still considered profitable: "On the other hand, it should be noted that by focusing dramaturgical elements, animated films can effectively achieve the same impact with a shorter runtime compared to live-action films under similar conditions" (Berichte und Informationen, 14 (666), 1959: 12).

Established in 1923, *Mayer's Filmbüro* – known as *Adi Mayer's Filmbüro* from 1938 and *Adi Mayer Film* from 1945 (*AMF* for short) – had already gained recognition as Austria's leading advertising film producer during the 1930s. Production was halted in 1944 due to the war but resumed shortly after its end in September 1945. The ensuing economic growth allowed the advertising film industry to thrive, with *AMF* producing over 70 cinema advertising films between 1946 and 1949. By 1960, the studio had created around 600 advertising films for cinema and television, including many animated films. Martin Bauer (1919–?), a key figure at the studio, was a screenwriter, cameraman, draftsman, and animator. Born in Graz (Styria), he discontinued his studies at the University of Applied Arts in Vienna after Austria's annexation into the German Reich in 1938. "In 1945 he resumed his artistic activities, and after a few years, in Graz, he made his first animated film, *Der böse Troll* (The Evil Troll, 1947), exhorting citizens to be careful with wood to heat their rooms and not to use too much" (Bendazzi (ed.) 2016b: 49). From 1953 onward, Bauer took on the main responsibility for the studio's animated advertising films at *AMF* in Vienna, where he experimented with various animation techniques. Over time, the content and artistic style of his advertising animated films shifted away from *Disney*'s aesthetic toward a style reminiscent of the renowned *United Productions of America* (*UPA*) studio in the US. An example of this is *K(l)eine Zauberei* (No [Small] Magic, 1958), which advertised adhesive furniture films: "Sweepingly painted areas of color, in combination with quickly sketched objects consisting of a few strokes, form the backgrounds. The figure design is extremely simplistic, allowing a much more dynamic handling of the animation" (Renoldner 2010: 104). The first commercials combining live-action and animated film were also created, such as for the shampoo *Gloria* (1959). In *Keramische Fliesen* (Ceramic Tiles, 1959 or 1960), he presented "a combination of abstract elements of varying quality" (Renoldner 2010: 104). Leveraging 'Wienerlieder' (Viennese Songs, humorous Viennese folk songs), his commercials appealed particularly to those who could not afford a TV set in the post-war period: "They flocked to the cinema halls to have fun, and the animated folk song commercials were a part of it" (Bendazzi (ed.) 2016b: 49). In 1961, Bauer departed from *AMF* and embarked on a solo career as a commercial animator.

FBN-Film (Franz Bres-Nikar), founded by former actor Franz Bresnikar, emerged as another film production company focused on advertising in 1947. To accommodate the venture, the former storage rooms of the Austrian branch of *Metro-Goldwyn-Mayer* (*MGM*), located in an attic and damaged by bombings, were refurbished by 1948. Toward the end of the 1980s, an employee of the *Filmarchiv Austria* (Austrian Film Archive) took charge of the furnishings of the disbanded studio and documented the acquisition:

"It was hard to believe that this attic had once been a bombed-out ruin after the war and that nearly everything in it had been conceived or built by Bresnikar himself. Considering the acute shortage of materials and tools, and the fact that goods were only available with ration coupons, founding a film production company in the post-war period seemed almost impossible" (Gloger 1993: 19).

Established during the challenging period following the war, when necessities like food and clothing were still crucial, the studio's series *Fanfaren der Werbung* (Fanfares of Advertising) aimed to provide affordable advertising film production for small businesses. Franz Bresnikar, hailed as the "Austrian Walt Disney" by the media (as cited in Bohmann and Taylor 1972: 90), not only spearheaded the production of advertising films but also oversaw a series of animated films, with Paul Obczovsky serving as the principal illustrator. Obczovsky managed a small group of approximately five artists responsible for in-between frames and colorization.

Bresnikar, a trained actor, enacted certain scenes, which were then sketched and later animated by Obczovsky. "Work was done with equipment that was still quite improvised – a self-adapted and constructed animation camera, a makeshift sound studio, a hand-operated editing table, and a simple yet effective lab facility for film development" (Gloger 1993: 21).

One of the early significant assignments was creating a seven-part animated series for the Austrian Federal Ministry of Trade and Reconstruction, Department of Tourism. A memorandum dated May 7, 1949, mentioned the following: "During the peak of foreign tourism in Austria before 1938, the 'Austrian person' became an exceptional advertising asset. The Austrian way charmed foreign visitors, [...] making them feel more comfortable and welcomed than in any other country" (as cited in Karl 2021: para. 1). After a decade without significant tourism, *FBN* created 3-minute educational cartoons called *TIP-TOP in Österreich* (TIP-TOP in Austria) in collaboration with the Austrian Federal Ministry of Education to retrain Austrians to be good hosts (Figure 8.2). The initial three parts, *Sei höflich* (Be Polite), *Reinlichkeit* (Cleanliness), and *Redlichkeit* (Honesty), were released at the end of June 1951. "Animated films of this kind were considered an absolute rarity in Austria at that time, and the educational series featuring Tip and Top was considered a true novelty in the still-young Second Republic" (Karl 2021: para. 6). In 1952, four additional titles were released, including *Wegweiser im Verkehr mit Fremden* (Signposts in Dealings with Strangers) and *Warum Fremdenverkehr?* (Why Tourism?) as the final part of the series. A revised and considerably longer 7-minute version of this final film was intended for nationwide use in 1953. However, the *Wiener Lichtspieltheater-Verband* (Vienna Cinema Association) declined to associate such a lengthy film with the *Austria Wochenschau* (Austrian Weekly Review).

FIGURE 8.2 Cels featuring the character designs of Tip and Top from 1951. (Courtesy of Austrian State Archives, Vienna (ÖSTA/ADR, BMfHuW, Signatur 19b, Zl. 120161-V/34/1951).)

After completing this commission, Franz Bresnikar became interested in creating a commercial-free animated series. Inspired by the 1952 Olympic Games in Helsinki (Finland, summer) and Oslo (Norway, winter), a five-part series was created under the artistic guidance of Paul Obczovsky titled *Tierolympiade* (Olympic Games for Animals, 1953): *Aufruf zur ersten Tierolympiade* (Call to the First Olympic Games for Animals), *Training zur ersten Tierolympiade* (Training for the First Olympic Games for Animals), *Wassertraining zur ersten Tierolympiade* (Water Training for the First Olympic Games for Animals), *Sportparade* (Sports Parade), and *Tolles Training* (Great Training). Despite receiving cultural film funding and being suitable for international distribution due to the lack of dialogue, the financial success of the series was disappointing. Allegedly, competition from the USA played a role: "These films were initially successful, but when the Americans recognized competition in F.B.N., they began offering their films to cinemas at lower prices or even for free. Consequently, Austrian films were once again economically sidelined" (Gloger 1993: 22). Nevertheless, Bresnikar made one final attempt at an advertising-free animated film with *Die pritschelnde Venus* (Splashing Beauty, 1954), a satire on the Hollywood film *Badende Venus* (Bathing Beauty, 1944) featuring a duck in the leading role.

The lack of success of these films can be attributed to several factors. Firstly, Franz Bresnikar's reliance on black-and-white film due to economic constraints was limiting. Additionally, while his stylistic approach closely resembled *Disney*'s, he struggled to infuse the stories with enough suspense. Bresnikar's *FBN* studio continued producing animated advertising films until the late 1950s. However, due to his commitment to full animation, he couldn't compete with rivals who utilized different animation styles. Consequently, the studio transitioned to live-action films. In 1963, Paul Obczovsky, his main cartoonist, became one of the managing directors at the newly established advertising film producer *Art-Film GmbH*.[29]

Kurt Traum and cameraman Walter Maier co-founded another advertising film company named *Traum & Maier* in 1948. Before that, Traum received training at the *Graphische Lehr- und Versuchsanstalt* (Graphic Arts School) from 1939 to 1942 and then spent 5 months working at *Deutsche Zeichenfilm GmbH*. Initially, *Traum & Maier* specialized in producing animated puppet films, drawing inspiration from the style of Czech master Jiří Trnka (1912–1969), albeit without matching his level of proficiency. Despite this, their puppet animation *Brotmodenschau* (Bread Fashion Show, late 1950s) for the *Ankerbrot* bakery secured the top spot in an audience poll at an advertising film matinee. Additionally, their portrayal of puppets in stereotypical native attire joyfully indulging in cigarette smoking for the brand *Smart Export* (c. 1965) garnered attention. They also combined puppet and hand-drawn animation in the elaborate production *Hungerstreik im Schlaraffenland* (Hunger Strike in the Land of Cockaigne, 1955), in collaboration with Paul Obczovsky. Their hand-drawn animated films were stylistically reminiscent of 1950s design, albeit lacking the bold experimentation seen in the work of Martin Bauer. After overcoming initial challenges, they achieved relative commercial success and boasted prominent clients such as *Casali* (now part of *Manner AG*). Their blatant promotion of the company's alcoholic beverages in *Wer Sorgen hat…* (He Who Has Sorrows, 1958)[30] was characteristic of the era, positioning these drinks as a form of mental hygiene. While commercials like *Casali – Rum Kokos* (Casali – Rum Cocos, 1957) evoked the work of Oskar Fischinger (1900–1967), films such as *Napoli Golddessert* (Napoli Gold Dessert, 1966) were reminiscent of the *UPA* style.

Paul Lazarsfeld (also known as Elias Smith, 1901–1976) and Ernest Dichter (1907–1991), both Austrian pioneers, played key roles in advancing market and opinion research in the United States. Following their contributions, Austria experienced a surge in scientific interest in advertising. The *Werbewissenschaftliche Schriftenreihe* (Advertising Science Publication Series) was launched in 1947, and in 1949, the *Hochschule für Welthandel* (University of World Trade, now Vienna University of Economics and Business) introduced Europe's first university course on business advertising. The *International Advertising Conference* in London in 1951 led to the establishment of an annual *Advertising Week*, with Austria being one of the first host countries in 1953. This was a significant moment for Austria, especially with neighboring Germany absent for the second consecutive time. The growing importance of advertising films became evident through a 1956 initiative aimed at raising awareness of film as a powerful advertising medium, while also supporting film producers and improving the overall quality of their work. As part of this effort, a prestigious state prize was introduced, which included recognition for animated advertising films, such as *Nimm Urlaub vom Auto, fahr' mit der Bahn* (Take a Holiday from Your Car – Go by Train; *AFM* for the Austrian Federal Railways) in the late 1950s.

NOTES

1 On December 22, 1946, the movie was shown in various Viennese cinemas as part of Christmas events for kids. The German dubbed version premiered on April 8, 1947, at the *Internationale Filmfestwoche* (International Film Festival Week) in Salzburg, organized by the *Österreichischer Kulturbund* (Austrian Cultural Association). Starting in 1948, the film became part of the Austrian cinema program, while in Germany, it was included only from 1950.

2 The films encompassed Soviet, Czechoslovak, and Polish animated productions.

3 These theaters earned the nickname 'Schulschwänzer-Kinos' (Truancy Cinemas) because they started their programs early in the morning and quickly attracted students skipping school.

4 The ÖPZ was established in 1950 with financial support from the American Marshall Plan.

5 The film was screened in Austria no later than 1952. The Marshall Plan film *Eine Rettungsgeschichte* (Story of a Rescue, 1950), produced by Paul Grimault's French studio *Les Gemeaux*, also reached Austria in the 1950s.

6 In the late 1940s, Hermann Bieber established the *Österreichische Kinemathek* (Austrian Cinematheque), which can be considered the precursor to the *Filmarchiv Austria* (Austrian Film Archive). In 1949, Bieber received a loan from the *Gesellschaft der Filmfreunde Österreichs* (Society for Friends of Film in Austria) to expand his archive. Shortly after, his Cinematheque also became a member of the *International Federation of Film Archives* (fiaf). However, financial difficulties forced the Cinematheque to shut down in 1954. Following this, the Society for Friends of Film became one of the founding members of the Austrian Film Archive, established in 1955.

7 In the spring of 1938, a German-dubbed version of the movie was created in Amsterdam, Netherlands, but it was not screened in Austria due to its annexation into the German Reich.

8 Even after the end of the occupation, *Tschechoslowakische Filmwochen* (Czechoslovak Film Week) continued to be organized and received state sponsorship until at least 1980.
9 In 1907, Hermann Lemke published a catalog of films suitable for educational purposes in Germany, although these films were not created specifically for school use.
10 The year of death was obtained from Matthias Kasteiner at the registry office of the municipality of Wiener Neustadt (email to the author, dated December 18, 2023).
11 For details about the film's release, see the *Cultural Films* section in the following chapter.
12 The company's articles of association were signed on August 7, 1945, and the company was officially registered in the commercial register on September 4, 1945.
13 According to press reports, the Balkan states expressed interest in these Austrian animated film productions.
14 On February 17, 1953, the commercial court in Vienna declined to initiate bankruptcy proceedings due to insufficient assets. The company was formally dissolved on March 11 and was removed from the commercial register on September 16.
15 The company's articles of association were signed on September 10, 1946, and the company was officially registered in the commercial register on September 20, 1946.
16 The world-renowned *Wiener Sängerknaben* (Vienna Boys' Choir) was joined by Paul Hörbiger (1894–1981), one of Austria's most famous actors at the time, in this 'Heimatfilm.'
17 Elisabeth Leonore 'Lilly' Dillenz (née Hollitzer, 1896–1964), the wife of Richard Dillenz, directed the cultural films. Recognized not only as an actress but also as a pioneering aviator, she achieved international acclaim beyond Austria. In 1927, she made history as the first female passenger to fly across the Atlantic, creating a sensation in the US media. The flight had to be paused after experiencing propeller damage in the Azores. A few months later, Amelia Earhart (1897–1937), the American aviator, completed the first non-stop solo flight across the Atlantic.
18 On March 13, 1958, the company ceased operations and entered liquidation. Its registration in the commercial register was removed on November 25.
19 This is evident from a letter dated June 27, 1945 (facsimile provided by Marianne Weichberger), in which Johann Weichberger requested the allocation of suitable living and working space from the *Wohnungsamt der Stadt Wien* (Housing Office of the City of Vienna). In the same letter, Johann Weichberger claimed that he and his brother Kurt had "formed a professional artistic partnership for the production of hand-drawn color films [...], as it's the only way to handle our exceptionally demanding work." However, according to Johann Weichberger's daughter Marianne Weichberger (b. 1942), her uncle was employed in a completely different profession (telephone conversation with the author on September 24, 2024). It's likely that this statement was intended to convince the housing office to allocate two adjacent vacant apartments to their families.
20 The company's articles of association were signed on November 24, 1948, and the company was officially registered in the commercial register on December 8, 1948.
21 Marianne Weichberger provided the life data in a telephone conversation with the author on September 24, 2024.
22 Hella Soyka was also an illustrator, notably designing the character Benjamin Blümchen (Benjamin the Elephant), created by Austrian author Elfie Donnelly (b. 1950) in the 1970s. Additionally, she worked as a graphic designer for state television and organized puppet shows.
23 According to Peter A. Schauer (1930–2018), the election campaign film *Zwei Köche versalzen den Brei* (Two Cooks Spoil the Broth) marked one of the studio's earliest triumphs (Schauer 1999: 57). Alongside commissioned projects, independent endeavors like the film series *Peter und Paul – Die ungleichen Brüder* (Peter and Paul – The

Unequal Brothers) were also undertaken, representing a sort of revival of *Fritz & Fratz*, according to Johann Weichberger's daughter Marianne Weichberger (telephone conversation with the author on June 23, 2024).

24 According to Marianne Weichberger, her father, Johann Weichberger, was the mastermind behind the visual identity of state television ORF. He was responsible for designing the logos, including that of the news program *Zeit im Bild* (ZiB, A Time in the Picture), among other elements (letter from Marianne Weichberger to the author, dated March 16, 2024).

25 A year earlier, *Helios-Film* had already created a comparable animated film titled *Erfolg enorm…!* (Enormous Success…!, 1948).

26 The company's articles of association were amended on April 7, 1952, and the company's name was updated in the commercial register on April 29.

27 Susi Weigel, Else Weichberger, and Hella Soyka all worked as illustrators for the children's magazine *Unsere Zeitung* (Our Newspaper), which was published from 1946 to 1960.

28 An example of this is the publication of a trilingual edition in 2016, featuring texts in Arabic and Farsi, aimed at supporting German language learning and integration into Austrian society.

29 In the spring of 1967, Paul Obczovsky left *Art-Film*, which was later renamed *Ufa-Werbefilm GmbH*. The studio's dissolution was decided in December 1977 and finalized in 1978.

30 The film was created in collaboration with the South Tyrolean artist Carlo Raffeiner.

9 "For a Piece of Heart" *Austria's Animated Reanimation*

"Österreich ist frei!" ("Austria is free!") proclaimed Leopold Figl (1902–1965), the Austrian Foreign Minister at the time, after the signing of the State Treaty on May 15, 1955. This historic event not only restored Austria's sovereignty but also ended the 10-year Allied occupation. According to Holger Lang (b. 1964), this pivotal moment marked a "'rebirth' of film and animation in Austria" (Lang 2019: 87). This revival also extended to artistic expression. Previously, Austrian animators had tried to emulate *Disney*'s style, but they began developing a distinct approach reminiscent of the American *UPA*. This transition foreshadowed the avant-garde style that would dominate from the 1980s onward. Moreover, the launch of Austrian television's test run in 1955 provided new opportunities for animated filmmakers. However, by this time, many animators had already abandoned their struggle to survive in the industry, leading to yet another significant generational shift in Austrian animation.

A NEW BRUSHSTROKE: EMERGING STYLES IN ANIMATION

The Austrian post-war animated film industry was initially dominated by animators who had either worked or received their training before the war. However, in the late 1950s, a new generation of animators emerged, bringing fresh perspectives and innovative approaches. Among them was Richard Fehsl (b. 1937), who studied at Vienna's *Graphische Lehr- und Versuchsanstalt* (Graphic Arts School) from 1951 to 1956.[1] During his studies, Fehsl gained valuable experience at *Specht-Film* (Figure 9.1), where he met Ida Kozelka-Mocsàry (née Ida Mocsàry, 1920–2005) and Kálmán Kozelka (1924–2000), a couple who had fled Hungary for political reasons. The Kozelkas taught him the fundamental principles of animated film, and together, they collaborated on various animated advertising films. One of their notable works was the object animation film *Wünsche erfüllen* (Wishes Come True, 1957) for the household goods retailer *Slama*: "The film harmonized the world of images and the rhythm of the music with surprising success and was awarded many times" (Orosz 2011: 16). Additionally, beginning in 1958, a series of animated advertisements was produced for the German automobile manufacturer *Opel*. When the Kozelkas relocated to Germany near Stuttgart in 1961, Fehsl joined them, collaborating on instructional films at *Leonaris-Film* and employing his distinctive frosted cel technique. Two years later, the group went their separate ways – the Kozelkas moved to the Netherlands, while Fehsl returned to Vienna to pursue painting studies until 1967. During this period, he reconnected with *Specht-Film*, producing animated advertising films, including those for *Mont Blanc* in 1965. According to animation historian

DOI: 10.1201/9781003415442-11

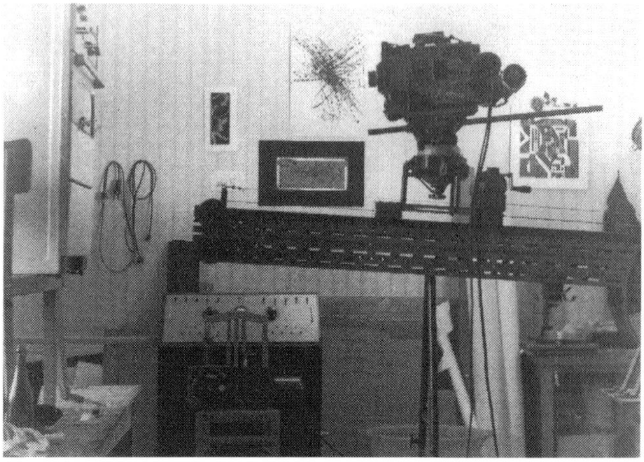

FIGURE 9.1 The camera crane used (and possibly even constructed) by Herbert Link to produce stop-motion films at *Specht-Film*. (Courtesy of Inge Link.)

Thomas Renoldner (b. 1960), Fehsl represents "a link between the boom of the 1950s and the new course that started in the 1960s and grew until the 1980s" (Bendazzi (ed.) 2016b: 50). Renoldner notes that Fehsl's animation style "fundamentally differed from all previously known animators in Austria" (Renoldner 2010: 114). Although he showcased his distinctive animation style in only a handful of independent works, Fehsl remained a highly sought-after animator for various projects well into the 2010s, earning the title of an "old master of animation."[2] Among his notable contributions were the design of several animation sequences for the feature film *Dicht hinter der Tür* (Just Behind the Door, 1984) by Mansur Madavi (1942–2022) and his involvement in the film project *Een Midzomernachtsdroom* (A Midsummer Night's Dream, 1986), a hybrid of live-action and animation. This Dutch TV production was directed by Thérèse 'Tissa' David (1921–2012), a Hungarian-born director based in the USA, who also enlisted the Kozelka couple. As a close associate of the couple, Richard Fehsl excelled in creating the background animation for the project.[3]

Harold Dean 'Hal' Clay (1927–2015) also had an impressive international career. Born in the United States, he began working as an in-betweener at *Disney* at the age of 17. His career then took him on a global journey, with stops at educational institutions in San Francisco (USA), Paris (France), and Vienna (Austria). Along the way, he met notable figures in animation, including John Hubley (1914–1977). His travels eventually brought him to the picturesque Austrian province of Tyrol, where he met Flo Nordhoff (né Florenz von Fuchs-Nordhoff, 1914–1987), a Tyrolean animator who had originally trained in Munich, Germany.[4] Together, they collaborated on the film *Hands Up Mr. Rasnitchi* (1967), described as "a first independently produced animated film with experimental features" (Renoldner 2010: 114). Although the film was initially released in Germany and is often considered a German production, it clearly reflects a significant Austrian influence. For example, Nordhoff leveraged his connections with Austrian actor and cabaret artist Helmut Qualtinger (1928–1986), with whom he had previously worked on stage in the early 1950s, to have Qualtinger provide the voice for the film. Additionally, Nordhoff and Clay used photographs of Qualtinger and Austrian actress Tilla Hohenfels (1936–1994) to blend reality with surrealist fiction through the layering technique.[5] The film conveys a simple yet powerful message: many problems could have been avoided by not engaging in a simple handshake, a point illustrated by Adolf Hitler's (1889–1945) appointment as German Reich Chancellor in 1933, facilitated by a handshake from Paul von Hindenburg (1847–1934).

A FISTFUL OF SCHILLINGS: THE END OF THE ADVERTISING BOOM

Austrian television began its trial operations in 1955, initially broadcasting in the major urban areas of Vienna, Graz (Styria), Linz (Upper Austria), and Salzburg. Regular television programming started 2 years later, but it wasn't until 1959 that broadcasts were available on all weekdays. During this period, television also began incorporating advertising, tapping into a rapidly growing market: by 1968, the number of television sets had surged from fewer than 200,000 in 1960 to over a million, in a country with a population of around 7.3 million. One of the most notable figures in television advertising during this time was Hans Albala (1919–1976). Born in Vienna, Albala had to abandon his medical studies due to his Jewish heritage following the *'Anschluss' Österreichs* (annexation of Austria) into the German Reich and survived the National Socialist labor camps. After the war, he attended an art school in Linz (Upper Austria) and gained his first self-taught experience in animation. The shift to television advertising required a transition from elaborate individual films to short commercial series. Albala, "who can certainly be called the 'avant-gardist' of animated commercials in the 1950s and 1960s" (Renoldner 2010: 109), produced some of the era's most innovative work from his self-constructed animation stand. For example, in a commercial for the cognac brand *Bouchet* (1958), he made the letters interact with each other, transforming into different shapes across various scenes. He was also among the first to use photo animation in advertising, as seen in the commercial for the razor *Remington Roll-A-Matik* (1958).[6] His advertising films *Capriccio Italien* (Italian Capriccio, 1957) and *Humanic Varese* (1959) resembled the concept of 'visual music' found in the works of Len Lye (1901–1980) and Oskar Fischinger (1900–1967). According to his widow, Heidemarie Bernhard, there was no way Albala could have seen such films in post-war Austria: "He can therefore certainly be addressed as the first representative of experimental animation film in Austria" (Renoldner 2010: 113).

Between 1953 and 1961, Martin Bauer (1919–?) was primarily responsible for advertising animations at *Adi Mayer Film* (AFM) before starting his own independent business. He focused on expanding the expressive potential of animation by experimenting with the interplay between drawing and object animation. In his commercial series *Adeg* (1962), for example, he depicted a drawing hand creating a figure, reminiscent of early Fleischer brothers' films, which was then placed in a three-dimensional space and animated. Besides commercials, Bauer produced commissioned films that skillfully blended drawings with object animation. Notably, for the German television station *Zweites Deutsches Fernsehen* (ZDF, lit. Second German Television), he brought a Viennese song to life in *Blunz'nfilm*

(Blood Sausage Film, 1964), "a brilliant example of his ability in merging different techniques" (Bendazzi (ed.) 2016b: 49). Additionally, he developed an advertising film for the Austrian Socialist Party (SPÖ) during the 1966 National Council election. The film's content bore a resemblance to *Die Abenteuer des Herrn Antimarx* (The Adventures of Mr. Antimarx, 1930),[7] but its style introduced fresh ideas to Austrian stop-motion animation. Bauer also used the stop-motion technique to produce special effects for feature films, such as orchestrating a pair of gloves to magically play the piano in a scene from *Charley's Tante* (Charley's Aunt, 1963). However, by the mid-1960s, the advertising boom had waned, leading Bauer to close his studio in 1967 due to financial challenges.

"HOW ANIMATION WAS BORN": CULTURAL FILM CONTRIBUTIONS

In the late 1940s, the cultural sector faced a precarious situation, leading to a cultural crisis. To alleviate this hardship, the 'Kulturgroschen' (cultural penny), a controversial compulsory levy on every movie ticket sold, was introduced in May 1949. On the recommendation of Dr. J.P. Haustein (1888–1973), the film advisor to the Federal Ministry of Education, a portion of the funds collected through this levy was allocated to the production of cultural films. This initiative sparked a surge in cultural film production, with the number of producers in Austria rising from 54 in 1951 to 127 by 1960. Thanks to the cultural levy, Gustav 'Gustl' Peuker (1913–1988)[8] was able to release his animated puppet film *Der Siebenpunkt* (The Sevenpointer), mentioned in the previous chapter, as a cultural film through *Belvedere-Film*.[9]

A remarkable cultural film was produced in the late 1950s at *Centropa-Film* under the direction of Karl Stanzl (1916–1978). This project emerged from an international competition that collected over 3,000 children's drawings from Austria, Germany, France, Great Britain, Japan, the USA, and the Soviet Union. The best drawings were used to create the color film *Reise auf den Mond* (Journey to the Moon, 1958/1959). The film featured the futuristic sounds of the Heliophon, an electronic musical instrument invented in Austria and similar to today's synthesizer, and received the *Austrian Cultural Film Prize* in 1959. Following this, *Kinderträume* (Children's Dreams, 1961) was created from approximately 8,500 children's drawings collected from 11 nations. This film was showcased at the 11th Berlin International Film Festival in 1961 and also won the *Austrian Cultural Film Prize* that same year. The success continued with the third film, *Vergangenheit und Zukunft* (Past and Future, 1964), which garnered several international awards, including one in San Francisco, USA. Although these films cannot be technically classified as animated films, they underscored the significance of drawing in Austrian culture and highlighted Austria's role as a neutral country in the heart of Europe, bridging East and West during the Cold War.[10]

Erhard Amadeus-Dier (1893–1969), a Viennese filmmaker who had worked for *Deutsche Zeichenfilm GmbH* during the war, ventured into producing state-subsidized cultural films in the 1960s. After about 6 years of dedicated effort, he independently completed a marionette color feature film in 1966, based on the classic Grimm Brothers' fairy tale *Vom Fischer und seiner Frau* (The Fisherman and His Wife).[11] Once he had nearly single-handedly finished the film, Amadeus-Dier

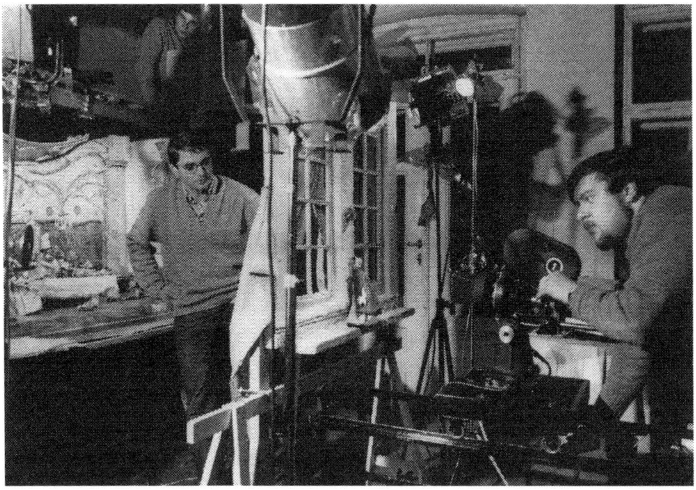

FIGURE 9.2 Herbert Link filming *Sterntaler* (Star Talers, 1968), directed by Walter Bannert (1942–2020, center). (Courtesy of Inge Link.)

brought filmmaker Herbert Link (1944–2018) on board for another marionette film titled *Sterntaler* (Star Talers, 1968) (Figure 9.2). In his younger years, Link was an avid amateur filmmaker with a passion for experimenting with animation. From 1962 to 1979, he created a significant number of commercials for *Specht-Film*, drawing on this early passion for film. Throughout his career, he created live action films and oversaw stop-motion ads at the studio, while his colleague Toni Zögl specialized in animated cartoons.[12]

During the 1960s, Linz (Upper Austria), Austria's third-largest city, emerged as a significant cultural film hub alongside Vienna. After the war, Alexander Hans Puluj (1901–1984), a pioneer of Austrian sound film, managed the *Froschberg Kino* (Frog Hill Cinema) in Linz. His son, Peter Puluj (1930–2017), later recalled, "We screened several shows every day, only featuring films with artistic merit" (Peter Puluj, as cited in Wurz 2016: para. 1). In 1949, A. Hans Puluj, along with his sons Peter and Axel Puluj (b. 1939), transformed an old horse stable adjacent to the cinema into the *Froschberg Filmstudio* to produce such films themselves.[13] However, the studio soon outgrew its space. After the death of Friedrich 'Fritz' Blaschko (1914–1963), the founder of *Blaschko-Film*, the Puluj "film family" (Sperner 1976: 99) took over his studio in Linz's industrial area and rebranded it as *Studio A* in 1965.[14] Following the acquisition, it rapidly gained recognition as the country's most advanced animation and short film studio. A. Hans Puluj had even greater ambitions – he aimed to establish a film seminar in Linz to allow students to observe foreign animation experts in action.

During that period, Prague-born A. Hans Puluj had already established contact with the animation artist Jan Švankmajer (b. 1934), who also hailed from Prague. After Švankmajer received an award for his first short film at the 13th *International Film Week Mannheim* (Germany) in 1964, Puluj invited him to Linz.[15] However, Švankmajer's vision for a comprehensive film project in Linz was deemed unattainable

FIGURE 9.3 Jan Švankmajer, along with his wife Eva and A. Hans Puluj, during the production of *Spiel mit Steinen* (A Game with Stones, 1965) at *Studio A*. (Courtesy of Thomas Ballhausen (Permission by Axel Puluj).)

by the studio. As a result, during a stroll along the Danube, he conceived the idea for a short film by observing the stones on the bank, critiquing a life cycle reduced to mere reproduction. Within a few weeks, the animated film *Spiel mit Steinen* (A Game with Stones, 1965) was created in a nearby farmhouse (Figure 9.3). Not only did it secure the Austrian Cultural Film Award in 1965, but it also achieved success at international festivals. This laid the groundwork for a crossroads of East and West European animated film, exemplified by Švankmajer's work. Following his lead, the Polish animator Witold Ney produced the animated film *...für ein Stück Herz* (...For a Piece of Heart, 1965) in Linz, satirizing the stereotypical nature of cowboy films. After being featured at the *Viennale* in 1966, the film's success motivated Ney to pursue additional projects in Linz, such as creating the animated film *Samariter 66* (Samaritan 66, 1965/1966).[16] In this film, a drowning man lures a passerby on a bridge by waving a bundle of banknotes, prompting the passerby to leap into the water, only to seize the money. In contrast, *Der kleine Bär* (The Little Bear, 1966) was a whimsical fairy-tale-animated film about a bear's adventures with the constellations on the Milky Way, which was featured at the 1967 Cannes Youth Film Festival. Czech artist Ivan Renč (b. 1937), a student of Jiří Trnka (1912–1969), created the animated film *Windstille* (Still Air, 1966/1967) in Linz, exploring the force of habit while crafting a film ballad with a timeless message. A project was also conceived under the supervision of Polish animator Witold Giersz (b. 1927), but it apparently did not come to fruition. In the late 1960s, Jan Švankmajer returned to Linz for a second animated film titled *Picknick mit Weismann* (Picnic with Weismann, 1968). Reflecting on this multinational collaboration, film historian and critic Goswin M. Dörfler (1922–2008) concluded:

"Thus, 'Studio A' not only emerges as a key hub for Austrian [...] short film production but also becomes a vital meeting point for East and West in the film industry. This role perfectly aligns with Austria's tradition as a small country at the heart of Europe, acting as a mediator and guardian of European culture" (Dörfler 1966: 17).

Leszek Kałuża (1930–2018), better known as Les Kaluza, was another internationally recognized filmmaker who briefly stayed in Linz. In 1947, he joined a newly established Polish animation studio, which later evolved into the esteemed *Studio Filmów Rysunkowych* (Studio of Animated Movies) in Bielsko-Biała.[17] During 1947/1948, he contributed to the creation of the first Polish post-war animated film, *Czy to był sen?* (Was This a Dream?), which was subsequently banned by the communist government upon its completion.[18] In 1958, when a team of animated filmmakers from Zagreb (formerly Yugoslavia, now Croatia) invited his team for a return visit, Kaluza traveled behind the Iron Curtain to Vienna, "the beautiful city I had read and heard about so much; the city I had so many plans for, which only I knew about. [...] I was in 7th heaven; I was breathing in freedom!" (Kaluza 2015: 97) This visit ultimately led to his decision to seek political asylum during a stopover in Vienna while returning from Yugoslavia to Poland. Guided by Władysław Nehrebecki (1923–1978), the creator of the legendary Polish animated characters *Bolek i Lolek* (Bolek and Lolek, 1962–1986), Kaluza found himself at the *Froschberg Filmstudio* in Linz, where he produced his first animated commercial for the Austrian beer brand *Gösser*. Upon returning to Vienna, he collaborated with the advertising film producer *Traum & Maier* and contributed illustrations to the magazine *Neue Wiener Illustrierte* (New Viennese Illustrated). During his brief stay in Austria before immigrating to the USA, Kaluza experienced a highly productive creative phase. In addition to creating various commercials, he was commissioned by *Studio A* to produce the animated film *How Man Was Born*, a loose interpretation of Charles Darwin's (1809–1882) theory of the creation of man.[19] His Viennese girlfriend Erna, who later became his wife in December 1959 before they emigrated, assisted him in creating the film. The pair also collaborated in Vienna on another animated film, with Kaluza developing the storyboard and sketching characters and backgrounds for the project funded by his friend, Mik.[20] Alongside Erna, Kaluza recruited colleagues from the commercial film studio *Traum & Maier*, and they enlisted a talented Viennese musician to compose the music. This collaboration resulted in a Western-style film titled *Gold*, featuring limited animation. After immigrating to the United States in 1960, the Austrian-Polish couple made significant contributions to American television. Initially, they worked at *Paramount* in New York, where they were involved in creating animated series such as *Popeye the Sailor* and *Casper the Friendly Ghost*.

Later, in 1964, they joined the team at *Hanna-Barbera* in Los Angeles, contributing to iconic series such as *The Flintstones*, *The Jetsons*, and *Yogi Bear*. Subsequently, at *Filmation* in LA, they worked on animated series like *Superman*, *Star Trek*, and *Tom & Jerry*. Their involvement in these renowned animated series highlights their substantial impact on popular culture. Additionally, according to animation historian Jerry Beck (b. 1955), Kaluza's animated short *Potpourri* (1972) was even considered for an Oscar nomination for *Best Animated Short* in 1973 (cf. Beck 2017).

In 1968, *Studio A* began producing non-animated commissioned films. By around 1970, the Linz film studio was sold, and the building was repurposed for other uses. *Studio A* then relocated its headquarters to the small town of Leonding in Upper Austria. This move marked the beginning of the studio's decline, culminating in its liquidation on July 11, 1972, and its removal from the commercial register on May 16, 1974.[21]

ANIMATING THE ANIMATORS: THE ART OF PUPPET FILMS

Richard Teschner (1879–1948), a pioneering puppeteer, sought to immortalize his rod puppets, inspired by the marionette theater of the Far East, on film as early as 1919. His puppet theater, established in Vienna in 1912, captivated even Gustav Klimt (1862–1918), the leading figure in Viennese Art Nouveau. Between 1926 and 1930, Teschner produced several films. Notably, in 1927/1928, he created a puppet sequence for the feature film *Der geheimnisvolle Spiegel* (The Mysterious Mirror, 1928) at the renowned German *Ufa* film studio. In this film, the protagonist gazes into a mirror and sees his future depicted by Teschner's puppets. Teschner's short film *Traum im Karneval* (Dream in Carnival, 1930), produced in collaboration with Max Goldschmidt, even garnered attention in the USA and received positive reviews in the New York magazine *Movie Makers* in 1931. Although Teschner's films were not animated, Austrian director and publicist Ernst Schmidt Jr. (1938–1988) regarded them as technologically equivalent to animated puppet films: "The technical perfection of Teschner's puppet performances renders animation techniques unnecessary for their filming; indeed, such techniques would have only detracted from the performances. Consequently, Teschner's puppet films are on par with the finest puppet-animated films" (Schmidt 1985: 35).

After Richard Teschner's passing, *Wiener Kunstfilm Walter Kolm-Veltée* created two marionette films based on his 'Figurenspiegel' (Figure Mirror): *Der goldene Brunnen* (The Golden Well) and *Marienlegende* (Marian Legend). These films were showcased at the 1951 Cannes Film Festival. A third film, *Prinzessin und Wassermann* (Princess and Aquarius), was in development in 1950 but was never completed. The project likely faced financial difficulties due to its ambitious nature, which involved elaborate color production and underwater scenes. Although marionette and puppet films were produced sporadically in the years that followed,[22] sustained large-scale production didn't occur until the mid-1960s, under the leadership of Johann 'Hans' Oswald Sindelar (1921–2014)[23] and Rudolf Enter (1927–2017).

Hans O. Sindelar is recognized as one of Austria's most exceptional animators. Having made animated films his career for an extended period, he stands out as one of the rare individuals who succeeded in this field without ever having to work in the advertising sector. From 1965 to 1980, Sindelar created over 100 films for the children's program of the *Österreichischer Rundfunk* (ORF, Austrian Broadcasting Corporation).[24] His journey into puppet animation was not initially planned. After acquiring a cine camera in 1945, following the war, and joining the *Klub der Kinoamateure Österreichs* (KdKÖ, Club of Amateur Filmmakers Austria) in 1946, Sindelar began by making live-action films. Dissatisfied with the performance and reliability of amateur actors, he turned to puppet animation, inspired by a film by Czech animator Jiří Trnka.[25] In the late 1950s, Sindelar produced the black-and-white film *Der Puppenmacher* (The Puppet Maker, 1958), where he interacted with the puppet character he brought to life, reminiscent of Max Fleischer's (1883–1972) animated series *Out of the Inkwell* (1918–1929). Additionally, in his colorful puppet film *Sindy Show* (1961), the trained musician brought popular tunes and chart-topping songs of the era to life, including *Souvenirs* (1959/1960) by American-German vocalist Bill Ramsey (1931–2021). The meticulous creation of the puppet costumes took weeks, followed by the painstaking animation of 10,000 individual shots. For his early films, Sindelar received assistance from Claus Scholz, who aided in the animation process, and Rudolf Enter, who crafted the puppet heads. Decades later, Sindelar looked back with fondness on the screening of his film at the 24th International Competition for the Best Amateur Films held by *Union Internationale du Cinéma d'Amateur* (UNICA) in Vienna in 1962: "It hit like a bomb. Despite the ban on applause at the International Competition, the audience stomped their feet, shouted, and who knows what else – it was the best day I've ever had with this film" ('Hans O. Sindelar' 2011, 00:00:38). The film earned a gold medal after thoroughly impressing the jury as well.[26] Following this success, Sindelar's career took an unexpected turn. His international recognition led to invitations for guest lectures at the University of Vienna and in Switzerland. Additionally, he attracted the attention of ORF, which commissioned a half-hour puppet film. However, the completion of *Circus Sindy* (1965/1966) was delayed due to Sindelar's animation assistant, who could only work on weekends because of his day job. This caused the originally estimated 6-month production to stretch to 15 months. Despite the financial risk of having only a verbal commitment from ORF and having already paid his assistant 15,000 schillings (approximately €8,000 today, adjusted for inflation), the film was eventually accepted, and the agreed fee was paid. *Circus Sindy* was premiered on television on May 30, 1966.[27]

In the early years of his career, Hans O. Sindelar produced longer puppet films, each running between 20 and 30 minutes. One of his first series, *Drei lustige Gesellen* (Three Funny Fellows, 1969–1971), followed the adventures of three traveling musicians. In *Abenteuer in Cucumbien* (Adventures in Cucumbia, 1968), he introduced vegetable characters for the first time, whimsically renaming Colombia to Cucumbia as a playful nod to 'cucumber'. The plot centered around two 'vegetable heroes' who arrive in the country to defeat a dragon infestation. However, various misunderstandings arise, the most notable being that the 'Drachen' (dragons) are actually 'Papierdrachen' (paper kites) flown by children from a neighboring country. In *Die Potatoes: Das Konzert* (The Potatoes: The Concert, 1974) and *Die Potatoes: Der Diebstahl* (The Potatoes: The Theft, 1974), Sindelar combined the musical theme with vegetable figures, featuring potatoes, crafted from insulating wire and felt, performing as a band. These figures became some of Sindelar's most iconic creations and were featured in a ten-part series in 1975. By the early 1970s, Sindelar had also begun creating much shorter films. For example, the ten-part series *Das Fragezeichen* (The Question Mark, 1973), *Gute Freunde* (Good Friends, 1975), and *Die Spieluhr* (The Musical Clock, 1976) were aired as *Betthupferl* (Bedtime Treat) and *Gute-Nacht-Geschichte für die Kleinsten* (Bedtime Story for the Smallest), each with a runtime of just under 5 minutes.

However, Hans O. Sindelar's versatility extended far beyond varying film lengths. While his work predominantly featured puppet films, it also encompassed a diverse range of animation techniques. For instance, *Kunibert* (1974) utilized cutout animation, while *Die Vogelscheuche* (The Scarecrow, 1977) was created using traditional hand-drawn animation. In addition to entertainment, Sindelar produced educational films, such as the cutout animation series *1-2-3* (1976), which was designed to introduce young children to numbers from 1 to 10, with a new number presented each day. Sindelar's films also explored a broad array of subjects. The aforementioned series *Drei lustige Gesellen* (Three Funny Fellows, 1969–1971) not only depicted Alpine culture but also ventured into exotic locales, as seen in *Die Urwaldeisenbahn* (The Jungle Railroad, 1971). He also tapped into the popular science fiction genre of the time with films like *SOS – Notlandung* (SOS – Emergency Landing, 1972), *Ausflug ins Weltall* (Space Trip, 1972), and *Weltraum-Zirkus* (Space Circus, 1973). Sindelar's ingenuity and skill were particularly evident in the film *Die geheimnisvolle Burg* (The Mysterious Castle, 1969), part of the *Drei lustige Gesellen* (Three Funny Fellows, 1969–1971) series. In this film, Sindelar choreographed a 'Schuhplattler' (a traditional folk dance) performed by two mouse figures. To overcome the challenge of air jumps in stop motion, he positioned the figures in front of a mouse hole made from black cardboard and used wires inserted through it to stabilize the characters. Sindelar regarded this film as one of his best-crafted works. His films, with a few early exceptions, were produced without dialogue, making them easily adaptable for international distribution. The ORF archives even preserve two of his films with Afrikaans titles: *Die Voëlverskrikker* (The Scarecrow, 1977) and *Die Mallemeule* (The Merry-Go-Round, 1977).

In terms of content, Hans O. Sindelar emphasized the importance of creating films with a moral message: "I never really aimed to make Kasperl films; instead, my goal was always to create films with messages that children could understand and that would also engage adults. I believe I succeeded quite well in that" (Sindelar 2011b, 00:03:31). For example, Sindelar's film *Nachbarn* (Neighbours, 1972) was a child-friendly adaptation of Norman McLaren's (1914–1987) Oscar-winning short film *Neighbours* (1952). In McLaren's original, two neighbors engage in a destructive fight over a flower growing on their property line. In Sindelar's version, the conflict centers on a vegetable. Both films illustrate the neighbors' descent into savagery, leading to the erection of a fence. However, in Sindelar's version, the eventual realization that the children are suffering and unable to play together prompts a reconciliation, echoing McLaren's message of "Love your neighbour": the neighbors tear down the fence and share the vegetable. Similarly, in *Hilfsbereitschaft* (Helpfulness, 1974), Sindelar underscored the importance of collective effort, showing how a major problem, such as a stuck tractor, can be solved when everyone, from grandpa to child, pitches in. In *Hilfe – Zauberei!* (Help – Magic!, 1979), a boy is pushed out of line by adults at various merchants until all the goods are sold out. When he receives a magic wand, he uses it to give the men horns and the women beards until they ask for his forgiveness for their inconsiderate behavior. These films effectively convey messages of cooperation, empathy, and forgiveness within communities and society as a whole.

After more than two decades of creating puppet films, Hans O. Sindelar retired from full-time production in 1980 but continued to make animated films occasionally. His retirement was not due to a lack of demand for his work, but rather the physical strain involved in his craft. Except for the music, primarily composed by Karl Grell (1925–2003), Sindelar managed every aspect of film production on his own – from designing the 15–17-cm-(6–7-inch) tall figures to bringing them to life on a 2.5-m-(2.7-yard) long and 1.7-m-(1.9-yard) wide stage using a crank-operated camera. The physical demands of repeatedly bending down for each camera shot made it increasingly difficult for him to continue working. His decision to retire came as a surprise to ORF, which had already allocated a budget for his 1981 productions. Although Sindelar was no longer producing puppet films when a television team visited him in 1997, he remained active in the film industry. Even at the age of 90 in 2011, he was still an enthusiastic artist, creating music and poetry.

Rudolf Enter (Figure 9.4) followed a similar path in life, receiving a film projector from his parents at the age of 12.[28] Tiring of regular movies, he obtained discarded film strips and painstakingly removed the emulsion. Inspired by *Disney*'s works, he meticulously drew his own in-between frames onto these film strips using ink and pen. After the war, Enter purchased a second-hand film camera and became involved with various amateur film clubs and associations. Initially, he focused on live-action films, until he once again found himself captivated by the "animation craze" (Rudolf Enter in 'Rudolf Enter: Puppen-Trick-Film-Leidenschaft' 2013, 00:03:16). To produce his animated films, he purchased 200 cels, meticulously washing and drying

FIGURE 9.4 A snapshot of Rudolf Enter taken on set. (Courtesy of Michael Enter.)

them for reuse. Using a stool as an animation stand, he mounted the camera through the grip hole. One of Enter's earliest animated films is preserved in the documentary *Besuch bei der Filmfachgruppe des Wiener Volksbildungsvereines* (Visit to the Film Section of the Viennese Popular Education Association, 1949), which showcases the association's film activities. *Disney*'s influence, which Enter claimed he only overcame later in life, is evident in the form of a mouse as the main character.

Like Hans O. Sindelar, Rudolf Enter began his professional career through an amateur film competition. Enter, a communications engineer at *Radio-Austria AG*, created the colorful animated film *Segen der Technik* (Blessing of Technology, 1965), "a lighthearted history of communication technology, from jungle drums to transoceanic cables" (Rudolf Enter, as cited in Filmpresse, 47 (1), 2011: 16). His work earned a bronze medal at the 1965 state championships of the *Verband Österreichischer Film-Autoren* (VÖFA, Association of Austrian Film Authors) in Weiz, Styria. Dr. Franz Hubalek (1917–2000), who was part of the jury, later hired Enter as an animator for educational films at the *Staatliche Hauptstelle für Lichtbild und Bildungsfilm* (SHB, Federal Office for Photography and Educational Film). During this time, SHB's animation department primarily focused on producing puppet films based on fairy tales.[29] Inspired by puppetry since childhood, Enter soon created his first animated puppet film, *Rotkäppchen* (Little Red Riding Hood, 1965/1966), followed by other films such as *Das tapfere Schneiderlein* (The Brave Little Tailor, 1966), *Hans im Glück* (Lucky Hans, 1973) (Figure 9.5), *Der Froschkönig* (The Frog Prince, 1975), *Frau Holle* (Mother Holle, 1975), and *Der gestiefelte Kater* (Puss in Boots, 1988).[30] Enter also worked on at least one hand-drawn animated film, *Bremer Stadtmusikanten* (Town Musicians of Bremen).[31] Later, two of his animated puppet films, *Dornröschen* (Sleeping Beauty, 1980) and *Die Sterntaler* (The Star Talers, 1986), were distributed by the *Institut für Film und Bild in Wissenschaft und Unterricht* (FWU, Institute for Film and Picture in Science and Education) based in Munich, Southern Germany, in 1990 and 1996, respectively.

Similar to Hans O. Sindelar, Rudolf Enter also employed a self-made, low-cost approach for his puppets, constructing their skeletal structures from a self-carved wooden corpus combined with wooden sticks, beads, and bent piano wire. Vrääth Öhner (b. 1965) from the *Ludwig Boltzmann Institute for Digital History* (LBIDH) considers Enter an animator in two senses: he not only animated films but also animated others to create films (cf. Vrääth Öhner in 'Rudolf Enter: Film-Animateur' 2020, 00:01:05). For instance, in the late 1980s, Enter produced a behind-the-scenes film titled *Puppentrickfilme – aus der Praxis, für die Praxis* (Animated Puppet Films – From Practice, for Practice, 1987)[32] and later authored the book *Puppen Trick Film – die Praxis* (Animated Puppet Film – the Practice, 1990), providing aspiring artists with step-by-step guidance on crafting wooden puppets.[33] Unlike Sindelar, Enter pursued his animation career as an amateur throughout his life, creating films part time. He remained an active member of amateur film clubs and even explored computer animation later in life. His short computer-animated films were featured in the ORF broadcast series *Videowelten* (Video Worlds, 2009–2014), showcasing amateur filmmakers' works, as recently as 2009 and 2010.[34] In addition to his animation work, Enter's remarkable legacy includes the *Breitenfurter Marionettenbühne*

FIGURE 9.5 Drafts from 1970 for the film *Hans im Glück* (Lucky Hans, 1973) by Rudolf Enter, originally envisioned as a hand-drawn animated film. (Courtesy of Michael Enter.)

(Breitenfurt Marionette Stage), which he and his wife, Helene Enter (1932–2018),[35] established in 1983 in Breitenfurt near Vienna. Remarkably, 40 years later, this stage continues to bring his scripts, sets, and puppets to life.

NOTES

1 Thomas Renoldner (b. 1960) stated that Richard Fehsl was born in Lower Austria (cf. Bendazzi (ed.) 2016b: 50). Márton Orosz (b. 1979) referred to him as "an Austrian animator of Hungarian origins" (Orosz 2011: 16). Fehsl confirmed his Hungarian origins during a telephone conversation with the author on June 28, 2023.

2 This is what the Vorarlberg artist Tone Fink (b. 1944), who produced the animated film *T. nicht füttern!* (Do Not Feed T.!, 2016) with Richard Fehsl, called him. Cf. https://www.tonefink.at/T-nicht-fuettern.html.

3 In an interview with the author, Richard Fehsl emphasized that his longtime colleague and lifelong friend, Ilse Kovacevic, played a crucial role in nearly all of his film projects, including *Dicht hinter der Tür* (Just Behind the Door, 1984) and *Een Midzomernachtsdroom* (A Midsummer Night's Dream, 1986). He believes her

contributions deserve equal recognition alongside his own (interview with Richard Fehsl and Ilse Kovacevic on February 17, 2024, in Vienna). For more details on their careers, refer to the article co-authored with Franziska Proksa (née Bruckner in 1981) in the *Encyclopedia of Animation Studies* (Bloomsbury Publishing).

4 His first animated film, *Die Purpurlinie* (The Purple Line, 1959/1960), was visually inspired by US productions and sought to depict human moods allegorically through abstract landscapes and figures.

5 The film is reminiscent of the animated sequences from the British TV series *Monty Python's Flying Circus* (1969), which was produced 2 years later.

6 During that period, photographic posters began to replace hand-drawn advertising posters.

7 This film was "a satire of an anti-Marxist petty bourgeois, the Heimwehr [a right-wing paramilitary organization], and Strafella" (Roy 2020: 694). Franz Georg Strafella (1891–1968), a member of the Christian Social Party, was confronted with several allegations, including corruption, by the Social Democrats in the early 1930s, leading to a significant political crisis.

8 The year of death was obtained from Matthias Kasteiner at the registry office of the municipality of Wiener Neustadt (email to the author, dated December 18, 2023).

9 The specific release date remains uncertain, but it can be narrowed down to the period between 1947, which marks the film's press presentation, and 1951, the year when *Belvedere-Film* ceased operations. Following the closure of *Belvedere-Film*, established in 1946, several films were pilfered by Soviet occupation forces. Among these might have been *Der Siebenpunkt* (The Sevenpointer), a film now categorized as lost.

10 As early as 1952, the Austrian branch of the US *Economic Cooperation Administration* (ECA) created a film called *Wir zeichnen* (We Draw) featuring children's drawings. The film accordingly featured several pro-American scenes, such as a kiss between a Native American and a man in alpine attire, and the rescue of residents from a burning house using an American flag as a safety net.

11 In January 1962, there were press reports about the project: "The painter Erhard Amadeus Dier has spent the past two years developing the groundwork for a color feature film using marionettes" (Böhm 1962 [no pagination]; special thanks to Nikolaus Domes from the Vienna Künstlerhaus Archives). The completion of the film, supported by the Ministry of Education, was announced in the *Austrian Yearbook 1966* (Bundespressedienst (ed.) 1967: 194).

12 Herbert Link was a lecturer at the Academy of Fine Arts Vienna from 1989 to 2006, where he guided the production of numerous student-animated films (email from Inge Link to the author, dated June 24, 2023).

13 The company was officially registered in the commercial register in 1950.

14 The company's articles of association were signed on April 20, 1965, and the company was officially registered in the commercial register on May 12, 1965.

15 A. Hans Puluj himself entered the competition with his film *Quo Vadis – Moderne Kunst?* (Quo Vadis – Modern Art?, 1962), but did not receive an award.

16 The film production began in 1965 under the working title *Samariter 65* (Samaritan 65), in collaboration with Witold Musiałowicz, a co-founder of the School of Animated Film in Łódź, Poland. From 1977 onward, *Samariter 66* (Samaritan 66) was also distributed as an educational film by the German FWU (email from Andrea Löhr to the author, dated August 11, 2023).

17 Bielsko-Biała is often called 'Little Vienna' due to its similar architecture.

18 Today, the approximately 11-minute anti-war film is considered lost.

19 Although the film was likely completed by 1960 when Les Kaluza immigrated to the USA, it was not released until 1967. It is possible that the release was delayed to address potential production lulls, given that no other *Studio A* project was reported for cultural film funding in 1967.

20 The individual in question may have been the Danish cartoonist Henning Dahl Mikkelsen (1915–1982), who used the signature 'Mik' for his comics. Lars Jakobsen (b. 1964), the author of a biography about Mik, confirms that Mik was in Vienna during the late 1950s as part of an extended European trip with his wife and children. However, since Les Kaluza, who claimed to have lived with his friend Mik, did not mention any family, Jakobsen considers it unlikely that the Mik in question is the same person (emails to the author, dated July 11 and 12, 2023).

21 Despite this, the Puluj 'film family' remained committed to the industry, with the *Froschberg Filmstudio* rebranded as *Puluj Filmproduktion* in the early 1970s and expanding its production to include image and advertising films. Andrij Peter Puluj (b. 1960) has successfully managed the company since 1997, now in its third generation, and has also been running a local television station alongside his sister Sabine Puluj since 2004.

22 Apart from the aforementioned marionette films by Erhard Amadeus-Dier and the puppet film by Gustl Peuker, other films were produced outside Vienna with the assistance of the *Salzburger Marionettentheater* (Salzburg Marionette Theater), including *Salzburger Marionetten* (Salzburg Marionettes, 1947) and *Der Diamant des Geisterkönigs* (The Diamond of the Ghost King, 1963).

23 The year of death was obtained from Elisabeth Essl at the Citizen Service Office of the municipality of Kreuttal (email to the author, dated October 20, 2023).

24 The book *Animation: A World History* (Bendazzi (ed.) 2016b: 196) states that Hans O. Sindelar created 107 films. However, in a 2011 interview, Sindelar mentioned having made 125 films (cf. Sindelar 2011b, 00:03:12). Including *Sindy Show* (1961), a total of 101 films were identified during this project, although the records before 1972 are incomplete.

25 Thomas Renoldner therefore pointed out that Hans O. Sindelar frequently missed the opportunity to fully exploit the unique possibilities of animated film, opting instead to tell stories that could have been depicted using live actors (Renoldner 2010: 128).

26 Hans O. Sindelar mentioned that he had previously participated in the national competition of the KdKÖ with the film, where he 'only' received a silver medal. He attributed this outcome to the association head's unfavorable disposition toward him (cf. Sindelar 2011a, 00:13:00).

27 In a 2011 interview, Hans O. Sindelar mentioned his television career spanning from 1962 to 1980 (cf. Sindelar 2011b, 00:02:59). It seems that Sindelar regarded the 1962 broadcast of his amateur film *Sindy Show* (1961) as the starting point of his television involvement, though most sources mark the beginning of his work with ORF – and the production of *Circus Sindy* – to 1965, with its premiere occurring in 1966.

28 During an interview in 2011, Rudolf Enter recalled receiving the projector at the age of 10 or 12 (cf. Filmpresse, 47 (1), 2011: 16). Additionally, during an author talk at a short film night in 2012, he stated that he was 12 years old at the time (cf. Pezold 2012, under 'Ein Urgestein der Trickfilmszene').

29 It is evident that they based their approach on the distribution program of the *Reichsanstalt für Film und Bild in Wissenschaft und Unterricht* (RWU, Reich Institute for Film and Picture in Science and Education), which also supplied Austria with educational films during its annexation into the German Reich (1938–1945). Beginning in 1935, the German Diehl brothers consistently produced puppet animation films, particularly fairy tale adaptations.

30 Special thanks to Peter Eiselmair and Gerhard Kaiserseder from Education Group GmbH, Linz, for providing the opportunity to view some of these films.

31 The film's production year remains unknown, but it predates September 1, 1971, as it was first listed in a distribution program published on that date. *Hans im Glück* (Lucky Hans, 1973) was initially also planned as a hand-drawn animated film, as evidenced by drafts from Rudolf Enter's estate dated 1970 (thanks to Michael Enter).

32 According to VÖFA archivist Egon Stoiber, the film was created for the annual *Internationale Puppentheatertage Mistelbach* (International Days of Puppetry Mistelbach), Austria's largest puppet theater festival (email to the author, dated August 21, 2023).

33 In Rudolf Enter's estate, another self-published guidebook titled *Kraut und Rüben: Aus der Praxis für die Praxis von Film- und Video-Amateuren* (Topsy-Turvy: From the Practice for the Practice of Film and Video Amateurs) has been preserved (thanks to Michael Enter).

34 These were animated films based on brief jokes, featured as closing segments in the programs.

35 Michael Enter provided the life data in a telephone conversation with the author on October 20, 2023. Helene Enter, also known as Helli, Hely, or Helly, worked as a costume designer and camera assistant on many of her husband's films.

10 "Cinema Is Not Movement"
Animated Experiments

During the post-World War II avant-garde movement, also known as neo-avant-garde, "Austria, and especially Vienna, were among the major and leading European avant-garde centers" (Fähnders 2020: 14). The 1950s and 1960s witnessed the rise of the *Wiener Gruppe* (Vienna Group) and *Wiener Aktionismus* (Viennese Actionism) as prominent artistic movements. This phenomenon also had a direct influence on animated advertising films. Hans Albala (1919–1976), who operated his own studio and produced animated commercials between 1955 and 1965, is now recognized as the "first representative of experimental animation in Austria" (Renoldner 2010: 113).

In the past, the animation aspect of Austrian avant-garde films was often neglected in film-theoretical studies. As late as the 1990s, film theorist Scott MacDonald (b. 1942) observed: "The two areas of Austrian avant-garde film I am familiar with are Otto Mühl's 'material action films' and the formalist works of Peter Kubelka and Kurt Kren; both [Kubelka and Kren] worked frame by frame, but not as animators" (MacDonald 1995: 286). Ernst Schmidt Jr. (1938–1988) became one of the first to acknowledge a blurring of the "boundaries between animation and live-action film" (Schmidt 1985: 35) in avant-garde cinema.[1] However, he did not attribute any animation effect to Kurt Kren's (1929–1998) stop-motion film *2/60: 48 Köpfe aus dem Szondi-Test* (2/60: 48 Heads from the Szondi Test, 1960), arguing that "the individual images still remain recognizable as static photographs" (Schmidt 1985: 35). Nonetheless, Austrian avant-garde films are evidently linked to animation, featuring numerous hybrid works alongside purely animated films.

"KRITZI KRATZI": METHODS OF EXPERIMENTATION

Film scholar Franziska Proksa (née Bruckner in 1981) differentiated among three types of animation employed in Austrian avant-garde cinema (cf. Bruckner 2011: 77–80). Firstly, stop motion, a technique with a longstanding presence in Austria since 1914, was utilized in *1/57: Versuch mit synthetischem Ton* (1/57: Experiment with Synthetic Sound, 1957)[2] by Kurt Kren and in the pseudo-documentary *Steine* (Stones, 1964/1965) directed by Ernst Schmidt Jr. Other notable examples include *Zimmerlinde* (Indoor Lime, 1975) by Karl Neubacher (1926–1978) from Graz, which features the systematic reduction of an indoor plant to its trunk, and *Lichtblitze* (Light Flashes, 1981) by Lisl Ponger (b. 1947), in which single-frame shots were assembled to create a time-lapse effect.

DOI: 10.1201/9781003415442-12

According to Franziska Proksa, a second animation technique in avant-garde film is fast cutting, a method prominently featured in the cinematic works of Peter Kubelka (b. 1934) and Kurt Kren. Early examples by Kubelka include *Adebar* (1957), *Schwechater* (1958), and *Arnulf Rainer* (1960). Commissioned by the Viennese café of the same name, *Adebar* (1957) showcased black-and-white footage of dancing figures, arranged according to precise rules. As Petra Erdmann notes, it was "the world's first structural film" (film description at sixpackfilm.com) and is recognized as the inaugural representation of *Wiener Formalfilm* (Viennese Film Formalism), where form takes precedence over content. *Schwechater* (1958), also an advertising film, depicted women drinking beer, sponsored by the beer company of the same name, from champagne glasses. Kubelka's rhythmic montage of individual images in this film exemplifies the use of fast cutting in avant-garde filmmaking: "Cinema is not movement. Cinema is a projection of stills – which means images which do not move – in a very quick rhythm" (Peter Kubelka, as cited in Mekas 1970: 291). The client was so shocked by the outcome that the film wasn't even released – Kubelka had to secretly retrieve it from the film laboratory. In *Arnulf Rainer* (1960), named after the Viennese artist Arnulf Rainer (b. 1929), Kubelka interspersed individual frames of blank and black film with a soundtrack of background noise and silence. This created alternating sequences of light and darkness, silence and noise. "At the film's premiere, the entire audience, who had expected a documentary about Rainer, reportedly left the theater" (Schmidt 1985: 35). Kurt Kren also explored an artist's work in his film *11/65: Bild Helga Philipp* (11/65: Helga Philipp Painting, 1965). Helga Philipp (1939–2002) "is regarded as a pioneer of geometric abstraction in Austria" (Renoldner 2010: 122), with the concept of movement already inherent in her paintings.

The technique of direct animation, practiced by artists like Len Lye (1901–1980) and Norman McLaren (1914–1987), represents the third animation technique. In *Sonne Halt!* (Sun Stop!, 1962), described as one of "the first Austrian live-action avant-garde films" (Bruckner 2011: 79), Ferry Radax (1932–2021) employed direct animation: as a man fires at the sun, each shotgun blast releases swarms of dots and lines that stream toward it.[3] Ernst Schmidt Jr. repurposed leftover film stock to create a new film in *Filmreste* (Film Scraps, 1966), which he then painted over or etched with acid. In *Prost* (Cheers, 1968), he used a felt-tip pen to draw a line across a film strip until it reached the edge (Cheers!) and then continued in the opposite direction. He also created *Weiß* (White, 1968), where he punched holes in blank film using an office hole punch. That same year, Peter Weibel (1944–2023) created *Fingerprint* (1968) using his thumbprint. Kurt Kren's only foray into direct animation, *26/71: Zeichenfilm – Balzac und das Auge Gottes* (26/71: Cartoon – Balzac and the Eye of God, 1971), condensed the plot – the celebrated pleasure of breaking taboos – into just half a minute.[4] Additionally, a blend of live-action film and direct animation was explored by artists such as Bogdan Grbić (1935–2016), an immigrant from Belgrade, in his film *Kritzi Kratzi* (1972), which altered footage from Graz's city park, and Karl Kowanz (b. 1951) in his film *Miles Smiles* (1976), where party footage was scratched.

"BIRTH OF VENUS": THE FEMININE FORCE BEHIND THE ANIMATION FRAMES

In the early 1970s, Austrian animation underwent a significant transformation. Following the decline of animated commercials in the mid-1960s, there was a notable decrease in the number of animators, with most having either "passed away, emigrated, or increasingly dedicated themselves to the production of live-action films" (Bruckner 2011: 76). Only Hans O. Sindelar (1921–2014) and Rudolf Enter (1927–2017) continued producing animated puppet films for state television and the state-owned film department, while Richard Fehsl (b. 1937) and Ferdinand 'Ferry' Unger (1938–2011) remained the last advocates of hand-drawn animation. In addition to their individual projects, Fehsl and Unger collaborated closely for over three decades, including a partnership with the Italian production company *Corona Cinematografica* in the mid-1970s to create the animated fairy tale film *Die Sonne* (Il Sole/The Sun, 1976).[5] Their collaboration continued with projects such as the German educational film *Die Haut* (The Skin, 1996) and the German animated Bible film *Die Ostergeschichte* (The Easter Story, 2005).[6] Ferry Unger also gained recognition for his expertise as a cameraman for complex trick shots, notably producing a kaleidoscopic color play for the *Farbversuchsprogramm* (Color Test Program, 1969) of Austrian state television.[7]

Amid the decline of the animation film industry, there was a growing demand for a film funding law in Austria at the start of the 1970s. In response, the Austrian Federal Ministry of Education and Arts revised its approach to film funding in 1973. Previously, funds from the 'Kulturgroschen' (cultural penny, a tax on cinema tickets) were primarily allocated as structural or corporate funding, but the focus shifted to project-based funding. In July 1973, a 'Filmbeirat' (Film Advisory Board) was established to determine which film projects merited support based on their artistic and social significance. However, it wasn't until November 1980 that Austria finally introduced a comprehensive film funding law, making it the last country in Western Europe to do so. This law also included a 'small film funding' for experimental films and video art.[8] Perhaps due to the previous lack of support, there was a scarcity of emerging animation artists and avant-gardists in Austria during the 1970s: "New names from this period are rare" (Tscherkassky 1995: 64).

The fact that this 'gap' was filled by several significant female animation and avant-garde artists, "who confidently and militantly pursued their very own artistic concepts" (Renoldner 2010: 126), is particularly noteworthy. One such artist, VALIE EXPORT[9] (née Waltraud Lehner in 1940), attended the *Kunstgewerbeschule Linz* (School of Fine Art Linz) from 1955 to 1958 before moving to Vienna in the early 1960s and transitioning to film in 1965. "Although her oeuvre seemingly had no direct impact on practical work in animation, her radical attitude, multi-disciplinary approach, and her autonomous standpoint make her a clear identification figure for later-born artists" (Lang 2019: 92). Through her work as a filmmaker, she demonstrated that women artists could shape and utilize the medium of film according to their own preferences, including in the realm of animated film. Another remarkable artist is Moucle Blackout (née Christiane Engländer in 1935), who was born in Prague (Czech Republic) and moved to Salzburg at the age of 3. She studied at the University of Applied Arts Vienna[10] from 1958 to 1967 and produced her first film in 1969, but "she began to take more creative freedom starting in 1972 with her next film, *Die Geburt der Venus* (Birth of Venus)" (Tscherkassky 1995: 65). This film, created between 1970 and 1972, is notable for Blackout's use of photographs of four friends and a dead pig, combined into a photo-animation at a professional animation stand in Hamburg, Germany. She experimented with reflections along the central axis and, through explicit depictions, created a 'love story' set to the rhythm of three Beatles songs, using the pig to symbolize the woman as a sexual victim. These women artists have pushed boundaries and redefined the film medium to suit their artistic visions.

During the same period, Maria Lassnig (1919–2014) also ventured into the world of animation. After studying painting at the Academy of Fine Arts Vienna (1940–1944),[11] Lassnig initially pursued a career as a paintress in Austria and France. Encouraged by friends like American artist Nancy Spero (1926–2009), who predicted she would find success in New York, Lassnig relocated to the Big Apple in 1968.[12] However, her work was considered too Austrian for the US art scene, and it was described as "strange" and "morbid" (Kunz (ed.) 1989: 100). Undeterred, Lassnig found a new avenue for artistic expression in animation.[13] Around 1970, she enrolled in an *Animation Production Techniques* course at the School of Visual Arts (SVA) and acquired a film camera.[14] Between 1970 and 1976, she created nine 'canonical' films, along with numerous unfinished or unreleased works (cf. 'Filmography' in Kondor et al. (eds.) 2021: 151–180).[15] Her first hand-drawn animated film, *Encounter* (1970), brought her original drawings to life through single-frame animation, a process she referred to as "Beseelung (ensoulment)" (Kondor et al. (eds.) 2021: 157). In *Chairs* (1971), chairs moved to music like people, evoking the style of the first Polish animated film, *Flirt krzesełek* (Flirting Chairs, 1916 or 1917).[16] In the autobiographical animated film *Selfportrait* (1971), Lassnig humorously depicted herself as the "[Lady] Liberty of Austria" in a self-deprecating manner (Figure 10.1). In 1972, she was awarded the *New York State Council Prize* for this film. *Shapes* (1972) featured stencil spray-painted body silhouettes that gradually accelerated, blurring the lines between male and female. Similarly, *Couples* (1972) employed various techniques, including cutout animation, to explore communication and copulatory dysfunctions between genders by reducing bodies to fleshy organ beings. While her films did not prioritize professional camera and studio techniques, they all reflected, to some extent, her concept of "body-awareness-painting" (Maria Lassnig, as cited in Bruckner 2011: 86). Though feminist approaches were present in Lassnig's paintings, they were more prominently expressed in her films: "In my films, I definitely expressed my feminist ideas, but never in my paintings" (Maria Lassnig, as cited in Bruckner 2011: 92). Consequently, in 1974, Lassnig co-founded *Women/Artist/Filmmakers, Inc.*, an association of feminist film artists. Her feminist critique was particularly evident in *Art Education* (1976), where she humorously reinterpreted male-dominated art history.

Maria Lassnig may not have focused as much on film work as she did on painting, but her influence on Austrian animation is regarded as highly significant.[17] Animator and historian Thomas Renoldner (b. 1960) has even gone so far as to divide Austrian

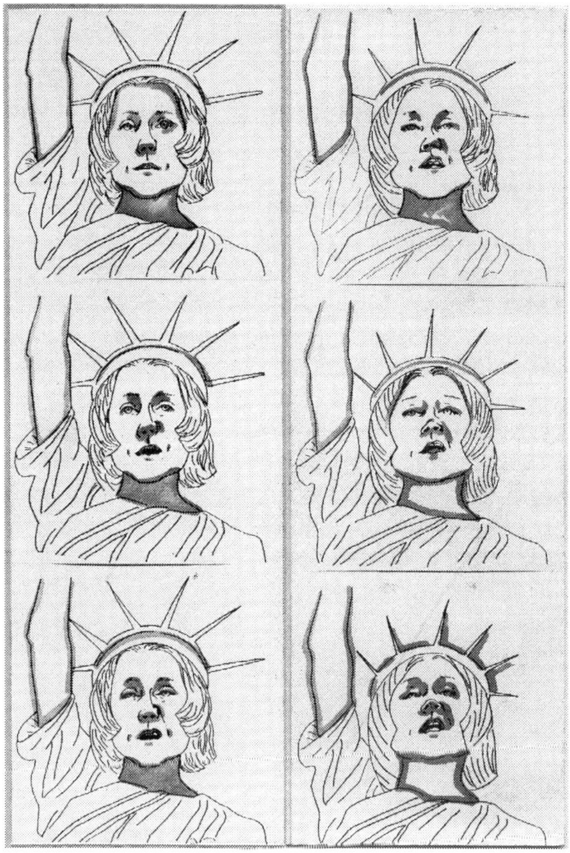

FIGURE 10.1 Maria Lassnig as 'Lady Liberty of Austria'; collage of single frames from the film *Selfportrait* (1971). (Courtesy of Archive of the Maria Lassnig Foundation, Vienna.)

animation history into "animation before Lassnig" and "animation after Lassnig" (Renoldner 2010. 41).[18] Since 2022, the prestigious *Maria Lassnig Golden Film Reel* has been awarded as the top prize in the international competition at the annual animation film festival *Tricky Women/Tricky Realities* in Vienna, with the award winners proudly carrying it out into the world.

Renate Kordon (b. 1952) is another notable female animator and one of the pioneering female animation artists in the avant-garde scene in Austria. Originally from Graz, Styria, she pursued architecture at the Technical University of Vienna and Graz from 1970 to 1974 before studying graphic design at the University of Applied Arts Vienna, where she graduated in 1978. Her foray into animation began during her student years, leading to the creation of her first 12-second cutout animated film, *Glühbirne* (Bulb, 1976). Three years later, she produced *Augenblicke* (Blinks of an Eye, 1979). With a scholarship, Kordon attended the animation and video class at the *École Nationale Supérieure des Arts Décoratifs* (ENSAD) in Paris, France, from 1980 to 1981, where she created the animated film *Hors d'œuvre* (1981). Notably, this film mesmerizingly showcased a play of black lines synchronized with the sound of zippers, undergoing constant transformation and challenging conventional viewing habits. In 1982, Kordon shared her expertise as a visiting artist professor at the Lawrence Institute of Technology in Detroit, USA. The emotional world was a pivotal element in Kordon's work from the beginning. For example, *Augenblicke* (Blinks of an Eye, 1979) explored the perception of time loss by portraying six moments as black images, ultimately declaring them a waste of time. In *Tageblätter* (Daily Drawings, 1980), 320 abstract structural drawings created between 1975 and 1980 were shown in fast motion, resembling a rollercoaster ride through the filmmaker's emotional world. Simultaneously, the resulting movement mirrored the very rhythm of the drawing process. After exploring the perception of time, *Passepartout* (1983/1984) shifted focus toward the perception of space – the film's rectangular frame was reflected in tables, windows, picture frames, and more. The orderly dominance of rectangles was intermittently disrupted by the recurring appearance of a bird's elegantly curved line, breaking through the structured confines (Figure 10.2).

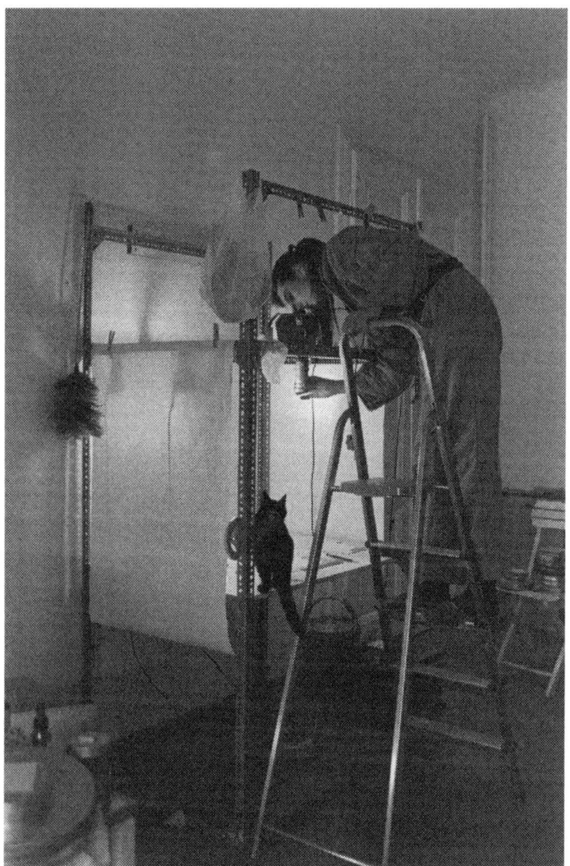

FIGURE 10.2 Renate Kordon, accompanied by her cat Kamikatze, capturing single frames with a 16-mm camera for her film *Passepartout* (1984) at her custom-built animation stand. (Courtesy of Renate Kordon.)

Renate Kordon's artistic work exhibited parallels to that of Maria Lassnig. Just as Lassnig critiqued the male-dominated art history in *Art Education* (1976), Kordon addressed and deconstructed the voyeuristic male gaze often depicted in the works of the 'old masters' in *Malerin* (Paintress, 1984). This film, which wasn't released to the public until 2008, features a recitation of the names of female artists, including Maria Lassnig and the German animator Lotte Reiniger (1899–1981). Another striking similarity to Lassnig's work is evident: "One is struck by the frequent focus on the body, which becomes the actual medium and catalyst of the animation and which is sometimes used and abused as a projection screen or reduced to stuttering individual frames" (Steinlechner 2013: 146). In *Buntes Blut* (Colourful Blood, 1985), a body was used as a painting surface, with its breathing movements appearing to animate the signs and symbols. Kordon's public art projects further expanded on the concept of the moving image, utilizing natural energies like wind and the earth's rotation instead of electricity to bring her art to life in public spaces:

"In *Windspiel Spielfeld* (Wind Chimes at Spielfeld, 1990/91), located at the border station to Slovenia above the twelve lanes of the highway, wind activates figure wheels that are suspended within a delicate steel network. As drivers pass through, their spatial perception shifts. In *Jahreszeiten-Sonnenuhr* (Sundial of the Seasons, 2009) in Schottwien at Semmering, movement is created by the Earth's rotation. The sun acts as the projector, while the main road through the town becomes the screen, displaying the moving shadow of the monumental bridge that spans the area. The artist marked the seasonal zones directly on the road" (Renate Kordon in an email to the author, dated November 7, 2023).

Throughout her extensive career, spanning over 40 years and nearly as many films, Renate Kordon has consistently demonstrated her passion for experimentation in cinema. Her work encompasses a wide range of techniques, from the paper-drawn animation of *Hors d'œuvre* (1981) and cel animation in *Passepartout* (1983/1984) to painted animation in *Buntes Blut* (Colourful Blood, 1985), clay animation in *Tonfilm* (Clay Film, 1986), and pixilation in *Raumfahrt* (Space Trip, 1989). Kordon's versatility extends to her film installations, with works such as *Trickptychon* (Trickptych, 1987)[19] using paper cutouts, *Echo* (1988) featuring modeling clay animation, *Jetzt für jetzt* (Now for Now, 1988) scratched directly onto film, and *Es schert* (Scissoring, 1989/1990) employing stop motion. Embracing the digital era, she ventured into computer animation with *Dancing Sculptures* (2001), showcasing line drawings that evoke steel figures on a photomontage. Even in the current decade, Kordon remains active, exemplified by her collaboration with Graz-based Australian musician Tamara Friebel (b. 1975) on the music video *Sun's a Sister* (2022). In this project, she utilized digital drawings on scanned, scratched slide material, further highlighting her innovative approach to animation.[20]

Bärbel Neubauer (b. 1959) moved from Klagenfurt (Carinthia) to Vienna in 1978 to study Stage Design and Film at the University of Applied Arts Vienna until 1983. Although the course primarily focused on stage design, Neubauer independently explored live-action film production starting in 1980. In 1983, she created her first partially abstract, partially figurative animated film, *OH,* by painting images on her room wall and filming them frame by frame. She then produced her first fully abstract film, *Mond und Tiger* (Moon and Tiger, 1984/1985), a 7-minute piece based on oil pastel drawings on paper. Notably, when the Austrian director Peter Schreiner's (1957–2023) film *Auf dem Weg* (On the Way, 1986–1990) was showcased at a film retrospective in 2020, he specifically requested *Mond und Tiger* (Moon and Tiger) as the supporting film:

"I appreciate the film because it embodies the essence of time-intensive creation – painted frame by frame – while also capturing the spontaneity of the creative process. The result is a captivating flow that draws the viewer into the action. For me, it exemplifies a core quality of cinema that I often encounter during editing: the emergence of something entirely new through the sequencing of shots – a flow that wasn't foreseeable in the initial concept or during filming but ultimately defines the film itself" (Peter Schreiner, as cited in Huber 2020a, under 'Auf dem Weg').

Before moving to Munich (Germany) in 1987, Neubauer explored various animation techniques. In her work *Dame* (Lady, 1985), she skillfully employed stop motion. Similarly, in *Zwischen Tier und Schatten* (Between Animal and Shadow, 1986), Neubauer utilized "the cutout technique in such a minimalist way that it outshone *South Park*" (Renoldner 2010: 138). Notably, Bärbel Neubauer, Moucle Blackout, Maria Lassnig, and Renate Kordon were among the pioneering advocates of a new, more feminine Austrian animation.

EVOLVING AUSTRIAN ANIMATION: FROM PERSONAL CRAFT TO TEAM ART

Another notable artist in the late 1970s was Herbert Werner Franke (1927–2022), a Viennese artist who had relocated to Germany after earning a doctorate in physics in 1950. Franke was an early adopter of computer graphics, beginning as early as the 1950s. Notably, in the early 1970s, he created the experimental computer film *Rotationen/Projektionen* (Rotations/Projections, 1970/1971), which was used as a background projection for an avant-garde ballet performance at the Bavarian State Opera's experimental stage in 1974 (Figure 10.3):

"By restricting the film to black and white, the graphic elements are accentuated: networks of lines, as well as parallel and circular strokes, are rendered with mathematical and geometric precision. These elements continuously fill the frame, expand, and then are gradually erased. This rigorous graphic approach and clarity define the distinctive style of his film *Rotationen* [Rotations]" (Jenewein 1978: 4).

Herbert W. Franke carried forward the legacy of Marc Adrian (1930–2008), an Austrian avant-garde filmmaker credited with creating Europe's first computer-generated film, *Random* (1963). In 1979, Franke co-founded *Ars Electronica*, an art and technology festival in Linz (Upper Austria). Peter Putz (b. 1954) is best known for his work on *Das Ewige Archiv* (The Eternal Archives), a dynamic encyclopedia capturing contemporary realities since 1980.[21] His interest in filmmaking was sparked by exposure to Norman McLaren's animated films during a study trip to Poznań (Poland) from 1977 to 1978.[22] With assistance from the film club in Poznań, Putz learned the basics of animation and created the film *Obuwie* (Shoes, 1977/1978),

FIGURE 10.3 Stills from Herbert W. Franke's *Rotationen/Projektionen* (Rotations/Projections, 1974). (Courtesy of ZKM Center for Art and Media Karlsruhe, Herbert W. Franke Archive (Permission by Susanne Päch).)

which consisted of 674 drawings depicting the metamorphosis of a shoe drawn with a felt-tip pen. Putz stated that the film was produced over a span of 6–7 weeks. This initial film won several awards at various film festivals, including those held in Bydgoszcz (Poland) in 1988 and Linz (Upper Austria) in 1989. When the morphing effect debuted in music videos during the mid-1980s, Putz created the animated film *Das Universum* (The Universe, 1985/1986), replicating the morphing effect using analog techniques.[23] Building on this innovation, in *Gelati Per Tutti* (1987), Putz artfully incorporated photographs from newspapers featuring individuals showcasing oversized objects like freshly caught fish or homegrown vegetables, which were then traced and altered. Additionally, in *TV Montezuma* (1987/1988), Putz combined live action and pixilation, drawing, and video art. From 1988 to 1989, he served as an artist-in-residence at the animation film department of Concordia University Montreal (Canada), where he and his wife, Barbara Putz-Plecko (née Plecko in 1956), co-produced the 20-minute film *Mont Real* (1988/1989), blending live action and animation. Lastly, between 1991 and 1993, Putz created numerous signations (animated title credits) for the children's program of *Österreichischer Rundfunk* (ORF, Austrian Broadcasting Corporation), utilizing a variety of analog and digital animation techniques.

In 1978, a short-lived animation collective called *Der Hammer* (The Hammer) was established, eventually giving rise to the *TRIFI Studio* in Vienna.[24] Although the group produced only one film, *Ohne Titel* (No Title, 1979),[25] co-founder Renate

Kordon later described this period, marked by intense film discussions, as "very intense" (Renate Kordon, as cited in Bruckner 2011: 83). Alongside Kordon, the founding members included future Oscar winner Zbigniew 'Zbig' Rybczyński (b. 1949) from Poland and his assistant Manfred Haspel (b. 1955). Starting in 1977, Rybczyński's ventures frequently took him between Austria and Poland. In 1982, he was granted political asylum in Austria and remained in Vienna until emigrating to the USA in 1983. During his time in Austria, he created films such as *Mein Fenster* (My Window, 1979) and *Schneideraum* (Cutting Room) aka *Media* (1979), with assistance from Haspel.[26] Rybczyński achieved "impressive visual effects using 35 mm techniques and intricate trick devices, creating the illusion of suspended gravity" (Schmidt 1982: 407). Haspel later went on to produce his own animated films, including *Kopflos* (Headless, 1980).[27] The fourth member, Hubert Sielecki (b. 1946), explored film and animation while studying at the University of Applied Arts Vienna from 1968 to 1973.[28] He then pursued animation and painting at the Łódź Film School (PWSFTviT) in Poland from 1975 to 1976 with the help of an international scholarship. Sielecki maintained close ties with the Austrian avant-garde scene in the 1970s, exemplified by his 1976 work with felt-tip pens on paper, which Ernst Schmidt Jr. captured using a single-frame technique, later becoming an animated scene in his feature film *Die totale Familie* (The Total Family, 1981). This connection led Sielecki to establish the *Studio für experimentellen Trickfilm* (Studio for Experimental Animated Film) in Maria Lassnig's master class at the University of Applied Arts Vienna in 1982, initiating a new era in Austrian animation.

A TRUE POET OF THE LENS: MAX VRECER

Maximilian 'Max' Vrecer (1951–2010) holds a special place in cinematography. Nicknamed "Mister Fantasy" (Profil, (12), March 21, 1983: 66) by the press and hailed as the "poet of the lens" (as cited in Ulrich 2004: 551) by Terry Southern (1924–1995), an author associated with Stanley Kubrick (1928–1999), Vrecer's passion for filmmaking began remarkably early. It is said that the renowned cinematographer and director harbored aspirations of a film career as early as 4 years old. He started shooting his first film at 15, using his father's Super 8 camera, and by 16, he was already working for the Styrian regional studio of Austrian television ORF, all while still attending school. One of his early works as a cinematographer, *Magic Graz* (1970), directed by Curt M. Faudon (1949–2019) and commissioned by ORF, garnered attention as the opening film of the *Viennale* (Vienna) in 1971 and as a competition entry at the Cannes Film Festival (France) in May 1972. However, Vrecer's innovative style faced criticism from the Austrian press for deviating from conventional norms: "With rapid camera movements and abrupt cuts, he [Vrecer] crafted an aesthetic and dynamism that many found challenging to adapt to at the time" ('Nachruf Max Vrecer' 2010, 00:00:18). This was followed by the tourism film *Wien zum Beispiel* (Vienna for Instance, 1972/1973), which was also screened at the *Viennale* and *Cannes Film Festival* in 1974, winning the *Prix ITB 74* at the *Internationale Tourismus-Börse* (ITB, International Tourism Exchange) in Berlin (Germany). Both films were honored with the *Austrian Cultural Film Prize*. Ultimately, Vrecer achieved international acclaim with his film *Österreich – In der Wiese liegen und mit der Seele baumeln* (Austria – Lying in the Meadow and

Dangling with Your Soul, 1976), produced for the Austrian National Tourist Office. The film, described as "an impressive film collage of captivating images, sophisticated tricks, and clever editing" (Profil, (12), March 21, 1983: 66), won first prize at ITB Berlin in 1977.

During this period, the ambitious self-taught filmmaker Max Vrecer also ventured into animated films, addressing a void in the 1970s.[29] In 1975, over the summer break, he utilized a school building in his Styrian hometown of Unterpremstätten, near Graz, to create the animated film *Der kleine schwarze Fisch* (The Little Black Fish, 1975/1976).[30] The production involved 12 local painters and graphic artists, all working "in Vrecer's characteristic haste" (Profil, (12), March 21, 1983: 66). Under the supervision of a lead draftsman from Vienna, around 10,000 phase drawings and watercolor backgrounds were produced in a drawing room, while Vrecer animated the characters at an improvised animation stand (Figure 10.4 and 10.5). Depending on the scene, a single movement required 80–250 individual drawings. The project,

FIGURE 10.4 The team working with Max Vrecer in the summer of 1975 in the art room of a school during the production of *Der kleine schwarze Fisch* (The Little Black Fish, 1976). (Courtesy of Bettina Haintz and Leah Vrecer.)

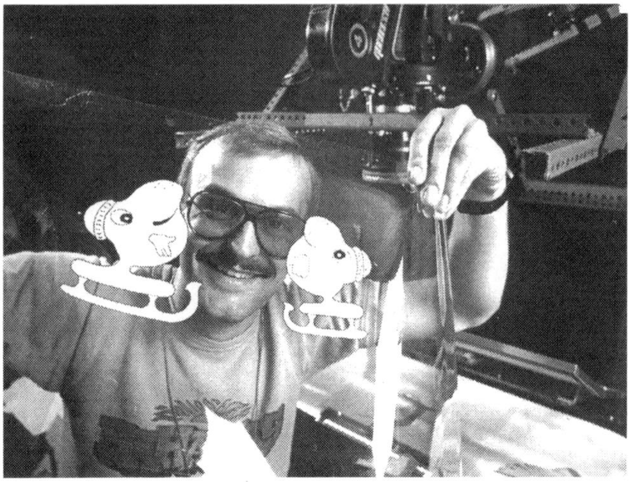

FIGURE 10.5 Max Vrecer in 1975, holding a cel from *Der kleine schwarze Fisch* (The Little Black Fish, 1976) at his improvised animation stand. (Courtesy of Bettina Haintz and Leah Vrecer.)

aimed at international distribution in multiple language versions, received financial backing from the cultural film funding provided by the Austrian Federal Ministry of Education and Art. Based on a Persian fairy tale, the film follows the adventurous journey of a small black fish seeking a more fulfilling life in the sea, far from the troubles of its home pond. The children's film, with a screenplay adapted by psychologist Thomas Schwinger (b. 1948), explores the theme of maturation through experiences:

"The characters include a militaristic crab, a sinister cormorant, mother figures, friends, clever types, and comedic ones. The fish itself is somewhat anti-authoritarian, cheeky, yet also humorous and immensely likable. I believe these characters and their adventures offer even the youngest children opportunities for identification" (Max Vrecer in 'Zeichentrickfilm 'Der kleine schwarze Fisch'' 1976, 00:02:48).

Starting in 1974, Max Vrecer incorporated animation and trick techniques into political advertising, creating election commercials for the *Österreichische Volkspartei* (ÖVP, Austrian People's Party) that featured "sophisticated stunts, slow-motion, and time-lapse effects" (Profil, (12), March 21, 1983: 66). Vrecer's work included producing two campaign films for then-Styrian governor Friedrich Niederl (1920–2012), which creatively blended animation and live-action footage. For example, in *Steirische Kraft* (Styrian Power, c. 1977), Vrecer incorporated an animation sequence where a slipper morphs into the shape of Austria and back again, followed by Niederl bending a tire in Styrian state colors, depicted in both animated and live-action scenes. In the film *Modell Steiermark* (Model Styria, c. 1977), aerial shots capture an eagle's viewpoint, transitioning into an animation featuring the "Styrian Power Egg" with Niederl's caricatured face, which later comes to life in front of the Federal Chancellery in Vienna. This is followed by an animation sequence created by the renowned Austrian cartoonist Manfred Deix

(1949–2016), a close friend of Vrecer. The sequence showed two Styrians preventing the 'disfigurement' of Styria by sawing down a skyscraper, followed by exaggerated peasants descending a mountain in Deix's distinctive style: "The Styrians are a wild mountain folk, fearlessly roaming all the valleys of the land. They're not entirely without danger, but they love their children." Niederl's final statement could also be seen as a nod to the film's self-irony: "Democracy also means questioning oneself."

At the end of the 1970s, Max Vrecer created the animated film *Hasiba* (1978) for Franz Hasiba (b. 1932), who was then the second deputy mayor of Graz. The film portrays little brownies guarding the city from the Graz clock tower and implementing Hasiba's political initiatives, such as halting high-rise construction, creating green spaces, expanding public transportation, building playgrounds, and revitalizing the old city. In their efforts, the brownies also resort to magic, using 'Hasiba' as their incantation. Similarly, Vrecer produced two elaborate CinemaScope advertising films with special effects for the then-Viennese deputy mayor Erhard Busek (1941–2022). In *Superman über Wien* (Superman Over Vienna, c. 1978),[31] an animated brownie contacts Busek for help when an excavator threatens to demolish a small house on the outskirts of Vienna. Busek, standing in front of St. Stephen's Cathedral, reveals a superhero costume under his jacket and flies over the Burgtheater and City Hall to the suburban area. Using the 'V sign' representing the *Volkspartei* (People's Party), he transforms the excavator into a toy vehicle, which then retreats without causing any harm, using a stop-motion technique. In *Superman gegen Dinosaurier* (Superman vs. Dinosaurs, 1983),[32] Vrecer incorporated Busek's colorful bird mascot, which Busek used to promote an ecological image. In this film, Busek shoos away a flock of animated birds from his office desk, which then attacks an animated dinosaur symbolizing the 'bureaucratic dinosaurs,' driving it out of the city.

Starting in 1979, Max Vrecer increasingly spent time working in Hollywood: "I was thrilled and impressed by the support, the atmosphere, the crew, and the professionalism" (Vrecer n.d. - b, under 'Poet der Linse'). At the time, Vrecer observed that while young film artists in Austria received initial support, they eventually hit a dead end where that support dwindled. In the "center of the film world" (Max Vrecer in 'Österreicher in den USA' 1985, 00:50:26), he not only worked on international advertising campaigns for major clients like *Sony* but also directed the music video *Olympia* (1984) for Sérgio Santos Mendes (1941–2024). Created during the 1984 Olympic Games in Los Angeles, Vrecer chose to use painted backgrounds in the video for cost efficiency – a technique he had hoped to implement upon his return to Austria, though he struggled to find a suitable artist there. According to Vrecer, Austria also lacked the boldness to undertake large-scale film projects like *E.T. the Extra-Terrestrial* (1982):

"There are certain ideas and concepts that, when you share them in Austria, people say, 'You can't do that here; that's only possible in Hollywood.' But the truth is, we'll end up making it happen in Austria, just from a base in Hollywood" (Max Vrecer in 'Österreicher in den USA: Los Angeles' 1985, 00:54:24).

In the mid-1980s, for instance, Max Vrecer created another ÖVP election commercial in Hollywood, employing an art illustrator for the backgrounds and small animations. It is rumored that even *Disney* approached Vrecer, but he chose to return to Austria in 1987, stating: "To me, Vienna and Austria are the most beautiful places in the world" (Vrecer n.d. - a). Even in 2009, shortly before his passing, Vrecer continued to dream of producing an animated feature film. In Austria, however, Max Vrecer is nearly forgotten, and his contributions to the world of animation remain almost invisible.[33]

NOTES

1 Ernst Schmidt Jr. is recognized as the filmmaker "who, during the 1980s, actively fostered the dialogue between avant-garde and animated film, both as an artist and as an author" (Renoldner 2010: 127).
2 The synthetic sound that gave the film its name was produced by scratching the soundtrack directly onto the film material.
3 In the original 1959 version of the film, Ferry Radax relied entirely on stop-motion techniques, but much of the film was destroyed during development. However, Radax incorporated the surviving stop-motion footage into the final version of the film.
4 During its screening, the film was "shown twice, in case the viewer missed something the first time" (Regina Cornwell, as cited in Canyon Cinema (ed.) 1992: 204).
5 The Italian-Austrian co-production was submitted for censorship in 1976: "It does not mean it was made that year, it means that the request by the company Corona Cinematografica to have a censorship visa was made in 1976 (March the 31st) and the censorship commission approved the same year (June the 1st)" (email from Andrea Meneghelli of the *Cineteca di Bologna*, dated February 15, 2024). An online database from the *British Film Institute* (BFI), which is no longer accessible, dated the film to 1974, while Eigner (2013: 102) placed it as early as 1968. The film was also aired on June 13, 1978, as part of the series *Märchen der Völker* (Fairy Tales of the Peoples) on the German TV channel ZDF (cf. Jerrendorf 1985: 148).
6 The film *Die Ostergeschichte* (The Easter Story, 2005) was re-edited and extended in 2009, following the recommendation of the production company *STUMM-FILM*, to make the narrative more suitable for children. Unfortunately, Ferry Unger's name was mistakenly left out of the credits in the revised version (email from Nikolaus Weißenhorn, dated February 27, 2024).
7 Even into the 1990s, Ferry Unger remained active as a graphic artist and animator on various ORF projects, including the award-winning documentary *Die Entstehung der Alpen* (The Formation of the Alps, 1997). This documentary was also adapted into a shortened version for distribution as an educational film in schools.
8 The law took effect in May 1981.
9 VALIE EXPORT conceives her artist's name both "as an artistic concept and logo, with the provision that it only be written in capital letters" (Mader 2007: 380).
10 The *Universität für angewandte Kunst Wien* (University of Applied Arts Vienna) attained university status only at the end of 1998; before that, it was known as the *Hochschule für angewandte Kunst Wien* (College of Applied Art Vienna) from 1970 to 1998 and the *Akademie für angewandte Kunst Wien* (Academy of Applied Art Vienna) from 1948 to 1970. This chapter will refer to it as the University of Applied Arts Vienna for simplicity.
11 Maria Lassnig completed her studies in December 1944, with her diploma being issued in January 1945.
12 Maria Lassnig mentioned another reason for her move to New York: "Of course, it would have been possible to stay in Paris, but all Paris was Pop – that meant: influenced by America – so why not go straight to the source" (Maria Lassnig, as translated in Lettner 2022: 191).

13 Maria Lassnig also hoped to find work at an animation studio specializing in commercials and short films, which would provide her with a means to support herself.
14 The exact start date of Maria Lassnig's attendance in the course varies by source, with dates ranging from 1968 to 1971.
15 The 28 films not typically included in the artist's canon were produced in both the USA and Austria. Notably, *Seasons* (1970) marks Maria Lassnig's debut in animation, where she employed stop-motion techniques to bring paper cutouts to life.
16 The drawings for the film were created in Kraków during World War I, when the city was still officially part of Austria-Hungary. The film was later shot in a studio in Vienna.
17 In Austria, Maria Lassnig created just one animation film: *Maria Lassnig Kantate* (Maria Lassnig Cantata, 1992/1993).
18 Thomas Renoldner described "animation before Lassnig" as an era focused on commercial and advertising films, whereas "animation after Lassnig" is seen as a period defined by predominantly independent artistic endeavors (Renoldner 2010: 41).
19 The title plays on the term triptych; it was an animated film installation at the Vienna Secession featuring three projectors.
20 In the 2010s, Renate Kordon concentrated on various projects in public art, film installations, objects, painting, and more. She is now returning to a more prominent role in the field of animation (email to the author, dated November 3, 2023).
21 *Das Ewige Archiv* (The Eternal Archives) is available online at www.ewigesarchiv.at.
22 Peter Putz, who studied in the department of poster graphics at an art academy in Poznań (Poland), also designed a poster as a tribute to Norman McLaren's films.
23 The film, which remained incomplete as a pencil test, was digitally edited and scored in 2019 and subsequently released under the title *Universum* (Universe).
24 The studio's name is likely a shortened version of the German word 'Trickfilm' (animated film).
25 The film was produced without a camera, utilizing drawn and stamped optical sound.
26 Although it is debatable whether Zbigniew Rybczyński's experimental works qualify as animated films, filmmaker Thomas Renoldner (2010: 133) acknowledges Rybczyński's profound impact on the Austrian animation scene. In 1984, Rybczyński returned to the University of Applied Arts Vienna for a guest lecture.
27 Franziska Bruckner (2011: 83) offers an alternative date for the film, placing it in 1982.
28 Hubert Sielecki's first animated film, *Underground-Kino* (Underground Cinema, 1968), was rediscovered by the artist in his basement in 2006.
29 Apart from the avant-garde movement and the works of Hans O. Sindelar (for state television) and Rudolf Enter (for the state film service), another animated film was produced: *Die Sonne* (Il Sole/The Sun, 1974) by Richard Fehsl and Ferry Unger, commissioned by an Italian client. Additionally, Unger produced the animated film *Boro Bya* (1971) directed by Mansur Madavi (1942–2022), though nothing else is known about it.
30 In 1983, a press article noted that the animated film was "still being shown to children all across Austria" (Profil, (12), March 21, 1983: 66).
31 The film's dating ranges from 1972 to 1983, with Max Vrecer's own date being 1979. However, it was most likely created in the lead-up to the 1978 Vienna state election.
32 Max Vrecer dated the film to 1981, while ORF placed it in 1983, aligning with the year of the Vienna state election.
33 For instance, in response to an inquiry on September 20, 2023, the *Viennale* archive was unaware that Max Vrecer's *Magic Graz* (1970) had opened the 1971 *Viennale*. However, the author later uncovered a contemporary source that confirms this (cf. Rathaus-Korrespondenz, March 25, 1971: 869).

11 New Austrian Animated Film
Postmodernism in Motion

In the early 1980s, a new era of Austrian animated film, referred to by Ernst Schmidt Jr. (1938–1988) as the "new Austrian animated film" (Schmidt 1985: 34), began to take shape. The surge in animated filmmaking, along with the expansion of styles and themes, was driven not only by the societal changes of the time but also by a significant shift in artistic paradigms. The 1980s are widely recognized by art historians as a pivotal decade for modern art, characterized by a stylistic pluralism that signaled the advent of postmodernism. The bold, self-assured, and critical imagery that emerged from the 'rediscovery of painting' also found expression in animated films. From a technical perspective, the Super 8 film format flourished during this period; introduced in the 1960s, it reached its peak in sales by 1980. The proliferation of Super 8 film programs and festivals in the early 1980s reflected a sense of optimism within the film industry. The Austrian animated film scene benefited significantly from this trend, evolving from a largely Vienna-centric activity – with few exceptions – to a nationwide phenomenon during the 1980s. Just as Austrian animated film began to adopt a more feminine character in the 1970s, it also embraced a more rural identity in this new era.

COUNTRYSIDE CREATIVITY: THE RISE OF RURAL ANIMATION

During the 1980s, Linz, the capital of Upper Austria, became a significant hub for Austrian animated film. A major catalyst for this development was the founding of *Stadtwerkstatt* (Urban Workshop), an alternative cultural center, in 1979. Among its founding members were prominent filmmakers such as Franz Blaas (b. 1955), Thomas Steiner (b. 1956), and Wolfgang Paul Georgsdorf (b. 1959). Other notable animation filmmakers from Linz during this period included Georg Ritter (b. 1956), Leo Schatzl (b. 1958), and Christian Ruckerbauer (b. 1957).

The illustrator Franz Blaas initially collaborated on various film projects with Wolfgang Georgsdorf and Thomas Steiner before directing an independent film whose title aptly captures its essence: *10 Minuten im Finstern sitzen mit kurzen hellen Abschnitten und dumpfer Musik* (10 Minutes Sitting in the Dark with Short Bright Intervals and Muffled Music, 1981).[1] Even after two decades, Blaas, now based in Vienna, continued to produce animated films. For example, in collaboration with Peter Hauenschild (b. 1958), he created the animated film series *Four Songs for Tiger Lillies* (2002), which visually interprets songs like *Devine* and *Russians* by the British anarchist band *The Tiger Lillies.*[2]

 DOI: 10.1201/9781003415442-13

After collaborating with Franz Blaas on the animated film *Die Gestaltung* (The Design, 1980)[3] and engaging in various independent film projects, Thomas Steiner pursued further studies at the *Studio für experimentellen Trickfilm* (Studio for Experimental Animated Film) at the University of Applied Arts Vienna in 1985/1986.[4] From 1987 onward, he focused on creating abstract animated films, initially employing traditional drawing techniques. A notable work from this period is *Ikonostasis* (Iconostasis, 1990), where he captured images of an installation of the same name, gradually intertwining them through increasingly rapid repetitions. Steiner later explored the dynamic potential of stained glass in his films, and from 2000 onward, he increasingly incorporated digital animation techniques into his work.

Wolfgang Georgsdorf, in collaboration with Franz Blaas, produced *Fascination* (1978), a film in which a kind of lava lamp was captured in sequential shots:

"The interruptions in the film created by the shutter release bridge the gap between rapid camera cuts and stop-motion, dramatically highlighting the shifting positions of the colored rings. This results in a mysterious, visually-musical object performance that could also be interpreted as an unconventional method of timekeeping" (email from Wolfgang Georgsdorf to the author, dated September 20, 2023).

Wolfgang Georgsdorf considers *Im Gehäuse* (In the Body Housing, 1981), which he co-produced with Georg Ritter, who served as his assistant, to be his first true animated film. A film program described the stop-motion sequence in this work as a "lyrical tumult of things" (Dziemballa et al. (eds.) 1983: [18]). In contrast, Georg Ritter condensed the duration of *Vierstunden* (Four Hours, 1982) to approximately 3 minutes by capturing an image every 4 seconds. In 2010, he co-founded the non-commercial television station DORF, later becoming its art director. This station also collaborates with the University of Art and Design Linz.

From the early 1980s to the late 1990s, Leo Schatzl explored the influence of mechanization and the manipulation of perception through technical means. In 1980, he released his first animated film, *Die Stadt ist ein Kreuz* (The City is a Cross). Additionally, in his animated film *Krieg etc.* (War etc., 1983), he created frame-by-frame animations using montage graphics and drawings of war toys, which he then electronically accelerated.

In the early 1980s, Christian Ruckerbauer created a series of 'single-frame films.' His work *350 Bilder von...* (350 Images of..., 1980/1981) displayed 350 drawings made between 1973 and 1981, each for just half a second. At the same time, *Familienfilm* (Family Film, 1980/1981) anticipated the later development of the computer effect known as morphing: "The faces of the family members are combined based on various precise concepts, to blend them into a unified whole while shifting the emphasis on individual faces" (Christian Ruckerbauer, as cited in Dziemballa et al. (eds.) 1983: [34]).

In Salzburg, a young Virgil Widrich (b. 1967) was inspired by a documentary about Walt Disney (1901–1966) and, at just 13 years old, created the animated film *Auch Farbe kann träumen* (Color Can Dream, 1980/1981). A year later, he brought a wooden insect monster to life in *Monster in Salzburg* (1982). Fast forward to 2002, Widrich received an Oscar nomination for his film *Copy Shop* (2000/2001), which skillfully blurred the boundaries between live action and animation.

In Innsbruck (Tyrol), Reinhold Bergmann (b. 1956) created notable animated films, including *Außervillgraten 1680–1980* (c. 1983), which utilized fast cutting to showcase all the gravestones in his hometown within just 30 seconds. Ansgar Schnitzer (1962–1993) also contributed to the Super 8 scene in Innsbruck with animated films like *Die Schlacht der Halmamandin* (The Battle of Halmamandin, c. 1983).[5] Additionally, animated films were produced in Vorarlberg, Austria's westernmost province, during the 1980s. Tone Fink (b. 1944), who would later become a founding member of *ASIFA Austria*, created the 22-minute stop-motion film *Fliegenfängerfahnen* (Flycatcher Flags, 1981). Collaborating with the "old master" Richard Fehsl (b. 1937),[6] he produced *Aus der Luft gegriffen* (Plucked Out of Thin Air, 1983), described as "a kind of animated sketchbook in which a series of disconnected ideas, fantasies, and studies are set in motion" (Renoldner 2010: 142). Vorarlberg's cultural isolation from the rest of Austria positioned Fink as a cultural outsider in a positive way, enabling him to challenge prevailing artistic conventions through his experimentation with a diverse range of materials.

TOM & JERRY IN VIENNA: THE STUDIO FOR EXPERIMENTAL ANIMATED FILM

In May 1983, the Austrian Film Museum curated its most extensive retrospective of animated films to date. The event was held under the patronage of Charles Martin 'Chuck' Jones (1912–2002), the legendary American animated filmmaker, who also attended as the guest of honor. The retrospective, titled *On the History of Animated Film*, presented entertainment films by *Disney* and others alongside avant-garde films on an equal footing. As part of the event, Chuck Jones himself presented his best films and live drew his most popular characters during a two-part lecture titled *Chuck Jones and the Joy of Animation* in front of an audience.

Film education was directly influenced by the growing interest in animated films. Established in 1952, the Film Academy Vienna served as the only university-level training center for the Austrian film industry. It wasn't until 30 years later that the University of Applied Arts Vienna founded the second training center for aspiring Austrian filmmakers, focusing exclusively on experimental animated film. The *Studio für experimentellen Trickfilm* (Studio for Experimental Animated Film) was launched at the end of 1982, thanks to the efforts of Prof. Maria Lassnig (1919–2014).

In 1980, Maria Lassnig made history as the first woman in the German-speaking world to hold a professorship in painting at the University of Applied Arts Vienna.[7] With a vision to establish an experimental animated film studio, she made this a key objective within her *Meisterklasse für Gestaltungslehre und experimentelles Gestalten* (Master Class for Design Theory and Experimental Design).[8] In October 1982, Lassnig brought on Hubert Sielecki (b. 1946), a fellow Carinthian, as a lecturer. Sielecki, who came highly recommended by Ernst Schmidt Jr., had studied animation at the film academy in Łódź, Poland, thanks to a scholarship. He was tasked with setting up an animation studio in a small 12-m^2 adjoining room, initially equipped with just a camera and a single-frame device (Figure 11.1). Sielecki humorously called it "the smallest film studio in the world" (Sielecki 1990: 95).[9] While he

FIGURE 11.1 Hubert Sielecki in 1984 at 'the smallest film studio in the world.' (Photographer: Jurislav Tscharyiski. Courtesy of Hubert Sielecki.)

began constructing his own animation stand, students started working on their first animation sequences. The initial trick exercises were recorded in December 1982, with the university covering the material and copying costs, while the Austrian public service broadcaster *Österreichischer Rundfunk* (ORF, Austrian Broadcasting Corporation) provided expired reversal film stock for these exercises and managed the film development process. By June 1983, the studio had expanded to include sound equipment, and Sielecki even built his own mixing consoles, which facilitated the production of the first sound films.[10] During his visit to Vienna, Chuck Jones was invited to the studio: "He was so impressed by the students' early experimental exercises that he gifted the university studio an authentic Hollywood animation light table, one that had once been used to animate 'Tom and Jerry'" (Hubert Sielecki, as cited in Bruckner 2011: 118).[11]

The first seven permanent students in the master class were Sabine Groschup (née Spatt in 1959), Guido Hoffmann (b. 1960), Gudrun Kampl (b. 1964), Rob Kasseckert (b. 1956), Renate Kordon (b. 1952), Mara Mattuschka (b. 1959), and Stefan Stratil (b. 1963). Through painstaking, often months-long efforts, they created 1- to 5-minute films, each distinct in style. Beyond animation, the students experimented with painting and collage techniques, integrating music, dialog, and sound to craft artificial film worlds. Notable early works include *Earth is an Exploding*

Building (1983) by Rob Kasseckert, a surrealist commentary on the dangers of nuclear war, and *Prometheus* (1983) by Stefan Stratil, a politically charged futuristic superhero tale in which the protagonist challenges a fascist ruling class and its robots. Sabine Groschup brought film equipment to life in *Komeru Kanfas* (1983), while Mara Mattuschka's *Vegetarisches Restaurant* (Vegetarian Restaurant, 1983) presents a dialog between a diner and his food. Gerlinde Thuma (b. 1962) produced *Abanaleballade* (A Banal Ballad, 1984), a somber black-and-white frame-by-frame animation depicting the episodic life of a bird. In her pixilation film *Nabel Fabel* (Navel Fable, 1984), Mara Mattuschka visualized the birth process by attempting to free her head from a stocking. Renate Kordon used abstract cutout silhouettes in *Olympus* (1984) to evoke an underwater world. A defining characteristic of the university studio was its near-complete rejection of the cel animation technique, which was prevalent in major studios at the time.

Within a year, the studio produced approximately 80 minutes of footage. By 1989, a total of 6 hours of material had been presented to the public. To foster international connections, the studio not only hosted guest speakers like the Polish-born Oscar winner Zbigniew Rybczyński (b. 1949) but also actively participated in various international film festivals. For example, in the spring of 1984, several students showcased their work at the second *Internationales Trickfilm-Festival Stuttgart* (ITFS, Stuttgart International Festival of Animated Film) in Germany. This led to further invitations, including one to a festival during the 1984 Summer Olympics in Los Angeles (USA). At the 1988 *Berlinale* in Berlin (Germany), 11 films were screened, and during the ITFS that same year, the term *Wiener Trickfilmschule* (Vienna School of Animated Film) was coined: "a label that gradually became synonymous with exceptionally inventive productions. The founding of this studio proved to be a pivotal catalyst for a wide range of creative activities" (Putz 1988: 32). Starting in the fall of 1984, students from the University of Klagenfurt (Carinthia) increasingly utilized the animation studio at the Institute for Educational Technology and Media Education for their projects, resulting in the creation of "remarkable short and experimental films" (Putz 1988: 32) there as well (Figure 11.2).

ASIFA AUSTRIA: THE GENESIS OF A CREATIVE MOVEMENT

In the early days, graduates in Vienna faced a challenging situation, as opportunities to pursue independent and cost-effective animation filmmaking beyond the university were scarce. This lack of prospects led Hubert Sielecki to establish an Austrian branch of the international animation umbrella organization *Association Internationale du Film d'Animation* (ASIFA) after meeting with John Halas (1912–1995), then president of ASIFA, at the *Annecy International Animation Film Festival* in 1984. The founding members, alongside Sielecki, included ten students,[12] as well as seasoned animators like Richard Fehsl, Ferry Unger (1938–2011), and Peter Putz (b. 1954).[13] Manfred Haspel (b. 1955), who was a member of the artist group *Der Hammer* (The Hammer) alongside Sielecki, also joined the effort. The team was completed by Gerda El-Masri (1941–2018), a graphic designer for the Austrian drama *Dicht hinter der Tür* (Just Behind the Door, 1984), and Tone Fink from Vorarlberg,

FIGURE 11.2 Student Claudia Hassler and some of her single frames at the animation stand at the University of Klagenfurt in 1984. (Courtesy of ewigesarchiv.at (Peter Putz).)

who had previously created the stop-motion film *Fliegenfängerfahnen* (Flycatcher Flags, 1981) before the university studio was established. *ASIFA Austria*'s mission was to promote experimental animated film both nationally and internationally.

ASIFA Austria became an official association on March 5, 1985, with nearly all artists involved in animated film joining to foster connections within the community and with the broader industry. After several broadcasts of the students' work on German and Austrian television, the ORF commissioned a 45-minute compilation film in 1986, paving the way for a shift toward commercial animated filmmaking. Fifteen students, together with Hubert Sielecki, collaborated on the film *1x1 des glücklichen Lebens* (The ABC of a Happy Life, 1986/1987). Each student contributed their distinctive style, culminating in a visually diverse and stunning collective work (Figure 11.3).[14] This project can also be seen as a representative sample of student films from the 1980s. The film premiered at the *Berlinale* in Berlin (Germany) in February 1987,[15] and by American standards, it could be considered Austria's first animated feature.[16] The film's proceeds were split equally: half went to the participating artists, while the other half was allocated to maintaining and expanding the *ASIFA Studio*, covering expenses such as rent, renovations, and the acquisition of essential equipment.[17]

Subsequently, additional commercial commissions were secured, such as instructional safety videos (e.g., promoting helmet and safety belt usage) commissioned by the Austrian Federal Ministry of Transport. Additionally, *DoRo Produktion* showed interest in producing animated music videos. By the late 1980s, the studio's workload had grown so much that some individual projects had to be postponed. However, the *ASIFA Studio* was able to expand further, including the addition of a sound studio, thanks to the generated income.

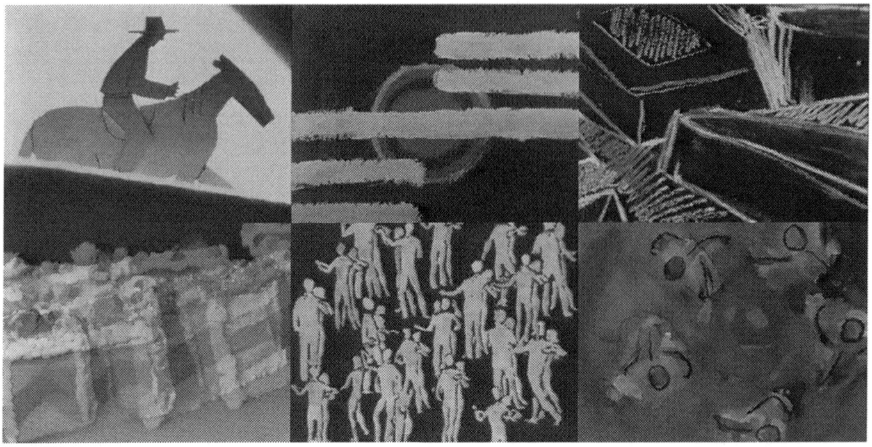

FIGURE 11.3 Stills from *1x1 des glücklichen Lebens* (The ABC of a Happy Life, 1987). (Courtesy of Jürgen Hagler and Remo Rauscher (Permission by Nikolaus Jantsch and Hubert Sielecki).)

FROM EXPERIMENTATION TO EXCELLENCE: ANIMATION IN THE LATE 1980S

The university's animation studio remained highly productive during this period. Although film production was an optional component of the master class, over 30 films were created between 1985 and 1987. For example, in the animation *Knochen* (Bones, 1985), Guido Hoffmann animated a human skeleton that disintegrated and reassembled into grotesque figures, only to collapse again to the beat of drums. Roland Schütz (b. 1962) created *MeYou* (1985), where two bodies emerged from a blue and a red dot, merging in a symbolic act of love before returning to their original forms. Mara Mattuschka's *Kugelkopf* (Ball-Head, 1985) used pixilation to transform a human head into the ball head of a typewriter, which then typed letters on a disk to classical music. Irene Hohenbüchler (b. 1964) highlighted the importance of music in these films with *Konphon* (1986), a portmanteau of 'Kontrabass' (double bass) and 'saxophone.' As Hubert Sielecki noted: "Everyone assumed the music was taken from a jazz record, unaware that it was actually improvised by a single musician" (Hubert Sielecki, as cited in Bruckner 2011: 127). In *Club* (1986), James Clay (b. 1958) parodied the legendary ORF talk show *Club 2* (1976–1995) by animating plasticine figures that incoherently repeated original quotes until a participant's final outburst.[18] Meanwhile, in his *Vorrang* (Right of Way, 1987), a traffic sign pictogram of a car transformed into a traffic hooligan through frame-by-frame animation, and Susanne 'Susi' Praglowski created a sand animation titled *Sand* (1987).[19]

Personnel and spatial changes took place in 1988. From 1988 to 1990, Martin Fritz (b. 1963) took on a teaching role and became the second assistant at the university studio, focusing primarily on managing distribution and sales.[20] During this period, the master class was relocated from the university's main building to an adjacent one, providing more space for the studio but also resulting in a physical separation between the animation and painting studios. As the new premises were not ready for use in 1988, the animation studio had to be temporarily housed in a room unsuitable for sound recordings until 1989. "An entire year was lost, stalling all momentum. It took years for the new studio to regain its footing. Films were still produced, but only through significant effort" (Hubert Sielecki, as cited in Bruckner 2011: 130). Film production dropped to 7 films in 1988 but rebounded to 15 in 1989. However, upon completion of the new premises in 1989, another setback emerged: the ORF shut down its film-copying plant due to the transition to video. As a result, the university had to cover the costs of film material and development, leading to a shift toward video production and the acquisition of appropriate equipment.

Notable films from this period include *Kaspar* (1988) by Monika Wibmer (b. 1961) and *Der Mensch mit den modernen Nerven* (The Man with Modern Nerves, 1988) by Stefan Stratil and Bady Minck (b. 1959), both employing pixilation techniques. Sabine Groschup's *Haus* (House, 1988) showcased a vibrant blend of modified base, cel, and stop-motion animation. Similarly, *Der Fisch* (The Fish, 1989) by Susi Praglowski combined various animation styles, from pixilation to cutout and stop-motion. Britta Keber (b. 1960) took a more geometric approach in *Geo Neo* (1989), where she used frame-by-frame animation to animate geometric shapes in sync with the rhythm of a traditional 'Schuhplattler' (traditional folk dance).

At the end of the 1980s, the *Studio für experimentellen Trickfilm* (Studio for Experimental Animated Film) had achieved remarkable success. It secured 3 hours of television airtime across Austria, Germany, Switzerland, and the UK and earned 6 awards at international film festivals. "The outlook is promising: After a prolonged slumber, Austrian animation has not only been reanimated but has also become one of the most vibrant and creative branches of the nation's film production" (Putz 1988: 32). In the spring of 1989, an exhibition project titled *Reverse Angle: New Art from Vienna in Chicago* was organized in Chicago (USA) by a group of artists led by Erich Praschak (b. 1955). This project featured a binational parallel exhibition with works from both American and Austrian artists. Additionally, 30 Austrian film artists presented experimental and animated films, further contributing to the global recognition of Austrian experimental animated films.

NOTES

1 Like many experimental films from that era, this one also resists precise classification. Franz Blaas, the creator of the now-lost film, does not consider it an animated work: "It wasn't an animated film. Instead, I used my Super 8 camera to capture brief, heavily overexposed shots of wooden figures carved by an artisan in the Steyr Valley [...] which I filmed between windowpanes with the sun as a backdrop. Around 5–7 of these blinding sequences were interspersed with longer periods of darkness. The idea was to create a film that underscores how the darkness in the cinema is reflected within the film itself" (email from Franz Blaas to the author, dated September 27, 2023).

2 The fourth part of the series was never produced after Peter Hauenschild relocated to Linz (email from Franz Blaas to the author, dated September 27, 2023).

3 Email from Thomas Steiner to the author, dated September 20, 2023.

4 The *Universität für angewandte Kunst Wien* (University of Applied Arts Vienna) attained university status only at the end of 1998; before that, it was known as the *Hochschule für angewandte Kunst Wien* (College of Applied Art Vienna) from 1970 to 1998. This chapter will refer to it as the University of Applied Arts Vienna for simplicity.
5 The exact production year of the two films by Reinhold Bergmann and Ansgar Schnitzer remains unknown, but both were showcased at the *Filmfestival tropisch* (Film Festival Tropical) in Innsbruck (Tyrol), which took place from January 11 to 22, 1983.
6 Nearly 30 years later, the two artists collaborated again on *vers.augt* (2011) and *T. nicht füttern!* (Do Not Feed T.!, 2016).
7 It appears that this decision wasn't driven by the progressiveness of the decision-makers, who had initially intended to recruit Joseph Beuys (1921–1986) for the master class. Maria Lassnig, ranked second, was awarded the professorship only after Beuys declined the offer.
8 Although Maria Lassnig produced numerous animated films in the USA between 1970 and 1976, she clearly regarded her role at the *Studio for Experimental Animated Film* as that of a mentor, distancing herself from direct involvement in film production.
9 Since the room also doubled as an assistant's workspace for Hubert Sielecki, only about half of the space was actually available for the animation studio.
10 By that point, around 60 minutes of silent animation exercises had already been completed.
11 Though seldom used today, the animation light table remains a fundamental part of the studio's equipment.
12 The ten founding student members were Renate Kordon, Bady Minck, Stefan Stratil, Sabine Groschup, Mara Mattuschka, Gerlinde Thuma, Susi Praglowski, James Clay, Guido Hoffmann, and Rob Kasseckert.
13 Since 2020, Peter Putz has held the title of honorary member of *ASIFA Austria*.
14 The studio was honored with a recognition award from ORF for the film's overall production.
15 The television premiere aired on June 19, 1987, as part of the program series *kunst-stücke* (Art Pieces, 1981–2002).
16 According to the *Academy of Motion Picture Arts and Sciences*, which awards the Oscars, a feature film must have a runtime of at least 40 minutes. However, most European festivals, including the *Annecy International Animation Film Festival*, require a minimum of 60 minutes. Consequently, the film was classified as a "collective feature film" only in *Animation: A World History* (Bendazzi (ed.) 2016b: 197).
17 The fixed costs in the early years were also covered by donations, with Hubert Sielecki providing the initial equipment.
18 The film recalls a notorious German television scandal from 1971, in which a talk show guest unexpectedly pulled out an axe and smashed the studio table.
19 After completing her studies, Susi Praglowski pursued training in psychotherapy, where she continued to incorporate animation into her practice. In 2010, she created an animated film using student drawings on the theme of fear. This film served as the backdrop for a school dance group's performance of Michael Jackson's (1958–2009) song *Thriller* (1982).
20 Between 4 and 7 copies of each completed film were produced and sent to festivals across Europe and America.

12 Ink and Pixels Unite

The Evolution of Animation in the Digital Age

The 1990s marked a new chapter for the *Studio für experimentellen Trickfilm* (Studio for Experimental Animated Film) at the University of Applied Arts Vienna. It was a period defined by the completion of a second major project on the one hand and a significant personnel transition on the other. After Maria Lassnig's (1919–2014) retirement in 1989, the master class faced a year-long leadership gap. Nana Swiczinsky (b. 1969), who joined the class in 1989 as the sole new student, described herself as a "missing link between the old and new generation" (Nana Swiczinsky, as cited in Bruckner 2011: 133). Simultaneously, a conflict arose among the students, as "some of them questioned whether the concept of the class was truly rooted in the purely artistic branch" (Johanna Freise, as cited in Bruckner 2011: 133). Despite the students' preference for a female leader, the professorship was awarded to Christian Ludwig Attersee (né Christian Ludwig in 1940) in 1990.[1] Under his leadership, several structural changes were introduced, including the integration of the tapestry class, which had been at risk of dissolution, and the renaming of the master class to *Meisterklasse für Malerei, Animationsfilm und Tapisserie* (Master Class for Painting, Animation Film, and Tapestry). The animation studio was also rebranded as the *Studio für experimentellen Animationsfilm* (Studio for Experimental Animation). Organizational shifts followed, with Stefanie Andrej taking on administrative duties, allowing Hubert Sielecki (b. 1946) to focus on artistic and technical tasks. Despite these transitions, the studio maintained its creative momentum, producing 28 animated films between 1990 and 1992.

FROM PAPER TO PIXELS: RESISTANCE WAS FUTILE

Founded in 1988 by Hubert Sielecki, *Animotion Films* was established to facilitate collaboration between the university studio and *ASIFA Austria* on various projects. The first major undertaking was a follow-up episodic film commissioned by *Österreichischer Rundfunk* (ORF, Austrian Broadcasting Corporation), provisionally titled *Planetenreise* (Planet Journey). This ambitious project aimed to support young artists in entering the film industry, involving 28 illustrators, painters, and musicians.[2] Preparatory work took place during a 3-month symposium in the summer of 1989, where teams of up to eight people developed the content and soundtrack for each segment. After 14 months of production, the approximately 43-minute film *Life Show* premiered on television on October 12, 1990, and was later featured at various festivals.[3] The film's colorized pixilation framework follows an angler who saves a drowning man, only to be abducted by a camera crew. As a participant in the

DOI: 10.1201/9781003415442-14

Life Show, the angler is connected to a device that extracts his dreams and thoughts, which are visualized through various animated sequences. Ultimately, after being drained of his thoughts, he is thrown back into the water and rescued by another angler, who then faces the same fate, perpetuating the cycle. Much like the previous project *1x1 des glücklichen Lebens* (The ABC of a Happy Life, 1986/1987), *Life Show* employed a wide range of animation techniques, including model animation, cutout animation, and modified-base technology. The program, which even featured a claymation band, provided a comprehensive overview of the diverse student work, in both content and technique (Figure 12.1).

In addition to managing the major ORF project, the *ASIFA Studio* also produced advertising films for various companies, including the computer manufacturer *Compaq*. Beyond the *ASIFA Studio*'s projects, students also took on private-sector commissions. A notable example of the strong connection between academic studies and the private sector was the music video *Käpt'n Knödl im Dreck* (Cap'n Dumpling

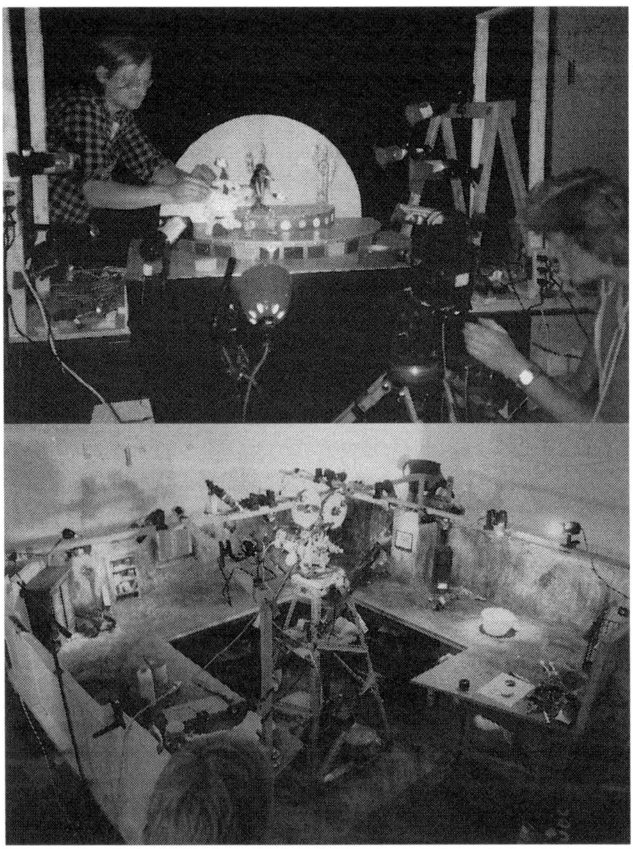

FIGURE 12.1 Stop-motion shots for *Life Show* (1990). Top: James Clay with his claymation figures of the Mexican band 'Los Embryos,' while Paul Braunsteiner operates the camera. Bottom: Model construction for single-frame pan shots at the *ASIFA Studio* in Vienna. (Photographer: Hubert Sielecki.)

in a Mess, 1993) for the Tyrolean band *Die Knödel* (The Dumplings, active from 1992 to 2000). This *Star Wars* parody, produced by the private *Haspel Trickstudio* (Haspel Animation Studio), featured contributions from students Thomas Renoldner (b. 1960) and Nana Swiczinsky, alongside artists Georg Dienz (b. 1964) and Pepi Öttl (b. 1959). Meanwhile, in 1993, the *Studio für experimentellen Animationsfilm* (Studio for Experimental Animation) chose to focus more on artistic animation films and training, leading to a formal separation from the *ASIFA Studio*.[4] Following the introduction of a summer break, the university studio's output slightly decreased, resulting in the production of 18 animated films between 1993 and 1996.

During the 1990s, the university studio underwent significant technical changes. New equipment, including a sound studio sampler and the U-matic video format for low-cost animation exercises, was acquired. The studio consciously chose to forgo computer animation in favor of retaining the 16-mm film format, allowing it to obtain previously unattainable equipment, such as animation stands from decommissioned sources. However, by the late 1990s, the costs associated with film stock and processing had become unsustainable, with film development alone consuming the studio's entire annual budget. The graduation film *Sonne, Salz und Meer* (Sun, Salt, and Sea, 1997) by Daniel Šuljić (b. 1971) – an animated depiction of a Croatian village by the sea enduring harsh winds, created using coffee powder – marked the end of 16-mm film production at the university studio. "For some students, the shift from analog to digital technology was a reason to discontinue their studies" (Bruckner 2011: 146). While most films continued to be hand-animated and digitally recorded, the shift to digital production transformed the conceptual approach to filmmaking. This transition also made it easier to bring creative ideas to life in animated film. One of the studio's earliest digitally recorded films was *Tanzschule Goya* (Goya Dance School, 1997/1998), a pixilation frame-by-frame animation by Ulu Braun (b. 1976).[5] The film features a looped sequence depicting a matador being stabbed by a bull, choreographed in a way that transforms the death struggle into a dance.

The studio's transition to digitalization extended into the new millennium. From 2002 to 2010, Austrian filmmaker Erwin Wagenhofer (b. 1961) held a faculty position at the university, overseeing the studio's technical equipment. After his tenure, Indian film artist Praved Krishnapilla took over the role of teaching film technology in 2010. Known as "an expert in all computer systems and the internet," he "continues to lead the studio alongside former student Niki Jantsch, upholding the tradition of 'painting in motion' in the spirit of Maria Lassnig" (Hubert Sielecki, email to the author, dated January 18, 2024). That same year, Hubert Sielecki retired, though he remains a prominent figure in Austrian animation to this day.

LICKING DUCKS AND CREATIVE MINDS

Inspired by their involvement in the large-scale film project *Life Show* (1989/1990), artist Paul Braunsteiner (b. 1948) and student Josef 'Sepp' Nermuth decided to create their own film in a similar style. The pixilation and stop-motion film *Die Jagd* (The Hunt, 1991/1992) begins from a dog's perspective during a walk but takes a dark turn when the dog disobeys and is shot by the hunter. In a surprising twist, the hunter transforms into a dog at the film's conclusion, causing the cycle to repeat itself.[6] In 1991, Braunsteiner and Nermuth teamed up with Hubert Sielecki and Luise Buisman (b. 1943), who did not have a traditional university background, to establish the film collective *A.S.K.* This group went on to create multiple no-budget projects between 1992 and 2001.

During the years 1993 to 1997, close friends Oliver Marčeta (b. 1969 in Onek, Slovenia) and Daniel Šuljić (b. in Zagreb, Croatia) were the dominant figures in the university studio's production scene, accounting for over half of the films made during this period. Their work gained international recognition, being showcased at numerous film festivals and winning several prestigious awards. Reflecting on their time in the studio, Marčeta recalled: "We practically lived there. We worked tirelessly from dawn till dusk" (Oliver Marčeta, as cited in Bruckner 2011: 143). In *Evening Star* (1993), Šuljić used a sophisticated cutout animation technique, employing cutout newspaper portraits of athletes, politicians, and models to create sequences that highlighted the interchangeable nature of individuals in our society. Meanwhile, Marčeta told the tragic story of a cowboy in *Jesus von New Orleans* (Jesus of New Orleans, 1994) using 3D stop-motion animation. Šuljić's film *LeckDonalds* (LickDonald's, 1995) cleverly referenced the globally recognized fast-food chain while introducing a touch of eroticism into the otherwise conservative world of Donald Duck (Figure 12.2). Starting in 1997, Šuljić continued his work at *Zagreb Film*, where he produced *Kolač* (The Cake, 1997), a rare example of cinematic glass painting that

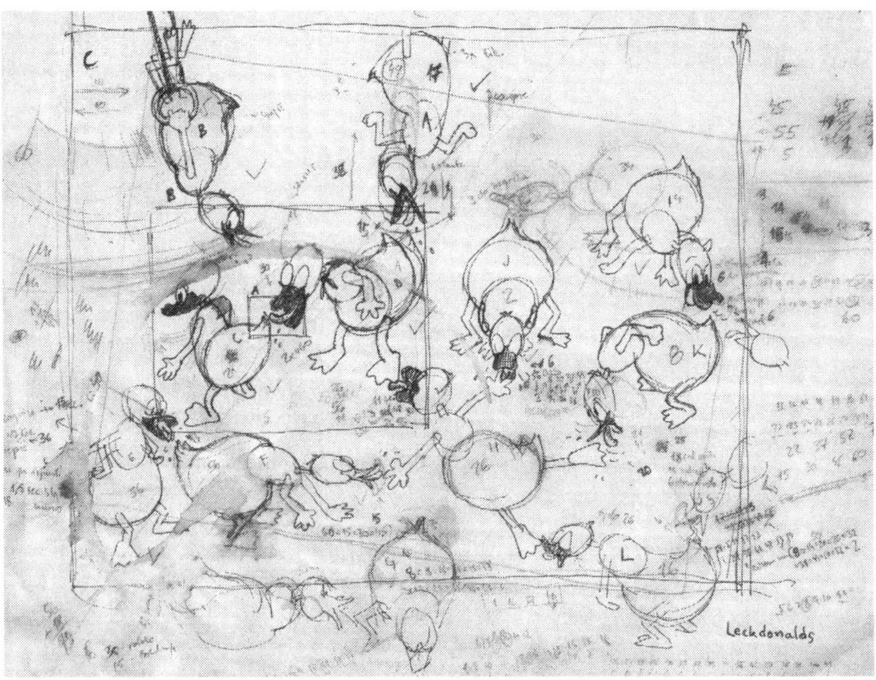

FIGURE 12.2 A drawing for *LeckDonalds* (LickDonald's, 1995) by Daniel Šuljić, "which functioned simultaneously as the initial concept, storyboard, and script – everything rolled into one." (Courtesy of Daniel Šuljić.)

depicted a group's conflict over a cake, leading to their mutual destruction alongside the sweet treat.

Martin Anibas (b. 1961) was one of the students who focused on creating abstract rather than narrative films. In his 'moving paintings,' he employed various techniques on paper or worked directly on the film material, producing both expressive abstractions and figurative allusions. Between 1989 and 1993, he created 16 independent films in the university studio. In his direct animation *Pluieblau* (Pluie Blue, 1990), Anibas painted abstract figurative imagery directly onto the film stock. The frame-by-frame animation *Bild 15/16* (Picture 15/16, 1993) featured melancholic watercolors where black ink strokes intertwined with violet hues. Various shapes oscillated within the abstract composition, evoking antennae, power lines, or musical staves. A year later, Anibas exhibited the watercolors that inspired the film, arranging them into a horizontal strip onto which the film was projected.

Iby-Jolande Varga (b. 1961) pursued music studies before enrolling in a 5-day course at the *Studio für experimentellen Trickfilm* (Studio for Experimental Animated Film) in 1987. Following this, she focused on animated film as a self-taught artist. Her efforts were recognized with a youth award and state film funding for a pop-up book and puzzles, which served as the basis for her plans to create a two-part animated film. Between 1988 and 1990, this resulted in the creation of *Neue Kristalle* (New Crystals, 1990) and *Hin zum Ozean* (Towards the Ocean, 1990). Continuing her artistic journey, Varga produced films such as *Kleiner Skulpturen Garten* (Little Sculpture Garden, 1995), which involved the construction of ten sculptures from 273 individual parts cut from plywood panels and their animation through the replacement technique. The sculptures underwent reassembly 9,760 times using 1,215 additional elements: "The film stands out as one of the most captivating animation experiences because, despite the viewer's intellectual grasp of the technique and the rigidity of the material, the movements are perceived as remarkably fluid and organic" (Renoldner 2010: 142). From 2002 onward, Varga also embraced digital technology, creating interactive works such as *Klanggärten* (Sound Gardens, 2013).

While many Austrians went to Germany to study animation film production, Ulf Stäger (b. 1966) was among the few Germans who relocated to Austria. After training as a city planner in Berlin from 1985 to 1987, he joined Maria Lassnig's master class. His film *Duocity* (1992) reflected his urban planning background by artistically comparing Vienna and Berlin through silhouettes. Initially depicted in a naturalistic style, the cities in the film gradually became more abstract and simplified. Inspired by the restlessness of the big city and capturing the essence of bustling urban life, the film was screened at various international festivals from Paris (France) to Hiroshima (Japan). Following an internship at the animation department of the German television station *Westdeutscher Rundfunk* (WDR, West German Broadcasting) in 1993, he created numerous other short films, including *Doppelgänger* (Doppelganger, 1997), a sort of sequel to *Duocity* (1992). Through his company, *Ulf Staeger Filmproduktion*, he not only produced his own short films but also worked on commissioned projects such as the puppet animation film *Auf dem Gletscher* (On the Glacier, 2011) directed by Norbert Hobrecht.

Thomas Renoldner began his journey in experimental filmmaking in 1980 and later honed his skills by attending Maria Lassnig's master class in 1989. His early student film, *Würfel* (Cubes, 1990), featured puzzle cubes dancing to 1960s pop music, resulting in ever-changing displays of colors and shapes due to the eclectic combination of their designs. Similar to the films of Martin Anibas, with whom Renoldner occasionally collaborated, his work emphasized the significance of music, abstraction, and the manipulation of perceptual norms. In subsequent films like *Bunt* (Colorful, 1991) and *Rhythmus 94* (Rhythm 94, 1994), the synchronization of sound was intricately linked with visuals and spatial awareness. A highlight of Renoldner's career was the international success of his film *Don't Know What* (2019), which was showcased at more than 100 festivals, earning multiple awards and an Oscar nomination.

Nana Swiczinsky, who collaborated with Thomas Renoldner on the music video *Käpt'n Knödl im Dreck* (Cap'n Dumpling in a Mess, 1993), created deeply personal animated films during her early academic years. Her frame-by-frame animation *Das ungehobelte Pack* (The Boorish Bunch, 1991) portrayed two characters dancing in an animalistic manner to drum rhythms, eventually leading to a drinking binge: "I was inspired by the studio's vibe at the time" (Nana Swiczinsky, as cited in Bruckner 2011: 139). In *Bio-Graphics* (1992), she autobiographically depicted her artistic growth from childhood doodles to animated filmmaking. In 1997, she transitioned to a career as a freelance animator, and her film *Wieder Holung* (Repetition, 1997) won first prize in the Best Animation category at the *Cinetexas Film Festival* (Austin, USA) in 1998. Swiczinsky also engaged in international projects and served as a storyboard artist for the German-Canadian co-production *Die Säulen der Erde* (The Pillars of the Earth, 2010), which was also broadcast as a miniseries in the USA.

During her tenure as a professor from 1980 to 1989, Maria Lassnig maintained a low profile in student film work, opting instead to play a supportive role as a mentor. However, she dedicated herself to creating a large-scale *Anti-Kriegsfilm* (Anti-War Film) between 1977 and 1998, aiming to highlight the absurdity of war from ancient times to the modern era.[7] Her estate includes numerous drawings, models, photographs, scripts, and a 2-minute film fragment (Figure 12.3). This project serves as a crucial link between her animated films of the 1970s, influenced by the US film industry, and her final completed animated work, *Maria Lassnig Kantate* (Maria Lassnig Cantata, 1991/1992), in terms of both chronological progression and stylistic evolution.

After years of contemplating a film based on her life story, Maria Lassnig was finally inspired to create the music video *Maria Lassnig Kantate* (Maria Lassnig Cantata, 1991/1992) at the suggestion of Hubert Sielecki. Using the melody of an old song as a foundation, Lassnig composed the lyrics and performed the song in various costumes against a backdrop of specially crafted animated films. In a nod to her earlier work *Selfportrait* (1971), Lassnig even appeared as the Statue of Liberty, holding a can of Coke instead of a torch. The project took nearly 2 years to complete, primarily due to the complex animations. Collaboration with Sielecki was essential, as he not only co-wrote the script with Lassnig over several months but also played a pivotal role in organizing the production:

"I secured the funding, oversaw the technical direction, and managed everything using my personal 16 mm film equipment. I handled the subsidies and paid the

FIGURE 12.3 Maria Lassnig while drawing her *Anti-Kriegsfilm* (Anti-War Film) in the 1980s. (Courtesy of Archive of the Maria Lassnig Foundation, Vienna.)

team members – Paul Braunsteiner, Josef Nermuth, and Brigitte Berchtold – while Lassnig and I declined any fees. For years, I managed the festival submissions, including all correspondence, entries, and shipping (35 mm), and organized international screenings in museums and galleries. I also took care of the distribution until Sixpackfilm eventually took over. Not to mention, I composed the music, played the self-built hurdy-gurdy, and accompanied it with an Irish tin whistle. All the sound engineering was also my responsibility" (Hubert Sielecki, email to the author, dated January 18, 2024).

The film celebrated its international premiere in 1993 at the *Berlinale* in Berlin (Germany). "To this day, the film is an international hit with its catchy final chorus" (Isabelle Reicher in Kondor et al. (eds.) 2021: 159).

Outside the University of Applied Arts, artists also began experimenting with animated film in the 1990s. For instance, Thomas Korschil (b. 1968) studied at the *San Francisco Art Institute* (SFAI) from 1987 to 1991, where he created *Spring* (1991). By meticulously adjusting the depth of field on a camera lens focused on a harbor scene frame by frame according to a specific time scheme, he produced a mesmerizing visual experience. Albert Sackl (b. 1977), a native of Graz (Styria), trained under Viennese filmmaker Peter Kubelka (b. 1934) at the *Städelschule* (Städel School) in Frankfurt (Germany) from 1997 to 2000. During this period, he created time-lapse films using single-frame animation to depict extreme activities, such as 44 hours of television viewing in *Fernsehfilm* (TV Movie, 1997) and the consumption of 50 cigarettes in 4.5 hours and 2 L of wine in 2.5 hours in *Rauchen und Saufen* (Smoking and Drinking, 1997).

In the early 1990s, Ursula Pürrer (b. 1962), Dietmar Schipek (b. 1959), and Ashley Hans Scheirl (also known as Angela Hans Scheirl, b. 1956) collaborated on the 84-minute feature film *Rote Ohren fetzen durch Asche* (Flaming Ears, 1991/1992), breaking away from traditional cinematic norms. The film not only fused various commercial cinema genres but also employed an array of techniques, including animation, model building, and trick shots. Another remarkable work from this period was Ernst Schmidt Jr.'s (1938–1988) trilogy *Denkwürdigkeiten eines Nervenkranken* (Memoirs of My Nervous Illness, 1986–1993), based on the book of the same name by German writer Daniel Paul Schreber (1842–1911). Schreber, who suffered from paranoid schizophrenia, sought to convey his visions and ideas through his writings, creating a system that was entirely coherent and logical – but only in his own mind. The collective film project attracted a distinguished roster of contributors from the Austrian animated film scene of the 1980s and 1990s, including Christian Ludwig Attersee, Sabine Groschup (b. 1959), Wolfgang Georgsdorf (b. 1959), Gudrun Kampl (b. 1964), Renate Kordon (b. 1952), Kurt Kren (1929–1998), Mara Mattuschka (b. 1959), Bady Minck (b. 1956), Lisl Ponger (b. 1947), Susi Praglowski, Roland Schütz (b. 1962), Hubert Sielecki, Stefan Stratil (b. 1963), and Gerlinde Thuma (b. 1962). After Schmidt's passing, the project was completed in 1993 by Peter Tscherkassky (b. 1958).[8]

'SILICON DREAMS' FROM AUSTRIA

Although Austria occasionally pioneered computer animation – Marc Adrian's (1930–2008) *Random* (1963) is cited as possibly the first computer-generated film in Europe (cf. Bruckner 2011: 80–81) – Thomas Renoldner noted in 2010 that "Austria's insignificance in the commercial sector of computer animation remains striking" (Renoldner 2010: 149). The lack of funding structures, specialized training, and production facilities contributed to this situation. When Ferdinand 'Ferry' Unger (1938–2011) aimed to create computer animations at the newly established *Telemotion* film studio in Vienna in 1989, he had to travel to Germany to take a basic course.[9] Notably, *Telemotion* was the first film production company in Central Europe to directly connect a *Silicon Graphics International* (SGI) computer, specialized in graphic design, to a video studio for recording and integrating 3D animations into films. "We truly did pioneering work," remembered Gerald 'Gerry' Kreisel (b. 1966), the studio's technical director at the time. He noted that Ferry Unger was "the first (in Central Europe, or even globally?) to embrace the challenge of 3D computer animation as a professional animator, at a time when there was little experience with this technology" (email to the author, dated October 2, 2023). This led to the creation of documentaries and educational films featuring computer-generated imagery, including the acclaimed film *Die Entstehung der Alpen* (The Formation of the Alps, 1997)[10] and the six-part series *Stadtentwicklung am Beispiel Wien* (Urban Development Using the Example of Vienna, 2001).

In Austria, several ambitious initiatives emerged, particularly in the non-commercial, artistic sphere. One notable project was launched at the same location as the *Studio für experimentellen Animationsfilm* (Studio for Experimental Animation). In 1986, under the leadership of Peter Weibel (1944–2023), the University of Applied Arts established a *Meisterklasse für Visuelle Mediengestaltung* (Master Class for Visual Media Design), where computer animation became a key focus. During her studies there, German-born Christine Meierhofer (b. 1966) introduced the concept of *Kettenanimation* (Chain-Animation, 1992/1993), representing "a bold statement from a new generation of artists exploring video and computer animation" (Renoldner 2010: 145). Within a year, 45 artists, primarily teachers and students from the media class, brought this project to life:

"Based on the principle of *cadavre exquis*, the artists worked together according to the following rules: the first artist was given an image on a floppy disk and this image was the starting point for an animation sequence of up to 2 minutes. Each artist had to finish the work in one week; afterward, the artist passed over the image of the sequence to another person on a floppy disk. After exactly 45 weeks, a 21-minute computer animation was created" (Hagler and Rauscher 2022: 184).

The result was a correspondingly diverse mix of techniques and aesthetics, ranging from geometric abstractions to conceptual test works. During the late 1980s and 1990s, video productions emerged that incorporated computer-aided animation, either partially or entirely. Another collaborative project from the media class was *Wirehead* (1993–1996), a half-hour, patchwork-style film in which Norbert Pfaffenbichler (b. 1967) and Timo Novotny (b. 1973) interwove various clips and animations within a cyberpunk narrative framework. By the mid-1990s, the digital revolution had firmly taken hold of audiovisual production, and notably, Austria managed to establish a foothold in the commercial market, particularly in video game production.

Austria has a rich history of computer game production, though it often went unnoticed by the general public. Early attempts to program chess games for computers can be traced back to 1958 when a chessboard interface was developed for a vacuum tube computer at the Vienna University of Technology. Graphical computer games began to emerge in Austria in the mid-1980s, led by pioneers like Ronald Mayer (b. 1961), who was named *Software-Champion* by a computer magazine in 1985. Starting in 1984, Mayer programmed titles such as *Roadpainter* (1984) from his home, marking the beginning of Austria's contribution to early computer game development. The first commercial producers started to appear in the early 1990s. *Max Design*, founded in 1991 in Schladming (Styria) by brothers Albert and Martin Lasser, along with Wilfried Reiter, is considered the country's first significant development studio. Their business simulation *Cash* (1991), developed for the Amiga, marked the beginning of their influence in the industry. Within a few years, *Max Design* grew to become one of Europe's largest game developers. Their title *Anno 1602* (1998), another economic simulation, became the best-selling game by a developer from a German-speaking country, selling over two million copies. Along with its sequel, *Anno 1503* (2002), the studio achieved over 4.4 million sales. Despite this success, *Max Design* ceased operations in 2004 due to the prolonged development of *Anno 1503* (2002) and the migration of many talents from its rural location. The *Anno* series, later distributed by *Ubisoft*, continued to thrive, producing six sequels by 2019.[11]

Another key studio was *Neo Software*, founded in 1993 by Niki Laber, Hannes Seifert (b. 1971),[12] and Peter Baustädter (b. 1971)[13] in Hirtenberg (Lower Austria). That same year, they released the role-playing game *Whale's Voyage* (also known as *Distant Frontiers*) for the Amiga, but it was the burglary simulation *Der Clou!* (The Clue!, 1994), also available for PC, which marked their breakthrough. Success continued with titles like the strategy game *Die Völker* (Alien Nations, 1999), before being acquired by the American publisher *Take-Two Interactive* in 2001. Following the acquisition, the studio shifted its focus toward contract work, including porting the game *Max Payne* (2001) for the Xbox console. In 2003, the studio, now based in Vienna, was rebranded as *Rockstar Vienna* and took on the responsibility of porting several high-profile games for Xbox and PlayStation 2. Their work on titles such as *Max Payne 2* (2003) and two games from the *Grand Theft Auto* (GTA) series resulted in significant commercial success, including number-one hits in the USA and over $300 million in sales. The control scheme they developed for *Max Payne* also set new standards for third-person shooters on consoles that remain influential today. Despite these achievements, the studio, which had grown to around 100 employees, was shut down in 2006 due to the parent company's reorganization, which led to the closure of non-English-speaking studios. After the shutdown, most of the team formed a new studio, which was later acquired by the German publisher *Deep Silver*. However, this studio was eventually closed in 2010 when *Deep Silver* consolidated its resources in Munich.

The third major game developer in Austria was *JoWooD*, founded in 1995 in Ebensee (Upper Austria) by Dieter Bernauer-Schilcher (né Bernauer in 1969), Johann Reitinger (b. 1962), Johann Schilcher (b. 1961), and Andreas Tobler (b. 1972).[14] Their business simulation *Industriegigant* (Industry Giant, 1997) marked their international breakthrough, with the game being translated into 12 languages. *JoWooD* also served as a publisher in the relatively small computer game industry, releasing titles such as *Die Völker* (Alien Nations, 1999), produced by *Neo Software*. After going public in 2000, *JoWooD* expanded aggressively, acquiring several smaller development studios and distributors in Austria and Germany and establishing international sales offices in England and Japan by 2001. However, intense pressure from global competition nearly drove the company to insolvency in 2002, a crisis averted only through stringent restructuring and the successful release of *Gothic II* (2002). As *JoWooD* became increasingly driven by stock market pressures and quarterly performance, the focus on quality waned. This was evident in the releases of *Söldner: Secret Wars* (2004) and *Gothic 3* (2006), which were riddled with bugs, rendering them nearly unplayable at launch. The company also faced legal battles, such as with the Australian developer *Perception*, which had been contracted to create a licensed game for the TV series *Stargate SG-1* (1997–2007), a project that was ultimately canceled in 2006. *JoWooD*'s shift toward positioning itself exclusively as a publisher led to the closure of all five of its development studios in Austria and Germany. Although the acquisition of the Canadian publisher *DreamCatcher Inc.* in 2007 allowed *JoWooD* to enter the US market, it wasn't enough to prevent its decline. By 2010, the company experienced a severe drop in sales, which ultimately resulted in its insolvency in early 2011. By that time, the workforce had already dwindled to just 24 employees from a peak of over 200 (Figure 12.4).

In 2001, *thriXXX* demonstrated how to successfully avoid bankruptcy by pivoting its business strategy. After the Innsbruck-based company (located in Tyrol) failed in its late 1990s attempt to develop military flight simulations, it repurposed its 3D engine for erotic simulations like *3D Luder* (3D Slut, 2001). This strategic shift propelled *thriXXX* to become the global market leader in 3D erotic games. The company made headlines in 2010 when it planned to develop an erotic game for *Microsoft*'s

FIGURE 12.4 Dieter Bernauer-Schilcher at a typical workspace of the once-prominent gaming giant *JoWooD*. (Courtesy of Dieter Bernauer-Schilcher.)

Xbox Kinect controller. However, *Microsoft* quickly halted the project, stating that the Xbox is a "family-friendly console" (as cited in Steinschaden 2011, under 'Die Grenzen der Lust'). Similarly, the company's attempts to 'penetrate' *Apple*'s App Store were thwarted, and despite inquiries from China, *thriXXX* noted that "our websites are blocked there" (as cited in Steinschaden 2011, under 'Die Grenzen der Lust'). While *thriXXX* successfully entered the Japanese market with *Hentai 3D* (2001), the first Western 3D hentai sex game, the USA remains its most crucial market: "Large American companies or investors don't dare to enter the adult sector" (as cited in Steinschaden 2011, under 'Die Grenzen der Lust'), the CEO remarked, yet "Americans are buying it and playing like crazy" (as cited in Gasser 2012; para. 4). This success starkly contrasts with the moral standards in the "Holy Land of Tyrol" (as cited in Steinschaden 2011: para. 1). Despite their efforts to shake off the "grubby image" (as cited in Steinschaden 2011, under 'Produkte für Erwachsene') by producing high-quality products, *thriXXX*'s headquarters remain discreet, with neither a doorbell nor a logo.[15] Consequently, Austria's role in the production of erotic computer games remains almost invisible.

In 2001, another prominent Austrian game developer emerged: *Sproing Interactive Media*. Founded in Vienna by Harald Riegler and Gerhard Seiler, *Sproing* quickly became Austria's largest gaming company for over 15 years, employing more than 100 people as of 2016. The studio developed over 60 games across various platforms and genres. Notable releases included *Undercover: Operation Wintersonne* (Undercover: Operation Wintersun, 2006), a classic World War II (1939–1945) adventure game for PC, and *Panzer Tactics DS* (2007/2008), a turn-based tactics game for Nintendo DS, which debuted in North America and later won the prestigious *German Developer Award*. Starting in 2011, *Sproing* increasingly focused on free-to-play games funded through in-game purchases, with titles like *Asterix & Friends* – initially launched as a browser game in 2013 and later as a mobile game in 2016 – offering players a strategy-building experience. However, at the end of 2016, the company was forced to file for insolvency following the failure of a major project.

Despite efforts to restructure, including a reorganization process, the studio faced a second insolvency and ultimately closed its doors at the end of 2017. With the support of an investor, Harald Riegler successfully founded the development studio *Purple Lamp* in early 2018. Around 30 employees, including several veterans from *Sproing*, joined the team. As of 2022, the studio had grown to an international workforce of about 70 individuals and has gained significant attention with its games featuring the popular cartoon character *SpongeBob SquarePants*.[16]

After successfully co-developing the game series *Die Völker* (Alien Nations, 1999–2001) as art director, Thomas Schleischitz (b. 1976) co-founded *Rabcat Computer Graphics GmbH* in October 2001. As video game production became more complex, *Rabcat* adopted a strategy commonly used in the automotive industry: instead of creating its own games, it specialized in providing top-tier graphic assets. From the outset, *Rabcat* prioritized excellence over competing on price with low-wage countries. However, the early years proved challenging – by 2005, only Schleischitz remained of the original six founders (whose first initials had formed the company name), prompting a fresh start. *Rabcat*'s breakthrough came in 2004 when it secured its first major project: creating detailed 3D models of 100 vehicles for the racing game *Test Drive Unlimited* (2006) by *Atari France*. At that time, each model required two to three employees to work for an entire month, while the team consisted of just ten people. The 2008 economic crisis, along with the insolvency of several clients, prompted *Rabcat* to diversify. In addition to *Rabcat Game Art*, the company launched *Rabcat Gambling*, securing a key partnership in 2009 with the Austrian Lotteries, which became the majority shareholder in 2010. By 2013, *Rabcat* had established itself in the international iGambling market and had grown to 25 employees. Simultaneously, *Rabcat* partnered with the British studio *Playground Games*, collaborating on creating in-game environments for the *Forza Horizon* franchise (since 2012), published by *Microsoft Studios*. Therefore, *Rabcat* sent a team to Leamington Spa (UK) to work closely on the game's development. A pivotal moment came in 2013 when *Rabcat* embarked on its largest collaboration to date with *Blizzard Entertainment*. After 2 years of intensive test tasks, the company secured its first official contracts. This led to the creation of 20–25 characters for *Overwatch* (2016), which in turn caught the attention of *Epic Games*. Starting in late 2018, *Rabcat* began delivering one to two 3D models monthly for the cartoonish shooter *Fortnite* (2017). The company's continued success led to rapid expansion, growing to 45 employees in 2019 and 60 by 2024. Today, the company collaborates with major international clients such as *Disney Interactive Studios* and *Ubisoft*, contributing assets like vehicles, environments, characters, and weapons for iconic game franchises like *Alone in the Dark* (since 1992) and *GTA* (since 1997).

With the release of *Ori and the Blind Forest* (2015), the Austrian game developer *Moon Studios* achieved significant acclaim. The game was celebrated for its "gorgeous painterly aesthetic, lush environments, and fluidly rendered animations. Yet, despite all its praise, one of the most fascinating stories surrounding *Ori* is not the game itself, but the unique development team, Moon Studios, that brought it to life" (Agar 2015: para. 1). Founded in Vienna in 2010 by Austrian Thomas Mahler (formerly a Cinematic Artist at *Blizzard Entertainment*) and Israeli Gennadiy Korol (formerly a Senior Graphics Engineer at *Animation Lab*), *Moon Studios* quickly emerged as a global player. Despite its relatively low profile, the studio's partnership with *Microsoft Studios* in 2011 led to the release of *Ori* on Windows and Xbox One platforms in 2015. "The game drew initial inspiration from a marriage of both old-school gaming mechanics and traditional forms of both Japanese and Western animation" (Agar 2015: para. 1), which contributed to its success. *Ori* received multiple accolades, including the prestigious *Best Debut Award* at the 2016 *Game Developers Choice Awards* in San José, California (USA). A sequel announced in 2017, *Ori and the Will of the Wisps* (2020), followed, further cementing the studio's reputation. The success of these titles led to the expansion of *Moon Studios* to a team of 80 talents from over 40 countries by 2020, including Austria, Israel, the USA, Canada, and Australia. To streamline communication, the studio developed a custom tool named *Apollo*. Following allegations of poor management practices from former employees, *Microsoft* ended its partnership with *Moon Studios* in 2022. Consequently, the action RPG *No Rest for the Wicked* was released by the American publisher *Private Division* (a subsidiary of *Take-Two Interactive*) in the spring of 2024.

Today, studios of this scale are rare in Austria due to significant shifts in the computer games industry. The influence of international corporations has led to the specialization and diversification of local expertise. According to the *Game Development Studie 2019* (Game Development Study 2019), Austria had around 90 game developers, most of which were one-person or micro-companies with fewer than ten employees. A notable example is the developer duo *Clockwork Bird*,[17] creators of the indie game *Silicon Dreams* (2021).[18]

NOTES

1 Since 2009, the master class has been led by the American artist Judith Eisler (b. 1962), marking a return to female leadership.
2 In addition to the students, non-university artists also contributed to the project.
3 For example, the film was screened at the *Österreichische Filmtage* (Austrian Film Days, October 16–21, 1990) held in Wels, Upper Austria. Runtime estimates vary, ranging from 40 to 50 minutes. According to the film magazine *Filmkunst* (Cinematic Art), the film comprised 65,300 individual frames, which, at a standard PAL frame rate of 25 frames/s, would result in a runtime of approximately 43.5 minutes (Filmkunst (131), 1991: 29). The copy stored in the ORF archive has a runtime of 42.5 minutes. The television broadcast was part of the series *kunst-stücke* (Art Pieces, 1981–2002).
4 Furthermore, Hubert Sielecki experienced a lack of support from the graduates: "The graduates expected me to continue working for them as I had done in the studio, but that was simply not feasible since I was now focused on new generations of students. After eight intense years, I could no longer manage *ASIFA* on my own, so in 1993, I stepped back from all my roles and handed over the association to the graduates" (Hubert Sielecki, as cited in Bruckner 2011: 178).
5 Cf. Bruckner 2011: 148. In some sources, the film is listed as a 16-mm production. When asked, Ulu Braun speculated that he created it as a 'practice piece' on 16 mm, even though he generally favored digital filmmaking. The project involved overpainting and repeatedly re-filming copies of etchings by the Spanish painter Francisco de Goya (1746–1828): "I arranged Goya's images and made black-and-white copies. I then worked over these with charcoal, acrylic paint, and pencils, copying each step and further refining the images" (email to the author, dated August 26, 2024).

6 The film's title serves as a metaphor for the pursuit of wealth, with the hunter attempting to magically create gold in his basement.
7 While Maria Lassnig's body of work is generally apolitical, themes of war and violence are notably present, likely influenced by her personal experiences during World War II. She sought to confront these issues in her *Anti-Kriegsfilm* (Anti-War Film), envisioning a scene where Adolf Hitler (1889–1945), driving across a green meadow, drags a trench filled with skulls behind him, with swastikas crushing soldiers along the way. (For more information on Lassnig's *Anti-Kriegsfilm*, see Bormann 2021: 72–75.)
8 In a 2019 interview, Mara Mattuschka reflected on how so many animation artists became involved in the film project: "Ernst Schmidt Jr. was a frequent visitor to our Lassnig-Sielecki animation class. He reached out to young artists, inviting them to animate passages for the film. Many of us, myself included, took part. He managed to complete Part 1. Then, he was hospitalized with cirrhosis of the liver. Susi Praglowski stepped in to direct Part 2, aiming to finish the film posthumously with his materials. Peter Tscherkassky took over Part 3 and brought me on board to compose the music" (Mara Mattuschka, as cited in Klocker 2019: 4).
9 Rüdiger Morawetz, founder of *Telemotion*, recalled in a telephone conversation that the idea to incorporate computer animation was Ferry Unger's own initiative (telephone conversation with the author on October 2, 2023). The system was acquired with the stipulation that Unger would learn the fundamentals. According to Gerald Kreisel, Unger refined his skills through "learning by doing" after a basic course in Germany, with additional support from the manufacturer's telephone assistance (email to the author, dated October 2, 2023).
10 This 45-minute film, directed by Kurt Mayer (1951–2023), was featured in the ORF documentary series *Universum* (Universe, since 1987) and received the *Camera Alpin in Gold* award at the *Bergfilmfestival Graz* (Mountainfilm Graz) in 1998.
11 In the summer of 2024, *Ubisoft* announced *Anno 117*, the eighth installment in the series, set during antiquity.
12 Hannes Seifert (b. 1971) had already been creating computer games independently, including the text-graphic adventure *Der verlassene Planet* (The Abandoned Planet, 1989).
13 Peter Baustädter also gained recognition as a VFX artist, contributing to major Hollywood blockbusters including *Apollo 13* (1995), *Titanic* (1997), *The Lord of the Rings: The Two Towers* (2002), *The Day After Tomorrow* (2004), *King Kong* (2005), *X-Men: The Last Stand* (2006), *Fantastic Four: Rise of the Silver Surfer* (2007), *Jumper* (2008), and *Avatar* (2009).
14 Birth years provided via email by Dieter Bernauer-Schilcher.
15 Media reports suggest that even the CEO's mother is unaware of how her son earns his living (cf. Gasser 2012: para. 2).
16 In 2020, the studio was acquired by the Swedish company *Embracer Group*.
17 Since 2023, the developer duo has parted ways, leaving *Clockwork Bird* to continue as a one-person operation.
18 In the realm of aesthetics, 'Silicon Dreams' refers to the surreal imagery characteristic of CGI animations from the 1980s and 1990s.

Part 3

What Was Once Invisible

Austria's Animation Claims Its Place

13 From Sketches to Statues

Austria's Animated Ascent to the Oscars

The Austrian animated film industry entered the new millennium with a significant achievement: an Oscar nomination in 2002 for the short film *Copy Shop* (2000/2001) by Virgil Widrich (b. 1967), marking the first nomination for an Austrian short film. Following this honor, Widrich was praised as "one of the most acclaimed Austrian directors of our time" (*Kurzschluss* 2005, 00:42:54). However, in an ironic twist, this milestone for Austrian animation occurred in the *Best Live Action Short Film* category, as *Copy Shop* skillfully blurred the line between live-action and animation: "The film consists of 18,000 photocopied frames, making it neither strictly live action nor animation" (Romney 2001: para. 5). Consequently, despite this innovative success, Austrian animation remained almost invisible at the world's most prestigious film awards.

A decade later, in his introduction to the television program *Die Nacht der Avantgarde* (The Night of the Avant-Garde, 2012), Virgil Widrich expressed his own surprise at the international success of Austrian avant-garde film:[1]

"A few years ago, I came across the program of a Texas cinema showcasing a selection of the world's best avant-garde films. To my surprise, nearly half of them were from Austria. This is truly remarkable considering Austria's small size on the global stage. It's undeniable that over the past few decades – and especially in recent years – Austria's avant-garde film scene has been exceptionally vibrant. This surge in creative output has led many experts to question what makes Austria such a fertile ground for avant-garde filmmaking" ('Die Nacht der Avantgarde' 2012, 00:00:48).

A comprehensive exploration of the Austrian avant-garde film scene, which frequently incorporates animated film techniques, could easily fill entire volumes – and indeed, it already has. To illustrate the global impact of this movement, four avant-garde filmmakers whose work gained international recognition shortly after the turn of the millennium will therefore be highlighted as examples:

"Until recently, Austria's avant-garde film scene was primarily represented by Martin Arnold and his obsessive experimental film *Passage à l'acte* (1993), which reinterpreted a scene from *To Kill a Mockingbird* (1960). Another key figure was Peter Tscherkassky, known for his equally obsessive experimental film *Outer Space* (1998/99), which transformed scenes from *The Entity* (1982) with Barbara Hershey. In recent years, Virgil Widrich has also become a prominent name in this distinguished circle" (*Kurzschluss* 2006, 00:15:02).

Paul Wenninger (b. 1966) also garnered international acclaim with his pixilation film *Uncanny Valley* (2014/2015), making him the subject of the fourth profile.

DOI: 10.1201/9781003415442-16

RE-ANIMATION: PETER TSCHERKASSKY

Few names are as synonymous with Austrian avant-garde cinema as Peter Tscherkassky (b. 1958). Described as "the figurehead of Austrian avant-garde film" ('Österreicher in Venedig' 2010, 00:00:24), Tscherkassky is celebrated as "one of the most esteemed figures and connoisseurs of German-speaking avant-garde cinema: a brilliant thinker, a masterful craftsman, and an internationally acclaimed film artist" (*Kurzschluss* 2011, 00:19:43). In 1978, Tscherkassky was introduced to avant-garde cinema through a 5-day lecture series at the *Österreichisches Filmmuseum* (Austrian Film Museum) led by P. Adams Sitney (b. 1944), a renowned historian of American avant-garde cinema. This experience ignited his passion for the genre. By the end of 1979, he had acquired Super 8 equipment and embarked on a filmmaking career that continues to this day, encompassing over 30 films and earning more than 50 national and international awards.

Beginning in 1984, Peter Tscherkassky expanded his influence in the film world by working as a curator and organizing numerous avant-garde film festivals. His academic pursuits culminated in a doctoral degree from the University of Vienna's Institute of Philosophy in 1986, with a dissertation titled *Film + Kunst: Zu einer kritischen Ästhetik der Kinematografie* (Film + Art: Towards a Critical Aesthetics of Cinematography). Tscherkassky also shared his expertise through university teaching positions in Linz (Upper Austria) and Vienna from 1989 to 2006, alongside leading numerous seminars and workshops. In 1990, he co-founded *sixpackfilm*, a non-profit film distribution company that plays a crucial role in connecting Austrian avant-garde cinema with both domestic and international audiences. His leadership in the film industry was further solidified when he was appointed the artistic director of the newly established *Diagonale* film festival in 1993, a key event in Austria's cinematic calendar, a position he held for two editions until 1994.

Peter Tscherkassky's significance extends beyond his work as a filmmaker and advocate for avant-garde cinema; he is also a prolific contributor to film theory and history, a pursuit he began in 1984. His essays and articles, translated into more than 15 languages, have garnered international recognition. Notably, he edited *Film Unframed: A History of Austrian Avant-Garde Cinema* (2012), the first comprehensive English-language account of Austria's avant-garde film history.

Peter Tscherkassky's debut film, *Kreuzritter* (Crusaders, 1979/1980), retained a traditional narrative cinematic style. However, he quickly shifted his focus toward creating purely structural films, exploring the boundaries of form and technique. In *Sechs über Eins* (Six Above One, 1982), he showed all 720 possible combinations of six film frames, resulting in an abstract flicker animation film. This experiment, featuring varying shades of gray from pure black to pure white, marked a pivotal moment in his career: "I was satisfied and decided to devote myself to the relationship between the figurative image and its abstraction" (Tscherkassky 2005a: 120). While Tscherkassky is not an animator in the classical sense, animation techniques feature prominently in many of his works, demonstrating his innovative approach to film:

"I'm not sure I'm really interested in the question of genres and sub-genres, but I do indeed utilize a frame-by-frame technique, which could be seen in the tradition of pixilation; I use pre-existing film frames as material, which in themselves are still pictures. In this sense, you might think of my films as animated still frames and as such, as animation films" (Peter Tscherkassky, as cited in Wells and Hardstaff 2008: 156).

In *Ballet No. 3* (1982), Peter Tscherkassky meticulously reassembled 256 photographic prints of a continuous dance movement using the camera's single-frame function, creating entirely new, abstract movements. These were further altered through double and triple exposures, adding layers of complexity to the final composition.[2] Tscherkassky is particularly renowned for his innovative approach to re-animating found footage. His journey into this technique began in the early 1980s when he stumbled upon a shortened Super 8 version of a medieval film featuring a scene where a kidnapped woman is sold at a slave market. Reflecting on this, Tscherkassky remarked, "I immediately loved the idea of doing something parallel by 'kidnapping' foreign pictures and using them for my own purpose, like the barbarian who kidnaps the beautiful woman, but I never intended to become a 'pure' found footage filmmaker" (Peter Tscherkassky, as cited in Wells and Hardstaff 2008: 156). In *Freeze Frame* (1983), Tscherkassky's first film of this nature, he combined found footage with his own material to illustrate the uncontrollability of images. To achieve this, he repeatedly re-filmed the footage and overlaid the exposures on top of each other. In the film's climax, the projection is deliberately halted, causing the filmstrip to scorch from the heat of the projector lamp, thus breaking free from the projectionist's control. Originally presented as a live performance in Berlin (Germany) during the summer of 1983, the film version premiered in New York City (USA) in the late summer of that same year.

Peter Tscherkassky values the constraints of the given material but also relishes the challenge of transcending these boundaries; "Tscherkassky's 'kidnap' of material and his engagement with the re-imagining of the footage before him enables him to re-animate not merely the film itself, but the potential implications of its content, both formally and narratively" (Wells and Hardstaff 2008: 156). A year after *Freeze Frame* (1983), Tscherkassky created *Motion Picture* (1984), a film that references the Lumière brothers' iconic *La Sortie de l'Usine Lumière à Lyon* (Workers Leaving the Lumière Factory in Lyon, 1895). For this project – his first to be produced entirely in a darkroom[3] – Tscherkassky attached 50 unexposed 16-mm film strips to a wall. He then projected a still frame from the Lumière film onto these strips, exposing them in this manner, which mimicked a digital scan using purely analog methods. This approach allowed Tscherkassky to reconstruct the entire film image while ensuring that viewers could not reassemble it into the original Lumière footage, thus preserving the unique abstraction of his work (Figure 13.1).

Manufraktur (Manufracture, 1985), Peter Tscherkassky's second film created entirely in the darkroom and his first on 35 mm, is considered his inaugural work made purely from found footage material. Using contact printing, he fused two advertising films – one for pantyhose and the other for car tires. This cinematic experiment in spatial movement accelerated toward an apparent collision – but ultimately, it was only the film material that collided. The film's production was as intense as its pace: "I made the film *Manufraktur* as if in a trance. It took six days, working in fourteen-hour shifts, to complete the film" (Tscherkassky 2005a: 134). The title, which plays

FIGURE 13.1 The 50 film strips from *Motion Picture* (1984), arranged sequentially in front of the corresponding projection, featured in the *From a Dark Room* (2008) exhibition at *Galerie nächst St. Stephan*, Vienna. (Courtesy of Peter Tscherkassky.)

on the term 'Fraktur' (fracture) to reference the cinematic break, later became the name of Tscherkassky's 'film manufacture.'

Peter Tscherkassky's passion for distorting film material is evident in *kelimba* (1986). Here, he made a contact copy of a short 16-mm film strip featuring a dancer onto photographic paper, then copied it five times until the dancer was reduced to amoeba-like spots. These five copies were transferred onto overhead transparencies, cut out, glued onto several meters of 16-mm blank film, and finally filmed as a loop from the screen of the editing table with a Super 8 camera: "I remember the pleasure and fervor with which I indulged in these kinds of distortions, organizing the results around fundamental reflections on the nature of the filmic image and its representation of movement" (Tscherkassky 2005a: 136). *Shot-Countershot* (1987), though only 22 seconds long, humorously literalizes the shot-reverse-shot editing technique in a single take. Due to this clever approach, it has been described in film programs as "the shortest cinematic joke based on film theory" (Huber 2020b: para. 1).

This film, which avoids animation, "marks the earliest incarnation of Hollywood cinema in Tscherkassky's œuvre" (Horwath 2005: 34). While found footage played only a minor role in *tabula rasa* (1987/1989), it became more prominent in *Parallel Space: Inter-View* (1992). This film was based on the realization that although the film strip of a photo camera shares the same dimensions as a film strip, the 24×36mm photo captured is exactly twice the size of a film frame. The space captured by Tscherkassky with the photo camera was thus halved in the film projection. In the found footage sequence, Tscherkassky reversed the effect: by placing two televisions on top of each other, showing a scene from the American film *Wild River* (1960) on one and a self-made film on the other, and photographing them frame by frame, an alternating, flickering, interwoven double exposure of both films was created.

For *Happy-End* (1996), Peter Tscherkassky used the amateur film legacy of a seemingly childless couple, Elfriede and Rudolf, which the filmmaker Lisl Ponger (b. 1947) had acquired at a flea market. "Tscherkassky re-animates not merely the frames of the found footage, but also the couple's lives as abstract individuals symbolizing the common experience of an existence which relentlessly moves through rituals such as birthdays, weddings, public holidays and ultimately, death itself" (Wells and Hardstaff 2008: 156). By arranging the film material in reverse chronological order, the couple appears to grow younger, akin to *The Curious Case of Benjamin Button* (2008). Toward the end of their amateur film career (or the beginning of *Happy-End*), they used a remote shutter release and tripod, while at the beginning (or end of *Happy-End*), they filmed with a hand-held camera. Tscherkassky interwove these hand-held shots using double projection: "a rush of images accompanying the blissful ecstasy of the two actors, all the way to the finale, an exuberant dance by Elfriede leading into a freeze frame of her face, its expression conveying both joy and deep pain at the same time" (Tscherkassky 2005a: 148).

Peter Tscherkassky's internationally acclaimed CinemaScope trilogy (1998–2001) showcases his mastery of darkroom filmmaking at a time when digital recording threatened to eclipse analog film. By intentionally choosing CinemaScope – a widescreen format introduced in the 1950s to counter television's rising popularity – Tscherkassky sought to fully explore the artistic potential of analog media. After months of experimentation, Tscherkassky discovered a trailer for the British-French historical film *Mayerling* (1968), featuring a train entering a station from left to right. When he flipped the film upside down, the scene evoked the Lumière brothers' iconic *L'Arrivée d'un train en gare de La Ciotat* (The Arrival of a Train at La Ciotat Station, 1895), sparking the concept for *L'Arrivée* (The Arrival, 1997/1998). In Tscherkassky's version, however, the train is set on a collision course with its reflection, culminating in a dramatic crash – not just of the train, but of the film material itself. For *Outer Space* (1998/1999), Tscherkassky used scenes from the American horror film *The Entity* (1982). Each day, he meticulously exposed a few meters of raw film frame by frame, layering multiple images from the original footage (Figure 13.2). At the end of each day, he developed the film and left it to dry overnight, allowing him to review the results the next morning. Inspired by children's play, Tscherkassky employed a laser pointer to precisely capture even the tiniest details, crafting a complex and uniquely distinctive film collage. The extensive material generated during the creation of *Outer Space* (1998/1999) led to the final installment of

FIGURE 13.2 Peter Tscherkassky in his darkroom in 1998, meticulously crafting *Outer Space* (1999). (Courtesy of Peter Tscherkassky.)

the trilogy, *Dream Work* (2001). In this film, which mirrors the duration of a deep sleep phase, Tscherkassky overlaid up to seven different shots from *The Entity* (1982) onto each frame.[4] In a nod to American avant-garde artist Man Ray (1890–1976), who pioneered cameraless films in the 1920s by exposing shadow-casting objects directly onto film, Tscherkassky employed similar techniques. He directly exposed objects like needles, thumbtacks, and coarse salt onto his film stock, blending tactile, manual artistry with avant-garde cinematic exploration.

Until this point, Peter Tscherkassky had predominantly relied on a single source film for his found footage projects. However, for his next endeavor, he initially planned to combine amateur films, his own footage, and elements from a Hollywood production. Discovering a worn-out print of the Italian Western *The Good, the Bad and the Ugly* (1966), Tscherkassky sought "to transform a Roman western into a Greek tragedy" (Tscherkassky 2005b: para. 1). To achieve this transformation, Tscherkassky had the hanged villain of the Western descend into a kind of cinematic Hades, where he was confronted with the 'secret signs' of film labs and projectionists – those technical markers that appear at the ends of individual film reels, symbolizing the very conditions of his existence as a shadowy figure on screen. *Instructions for a Light and Sound Machine* (2005),[5] also shot in CinemaScope, served as Tscherkassky's swan song to the fading medium of analog film and its unique technical iconography (Figure 13.3).[6]

In *Coming Attractions* (2010), the first installment in his *The Rushes Series*, Peter Tscherkassky constructed a triangular relationship between the cinematically intertwined realms of advertising film, early cinema (particularly the 'Cinema of Attractions'), and avant-garde filmmaking. He drew from a 6-hour pool of test footage for various commercials, where models repeatedly performed the same actions in pursuit of the perfect take. What the advertisers deemed waste material became a goldmine for Tscherkassky – and the relentless repetition imbued the footage with a humorous, almost absurd quality. For *The Exquisite Corpus* (2015), a title inspired by the Surrealists' associative technique known as the 'exquisite corpse,' Tscherkassky

FIGURE 13.3 Peter Tscherkassky's darkroom during the production of *Instructions for a Light and Sound Machine* (2005). (Courtesy of Peter Tscherkassky.)

employed a 1960s nudist film as an entry point. This set the stage for a playful and subversive exploration of fragmented imagery, blending eroticism, humor, and the unexpected in a dreamlike collage:

"It takes nearly four minutes to arrive at this juncture before Tscherkassky blows his fuses in characteristic style. Images begin to flicker and tremble, intermingling and superimposing, nervously shimmering between positive and negative, diving headlong into over-, under-, and multiple exposures, split screens, and distortion effects. [...] Tscherkassky's is a rigorously analog film, manually composed one frame at a time out of moments from disembodied feature films, amateur and porn flics, as well as fragments of discarded advertising rushes – magic from the garbage can of commercial film" (Stefan Grissemann in Tscherkassky and Grissemann 2018: para. 9–10).

The latest addition to *The Rushes Series* is *Train Again* (2021), a title that pays homage to Peter Tscherkassky's earlier work, *L'Arrivée* (The Arrival, 1997/1998).[7] The train, a motif intertwined with cinema's history since its inception, serves as both a direct reference and a compelling metaphor in this context. Over 40 years after his first film, Tscherkassky's electrifying masterpiece reaffirms that cinema and analog film remain resilient, standing strong against the encroaching dominance of digital media. "I am the Don Quixote of the analog film era" (Peter Tscherkassky in *Kurzschluss* 2011, 00:26:45), Tscherkassky declared, encapsulating his unwavering commitment to preserving analog film. Through his work, the re-animation of analog film material will continue.

EXACTLY THE RIGHT TIME: VIRGIL WIDRICH

When Virgil Widrich first saw *Disney*'s *Bambi* (1942) in the cinema at age 6, he was so captivated that his parents had to explain that, unlike in the theater, he couldn't meet the 'actors' backstage: "That was his first formative impression of how the movies work, and how they differ ever so slightly to the theater" (Widrich et al. (eds.) 2012: 19). At the age of 12, Widrich began making his first films using a Super 8 camera. In December 1980, he created a 17-second animation sequence as a test. After watching a TV documentary about Walt Disney (1901–1966), Widrich was inspired to create his own animated film. Without access to traditional animation cels, he resourcefully used overhead transparencies, painting and cutting out a thousand of them. Within 5 months, the 13-year-old completed *Auch Farbe kann träumen* (Color Can Dream, 1980/1981), a film about a small drawn figure escaping into the real world – an early exploration of the blurred lines between fantasy and reality that would become a hallmark of his work. At 15, Widrich directed his first short film featuring professional actors: in *Monster in Salzburg* (1982), inspired by the *Godzilla* movies, the Austrian actress Libgart Schwarz (b. 1941), who was well-known in Germany, played a role. However, the film's true star was a 30-cm-tall wooden puppet with twisted hair, brought to life through stop-motion animation in miniature models of Salzburg's streets (Figure 13.4). That same year, Widrich also began delving deeply into film theory. By the end of 1985, he was accepted into the *Filmakademie Wien* (Film Academy Vienna), though he left after only a few weeks in 1986. In 1990, Widrich embarked on his first Hollywood venture, serving as an assistant to John Bailey (1942–2023) on the science fiction film *The Search for Signs of Intelligent Life in the Universe* (1991). Upon returning to Austria, he became one of the co-organizers of the *Diagonale*, one of the country's most important film festivals, which launched in 1993.

Virgil Widrich established his reputation as a multimedia artist in the late 1990s. In collaboration with Viennese director Martin Reinhart (b. 1967), he co-produced *tx-transform* (1998), a visual showcase for the innovative film process Reinhart had been developing since 1992.[8] Described as "his first truly experimental film" (*Kurzschluss* 2006, 00:18:09), *tx-transform* is both the title of the film and a patented advancement of the slit-scan technique, famously used in the mesmerizing 'Star Gate sequence' in Stanley Kubrick's (1928–1999) sci-fi classic *2001: A Space Odyssey* (1968).

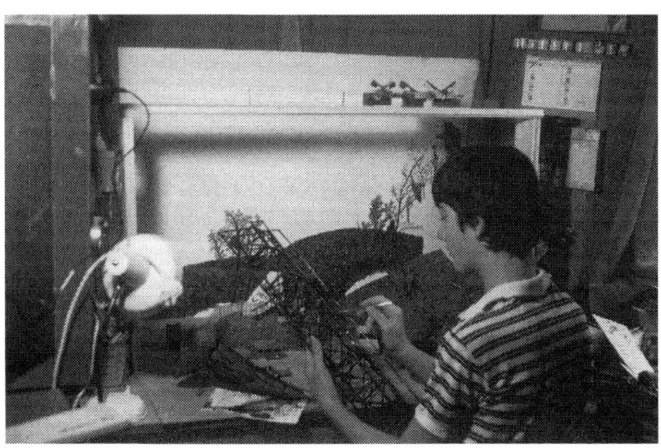

FIGURE 13.4 Virgil Widrich setting up model trick shots for *Monster in Salzburg* (1982). (Courtesy of Virgil Widrich.)

This groundbreaking process swaps the time (*t*) and space (*x*) axes: while traditional film captures an entire space in each frame over a brief moment (1/24 second), *tx-transform* inverts this, showing only a section of the space but capturing everything that occurs there over a given period. The result is an image where the left side represents the 'before,' while the right side shows the 'after.' This technique produces visionary visuals reminiscent of the concepts in Albert Einstein's (1879–1955) theory of relativity.

After his debut feature *Heller als der Mond* (Brighter Than the Moon, 1999/2000), Virgil Widrich went on to create the previously mentioned short film *Copy Shop* (2000/2001). In this Oscar-nominated work, a man duplicates himself until the entire world is populated by his copies, a narrative that can also be interpreted as a political allegory reflecting Austria's right-wing conservative government at the time. The film's production involved editing approximately 17,000 individual images on a computer, printing them out, and reanimating them using the single-frame technique (Figure 13.5). Although *Copy Shop* (2000/2001) did not win the Oscar, it garnered over 40 international awards. Widrich's subsequent short film, *Fast Film* (2001/2003), was similarly successful, earning more than 30 international accolades. In this experimental piece, Widrich referenced approximately 400 films from cinematic history by animating 10,000 paper figures and objects, thereby venturing into what was described as "uncharted short film territory" (*Kurzschluss* 2006, 00:15:37). The idea for *Fast Film* (2001/2003) emerged during the production of *Copy Shop* (2000/2001), where the sound of tearing paper was used for the film's soundtrack. The scraps that littered the floor inspired Widrich to deconstruct printed film images in a similar fashion. Over 2 years, a team of 12 animators collaborated with Widrich to bring this ambitious project to life. Following these successes, Widrich produced two short films for exhibitions: the surreal montage *make/real* (2010), composed of scenes from science fiction films for the exhibition *Roboterträume* (Robot Dreams) in Graz (Austria) and Basel (Switzerland), and the found footage film collage *warning triangle* (2011) for the exhibition *Fetisch Auto* (Car Fetish) in Basel. Between 2012 and 2014,

FIGURE 13.5 The 17,000 paper printouts for *Copy Shop* (2001), prepared ahead of the single-frame animation process in December 2000. (Courtesy of Virgil Widrich.)

FIGURE 13.6 Virgil Widrich during the filming of *Vienna table trip* (2016) in December 2015. (Courtesy of Virgil Widrich.)

Widrich developed *back track* (2014/2015), a 3D remix of feature films where scenes from the 1950s and 1960s were projected onto glass screens and photographed using the single-frame technique.

The promotional film *Vienna table trip* (2015/2016), commissioned by the City of Vienna, serves as Virgil Widrich's heartfelt tribute to his adopted city (Figure 13.6). Blending stop-motion and computer animation, the film conjures a microcosm of Vienna on a café table, set within a green box: butter spread on bread morphs into works of art; sugar cubes stack up to form an opera house where hazelnut slices dance; iconic Viennese motifs are projected onto napkins; the Danube spills from an overturned cup; and a miniature streetcar circles the rim of a plate. In the finale, the crockery forms the city's silhouette. Widrich also employed animation for the music video *Be My Rebel* (2017/2018), created for German singer Nena (née Gabriele Susanne Kerner in 1960) and British musician Dave Stewart (b. 1952), infusing the project with his signature imaginative style.

Shortly after, Virgil Widrich released *Light Matter* (2018), a film that challenged the very foundations of cinema and the collective experience of film viewing. Drawing on a psychological effect known since the 19th century, Widrich employed a rapidly alternating sequence of white, grey, and black frames to induce a subjective perception of color in the viewer's mind. In the same year, Widrich revisited and expanded upon the 20-year-old concept of *tx-transform* (1998) with *tx-reverse* (2018), where he artfully collided reality with cinema. Tragically, 2 years later, Widrich's life collided with a harsh reality when his and filmmaker Anja Salomonowitz's (b. 1976) 12-year-old son, Oskar Salomonowitz (2008–2020), passed away in an accident. A budding artist who had created his first animated film at the age of 6, Oskar left behind 206 drawings on flipbook paper. In a heartfelt tribute, Widrich honored his son's memory by transforming these drawings into an animated film, preserving Oskar's creative legacy:

"Oskar never showed me his drawings in detail because he did not want to showcase an unfinished film. At first, I had no idea whatsoever how the story should continue, and the beginning was very difficult for me. I practiced Oskar's stroke for a long time for fear of doing something wrong, but that's what definitely would have made my style be different from his, because he wasn't afraid at all. Oskar conceived his project as a flipbook and not necessarily as a film, but his stack would have been far too thick to flip through evenly. In the end, I would have suggested to him that we photograph his drawings and then turn them into an animated film with sound. I am sure he would have liked this format very much and it being screened in the cinema" (Widrich 2021: para. 2).

Virgil Widrich discovered the film's title in one of his son's math books, where a word problem posed the question of whether a train remains in a tunnel long enough to don a life-saving disguise. Under the solution, Oskar had scribbled: *Es ist genau genug Zeit* (There Is Exactly Enough Time) – and with that, the film's title was found. For Widrich, the task ahead felt like detective work, as he not only sought to continue the story in his son's spirit across the remaining 490 sheets of paper but also to track down the exact pencils from Oskar's belongings. Finally, in 2021, Widrich completed the story, drawing the final scenes and animating them himself: "For two weeks, Virgil sat hunched over the animation light table, and during that time, it was as if he had become 12 years old again" (*Making of Es ist genau genug Zeit*, 00:04:23). The poignant film resonated deeply with international audiences and juries alike, earning over 80 film awards – nearly twice as many as those won by his acclaimed *Copy Shop* (2000/2001). This heartfelt cinematic tribute to his son stands as a powerful monument to Oskar's memory:

"A very short film, infinitely sad and at the same time mischievous and playful. [...] The father [...] continues drawing the superhero tale, creating an animated film between deep mourning and carefree children's logic. Capturing the proximity of happiness and loss in the most succinct form" (Dinkla 2021: para. 1).

Since childhood, Virgil Widrich, who is currently working on an animated feature,[9] has been dedicated to blurring the boundaries between film and reality. His innovative approach to filmmaking and visionary works have earned him recognition as "one of our favorite directors" (*Kurzschluss* 2006, 00:14:50), according to the creators of the *Kurzschluss* (Short Circuit) series on the French-German cultural channel Arte. After *Copy Shop* (2000/2001) made history as the first Austrian film nominated for an Oscar in the *Best Live Action Short Film* category, Widrich has the potential to achieve the same feat in the *Best Animated Short Film* category.[10] Regardless, film critic Marina Pavido is convinced that "*Copy Shop* is present and future" (Pavido 2022: para. 1). It would indeed be the right moment – after all, *There Is Exactly Enough Time.*

DE-ANIMATION: MARTIN ARNOLD

Much like Peter Tscherkassky, with whom Martin Arnold (b. 1959) organized film retrospectives in the early 1990s, Arnold also achieved international acclaim for his deconstruction of found footage.[11] After studying psychology and art history at the University of Vienna, Arnold began making films in 1985. He now views his early work – the unfinished trilogy *O.T.* (Untitled, 1985–1989) – as "incomplete advance stages of his mature aesthetic" (Miessgang 2002: 15). Between 1989 and 1998, he produced three found footage films that Dirk Schaefer (b. 1971) described as "a trilogy of compulsive repetition" (as cited in Remes 2020: 129). For *pièce touchée* (Touched Piece, 1989),[12] Arnold painstakingly extracted 148,000 frames from an 18-second sequence of the Hollywood film *The Human Jungle* (1954) over the course of a year and a half, using a self-built optical printer. The Hollywood depiction of domestic intimacy was transformed into a 16-minute "mechanical ballet" (Häfele 2015: 11), meticulously choreographed with rhythm and movement, featuring symmetrical reflections, duplications, and forward and backward loops.[13] When the film premiered at the *Österreichische Filmtage* (Austrian Film Days) in Wels (Upper Austria) in 1989, Tscherkassky declared it "the most beautiful film of the festival" (Peter Tscherkassky in *Österreichische Film-Tage Wels 1989* 1989, 00:33:36).

For the 12-minute *passage à l'acte* (Transition Into Action, 1993), the second part of his trilogy, Martin Arnold reworked a brief 30-second breakfast scene from *To Kill a Mockingbird* (1962), this time also manipulating the audio track. Arnold's meticulous alterations transformed the mundane routine of a middle-class suburban family into a surreal nightmare. By dismantling and reconstructing the scene, he imposed a new rhythm, altering its meaning. For instance, the son's repeated slamming of the front door generates a soundscape reminiscent of machine gun fire. Similarly, the daughter's kiss on her father's cheek, played by Gregory Peck (1916–2003), is recontextualized through Arnold's looping technique – what could have been shifted toward a romantic implication instead becomes a rapid, machine gun-like repetition loop. "Text and images attack" (Martin Arnold in 'Arnold: Stadtkino' 1993, 00:00:31), Arnold noted in a television interview, emphasizing the aggressive power of his deconstructed visuals.

In *Alone. Life Wastes Andy Hardy* (1998), Martin Arnold meticulously deconstructed three Hollywood teen films featuring the fictional character Andy Hardy, portrayed by Mickey Rooney (1920–2014) alongside Judy Garland (1922–1969). This time, Arnold placed particular emphasis on musical elements. Through his deconstruction of Hollywood's cinematic codes – employing techniques of repetition and re-rhythmization – Arnold, with his background in psychology, unearthed underlying themes of violence and sexuality embedded within the 24 frames/s. Inspired by Austrian psychoanalyst Sigmund Freud (1856–1939), Arnold's meticulous approach transformed these seemingly innocent scenes into a kind of Oedipal drama, revealing the darker subtexts of classic Hollywood narratives:

"Moreover, Arnold's virtuosic image and sound editing creates a hypnotically rich rhythmic visual and sonic field which lends both grace and savagery to the films' analytical work. The physical vitality re-found in the image, accompanied by equally complex variations on the soundtrack, make his films work as dance and music as much as ironic inquiry" (Zryd 2004: para. 1).

Martin Arnold summarized the psychological aspect of his trilogy as follows: "The cinema of Hollywood is a cinema of exclusion, reduction and denial, a cinema of repression. If *pièce touchée* expresses sexuality and *passage a l'acte* aggression, then perhaps *Andy Hardy* finds melancholia" (Martin Arnold, as cited in Zryd 2004: introd.).

While Martin Arnold's earlier works were characterized by adding layers through repetition, his post-millennium approach involved stripping elements away instead.

According to Justin Remes, Arnold's films *Forsaken* (2002), *Dissociated* (2002), and *Deanimated* (2001/2002), all created for an exhibition, form "a trilogy of erasure" (Remes 2020: 129). In the 9-minute *Forsaken* (2002), two projection screens faced each other, showing scenes from the classic Western *High Noon* (1952). By digitally removing the film's characters, Arnold immersed viewers in a shootout set against a deserted backdrop. A similarly surreal scenario was crafted in the 8-minute film *Dissociated* (2002). Positioned between two screens, viewers watched Karen (played by Celeste Holm, 1917–2012) and Eve (played by Anne Baxter, 1923–1985) from *All About Eve* (1950), who, originally engaged in a heated exchange, now silently stared at one another due to the removal of their dialogue. Audiences could hear their breathing and swallowing, see them begin to speak – yet they remained voiceless, creating a powerful exploration of absence. The trilogy reached its climax with the 60-minute *Deanimated* (2001/2002). The story of the original movie *Invisible Ghost* (1941) seemed almost fated for Arnold's treatment: the protagonist, driven to madness after his wife leaves him, continues to live as though she were still present, celebrating their wedding anniversary each year. He instructs the butler to set a place for her at the table and speaks with his absent wife throughout the meal. Arnold's film magnifies this eerie sense of loss, as characters gradually disappear, leaving only faint traces of their existence.

Martin Arnold had two key motivations for creating a film in which he gradually erased dialogue and eventually entire characters digitally. First, he had long been intrigued by the idea of making a movie without actors, instead focusing on the camera moving through empty rooms while the audience followed its movement with a searching gaze. Second, Arnold was fascinated by the psychological dimension, allowing the protagonist's neurosis to spread from one character to another like a contagious disease: "They get the same symptom and start talking to thin air, and in the end, they all get lost" (Martin Arnold, as cited in Taanila 2001: para. 14). For this "radical cinematic operation" (*Neues vom österreichischen Film* 2002, 00:16:08), Arnold had to rely on a support team for the first time, as the frame-by-frame dissection would have been too labor-intensive for him to manage alone. Nevertheless, for him, it represented "the only true remake that is possible anymore: an exact recycling of empty spaces and encounters from yesterday's films" (Martin Arnold, as cited in Vogel 2002: para. 1).

Since 2010, Martin Arnold has been creating films that blend omission with repetition, often drawing on American animated films from studios like *Disney*: "My earlier films […] quite often got interpreted along the lines of sex and gender issues. At a certain point, I got tired of this and asked myself: What do we all have in common? Essentially, we all are animals, dressed and tamed animals" (Martin Arnold, as cited in André 2018: para. 2). The inspiration for his film *Shadow Cuts* (2010) came from a Japanese study on blinking, published in 2009. The study revealed that humans are blind for an average of 6 s/min. Additionally, the subjects blinked in unison when watching movie scenes, indicating that the brain coordinates blinks to align with moments when minimal visual information is missed. For *Shadow Cuts* (2010), Arnold reversed the final scene of a classic Mickey Mouse film, where Mickey cradles his dog Pluto. The two protagonists were repeatedly made blind by blacking out their eyes, and viewers also experienced brief moments of blindness due to flickering effects: "It's about seeing and overlooking, viewing habits and habits of overlooking" (Martin Arnold in 'Österreicher in Venedig' 2010, 00:03:42). Through his editing, Arnold stripped the family-friendly film of its innocent narrative, inviting viewers to reinterpret the relationship between the characters: "When a mouse falls for a dog, anything can happen" (Burger-Utzer and Arnold 2010: para. 4).

Soft Palate (2010), compared to Martin Arnold's earlier exploration of cartoon films, was a more solitary and fragmented experience. The film opens with a twitching hand, then shifts to pursed lips, a flickering tongue, and other disjointed details, until Mickey Mouse is finally seen sitting in a chair, emitting almost hypnotic snoring sounds (Figure 13.7) . *Self Control* (2011) follows a similar structure, gradually revealing the source of muffled thuds and screams. Through Arnold's minimalist and rhythmic editing, Tom (from *Tom and Jerry*) is transformed into a masochist. In a

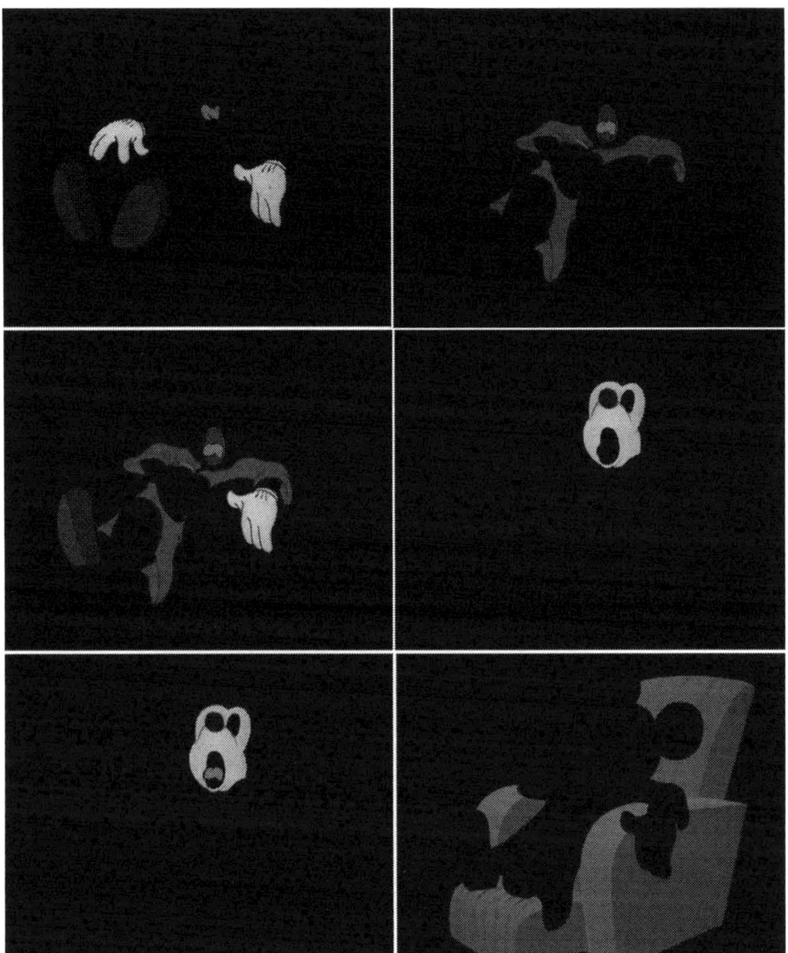

FIGURE 13.7 Stills from Martin Arnold's *Soft Palate* (2010). (Courtesy of Galerie Martin Janda, Vienna.)

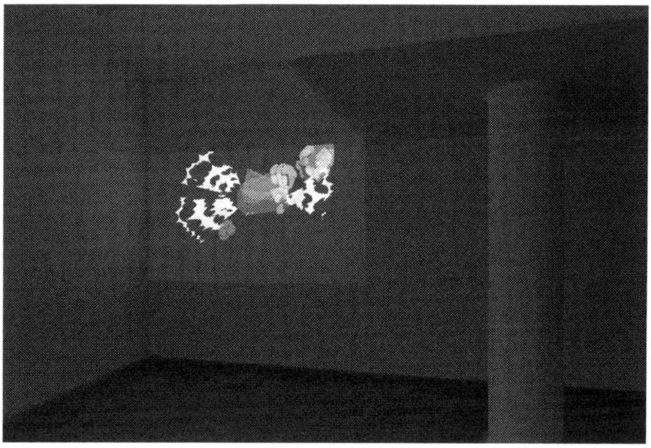

FIGURE 13.8 *Self Control* (2011), showcased in the exhibition *Martin Arnold: Elsewhere* (2013) at *Galerie Martin Janda*, Vienna. (Photographer: Lena Deinhardstein. Courtesy of Galerie Martin Janda, Vienna.)

scene where he repeatedly strikes his head with a brick out of frustration, he appears trapped in an endless loop of self-torment (Figure 13.8). A scream also haunts the viewer in *Haunted House* (2011). As the building's elements flicker in and out of view, the protagonist – of whom only fragmented glimpses are visible in the rapid sequence – seems to literally lose the ground beneath his feet (or paws), triggering a panicked, disorienting scream. Through these films, Arnold skillfully deconstructed familiar animated characters, revealing the darker, more unsettling aspects concealed within their seemingly innocent narratives.

In his later works, Martin Arnold completely detached the figures from their backgrounds, leaving them to float in what appeared to be a black void – still fragmented, of course. *Tooth Eruption* (2013) showcases tongues, hands, and, naturally, teeth swirling in chaotic motion, with sound editing that evokes the frantic screams of a monkey cage. In the brief film loops *Nix* (2013), *Hydra* (2013), and *Charon* (2013) – each lasting only a few seconds – parts of Pluto's face orbit his head like the moons of the same names around the dwarf planet Pluto. In *Whistle Stop* (2014), Daffy Duck becomes the victim of a relentless animation loop, where his beak, wings, and feet are isolated from their usual 'habitat' and wiggle against a stark black background.

Additional films in this style followed, including *Black Holes* (2015), *Elsewhere* (2016), and *Background Check* (2022). Among them, the most haunting was likely *Black Holes* (2015), where a partially visible Goofy appears to shoot himself in an endless loop. Martin Arnold's films served as both artistic and psychological studies; by isolating individual elements like beaks or hands, he evoked the industrial production process of classic US cartoons, where in-betweeners focused solely on drawing the parts of a character that would move in each scene. By extrapolating these elements, Arnold restored their original autonomy, allowing them to stand alone and reclaim their unique identity:

"Visually speaking, what I do is pull out some of these celluloid sheets from the pile of sheets with body-part drawings and break down the image to some of its original layers. Metaphorically speaking, I'm de-celing cel animation. Of course, I do it digitally, but if the original sheets were still available and I could have gotten access to them, I could also have done it in an analog way" (Martin Arnold, as cited in André 2018: para. 6).

At the same time, Martin Arnold's films functioned as psychological experiments, exploring complex emotions such as fear, aggression, frustration, vulnerability, and sexual attraction. Walter Benjamin (1892–1940) had already pointed out the inherent connection between cartoons and horror films, stating: "All Mickey Mouse films are founded on the motif of leaving home in order to learn what fear is" (Walter Benjamin 1931, as translated in Jennings et al. (eds.) 1999: 545). This insight aptly frames the trajectory of Arnold's work since *Deanimated* (2001/2002). Austrian psychoanalyst Sigmund Freud, the founder of modern psychoanalysis, succinctly captured the essence of this uncanny intersection: "Severed limbs, a severed head, a hand detached from the arm [...], feet that dance by themselves [...] – all of these have something highly uncanny about them, especially when they are credited [...] with independent activity" (Sigmund Freud 1919, as translated in Freud and Haughton 2003: 150). In this sense, Arnold can be seen as the Sigmund Freud of classic animation, dissecting the darker, unconscious layers of familiar cartoons.

THE ANIMATION CHOREOGRAPHER: PAUL WENNINGER

The dancer and choreographer Paul Wenninger began exploring animation relatively late in his career but with remarkable intensity. Throughout his choreographic work, he has consistently focused on the use of objects and bodies; in 1999, he co-founded the platform *Kabinett ad Co.* to create a space where artists from various disciplines could collaborate on body-centric projects without hierarchical constraints.

During his exploration of linear and time-delayed dramaturgy, Paul Wenninger encountered a creative limitation: "My approach to working with objects on stage, when I physically moved them, felt too slow to me" (Paul Wenninger, as cited in Rudle 2016, under 'Film als choreografisches Werk'). For Wenninger, animation became an extension of his choreography, much as it was an extension of painting for Maria Lassnig (1919–2014): "That's how I discovered pixilation: stop-motion animation with live actors" (Paul Wenninger, as cited in Rudle 2016, under 'Film als choreografisches Werk'). Speed plays a crucial role in Wenninger's work, evident not only in his dynamic time-lapses but also in his technical approach – while many animators use 15 frames/s in pixilation, he pushes the medium to its full potential with 24 frames/s. His films are choreographic works in which the body morphs into a moving object. To maintain precise control over these movements, Wenninger often positions himself in front of the camera or works closely with dancers, whose mastery of spatial and temporal manipulation proves essential to his animation process.[14]

For his films, Paul Wenninger chose the most basic form of animation – frame-by-frame – deliberately avoiding additional tools. His debut work, *trespass* (2012), delves into the theme of the body being confined within time and space, a constraint that gives rise to various forms of authority. Wenninger aimed to challenge these authorities by positioning the body itself as the primary force within space. His goal was to give the body a voice, to break free from its temporal and spatial imprisonment, thereby reclaiming autonomy and disrupting established power dynamics: "The goal was to turn the body into time and space, to transform time into space, and space into time" (Paul Wenninger in 'Werkschau Paul Wenninger' 2021, 00:03:08). In the film, he plays with the multiple meanings of 'trespass,' sending an avatar of himself on a global journey – all within the confines of his own four walls. The narrative is marked by repeated transgressions, where the outside world penetrates the cell-like prison from which the character, despite breathtaking images from across the globe, seems unable to escape. The film concludes with a poignant reflection on the fleeting nature of the body's prison, framed within technically and visually stunning animations.

In *Uncanny Valley* (2014/2015), Paul Wenninger explored the concept of the 'uncanny valley,' a term that describes the discomfort or acceptance gap people feel when encountering lifelike artificial figures. Wenninger not only played with this psychological phenomenon but also interpreted the term literally, connecting it to the eerie, desolate landscapes of trench warfare (Figure 13.9). Marking the centenary of the First World War's (1914–1918) descent into the static horrors of trench warfare in 1915, Wenninger depicted the harrowing struggle for survival of two soldiers in the trenches through an emotionally charged animated film based on found footage. The use of pixilation, which imparts a mechanical quality to the characters' movements, accentuates the mechanization of the conflict – widely recognized as the first industrialized war in human history. Wenninger further examined the tension between body and space by constructing each scene like a museum diorama, set within small, meticulously staged rooms. The imagery, captured with a six-axis, computer-controlled camera crane, evokes the perspective of drone footage a chilling parallel

FIGURE 13.9 The six-axis, computer-controlled camera crane positioned within the trenches during the filming of Paul Wenninger's *Uncanny Valley* (2015) in August 2014. (Courtesy of Paul Wenninger.)

to the surveillance and combat techniques employed in modern military conflicts: "I was especially intrigued by the choreographic dimension, the dynamic interplay between the camera's movement and the dancers' choreography" (Paul Wenninger in 'Schwerpunkt Wien und die Welt der Animation' 2016, 00:18:18). By the film's conclusion, the war is relegated to its rightful place – in a museum. Building on the meticulous construction of the film's imagery and the detailed process of creating the scenes, Wenninger later developed a stage performance that revealed everything left unseen in the film – a kind of 'making-of' that subtly conveyed the idea that, as the last witnesses of the First World War pass away, the conflict can only be represented as a carefully crafted reenactment.

For the short film competition *The Rhythm of Vienna*, organized by *Wien Tourismus* (Vienna Tourist Board) and *Vienna Independent Shorts* (VIS), Paul Wenninger teamed up with British filmmaker Susan Young to create *Dead Reckoning* (2016). The film captures a man's surreal journey around the 'Ringstraße' (Vienna Ring Road) – the grand boulevard that circles the historic city center – and later moves into neighborhoods shaped by migration. Rather than moving on his own, the protagonist's body is moved by the space around him, or as Wenninger described it, displaced by the city's architecture. The film captures the rhythm of the city and the cyclical nature of life, reflecting the rise and fall of its central character. Death is a constant presence, personified by a skeleton animated by Young, which even appears as a grumpy Viennese waiter. After a culinary adventure featuring traditional Viennese dishes like Wiener schnitzel, 'Kaiserschmarrn' (Emperor's Mess), and the city's renowned coffee specialties, the story – and the food – ultimately ends up in the toilet: "We weren't looking for the city's imperial beauty but rather for places where real life unfolds," Wenninger recalled (as cited in *Rathauskorrespondenz* 2016, under 'Dead Reckoning'). The film's concept was inspired by Young's observation during a visit to Vienna: the city, home to fewer living residents (around two million) than deceased in its central cemetery (around three million), remains deeply entwined with its morbid charm.

During the COVID-19 pandemic (in Austria from March 2020 to June 2023), a time marked by spatial restrictions like lockdowns across much of Europe, Paul Wenninger created his fourth film, *O* (2020/2021), in the isolation of a French villa (Figure 13.10). In this piece, Wenninger deliberately minimized bodily movements, allowing the surrounding space to move around him in elliptical orbits. Unlike in *trespass* (2012), the outside world does not intrude upon the scene; instead, it remains distant, depicting stormy times that eventually reveal themselves to be mere projections. The trembling 'O' at the film's opening also evokes the '0' of a coordinate system, symbolizing both the rush and stillness of space and time – a poignant reflection of the collective experience during the height of the COVID-19 pandemic. Viewers are drawn into the movement of the space, as Wenninger continues to view himself as a choreographer who considers the audience's gaze an integral part of the choreography: "What interests me is truly choreographing the viewer, integrating them into the choreographic idea" (Paul Wenninger in 'Werkschau Paul Wenninger' 2021, 00:10:04). Wenninger extends this exploration in his current work, challenging the hierarchy of perspective and anthropocentrism. In his latest project,

FIGURE 13.10 Paul Wenninger, during the spring of 2020, filming *O* (2021) inside a French villa. (Photographer: Claudine Roblez. Courtesy of Paul Wenninger.)

he positions exhibition visitors within a triangular arrangement of three screens, each displaying a drawn animal staring back at them. Through this experimental setup, Wenninger remains faithful to his guiding principle: "Art captivates me only as long as it remains an experiment" (Paul Wenninger, as cited in Rudle 2016, under 'Stolz auf die Töchter').

Norman McLaren (1914–1987) is widely regarded as the pioneer of pixilation, a technique he famously employed in his Oscar-winning film *Neighbours* (1952). Two decades later, Austrian puppet filmmaker Hans O. Sindelar (1921–2014) paid homage to McLaren's legacy – at least thematically – with his own film *Nachbarn* (Neighbours, 1972). Perhaps one day, Paul Wenninger, the Austrian Norman McLaren, will be similarly honored with an Oscar for his innovative contributions to the art of animation.

NOTES

1 When the book *Avantgardefilm. Österreich 1950 bis heute* (Avant-Garde Film. Austria. From 1950 to Today) was published in 1995, Austrian avant-garde film was regarded as more successful than its commercial counterpart (cf. 'Österreichische Avantgarde' 1995).
2 Soon after, *Ballett 16* (1984) was produced using the same 256 frames, but this time without any double or triple exposures.
3 Peter Tscherkassky set up his first darkroom for photographic work at the age of 14 in his family home. It was in this early darkroom that he created *Manufraktur* in 1985. In 1996, he relocated his darkroom to his country house in Lower Austria.
4 In *Outer Space* (1998/1999) – which earned a *Special Award for Innovation* at the *International Leipzig Festival for Documentary and Animated Film* (DOK Leipzig) in 1999 – Peter Tscherkassky incorporated up to 5 shots/frame.
5 *Instructions for a Light and Sound Machine* (2005) received the *Grand Prize* at the *Holland Animation Film Festival* (HAFF) in 2006.

6 In a TV interview, Peter Tscherkassky expressed his deep affection for analog film, stating, "I have a deeply sensual relationship with film. And when I say film, I mean analog film. I want to create works where I can physically engage with the material. [...] It's rooted in touch, and I strive to make films that bring this 'tangibility' – something that will soon vanish in the digital cinema of the future – viscerally alive once more" (Peter Tscherkassky in 'Österreicher in Venedig' 2010, 00:00:52).

7 Work on *Train Again* (released in 2021) commenced 18 years after *L'Arrivée* (The Arrival, 1997/1998), mirroring the way Austrian avant-gardist Kurt Kren (1929–1998) crafted his masterpiece *37/78 Tree Again* (1978) 18 years after *3/60 Bäume im Herbst* (3/60 Trees in Autumn, 1960). The end credits of *Train Again* pay tribute to legendary Kren.

8 Peter Tscherkassky initiated the first meeting between the two filmmakers in May 1997.

9 Refer to the chapter on animated features from Austria.

10 Although several Austrian animated films have successfully qualified for Oscar consideration – such as *Don't Know What* (2019) by Thomas Renoldner (b. 1960) and *Coming Home* (2019) and *The Zolle Suite* (2021) by Benjamin Swiczinsky (b. 1982) – none have yet secured a nomination in the *Best Animated Short Film* category (as of 2023).

11 From the outset of his film career, Martin Arnold rejected the idea of moving his work to the heart of the American film industry: "I have no desire to conquer Hollywood; I want to create small, nuanced works that people appreciate" (Martin Arnold in 'Auf-gerollt' 1990, 00:01:58).

12 The title alludes to a chess rule that requires a touched piece to be moved.

13 In 1998, filmmaker Albert Sackl (b. 1977) recreated the scene and titled his remake *nach "pièce touchée"* (after "pièce touchée", 1998).

14 Paul Wenninger's frequent appearances in front of the camera in his films were motivated by practical considerations rather than narcissism. As he explained in an interview, hiring an actor or dancer for several months would have been prohibitively expensive (cf. 'Werkschau Paul Wenninger' 2021, 00:11:05).

14 New Austrian Animation

A Return to Narrative Storytelling

"Austria's contribution to film history is essentially the avant-garde film." With these words, Austrian film historian Alexander Horwath (b. 1964) introduced his book *Avantgardefilm: Österreich. 1950 bis heute* (Avant-Garde Film: Austria. From 1950 to Today, 1995) on Austrian television ('Österreichische Avantgarde' 1995, 00:00:12). For a long time, avant-garde film also dominated Austrian animation. When Ernst Schmidt Jr. (1938–1988) coined the term "new Austrian animated film" (Schmidt 1985: 34) to describe the wave of Austrian animation that began in the early 1980s, he was mainly referring to avant-garde filmmakers. During this period, the *Studio für experimentellen Trickfilm* (Studio for Experimental Animated Film) at the University of Applied Arts in Vienna emerged as Austria's first university-level institution dedicated to animated film training. The dominance of this studio was so significant that, in his search for alternatives, Benjamin Swiczinsky (b. 1982) had to go to the Film Academy Baden-Württemberg in Ludwigsburg (Germany) to pursue his animation studies from 2006 to 2011. At that time, he was unaware of the artistically oriented *MultiMediaArt* program established in 1996 at the Salzburg University of Applied Sciences and found the other educational opportunities in Austria inadequate:

"While the University of Applied Arts offers an animation class focused on experimental film, the training there is purely artistic and lacks a holistic approach – unlike Ludwigsburg, where artistic elements are woven into a broader, comprehensive framework. On the other hand, Austrian universities of applied sciences teach technical skills, but they don't cover essential aspects like directing, film editing, or storytelling" (Benjamin Swiczinsky, as cited in Eigner 2013: 44).[1]

Together with his fellow Austrian students Johannes Friedrich Schiehsl (b. 1984) and Conrad Tambour (b. 1984), Benjamin Swiczinsky aimed to challenge the prevailing dominance of avant-garde film in Austria: "At the time, we felt there was an overwhelming focus on experimental films, which had a long and successful tradition in Austria, but very few filmmakers and studios dedicated to narrative, or more 'commercial' animation" (Benjamin Swiczinsky, as cited in Tschütscher 2021: para. 3). The trio did not intend to criticize the avant-garde scene, as they were often accused, but rather sought to expand the landscape of Austrian animation by introducing a new dimension:

"No, our goal was simply to prioritize storytelling, to put the narrative front and center, rather than concentrating on a specific technique or style. [...] But that doesn't mean it can't be artistic. It can still take any creative direction while telling a story that resonates and is accessible to people" (Benjamin Swiczinsky, interview with the author, July 5, 2023).

DOI: 10.1201/9781003415442-17

When the trio showcased their graduation films in Austria in June 2011, they seized the opportunity to make a splash by launching the animation studio *Neuer Österreichischer Trickfilm* (NÖT, New Austrian Animation). This bold move positioned them as leading figures of a new generation of Austrian animation filmmakers. That same year, *arx anima* – now arguably Austria's largest animation studio – was founded, followed by the establishment of *Salon Alpin* in 2012 and *LWZ Design & Animation* in 2014, among others.

FADED FRAMES: THE STORY OF *CINE CARTOON*

The story of the revival of narrative animated film in Austria would be incomplete without recognizing a nearly forgotten studio. In 1995, Michael K. Epstein (b. 1953)[2] founded *CINE Cartoon Filmproduktion* in Vienna, which gained a reputation as "the only Austrian production company specializing in the creation of animated series" (Der Standard, September 30, 2003c, under 'Über Cine Cartoon'). The studio employed a broad spectrum of animation techniques, including claymation, 3D computer animation, puppet and model animation, as well as traditional hand-drawn methods. Additionally, it ventured into animated commercials to "bring domestic animation back into the public eye" (Michael Epstein, as cited in Greuling 2003: 17). To maintain its series production, the studio relied on international partnerships for funding: "We would love to produce everything here [in Austria], but it's not financially feasible" (Michael Epstein, as cited in Gasteiger 2004: 27). This financial necessity led to an EU-supported collaboration between studios in Austria, France, and the United Kingdom, operating under the collective name *Fantasy Animation*.[3]

The studio's first notable achievement in series production came with *Taxi* (2000), a project conceived at the turn of the millennium by Franz Grabner (1955–2015) and writer Gebhard Birnbaumer. According to director Alexander 'Sascha' Wieser (b. 1959), the roughly 5-minute episodes were intended as thematic interludes for the television magazine *kreuz und quer* (Criss-Cross): "Due to the demands of current events, each episode had to be conceived and produced within just 3 weeks. It was incredibly stressful" (email from Alexander Wieser to the author, dated February 3, 2024). Produced in claymation by animator Franz Moritz (b. 1968) and featuring voice performances by well-known actors like Cornelia Lippert (b. 1953) and Wolfgang Böck (b. 1953), the series was initially slated for 26 episodes. However, despite its initial success and a planned collaboration with the British BBC, it was discontinued after just four episodes due to funding challenges (telephone conversation between Michael Epstein and the author on November 27, 2023).

The true breakthrough came with the French-German-Austrian co-production *Talis und die tausend Aufgaben* (Talis and the Thousand Tasks, 2000–2001), which the press hailed as "the first time an animated TV production was significantly developed in Austria" (Schmid 2002: 14). The series had its world premiere on Austrian television on October 26, 2001, coinciding with Austria's National Day. The original concept, developed by Austrian Alexander Wieser, follows the adventures of Talis, a squire, and his anteater companion as they undertake tasks assigned by the wizard Merlin.[4] The duo is transported through a magical door from the Middle Ages into the 21st century. The production processes were also "significantly developed in Austria" (Michael Epstein, as cited in Neues Volksblatt, October 25, 2001: 37). Wieser remarked that the series bore similarities to Disney productions: "The storytelling is very American, but the humor is distinctly European" (Alexander Wieser, as cited in Die Presse, October 23, 2001: 30).

The animations were created by the French company *Millimages*, with studios in France, Ukraine, and India, employing around 100 animators who produced a 15-minute episode each week: "The animation is done by hand, in black and white on paper, and only then goes to the computer. It's scanned and digitally colored" (Michael Epstein, as cited in Wallnöfer 2001: 30). The series, with a budget of around €6 million, was financed by France 3 (France), ZDF (Germany), and ORF (Austria). Post-production, including editing, sound effects, and mixing, along with German dubbing, was conducted in Vienna:[5] "We received the scenes in segments and assembled them according to the storyboard. The entire sound level is added, mixed in English, and then we do the German dubbing" (Michael Epstein, as cited in Wallnöfer 2001: 30). Despite Austria's significant role, the series is often cataloged as a French or French-German production, overshadowing Austria's contribution. A second season followed in 2002, and simultaneously, the studio partnered with Germany's *Ravensburger Film & TV* on the British animated series *Wilf the Witch's Dog* (2002), again managing the post-production and German dubbing.[6]

The series *Spirello* (Spirello Songs, 2002/2003), which premiered on Austrian television on October 4, 2003, was also based on a concept by Alexander Wieser. Based on children's songs, the series featured exotic animals with spiral spring legs and subtly promoted values such as tolerance, friendship, and helpfulness. This multinational co-production, with design contributions from Richard Fehsl (b. 1937),[7] was an Austrian-Czech-Finnish collaboration, released in more than half a dozen languages.[8] Vienna's *CINE Cartoon* studio not only developed all the storyboards but also produced 13 of the 26 episodes, making it "the first TV animated series conceived and primarily produced in Austria to air on ORF in over 50 years" (Kurier, September 25, 2003: 31).[9] The first season[10] had a budget of approximately €620,000, "well below the European average" (Michael Epstein, as cited in Greuling 2003: 17). The series' distinctive wax crayon aesthetic was achieved by drawing the characters directly onto Wacom tablets with special pens, with the artwork stored on a server accessible to partner studios from Germany to China (Figure 14.1). This visual style was designed to inspire children to recreate the characters through drawing, with a variety of related media such as books and CDs further enriching the experience.

In late 2003, an adaptation of Richard Strauss's (1864–1949) opera *Till Eulenspiegel* (1895) was announced as a "hypermodern animated spectacle" (Der Standard, September 1, 2003b: 12) (Figure 14.2). The project promised to break new ground: "The film will also be released in IMAX theaters, a completely new dimension for animated films. The technical challenge is immense – an IMAX frame is ten times larger than a 35 mm film frame" (Michael Epstein, as cited in Der Standard, September 1 2003b: 12). Simultaneously, the studio revealed plans for another feature film project, *TomTom*, based on the cartoon character created by Austrian Thomas Kostron, which was especially popular in Asia (Figure 14.3). Energized by these developments, film journalist Rodja Pavlik anticipated 2004 to be "a fateful year for Austrian animation" (Pavlik 2016: para. 1). However, the vision did not materialize as expected.[11] By mid-2004,

FIGURE 14.1 Storyboard drafts for the series *Spirello* (2003), created by Peter Höhsl in the distinctive wax crayon style envisioned by Richard Fehsl. (Courtesy of Thomas Bogner.)

FIGURE 14.2 Apprentice Simon Wieser animating Balduzius, the magical mouse from the *Till Eulenspiegel* project, in July 2004, wearing gloves to protect the drawing tablet from hand perspiration. (Photographer: Jürg Christandl.)

the ambitious large-scale *Till Eulenspiegel* adaptation had been scaled down to a roughly half-hour TV special, while *TomTom* was reimagined as another TV series.[12]

In 2005, Michael Epstein retired from the film industry, and, through Sascha Wieser's mediation, the studio was sold to film producer Thomas Bogner (b. 1958).

FIGURE 14.3 Character designs for the *TomTom* project by Peter Höhsl, inspired in part by the original figures created by Thomas Kostron. (Courtesy of Thomas Bogner.)

Despite this transition, the studio's ambitions remained high. That same year, plans were initiated for an animated feature based on the German cartoon series *WinneToons* (2002),[13] with six co-production partners – three from Germany and one each from Belgium, Luxembourg, and the Philippines. Although ORF reportedly expressed interest, Austrian film funding authorities ultimately declined to provide financial support. A cinematic adaptation was finally realized in 2009 – without Austrian involvement. Between 2007 and 2008, *CINE Cartoon* participated in the development of the German-Polish-Austrian feature film project *Winzig, der Elefant* (Tiny the Elephant), based on a children's book by Austrian author Erwin Moser (1954–2017). "Unfortunately, the film couldn't secure full financing and, as a result, was never produced," explained Norbert Lechner of the lead production company, *KEVIN LEE Filmgesellschaft* (email to the author, dated November 15, 2023). Only storyboard drafts from the Polish *Studio Miniatur Filmowych* remain as a testament to the unrealized project.

In the fall of 2008, ORF restructured its children's programming, shifting its focus from co-producing international formats to prioritizing in-house productions. "This change meant that CINE Cartoon lost the key partner it needed to secure domestic pre-financing for international project developments," explained Thomas Bogner (email to the author, dated January 22, 2024). As a result, the studio became increasingly reliant on film funding. The last major production for which *CINE Cartoon* provided animation was the Austrian-German documentary *Plastic Planet* (2009).[14] This was followed by a funded Christmas special for the Slovenian animated series *The BeBuzz*, titled *The BeBuzz and Christmas Hulabaloo* (2010), co-produced with the Slovenian studio *Qollective*.[15] During production, Bogner sold the studio but remained involved until the project's completion. By 2011, the studio's financial situation had worsened: ORF declined to purchase the half-hour TV film, and one of the film funding authorities "had concluded that animation was not considered film and therefore no longer eligible for film funding" (email from Thomas Bogner to the author, dated January 22, 2024). Without these crucial financial resources, producing animated films became unsustainable: "CINE Cartoon still exists as an LLC, but under a new name, with different owners, and it operates in a completely different business sector" (email from Thomas Bogner to the author, dated January 25, 2024). However, the void left by *CINE Cartoon* in the Austrian animation landscape was swiftly filled by the emergence of new studios, including *NÖT* and *arx anima*, both established that same year.

TRIPLING THE DOUBLE EAGLE: *NÖT*

Benjamin Swiczinsky, co-founder of the studio *Neuer Österreichischer Trickfilm* (NÖT, New Austrian Animation), was introduced to animation by his older sister, Nana Swiczinsky (b. 1969). While studying at the University of Applied Arts Vienna in Maria Lassnig's (1919–2014) master class and at the affiliated *Studio für experimentellen Trickfilm* (Studio for Experimental Animated Film), she also conducted an animation workshop at her 10-year-old brother's school. Enthralled by this new creative outlet, Benjamin Swiczinsky completed his first animated film, *Max Monkey* (1995), at just 12 years old. The project took 1–2 years to finish, starting with freehand drawings before refining the process through the creation of a storyboard. In a covert late-night session, Benjamin Swiczinsky and his sister shot the entire film at the University of Applied Arts' studio. By the age of 16, he submitted *School Revolution* (1999), an animated film made with friends Timur Tietze (then 12) and Philipp Fröhlich (then 13), to the 5th *Wiener Video & Filmtage* (Vienna Video & Film Days), where it won him his first award.

At just 17, Benjamin Swiczinsky was invited to appear as an "animation filmmaker" on ORF's children's television program, showing kids how animated films are made (*Confetti Clubbing* 1999, 00:13:14). However, producing such films turned out to be a time-consuming endeavor; Swiczinsky and his two friends had spent about a year and a half completing their 5-minute project *School Revolution* (1999). This lengthy process prompted him to explore live-action filmmaking, though his passion for animation remained.[16] For his entrance exam to the Vienna Film Academy, he created *Lockvogel* (Decoy Bird, 2002), a hybrid of live-action and animation, much like the famous *Who Framed Roger Rabbit* (1988).[17] Swiczinsky took on multiple roles, serving as director, lead actor, cameraman, screenwriter, and editor. In 2003, he submitted the film to the *Shorts on Screen* competition, which debuted in collaboration with ORF after being announced at the 2002 *Diagonale* festival. Modeled to nurture young talents aged 16–30, the competition was inspired by the Oscar-nominated short film *Copy Shop* (2000/2001) by Salzburg director Virgil Widrich (b. 1967), co-financed by ORF.[18] Participants competed in local contests within their federal states, with winners advancing to the national finals at the *Diagonale* in Graz.

The 20-year-old Benjamin Swiczinsky emerged as the winner from a pool of over 100 competitors, securing the top spot in the regional competition for Vienna. His formula for success was remarkably simple – having noticed an increasing number of grim and pessimistic entries at youth film festivals, he chose to take a humorous approach. With characteristic Viennese charm, he told the story of a would-be suicide whose plan is thwarted by a newfound love for life. This lighthearted tone helped the film stand out at the 2003 *Diagonale*, where it competed against predominantly darker works, eventually securing Swiczinsky a shared victory with the Burgenland entry.

After studying journalism and film studies at the University of Vienna from 2004 to 2006, Benjamin Swiczinsky moved to Ludwigsburg (Germany) to attend the Film Academy Baden-Württemberg, where he studied from 2006 to 2011. With his award-winning animated graduation film *Heldenkanzler* (Heroic Chancellor, 2011), he delivered a satirical take on the history of Engelbert Dollfuß (1892–1934), Austria's authoritarian chancellor from 1933, and the rise of fascism.[19] Swiczinsky sought to make this complex chapter of history accessible to international audiences unfamiliar with the figure. During his time at the academy, Swiczinsky met fellow Austrians Johannes Schiehsl and Conrad Tambour. Both had previously attended the Higher Federal Institution for Graphic Education and Research (known as 'die Graphische') and, at the age of 19, created the award-winning 3D-animated film *Finitio* (2003)[20] as their final project – a pioneering achievement in the school's history: "Alongside our graphic design studies, we taught ourselves animation, and thanks to the school's lenient policies, we were able to make an animated film for our diploma," explained Johannes Schiehsl (as cited in *Filmverband Sachsen* 2017: para. 6). Schiehsl, who had been creating animated films with *Lego* bricks and colored paper since age 6, spent a year in Zlín (Czech Republic), studying traditional animation techniques after completing his civilian service. Tambour, meanwhile, had already begun his studies at the Film Academy Baden-Württemberg. Both used humor to tackle serious themes in their award-winning graduate films: Conrad Tambour's *Der Besuch* (The Visit, 2010) addressed dementia, while Johannes Schiehsl's *366 Tage* (366 Days, 2011) examined the merciless efficiency of a calculated healthcare system through the perspective of a civilian service worker.[21] Their films were distinctly Austrian, not only due to the inclusion of well-known Austrian actors and comedians as voice talent but also through cultural references – *366 Tage* (366 Days, 2011) even had its protagonist navigating his regimented daily routine to the music of the iconic *Radetzky March* (1848).

The Eagle Has Landed

After their three graduation films premiered to little fanfare at the Film Academy Baden-Württemberg, the trio devised a daring plan:

"We just thought, we wanted a proper premiere, not just at the film school – plus, these were all Austrian films in a way. So, we decided to team up, which gave us enough material for a nearly feature-length screening, and we could rent out the Filmcasino in Vienna. The idea just kept evolving from there."[22]

On June 14, 2011, their vision became reality. The Filmcasino was packed with a crowd that included prominent voice actors from their films, such as Erwin Leder (b. 1951) and Peter Hörmanseder (b. 1970), along with invited press and a lively audience. To take full advantage of the media attention, the trio announced the founding of their animation studio, *Neuer Österreichischer Trickfilm* (NÖT, New Austrian Animation), right on the spot. Their strategy worked; two TV crews, numerous print and online journalists, and curious onlookers filled the venue, prompting a second screening to accommodate the unexpected turnout. "We couldn't have predicted this success," remarked Benjamin Swiczinsky (as cited in *Forschen & Entdecken* 2012: 25). Among the attendees were representatives from various production companies. By July, *Dor Film* had already approached *NÖT* with an offer to work on the third season of the animated series *Hexe Lilli* (Lilly the Witch).[23] The offer caught the trio off guard, as they hadn't officially registered the studio yet or secured office space. By August, they found themselves in Berlin (Germany), where they were provided with an apartment – "a director's flat-share" – to work from: "In a way, the founding of *Neuer Österreichischer Trickfilm* came out of Berlin." The official company registration followed later in the fall.

The project was both a professional and personal challenge for the trio. Although Johannes Schiehsl and Conrad Tambour had previously attended 'die Graphische' together, the experience of living and working so closely was new for all three: "We still had to get to know each other properly while simultaneously directing [...] and finding a shared style." As a result, it took about a year just to complete the first episode, and only then did they manage to establish a consistent workflow. The team produced the series from Berlin for around 2.5 years, "but honestly, it was a bad arrangement – three directors working on one series, and we were completely tied to it, so we could hardly do anything else." Taking on such a large project immediately after graduation was a double-edged sword for the trio. While it was an incredible opportunity, the artistic freedom they had enjoyed as students was greatly diminished. They had to adhere to strict guidelines on everything from color schemes (not too dark) and character proportions (neither too fat nor too thin) to content (no overly intense conflicts). Budget constraints led to outsourcing the animation to Vietnam, a common practice but one fraught with difficulties: "The problem is that it's not a co-production on equal footing. You never actually speak to the people doing the work [...] instead, you deal with a supervisor." This resulted in several scenes needing rework because the animators in Asia didn't fully understand the story. Despite these hurdles, the project was completed in 2014, though delayed. Another brief foray into the world of TV series followed in 2015 with the animated short *Der Maulwurf und der Regenwurm* (The Mole and the Earthworm) for the German children's series *Ich kenne ein Tier* (I Know an Animal, 2012–2019) (Figure 14.4).

FIGURE 14.4 Benjamin Swiczinsky working at the digital animation table in the *NÖT* studio, August 2015. (Courtesy of *SWICZ Animation*, Vienna (Benjamin Swiczinsky).)

While working on *Hexe Lilli* (Lilly the Witch) in Berlin, the trio frequently took breaks to pursue other projects in Vienna. One notable endeavor arose in connection with the 90th birthday of Austrian composer and singer Georg Kreisler (1922–2011). The French-German cultural broadcaster Arte had planned a documentary about Kreisler, but his unexpected passing during the preparation phase left gaps in the scheduled interviews. To address this, the project *Kreislers musikalische Stolpersteine* (Kreisler's Musical Stumbling Blocks)[24] was conceived, inviting 15 students and graduates from German film schools to create film interpretations of his songs. Benjamin Swiczinsky contributed *Die Telefonbuchpolka* (The Phone Book Polka, 2012/2013), his first humorous exploration of societal diversity and migration themes.[25] He used a collage of historical photos from Bohemian newspapers to craft a visual style reminiscent of an illustrated poetry album. This project marked the first of about a dozen music videos *NÖT* would produce for artists across Austria, Germany, and Italy. Among these were five videos directed by Conrad Tambour for Styrian musician Krawauli (real name Kurt Gaulhofer, b. 1955) between 2016 and 2021.

After their graduation films were featured at the 2011 *Content Award Vienna*, where two of them earned accolades, the trio was invited to create the official *Content Award Trailer* (2012) for the following year. Numerous commercial projects followed, including campaigns for *Wien Energie* (an energy provider), *Wiener Zeitung* (the world's oldest daily newspaper until its print edition ended in 2023), the Federal Ministry for Climate Action, the car brand *Smart*, and animated sequences for British TV channel ITV as part of their 2018 FIFA World Cup commercial. Their versatility and experimental spirit were further displayed in projects like *The Clown* (2018) for Austria's first virtual reality ghost train, *Die Bücherwürmer* (The Bookworms, 2019) for an augmented reality tour at the Austrian National Library, and the interactive show *Der kleine Häwelmann* (The Little Haverman, 2021) for the Planetarium Hamburg (Germany).[26] In 2018, to mark the 100th anniversary of

Austrian architect Karl Schwanzer (1918–1975), Benjamin Swiczinsky ventured into print with his graphic novel *Schwanzer: Architekt aus Leidenschaft* (Schwanzer: Architect. Visionary. Maestro.), praised as a tribute "full of respect, factual knowledge, a dash of humor, and confident artistic style" (Marboe 2018: para. 8).[27]

Starting in 2013, *NÖT* became a regular contributor to feature-length documentaries and films from Austria and Germany. For the comedy *Zweisitzrakete* (Two-Seater Rocket, 2013), the team animated two pigeons that humorously commented on the unfolding events, reminiscent of the Muppet duo Statler and Waldorf. In the coming-of-age film *Beautiful Girl* (2015), they handled digital post-production, adding visual effects like floating pollen and stabilizing drone footage. For *Der Vampir auf der Couch* (Therapy for a Vampire, 2014), they crafted animated type designs for both national and international versions. In *Gruber geht* (Gruber Is Leaving, 2014/2015), they not only created visual effects (VFX) but also designed a fictional cartoon series featured within the film. For the historical documentary *Diplomatische Liebschaften* (Diplomatic Affairs, 2013/2014), *NÖT* designed animated paintings and maps, while for *Macht Energie* (Energized, 2013/2014), they produced explanatory videos and infographics. The team also created animated segments for *Auf Ediths Spuren* (Tracking Edith, 2016) and designed 2D animations, artwork, and 3D assets for *Kleine Germanen* (Little Germans, 2018/2019). This wide array of projects demonstrated *NÖT*'s versatility and ability to elevate storytelling through creative visual solutions.

Eagle's Travels to Hollywood

In 2014, by chance, *NÖT* became involved in the production of the Hollywood film *A Hologram for the King* (2016), starring Tom Hanks (b. 1956). German director Tom Tykwer (b. 1965) was searching for a producer for the film's animated opening sequence when he came across a DVD featuring graduation films from the Film Academy Baden-Württemberg. Benjamin Swiczinsky's *Heldenkanzler* (Heroic Chancellor, 2011) caught his attention: "Basically my cell phone rang, and Tom Tykwer was on the phone and asked me if I could come to Berlin as soon as possible" (Benjamin Swiczinsky, as cited in Amidi 2016: para. 3). Following this meeting, Swiczinsky received footage from Boston (USA) and Berlin (Germany), set to Tom Hanks performing Talking Heads' *Once in a Lifetime* (1981). He was also given a draft script with a placeholder marked only as "dream sequence/music video" (as cited in Amidi 2016: para. 4), allowing him full creative freedom to develop the storyboard and design concept, which focused on the economic crisis and its effects on the film's protagonist. Swiczinsky was assisted by Santiago López Jover (b. 1980), a Spanish animator based in Austria, who later served as animation director for the Austrian animated feature *Rotzbub* (Snotty Boy, 2021). "We then did most of the stuff in our studio in Vienna and stayed in close contact with Tykwer, production designer Ulrich Hanisch, and editor Alexander Berner via Skype, email, and telephone. And occasionally there were meetings in Berlin together" (Benjamin Swiczinsky, as cited in Amidi 2016: para. 3). One of the most challenging tasks, according to Swiczinsky, was designing the animated version of Tom Hanks, which went through numerous revisions (Figure 14.5): "It ended up being a somewhat younger Tom Hanks, like an

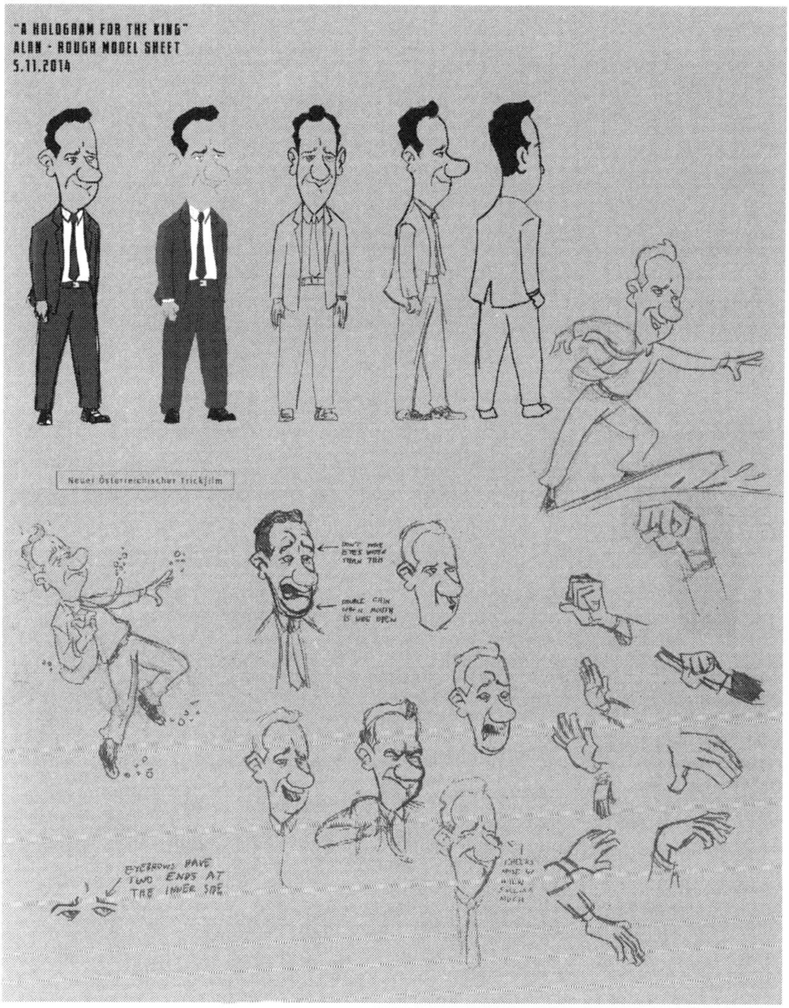

FIGURE 14.5 Preliminary character design of the animated Tom Hanks from November 2014 for the film *A Hologram for the King* (2016). (Courtesy of *SWICZ Animation*, Vienna (Benjamin Swiczinsky).)

18-year-old version of him. The design ideas for the main character were exchanged back and forth endlessly. In the end, it became an idealized version of Tom Hanks." Despite the pressure to complete the work within a tight timeframe of just a few months, the film's release was delayed until 2016. In the final cut, much of the elaborate animation was scaled back, leaving only a few animated sequences featuring banknotes and coins: "After the finished piece was handed in, Swiczinsky learned that significant chunks of the sequence would be cut because the filmmakers deemed that it didn't fit the evolving tone of the overall film, which had become slower-paced" (Amidi 2016: para. 7). As a result, Austria's contribution to this Hollywood production remained almost invisible.

In celebration of their fifth anniversary in 2016, the *NÖT* team ventured into new territory. That July, they premiered the first episode of what they dubbed the "first German-language animation web series" (Swiczinsky 2022: para. 1) on YouTube. Inspired by Walt Disney (1901–1966), who reportedly could make a film in just a month during his early years, the trio aimed to release a new episode monthly: "I thought, if it worked in the 1920s or whenever, it should work now too." By October, they had released four episodes of *Birne, Schädel & Haupt* (Nob, Crown & Head, 2016–2017), directed by Benjamin Swiczinsky. To complete a full season of 12 episodes, they launched a crowdfunding campaign in October 2016. However, they raised only €5,000 of the €20,000 target. Despite the shortfall, two more episodes were produced in 2017 – directed by Conrad Tambour (episode 5) and Swiczinsky (episode 6) – before the project was ultimately shelved. The series, which later aired on television, was semi-autobiographical, featuring a three-headed eagle inspired by the double-headed eagle of the Austro-Hungarian monarchy, also used as the studio's logo: "It came about because we had this logo of a three-headed eagle and thought it could be turned into a cartoon character. That eagle represented us – the three heads – and it held a pen and a mouse, symbolizing analog and digital creation." The series' plot, centered on the eagle's unfulfilled dream of producing an animated film, mirrored the team's own challenges with limited funding and difficult production conditions. The project began during a period of low workload: "There weren't many commissions coming in, and we had the time to make something. That's how it all started. I think there simply wasn't anything else going on at the time." In the final episode, *Eagle* (2017), an American bald eagle appeared as a shady investor, promising to finally fulfill the dream of making an animated film in the style of *Pixar*.[28]

Benjamin Swiczinsky's short film *Coming Home* (2019), a sharp satire on migration, also had strong ties to American culture. The film envisions a scenario where Native Americans win a war against the 'cowboys,' prompting then-US President Donald Trump (b. 1946) to announce the return of all 'immigrants' to Europe, Africa, and Asia. Swiczinsky intentionally hired American voice actors to lend authenticity to the project. While the exaggerated character depictions faced criticism for potential racial insensitivity, Swiczinsky intended to satirize racism itself, portraying "how an idiot imagines the world" ('Videostatement Benjamin Swiczinsky' 2020, 00:01:24). For Swiczinsky, whose family has Polish, Russian, and Austrian roots, the film served as a critique of the absurdity of ethnic origin debates. As the 'cowboys' in the film set off for their supposed 'homelands,' Swiczinsky, with this work, began his first journey toward the Oscars.[29]

An Eagle under the Radar

After *NÖT* had contributed to several documentaries and feature films, an opportunity arose in the late 2010s for the team to participate in a full-length animated feature for the first time. While working on the TV series *Hexe Lilli* (Lilly the Witch, 2014) in Berlin, the team established contact with German director Ralf Kukula (b. 1962). Kukula sought to portray the 'Peaceful Revolution' in Germany in 1989 from a child's perspective. Having previously encountered Benjamin Swiczinsky's *Heldenkanzler* (Heroic Chancellor, 2011) as a juror, Kukula was already familiar with *NÖT*'s work: "The mutual respect for each other's artistry, combined with the Austrian involvement in key historical events – such as the Paneuropa Picnic and the opening of the border fence between Hungary and Austria – secured the commission for the Viennese team" (Wagner 2019, under 'Mehr als 2600 Bilder'). For *Fritzi: Eine Wendewundergeschichte* (Fritzi: A Revolutionary Tale, 2019), *NÖT* was involved in the early development phase, contributing to the storyboard and set design. Under the coordination of Benjamin Swiczinsky and the artistic direction of Conrad Tambour, the team created approximately 2,650 drawings for the film:

> "As a storyboard artist, you act as the first director, translating the abstract screenplay (by Beate Völcker) into spatial relationships through rough sketches while defining the basic characteristics of the figures. You also serve as the initial cinematographer, since, unlike in live-action films, animation requires drawing every perspective – the angles from which the characters are seen – and indicating whether they are speaking. Additionally, you must plan the dialogue length, determining how many frames are needed to synchronize with the spoken lines" (Conrad Tambour, as cited in Wagner 2019, under 'Erste Regie, Kamera und Charaktere').

For the set design, *NÖT* secured the talents of Johannes Mücke (b. 1976), a German-born architect and production designer based in Vienna, renowned for his collaborations with director Roland Emmerich (b. 1955).[30] While these initial storyboards and set designs greatly influenced the film's final visual style, Austria's contribution went officially uncredited, with the film marketed as a German-Luxembourgish-Belgian-Czech co-production. Although Benjamin Swiczinsky and Conrad Tambour were credited, it was in less prominent positions. Swiczinsky described this as "very frustrating," noting that Austria's involvement was limited to the development phase due to funding constraints and did not extend into production, making it too marginal for formal recognition.[31] Once again, Austria's role remained invisible.

Eagle's Final Flight

The COVID-19 pandemic (which lasted in Austria from March 2020 to June 2023) immediately impacted the *NÖT* team: "The commissions disappeared almost overnight, leading to a significant reduction in client work, but only during the initial phase." Like many other businesses, *NÖT* had to pivot to remote work. An ongoing advertising campaign for the *Rote Nasen Clowndoctors* (Red Noses Clown Doctors), initially planned to feature monthly films similar to *Birne, Schädel & Haupt* (Nob, Crown & Head, 2016–2017), was scaled back and delayed. Although no new commissions came in during 2020, the pandemic eventually led to unexpected opportunities, including a project for the L.A. Opera.

This US project came about more by chance. After Ron Diamond (b. 1958) of *Acme Filmworks* first noticed Benjamin Swiczinsky's trailer *Only Human* (2010) for the FMX Conference in Stuttgart (Germany),[32] he began offering him smaller commissions, mainly in advertising. However, it wasn't until promising negotiations for a Netflix project fell through and commissions dwindled during the pandemic that *NÖT* found the time for a more substantial undertaking. This led to the collaborative effort *The Zolle Suite* (2021), in which three international animation directors each contributed a segment to create a cinematic adaptation of the opera *Zolle* (2005) by Chinese-American artist Du Yun (b. 1977).[33] Through these filmic interpretations, the L.A. Opera aimed to generate digital content to make up for the COVID-related cancellation of live performances. Swiczinsky was instructed to let the music inspire him without knowing the opera's narrative in advance. For his contribution, the middle segment *Climax* (2021), he embraced the challenge of visually depicting wind, which typically manifests only through its effects: "The idea was to reverse that – make the visible invisible and the invisible visible." This film marked Swiczinsky's second journey toward Oscar consideration.

Shortly before *NÖT* disbanded, Benjamin Swiczinsky embarked on another animated feature project: *Johnny & Me: Eine Zeitreise mit John Heartfield* (Johnny & Me: A Journey Through Time with John Heartfield, 2021/2022), which premiered on June 12, 2023, at the *Annecy International Animation Film Festival.* This film showcased Swiczinsky's most extensive animation work for a feature film to date. The story follows a female graphic designer who travels through a time tunnel into the studio of John Heartfield (né Helmut Herzfeld, 1891–1968), the renowned inventor of photomontage and a pioneer of politically charged art. To bring Heartfield to life in the film's 15-minute live-action framing sequence, filmed in Vienna, an intricate cutout technique was used. The character was crafted from layered cardboard and animated through stop-motion on a blue-screen stage, later composited into the live-action scenes.[34] Swiczinsky, who also designed the character, worked with four animators to complete the animation and compositing over 3 months in the summer of 2022 at the *ASIFA Austria* studio (Figure 14.6).

The work was particularly demanding, as the cardboard figures wore out with each use, necessitating constant rebuilding and replacement of individual parts: "It was incredibly stressful." Beyond the challenge of creating lip-synced mouth movements, Benjamin Swiczinsky and his team had to carefully match the outdoor lighting of the live-action scenes. Despite his limited experience in stop-motion, Swiczinsky

FIGURE 14.6 Birgit Scholin (b. 1984) animating the cardboard figure of John Heartfield in the *ASIFA Austria* studio, August 2022, for *Johnny & Me* (2023). (Photographer: Ernst Miesgang. Courtesy of *SWICZ Animation*, Vienna (Benjamin Swiczinsky).)

found the hands-on nature of the project refreshing: "I love working with tangible materials. It's nice to take a break from the computer, though both methods have their advantages and disadvantages."[35] In addition to the partially animated framing sequence, fully animated flashbacks depicting John Heartfield's life were created by a German team in Berlin, adding further depth to the narrative of this pioneering artist.

In a sense, *NÖT* fell victim to the pandemic in two ways. The studio's tenth anniversary was planned to be celebrated with an opening gala for the *Best Austrian Animation Festival* on November 23, 2021. However, a nationwide lockdown that began on November 22 forced the event's postponement to April 26, 2022. By then, the gala had transformed into a farewell party, as the studio announced its dissolution. The pandemic's restrictions had contributed to the team growing apart: "Everyone had developed in slightly different directions." In 2022, Benjamin Swiczinsky launched his own company, *SWICZ Animation*;[36] Johannes Friedrich Schiehsl founded *JFS Animation*; and Conrad Tambour shifted his focus to art projects that critically engage with sociopolitical issues. During its decade-long run, *NÖT* helped shape Austrian animation with visionary ideas, international collaborations, and experimental daring, like few other studios. Despite the challenges, Swiczinsky remains deeply committed to *NÖT*'s vision of producing narrative animated films.

One of *NÖT*'s enduring legacies is the *Tricktisch* (animators' table), a regular meetup for animators and animation enthusiasts. After returning to Austria following their studies and work on the TV series *Hexe Lilli* (Lilly the Witch, 2014) in Germany, Benjamin Swiczinsky, Johannes Schiehsl, and Conrad Tambour found themselves disconnected from the Austrian animation scene and its ongoing projects. In response, they established the *Tricktisch* (animators' table) as a platform for networking and exchanging ideas with other filmmakers. However, the pandemic forced a pause in these meetings, and after *NÖT* disbanded, there was a real risk the gatherings would cease altogether. To preserve the tradition, Swiczinsky revived the concept by organizing the *Neuer Tricktisch* (new animators' table) on January 27, 2023. This initiative aimed to continue many prior, often unsuccessful, efforts to unite Austria's fragmented animation landscape – still dominated by small studios and independent creators – into cohesive production collectives, while positioning Vienna as a central production hub. The *Tricktisch* (animators' table) bridges these microcosms, uncovering a diverse and often surprising array of Austrian animation talent, and offering fresh insights even to seasoned industry insiders. Its broader goal is to bring Austrian animation out of its long-standing invisibility.[37]

"WE ANIMATE": *ARX ANIMA*

Founded in Vienna in 2011, the award-winning animation studio *arx anima* has established itself as a prominent player in the European animation industry – and beyond. "We started as a studio providing animation support for other productions in need of assistance" (as cited in Fischer 2022: 64), recalled Christoph 'Kris' Staber (b. 1979), who co-founded the studio with Dunja Bernatzky (b. 1978). The choice to base the studio in Vienna, despite intense competition from Asia, was deliberate: "I studied in England and America [...].[38] After spending a significant amount of time in those places, you come to appreciate just how fantastic the quality of life is in Vienna. And if you want to live in this wonderful, artistically inspiring city, you have to bring the work here," explained Staber (as cited in Flossmann 2019: 24).

In addition to VFX, video games, and art installations, *arx anima* produced animated advertisements for notable clients such as the *Österreichische Nationalbank* (ÖNB, Austrian Central Bank) and *Walt Disney Records*. Their work has gained international recognition, appearing on platforms ranging from linear TV channels like Cartoon Network to streaming services such as Netflix and Amazon Prime, as well as in esteemed venues like London's Royal Opera House and the 2012 Olympic Games. Today, *arx anima* specializes in high-end character animation and development.

The studio's breakthrough came with its first commissions for the *Talking Tom & Friends* franchise, created by game developer *Outfit7*.[39] "We produced the initial promotional trailers for *Outfit7*'s newly launched apps," recalled Dunja Bernatzky. "At that time, *Outfit7* was a team of just 12, and within three years, they had grown to 500" (email from Dunja Bernatzky to the author, dated February 27, 2024). In the spring of 2012, *arx anima* released *Talking Tom and Ben News: World Cleanup 2012*, the first animated film in the popular franchise, which quickly garnered over 12 million views on YouTube within just a few months. That summer, under the direction of Austrian filmmaker Toni Weiss – who has since become a prominent director of CG character animation films – the studio created the animated music video *You Get Me* (2012) for *Walt Disney Records*. With a 25-member team, *arx anima* managed the entire production process, from script development to final animation, capturing the essence of *Disney*'s iconic style. "We are exceptionally proud to produce an animated film for the world's leading name in animation entertainment," remarked Christoph Staber (as cited in Staber and Weiss 2012: para. 4).

Thanks to the tremendous success of the video – amassing over 400 million views on YouTube as of 2024 – *arx anima* solidified its relationship with *Outfit7*, which soon commissioned the studio to produce a 52-episode web series titled *Talking Tom & Friends* (TTF). This marked *arx anima*'s first large-scale project, establishing the studio as a major player in the global animation industry. "Everything, from concept and scripts to design and post-production, is handled by us," said Christoph Staber (as cited in Fischer 2022: 64). For this ambitious endeavor, the studio employed up to 150 international collaborators. Approximately 90 team members, divided into ten groups, worked across two locations in Vienna, while the writers' room, responsible for developing the scripts, was based in Los Angeles (USA).[40] Freelancers from Spain, Japan, and South America also contributed to the production. The pilot episode premiered on December 23, 2014, with subsequent episodes released between April 30, 2015, and December 22, 2016. The series, which was also streamed on Netflix and aired on TV worldwide, was a phenomenal success, attracting 350 million views per month. Two additional seasons of 26 episodes each followed, with the final episode released on December 27, 2018.[41] Throughout the 104 episodes produced by *arx anima*, the studio not only cemented its reputation but also demonstrated its rapid technical advancements (Figure 14.7).[42]

With a total runtime exceeding 1,000 minutes, the production was equivalent in scale to approximately 16 feature films. By the late 2010s, *arx anima* began directly

FIGURE 14.7 A view of the *arx anima* studio during the production of *Talking Tom & Friends* in April 2016. (Photographer: Roland Ferrigato. Courtesy of *arx anima*, Vienna (Dunja Bernatzky).)

participating in feature-length projects. For the German animated feature *Der kleine Rabe Socke: Suche nach dem verlorenen Schatz* (Raven the Little Rascal: Hunt for the Lost Treasure, 2019), *arx anima* managed 2D animation, clean-up, and cel shading. In *Die Heinzels: Rückkehr der Heinzelmännchen* (The Elfkins: Baking a Difference, 2019), the studio handled the final look development. Additionally, *arx anima* co-produced the German-Austrian animated feature *Die Häschenschule: Der große Eierklau* (Rabbit Academy: Mission Eggpossible, 2022), creating an Austrian-language version that became Austria's most successful minority co-production of 2022.[43] Starting in the fall of 2022, the studio worked on *Die Heinzels: Neue Mützen, neue Mission* (The Super Elfkins), another German-Austrian co-production released at Christmas 2024. In this sequel, the Elfkins family from the first film encounters a Viennese Elfkin gang. Several other animated features are currently in development and financing, including the German-Austrian project *Seeräuberin Moses* (Pirate Mo). The studio is also involved in high-profile series projects, such as *Chill mal, Zeus!* (Chill Out, Zeus!), a Greek mythology-themed show, in collaboration with Benjamin Swiczinsky, co-founder of *NÖT*.[44] Moreover, in collaboration with *Geyrhalter Film*,[45] *arx anima* is developing an animated series based on the beloved book series *Geschichten vom Franz* (Tales of Franz) by acclaimed Austrian author Christine Nöstlinger (1936–2018). Spanning 19 volumes published between 1984 and 2011, the series follows the childhood adventures of a young boy growing up in Vienna, from kindergarten to the age of 9. Translated into 28 languages and distributed across Europe, Asia, the UAE, as well as North and South America, the books' international success highlights the vast market potential for this animated adaptation.

There is a strong connection between *arx anima* and the Vienna-based *Samsara Filmproduktion*, which began in 2020 with their collaboration on *Rubikon* (2022). Touted as Austria's first science fiction film produced to Hollywood standards,

Rubikon (2022) represented a major milestone in Austrian cinema. After filming concluded in late 2020, *arx anima* undertook the extensive 9-month VFX post-production process, with Franz Brandstätter from the Film Academy Vienna serving as visual effects supervisor.[46] The studio leveraged its state-of-the-art render farm – one of Europe's most advanced – featuring 1,700 CPU cores and 20 TB of RAM to achieve high-quality results. The production, however, was not without its challenges. With Austria under continuous lockdowns due to the COVID-19 pandemic (March 2020 to June 2023), the VFX team, composed of international artists, had to work entirely remotely. Despite a modest budget of just €3 million – a stark contrast to the $250 million budget of Hollywood's *Avatar: The Way of Water* (2022) – *arx anima* delivered 86 Hollywood-quality VFX shots, resulting in a visually impressive film achieved with limited resources.

For the animated feature project *Operation Oma* (Mission Granny), developed by *arx anima* and *Samsara Filmproduktion*, the partners won an award at the 2022 *Junior Entertainment Talent Slate* (JETS) initiative during the *Berlinale* (Germany). Loredana Rehekampff (b. 1985) of *Samsara Filmproduktion* described the film's distinctive concept: "Usually in animated films grandmothers are always sweet and a bit boring, in ours, she's such a real 'badass' character with [...] a pipe and a trench coat" (Loredana Rehekampff, as cited in Hairapetian 2022: para. 3). During the initiative, potential co-production partners were actively pursued for the spy film, set in Vienna and drawing inspiration from *The Third Man* (1949). As Dunja Bernatzky from *arx anima* clarified, there were no specific preferences for collaborators: "Personally, we don't have any preferences; the parameters are rather determined by funding, technical possibilities, and talent" (Dunja Bernatzky, as cited in Hairapetian 2022: para. 3).

The international scope of *arx anima*'s animation projects is exemplified by their upcoming animated feature *Monster Mia* (Monstrous Mia), slated for release on Halloween 2026. This marks the studio's first majority co-production.[47] Dunja Bernatzky explained: "Since a large portion of the team working on *Talking Tom* in Vienna was of Spanish origin, and we consistently had top talent in Spain, we spent years actively developing a studio there. A joint venture with Nico from *Lightbox* was a logical step" (email to the author, dated February 27, 2024). In partnership with *Lightbox Entertainment*, the producer of the successful *Tadeo Jones* animated film series (2012–2022), *arx anima* co-founded *arx Light* in 2021. The collaboration set ambitious goals: "A joint venture, the partnership aims to produce an animation feature every two-and-a-half years with an around €10 million ($12.1 million) budget" (Mayorga 2021: para. 2). The project also includes the German studio *Peng! Boom! Tschak! Films*, further broadening the cooperative efforts behind *Monster Mia* (Monstrous Mia).

Over the years, *arx anima* has grown into an international network, establishing studios in Madrid (*arx aniMAD*, Spain), Leipzig (*arx anima MD*, Germany), and Frankfurt (*arx anima Hessen*, Germany). Dunja Bernatzky explained: "Producing an animated film takes years, and to maintain a stable team with ongoing development opportunities, we quickly realized that we needed to expand beyond Austria" (email to the author, dated February 27, 2024). By leveraging global expertise, dedication, and bold ambition, *arx anima* continues to deliver Hollywood-quality animation projects from the heart of Vienna.

INVISIBLE ANIMATION IN THE HINTERLAND

Even as recently as 2010, Thomas Renoldner (b. 1960) noted: "Austria's insignificance in the commercial sector of computer animation remains striking" (Renoldner 2010: 149). However, despite limited visibility and public awareness, several smaller Austrian studios specializing in digital post-production (including 3D animation and VFX) have quietly emerged in recent years, contributing to major Hollywood productions. A standout figure in this field is Viennese artist Christoph Schinko, who began his career in 1999 as a 3D animator for TV series at *Asset Media International* in Germany after studying 3D Animation & Visual Effects at the *Vancouver Film School* (VFS) in Canada. By 2002, he was involved in his first feature film project as a character animator, and by 2003, he had joined *Cinesite Europe* in London, contributing to Hollywood films like *Harry Potter and the Prisoner of Azkaban* (2004) and *The Hitchhiker's Guide to the Galaxy* (2005). Schinko's notable contributions include the pre-visualization and character animation of the iconic facehugger in *Alien vs. Predator* (2004) and VFX animation for *King Arthur* (2004), where he animated the cracking ice of a frozen lake and enhanced battle scenes with fire and fallen bodies. From 2007 to 2008, he worked at the British *Moving Picture Company* (MPC) on character animation for *The Chronicles of Narnia: Prince Caspian* (2008). After spending a decade abroad, Schinko returned to Vienna and founded *CS Film & Animation* in 2011, focusing on 3D animation and digital post-production. His studio has contributed to notable Austrian and German films like *MindGamers* (2015) and *Ballon* (Balloon, 2018), while also playing a key role in Hollywood blockbusters such as *Jurassic World: Fallen Kingdom* (2018), *Serenity* (2019), *Shang-Chi and the Legend of the Ten Rings* (2021), and *The Northman* (2022). Schinko's diverse portfolio also includes contributions to TV series like *Outlander* (2018), *Watchmen* (2019), *Hanna* (2021), and *She-Hulk: Attorney at Law* (2022), demonstrating the growing global demand for high-quality VFX and 3D animation 'made in Austria.'

Another Austrian studio making waves in international projects is *Kaiserlicht*, co-founded by visual effects specialist Felix Geremus (b. 1983) and Alexander Siquans (b. 1983) in July 2015. Geremus, who previously worked on *Guardians of the Galaxy* (2014) for *MPC Film* and Marvel's *Avengers: Age of Ultron* (2015) for *Trixter*, teamed up with Siquans to establish the Vienna-based post-production studio specializing in VFX, animation, and motion design. The duo's journey began with degrees in media technology from St. Pölten University of Applied Sciences (Lower Austria), followed by 7 years of invaluable experience in the advertising industry. Reflecting on their advertising careers, Siquans remarked: "What made it interesting was that each spot told a new story while maintaining a consistent thread. I believe that's something often missing in today's advertising" (Alexander Siquans, as cited in Giesinger 2015: 19).

Despite their international success, Felix Geremus and Alexander Siquans ultimately chose to return to their roots in Austria. "We're both Viennese, and after spending enough time abroad, you just long for a return to beautiful Vienna," Geremus explained (as cited in Giesinger 2015: 19). Now, they are determined to reverse the trend of outsourcing Austrian projects overseas and instead aim to attract international productions to Austria. "Large-scale projects can absolutely be realized

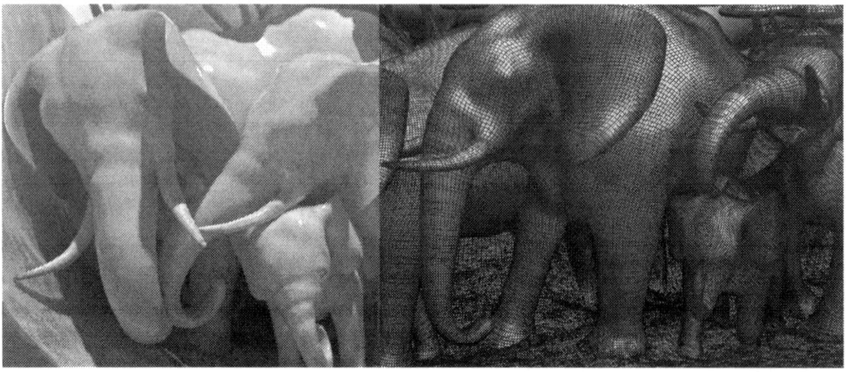

FIGURE 14.8 An animated ivory carving of an elephant herd, depicted after and before the final rendering, created for the title sequence of the award-winning Netflix documentary *The Ivory Game* (2016). (Courtesy of *Kaiserlicht*, Vienna (Felix Geremus).)

here, too. Our long-term goal is to establish Austria as a strong hub for visual effects," added Siquans (as cited in Giesinger 2015: 19).

For the award-winning Netflix documentary *The Ivory Game* (2016), *Kaiserlicht* created both the graphic inserts and the opening title sequence (Figure 14.8). Their expertise was further highlighted in the multiple award-winning documentary *Sea of Shadows* (2018/2019), distributed globally by National Geographic. Working closely with Austrian director Richard Ladkani (b. 1973), they created the title sequence, featuring a dramatic 4K-rendered scene of a fish entangled in a ghost net – marking the studio's first foray into 4K rendering. Reflecting on their work for *The Arctic: Our Last Great Wilderness* (2020/2021), the team described it as "our first giant screen project" (Geremus n.d.: para. 1). Since the film was released in IMAX format, the computer-generated imagery (CGI) visualizations of animal migration routes required 6K rendering, presenting a significant technical challenge. For Netflix's four-part documentary *Meltdown: Three Mile Island* (2022), *Kaiserlicht* developed a series of detailed explanatory animations. The studio also created maps, character inserts, and explanatory animations for the independent US documentary *Make People Better* (2022), available on platforms such as iTunes and Amazon Prime Video.

The production of the feature film *Hinterland* (2021), directed by Academy Award winner Stefan Ruzowitzky (b. 1961), garnered international attention. To recreate 1920s Vienna for this historical thriller, the film was shot almost entirely in front of a blue screen, with expressionistically distorted buildings digitally added during post-production. "I've never attempted anything like this before. While there are computer-generated effects in almost all my films, never in such density," Ruzowitzky remarked (as cited in Greuling 2021: para. 5). Although filming was completed by the end of 2019, constructing the virtual world around the actors required an additional year. Oleg Prodeus of *Prodeus Productions*, who had previously collaborated on Virgil Widrich's *Vienna table trip* (2016), led the early design phase as Digital Design Art Director. These designs were later animated by the Belgian *Benuts Studio*, with further VFX provided by *Kaiserlicht*. Ruzowitzky described the film as an "experimental film" in the press kit, highlighting its bold visual style, where VFX is deliberately showcased rather than hidden (Constantin Film (ed.) 2021: [13]). With *Hinterland* (2021), Austria's avant-garde cinema has successfully ventured into the international mainstream.

ANIMATION AS 'COVID-COMPLIANT' FILMMAKING

"You need to have to do a bit of animation as well, cause that's what everyone does now – image is moved now," British animator Paul Barritt advises students in his illustration course (interview with the author on June 8, 2023). Indeed, Austria now hosts numerous studios that create a wide range of animated content, including commercials, explainer videos, corporate films, social media videos, event films, product videos, and animated graphics. Studios like *LWZ Design & Animation*, *Studio Citron*, and *Polarfux* are at the forefront of this movement.[48] In recent years, public institutions have increasingly turned to animated films for their campaigns, often gaining significant media attention. The COVID-19 pandemic, with its series of nationwide lockdowns starting in March 2020, further fueled this trend, as animated films offered a 'COVID-compliant' way to produce content with minimal human interaction.[49]

For instance, during the pandemic, the Vienna-based video agency *News on Video* had to shift to remote work, making large-scale shoots impossible. Nevertheless, their graphics department continued producing animations without interruption. One notable project was an animated explainer video commissioned by the City of Vienna, titled *Das Coronavirus Kindern einfach erklärt* (The Coronavirus Simply Explained to Children, 2020). The two-minute film gained international attention, reaching three million people on Facebook within a week and accumulating around 750,000 views on YouTube. It was also featured on numerous school websites in Germany: "We even received a request from Romania to distribute the video with Romanian subtitles. The City of Budapest [Hungary] also expressed interest" (Michael Ludwig and Jürgen Czernohorszky, as cited in *Rathauskorrespondenz* 2020: para. 2).

In the spring of 2021, a public information film commissioned by the government sparked significant controversy: "A video released by the Ministry of Foreign Affairs, which uses animation to graphically illustrate the impact of a nuclear bomb being dropped on Vienna, has caused confusion and outrage" (Salzburger Nachrichten, January 25, 2021: 12). The video was published to mark the entry into force of the *Treaty on the Prohibition of Nuclear Weapons* (TPNW) on January 22, 2021, a treaty Austria helped spearhead. Critics, including Vienna's Mayor Michael Ludwig (b. 1961), condemned the video as unnecessary fearmongering, especially amid the ongoing COVID-19 crisis.

The Austrian Federal Ministry for Climate Action's *Mission 11* energy-saving campaign, launched in the summer of 2022, also attracted significant media attention. Aimed at helping Austrians reduce their energy consumption by 11%, the campaign featured advertising concepts developed by the agency *Jung von Matt DONAU* (JvM), which were animated in motion design by the Vienna-based *bounty.studio*. However, the €3.6 million campaign was met with criticism – not only for its name, which evoked the Apollo 11 mission, and its overly simplistic energy-saving tips but also for its design, which closely resembled the corporate branding of an Austrian electric car manufacturer. For another controversial campaign by the same ministry, *JvM* collaborated with British *Feral Child Studio* to produce *Österreich ist nicht ganz dicht!* (Austria Is Not Completely Tight!, 2023). The film, which combined live-action with animation and echoed the style of *Who Framed Roger Rabbit* (1988), promoted government subsidies for thermal building renovations. In the advertisement, leaky windows and doors are depicted as animated characters in a real house. While some praised it as "a particularly clever campaign […] that slightly resembles the Disney style" (Bonn 2023: para. 1), it faced heavy criticism due to the double entendre in its title.[50]

While this film production was outsourced to the UK, the opposite occurred with a British Greenpeace campaign: the animated short *There's a Rang-Tan in My Bedroom* (2018) was directed by Philipp 'Lip' Comarella (b. 1985) and Simon Griesser (b. 1979) of the Austrian animation studio *Salon Alpin*. Originally from Bolzano (Italy), Comarella worked at several advertising agencies – where he crossed paths with Tyrolean native Simon Griesser – while pursuing his studies in graphic design and advertising at the University of Applied Arts Vienna.[51] Their collaboration began with Comarella's mixed-media graduation film *Viel besser jetzt* (Much Better Now, 2011),[52] which led to the founding of *Salon Alpin* in January 2012. The studio, operating on a decentralized model – with Griesser now based in Lisbon (Portugal) – quickly earned recognition for animated commercials and video game animations, including work on the award-winning game *Old Man's Journey* (2017).

There's a Rang-Tan in My Bedroom (2018), created for Greenpeace, tells the story of a young orangutan wreaking havoc in a child's bedroom. When asked why it is there, the orangutan explains that humans have invaded its habitat, destroyed the rainforest, and killed its mother. This touching and timely film won the prestigious *Annie Award* for *Best Animated Television/Broadcast Commercial* in Hollywood in 2019, but it had already garnered international attention during the 2018 Christmas season. After Greenpeace successfully launched the film in the summer of 2018, British supermarket chain Iceland attempted to use it as its Christmas TV advertisement to promote its ban on palm oil. However, the commercial was blocked from airing by the UK non-governmental organization Clearcast, sparking an international outcry. Headlines from Australia to the USA accused Clearcast of political censorship. On social media, the alleged ban went viral, and within 24 hours, the film had garnered three million views. By mid-November 2018, the film had reached 30 million views, and by mid-December, it had surged to 70 million.

Contrary to popular belief, the advertisement wasn't officially 'banned,' which would have required action by a governmental body like the *Advertising Standards Authority* (ASA). The idea that the advertisement was blocked for its political content was also incorrect. In reality, it was not approved for broadcast because the *UK Code of Broadcast Advertising* (BCAP Code) prohibits advertisements from political organizations, including Greenpeace. Despite this, Iceland hailed the film as "the most successful Christmas TV ad of all time" (Walker 2018: para. 1) – even though it never aired on television. Although the controversy made headlines in Austria as well,[53] the significant involvement of Austrian production talent in the campaign went largely unnoticed and remained almost invisible in the broader coverage.

NOTES

1 This statement referred to the art of storytelling through cinematic editing techniques, as the technical aspects of editing using software are indeed covered in courses at universities of applied sciences (email from Benjamin Swiczinsky to the author, dated November 20, 2023).
2 In 1996, Michael Epstein assumed the role of Austria's representative on the board of directors of *CARTOON – European Association of Animation Film*, a non-profit organization headquartered in Brussels (Belgium). He succeeded Hubert Sielecki (b. 1946), who had held this position from 1992 to 1996.
3 Email from Michael Epstein to the author, dated November 26, 2023.
4 Alexander Wieser's original concept, proposed to Michael Epstein shortly after the founding of *CINE Cartoon*, initially featured a porcupine as the animal hero of the series. However, following discussions with French partners, the character evolved into a squire with spiky hair.
5 The series was dubbed at the recording studio of Alexander Wieser, who also conceived the original concept for the show.
6 The series, reportedly initiated by *CINE Cartoon*, was based on the children's book series *The Witch's Dog* (first published in 1998) by Scottish author Frank Rodgers (b. 1944).
7 Peter Höhsl (b. 1967), the lead animator at the time, recalled: "I developed the digital workflow for the series, as the wax crayon style specified by Richard Fehsl would have been too time-consuming to execute with traditional techniques" (email to the author, dated January 17, 2024).
8 The series was dubbed not only in German, Czech, and Finnish but also in English, Slovak, Swedish, and Norwegian. "Negotiations are currently underway with Italy, France, and Belgium" (Michael Epstein, as cited in Greuling 2003: 17).
9 On August 19, 2005, a live show featuring life-sized *Spirello* puppets was recorded in front of a live audience of children. The event served as a pilot for a planned series titled *Spirello Party*.
10 By the end of 2003, attempts to secure financing partners for additional seasons were made, but ultimately proved unsuccessful.
11 Rodja Pavlik's excitement stemmed not only from the upcoming projects at *CINE Cartoon* but also from the development of *Total Fred* (Totally Fred), a computer animated series launched by *SPECTRUM Trickfilm*, directed by Alexander Noëlle. This EU-funded series, based on the comic by Harald Havas (b. 1964) and Reinhard Kiesel (1961–2019), resulted in a 5-minute pilot and seven short episodes produced between 2003 and 2005. Despite parts of the series being created in English, Havas did not anticipate an export to the US, explaining: "With a European animated series, there are really only two viable markets: Europe and Asia. The US is a monolithic block that doesn't let anything in. They produce a vast amount of their own content and are focused on exporting it" (Harald Havas, as cited in Pavlik 2004: 29).
12 Neither project progressed beyond a trailer or test reel. For more details, refer to the chapter on animated feature films.
13 The series drew inspiration from the *Winnetou* stories by German author Karl May (1842–1912). Its title is a portmanteau, blending 'Winnetou' with 'cartoons.'
14 With Thomas Bogner serving as producer of the film at *Neue Sentimental Film*, it was a logical step to consolidate the resources of both studios. The animation was overseen by Peter Höhsl, who had also acted as the lead animator for the *Till Eulenspiegel* project.
15 The film aired slightly later than planned, premiering on Slovenian television on December 31, 2010.

16 There was another reason for this shift: "I thought to myself, now that I'm an adult, it's time to move on from cartoons" (Benjamin Swiczinsky, interview with the author on July 5, 2023).

17 Benjamin Swiczinsky later heard indirectly that his rejection from the Vienna Film Academy was allegedly due to the film's implied eroticism. Shortly afterward, he made a second unsuccessful attempt to gain admission with the short film *Krieg* (War, 2003), an outcome he would later view as a fortunate twist of fate. (Benjamin Swiczinsky, interview with the author on July 5, 2023)

18 Refer to Chapter 13 for further details.

19 Among its numerous awards, the film received the *Lotte Reiniger Promotion Award for Animated Film* at the 2012 *Internationales Trickfilm-Festival Stuttgart* (ITFS, Festival of Animated Film Stuttgart). During the festival, Benjamin Swiczinsky attended a lecture by the author, as he revealed in an interview on July 5, 2023.

20 The film had its public debut at the 7th *Wiener Video & Filmtage* (Vienna Video & Film Days) in 2003 and was also reportedly screened at the Graz *Diagonale* (Styria) in 2004.

21 The film was frequently compared to the Austrian feature *Komm, süßer Tod* (Come Sweet Death, 2000), which had premiered in cinemas just before Johannes Schiehsl began his civilian service.

22 Unless otherwise indicated, all quotations in this subchapter are taken from the author's interview with Benjamin Swiczinsky, conducted on July 5, 2023, in Vienna.

23 *Dor Film* had previously served as a co-producer for two part-animated feature films centered around Hexe Lilli (Lilly the Witch), produced in Germany in 2009 and 2011. The company also handled the dubbing of the series' third season in Vienna.

24 'Stolpersteine' (literally 'stumbling stones,' metaphorically 'stumbling blocks') are memorial plaques set into the ground to commemorate Jewish individuals persecuted during the Nazi regime. While Georg Kreisler survived the Holocaust, he and his family were forced to emigrate to the United States, and he led a restless life even after the war's end.

25 Benjamin Swiczinsky further explored this theme in his film *Coming Home* (2019), which is discussed in more detail later.

26 The production was nominated for the *Janus Award* at the 2022 *FullDome Festival* in Jena (Germany), the leading international festival for fulldome shows.

27 Although Benjamin Swiczinsky is the son of an architect himself, the project, initiated by Martin Schwanzer (1952–2020), the younger son of architect Karl Schwanzer, came to him by chance through indirect channels. While Swiczinsky expressed interest in creating another graphic novel, the lack of funding for comics in Austria and his limited time for independent projects have hindered further development. (Interview with the author on July 5, 2023.)

28 On the drawing board of the three-headed eagle, there is a corresponding reference to *Toy Story* (1995), which has already made an appearance in the second episode of the series: two bearded men, one dressed as a cowboy and the other as an astronaut, embracing in front of a sign that reads 'TOL STOY: War and Peace.'

29 With this film, Benjamin Swiczinsky qualified for the longlist, from which the 2021 Oscar nominations were chosen.

30 Johannes Mücke later worked as a set designer on the Austrian sci-fi film *Rubikon* (2022); refer to the subchapter on *arx anima* for more details.

31 As of 2023, Benjamin Swiczinsky and Conrad Tambour were listed as "uncredited" on IMDb for the film, despite being acknowledged in the end credits. Benjamin Swiczinsky remarked: "I even considered uploading a screenshot of the credits because the IMDb entry is simply incorrect" (interview with the author on July 5, 2023).

32 FMX defines itself as a *Conference on Animation, Visual Effects, Games, and Immersive Media.*

33 In addition to Benjamin Swiczinsky, who crafted the middle segment, the project featured contributions from Canadian artist Steven Woloshen (b. 1960) and Norwegian artist Kristian Pedersen (b. 1980).

34 The use of layered cardboard was designed not only to enhance the figure's three-dimensional effect but also to optimize how it interacted with light. The lighting conditions were carefully recreated to match those of the film set, ensuring visual consistency.

35 The team also visited the set of *Sine Meta Drom* (2022), a hybrid film produced concurrently in Vienna. Created as a pandemic project by the *Odeon* theater group, directed by Max Kaufmann (b. 1976), the film features a highly detailed model of Vienna's Praterstern transportation hub, painstakingly crafted over the course of a year by artist Eva Grün (b. 1975). Even the pigeon droppings were meticulously replicated using a mixture of dirt, water, and white acrylic paint. The film alternates between live-action and stop-motion sequences, with the daily life around Praterstern reenacted by theater actors and 60 puppets designed by Miriam Salzer.

36 Through his studio, *SWICZ Animation*, Benjamin Swiczinsky collaborates with various partners, including *arx anima*; further details can be found in the following subchapter.

37 Since 2023, *ASIFA Austria* has also been holding regular member meetings, approximately once a month, where a member's work is showcased.

38 Alongside his international studies, Christoph Staber received training from animators at *DreamWorks*, *Pixar*, and *Disney*.

39 The franchise evolved from the mobile game app *Talking Tom Cat*, first released in July 2010.

40 Tom Martin (b. 1964), head writer for the first season, had previously written for *The Simpsons* from 1999 to 2001. The voice cast was also assembled in Los Angeles (USA).

41 Seasons 4 and 5, released between 2019 and 2021, were produced by the Spanish studio *People Moving Pixels*.

42 Alongside the 104 episodes from seasons 1 to 3, *arx anima* also produced ten episodes of the short film series *Talking Tom Shorts* (2014). Additionally, the studio was responsible for nearly all game trailers released by *Outfit7* prior to 2015.

43 Minority co-production refers to the "production of a feature film where the producers of national origin provide less than the largest share of financing" (UNESCO Institute for Statistics, available online at https://uis.unesco.org/en/glossary).

44 As of the interview with the author on July 5, 2023, Benjamin Swiczinsky was in the midst of preliminary work for the series.

45 *Geyrhalter Film* has already produced two feature films based on the book series: *Geschichten vom Franz* (Tales of Franz, 2022) and its sequel, *Neue Geschichten vom Franz* (New Tales of Franz, 2023).

46 The Austrian visual effects studio *VAST* also contributed to the production. *VAST* is known for its work on high-profile projects like the fourth season of *Star Trek: Discovery* (2021/2022) and the Hollywood film *Asteroid City* (2023).

47 Majority co-production refers to the "production of a feature film where the producers of national origin provide the largest share of financing" (UNESCO Institute for Statistics, available online at https://uis.unesco.org/en/glossary).

48 Founded in 2014, *LWZ* Studio has created a range of commissioned projects, including informational videos for the City of Vienna. *studio citron*, a creative network with a strong emphasis on motion design, has worked with clients like Austrian Airlines and Statistics Austria. Similarly, *Polarfux*, specializing in motion design, has served clients such as the Austrian Patent Office and the Austrian Federal Railways (ÖBB).

49 In April 2021, a film produced in the context of a Viennese youth center was described as follows: "They created the film – COVID-compliant – as an animated production" (*Wiener Jugendzentren* 2021: para. 2). Austrian animator Paul Wenninger (b. 1966)

similarly noted in a TV interview that the lockdowns had minimal impact on his filmmaking process, as his work had long been a largely solitary endeavor (cf. 'Werkschau Paul Wenninger' 2021).

50 In German, the phrase "nicht ganz dicht sein" (not being completely tight) can also be used as an insult, suggesting someone is "not of sound mind." In 2021, the ministry had already launched another campaign with a similarly provocative title, *Österreich holt die Leichen aus dem Keller* (literally Austria Takes the Skeletons Out of the Closet, aka What's That Lurking in the Basement?), featuring a puppet film produced by the British studio *Blinkink* to promote the replacement of outdated heating boilers.

51 Simon Griesser studied Multimedia Art at the Salzburg University of Applied Sciences from 2000 to 2004.

52 The film also featured contributions from Christoph Staber, co-founder of *arx anima*.

53 For instance, see Salzburger Nachrichten, November 17, 2018: 21.

15 Thrice the First

The Quest for Austria's First Animated Feature

"Six Austrians in the Top Five" was once a headline in an Austrian sports newspaper. It initially inspired Austrian postcard artist Hias Schaschko to create a humorous postcard and later became the title of a book by Dirk Stermann (b. 1965), a German cabaret artist based in Austria.[1] A similar oddity exists in Austrian animation – three films are regarded as the country's first animated feature.

The dream of producing an animated feature film in Austria is nearly as old as Austrian animation itself. Just four years after *Ideale Filmerzeugung* (Ideal Filmmaking, 1913/1914) – the earliest known Austrian animated film – Peter Eng (1892–1939) attempted to convince his employer, Sascha Kolowrat-Krakowsky (1886–1927), the owner of *Sascha-Film*, to embark on such an ambitious project:

"That was in 1918. Every other day, I sent him a registered letter saying: 'Most Honorable Count! Provide me with 50 people, and I pledge to deliver a feature-length [animated] comedy within two months.' The response I received was: 'My dear Peter Eng, we are not in America; perhaps sometime in the future. Yours, Sascha Kolowrat.' A decade later, Hollywood rose to the challenge" (Eng 1936: 2).

On May 20, 1919, the *Institut für Kulturforschung* (Institute for Cultural Research) premiered the film cycle *Menschheit* (Humanity) or *Neue Menschheit* (New Humanity). This collection comprised six short films by Berthold Bartosch (1893–1968) with a combined runtime of approximately 50 minutes. Although this 'package film' might be considered feature-length by British and American standards, it doesn't fully qualify because a lecture interrupted the screening.[2] The first four segments were shown under the title *Staatenschau* (National Exhibition, approx. 22 minutes), followed by the remaining two parts as *Völkerschau* (Ethnographic Exhibition, approx. 28 minutes).

A year later, another attempt was made when the management of *Astoria-Film* – one of the major film studios of the interwar period alongside *Sascha-Film* – changed hands: "In February 1920, when Robert Reich took over as the new director, he was particularly committed to animation, which he had previously employed for advertising in his own company and now aimed to produce in feature-length form" (Payer 2000: 177). However, this plan never came to fruition. By June 1920, the company's management was restructured once again. Under Ladislaus Tuszyński (1876–1943) and Peter Eng, who became the new heads of the animation department, only animation sequences for live-action feature films were created. A notable exception was the approximately half-hour-long animated film *Die Jagd nach dem Kopfe* (The Hunt for the Lost Head, 1920), described as "the longest existing animated film" (Neue Kino-Rundschau, July 3 1920a: 14) – a title it held for many decades.

DOI: 10.1201/9781003415442-18

In the 1970s, when Austrian state television (ORF) commissioned its first animated feature, it turned out to be a spin-off of the Japan-produced series *Die Biene Maja* (Maya the Honey Bee, 1975–1980). *Die Biene Maja: Ihre schönsten Abenteuer* (Maya the Honey Bee: Her Most Beautiful Adventures, 1977), also produced in Japan, was essentially a compilation of several episodes from the series. It wasn't until a decade later, with *1x1 des glücklichen Lebens* (The ABC of a Happy Life, 1987), that Austria produced its first "collective [animated] feature film" (Bendazzi (ed.) 2010b: 197). However, with a runtime of around 45 minutes, it qualifies as a feature film only by British and American standards.[3] The same applies to *Life Show* (1990), a roughly 43-minute animated film that was hailed as Austria's longest until 2016.[4] Featuring a framing story, *Life Show* (1990) could be considered Austria's first 'collective narrative [animated] feature film,' following in the footsteps of its predecessor.

Martin Arnold (b. 1959) is not a traditional animator, but he utilized animation techniques in his found-footage films by meticulously manipulating the source material frame by frame. In *Deanimated* (2001/2002), Arnold reworked the 60-minute Hollywood film *Invisible Ghost* (1941) through digital manipulation of nearly every frame. Using software originally developed to make animals appear to talk in films, he selectively removed dialogue segments. As the film progressed, entire actors gradually vanished, their absence seamlessly filled through digital compositing, until the camera ultimately wandered through empty rooms. While Arnold created his earlier short films independently, this ambitious project required the support of a team:

"On the older films, I worked just on my own as a one-person production team. Now I have producers and a team of three co-workers, with one person in charge of the technical part of the production, a technical supervisor. It's the first time I'm working in a team. This is absolutely necessary – otherwise, I would only be able to show the film maybe two weeks before I die! It's so time-consuming that it takes forever. We'll have an output of something like five seconds per day per person. That's not very much for a 60-minute movie" (Martin Arnold, as cited in Taanila 2001: para. 16).

Given its runtime and frame-by-frame editing, one might question whether Martin Arnold's feature film, with its 'de-animation,' could also be considered an animated feature film in some sense. The productions from Vienna's *ZOOM Kindermuseum* (ZOOM Children's Museum) should also be considered in the search for Austria's animated feature films. Between 2007 and 2014, the Workshop *Lab Club* offered visitors the chance to contribute to a large-scale film project on weekends, public holidays, and during school vacations.

"The children and youngsters who come into the ZOOM Animated Film Studio pick up where the participants before them left off. Over the course of half a year a film is put together, combining the efforts of up to 700 kids from many nations. The completed animated film is shown in movie theaters, is available on DVD at the ZOOM, and can be viewed and downloaded on the website" (Kaiser 2014: 184).[5]

Fourteen films in total were produced, with runtimes ranging from 30 to 55 minutes. While these films may be considered too short to qualify as feature-length by European standards, half of them meet the 40-minute minimum runtime required for feature films according to British and American guidelines – from *NINA & NICO und das Geheimnis des Mäusekönigs* (NINA & NICO and the Secret of the Mouse King, 2007), which runs 49 minutes, to *Im Finsterland* (In the Dark Land, 2014), with a runtime of approximately 54 minutes. Like *1x1 des glücklichen Lebens* (The ABC of a Happy Life, 1987), these films could be classified as 'collective animated feature films.'

Meanwhile, the Austrian-German production *Rotzbub* (Welcome to Siegheilkirchen, *aka* Snotty Boy, 2021) was celebrated in the press as "the first animated feature film with a majority Austrian contribution" (Fuchs 2021: introd.), premiering at the *Annecy International Animation Film Festival* on June 14, 2021. However, few realized that nearly 6 years earlier, almost to the day, the 84-minute animated film *Noron* had its cinematic debut on June 12, 2015, at *Kinothek Lustenau*, a small theater in Austria's westernmost province of Vorarlberg. Despite also premiering in Vienna at *Top Kino* on November 27, 2015, *Noron* (2015) has largely faded from memory – even by 2023, it remained absent from both IMDb and Wikipedia.[6]

But which film truly deserves the title of Austria's first animated feature? Benjamin Swiczinsky (b. 1982) offered a balanced view in an interview with the author on July 5, 2023: chronologically, *Noron* (2015) is the first, while *Rotzbub* (2021) claims the title from a commercial perspective. Interestingly, even *Noron*'s director, Walter Zwiener (b. 1953), referred to his work as an "art film" (interview with the author on September 26, 2023). If *1x1 des glücklichen Lebens* (The ABC of a Happy Life, 1987) is included, Austria might be the only country in the world with three distinct films vying for the title of its first animated feature film.

AN ANIMATED SHOWDOWN: AUSTRIA'S RACE TO THE FIRST FEATURE

At the same time that ORF commissioned *1x1 des glücklichen Lebens* (The ABC of a Happy Life, 1987) in 1986, Virgil Widrich (b. 1967) envisioned a science fiction film set in a microscopic universe (Figure 15.1).[7] However, it wasn't until 2011 that development on the animated feature *Micromeo* began, with progress continuing over the years. In 2013, a trailer was produced along with an initial script, co-written with French screenwriter Jean-Claude Carrière (1931–2021), which was revised by 2014. After an extended hiatus, the screenplay underwent further revisions in 2017, with both Austrian and Luxembourgish production companies joining the still-in-development project as of 2023.

Another as-yet unrealized feature film project comes from Stefan Stratil (b. 1963), a founding member of *ASIFA Austria*. Stratil, known for animated films such as *Der Mensch mit den modernen Nerven* (The Man with Modern Nerves, 1988) and *I'm a Star!* (2002), as well as his curatorial work at *ASIFA Austria*'s ASIFAKEIL exhibition space, has also achieved success in commercial animation. Beyond creating music videos for the German band *Der Plan*, he has contributed to several award-winning advertisements. His first animated spot, *Tichy* (1986), made in collaboration with Bady Minck (b. 1956) and Sabine Groschup (b. 1959) for the famous Vienna ice cream parlor of the same name, won the *Creative Club Austria*'s *Golden Venus* award for *The Best Austrian Commercial of the Year.* Between 2000 and 2002, Stratil also created a comic series and, once again partnering with Bady Minck, produced several animated commercials for the multimedia advertising campaign *Spacy* by the mobile provider *mobilkom austria*.

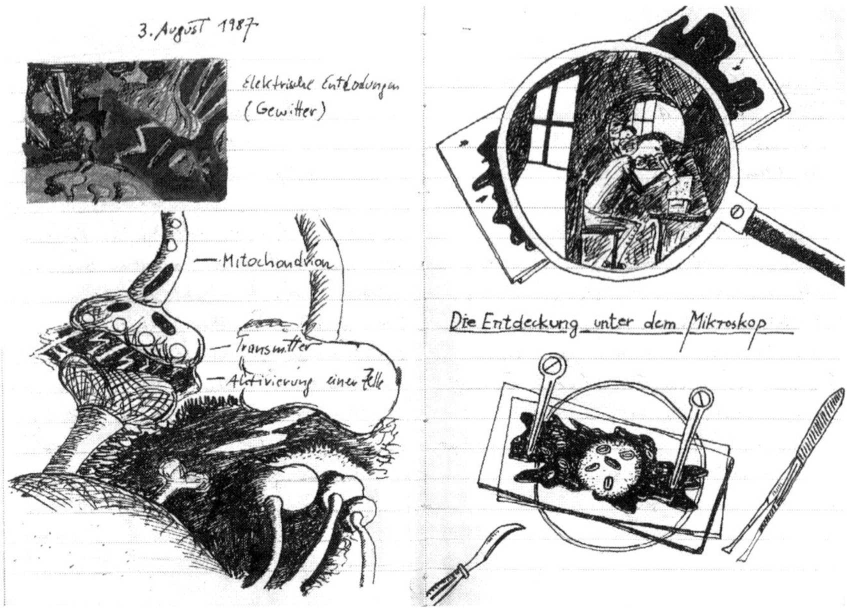

FIGURE 15.1 Early sketches from 1987 by Virgil Widrich for *Micromeo*, an animated feature film still in development as of 2023. (Courtesy of Virgil Widrich.)

In 2010, the Luxembourg and Vienna-based production company *AMOUR FOU* secured funding for the development of Stefan Stratil's animated feature film project *Bionet*, including support for the screenplay. Further backing came in 2011 from film funding bodies in both Austria and Luxembourg. Bob Baker (1939–2021), renowned for his work on several films in the iconic British *Wallace & Gromit* series (since 1989), was brought on as co-author for the ambitious project. In the spring of 2014, the film's concept was unveiled: inspired by the world's largest known organism – a fungus network spanning 9 km^2 beneath Oregon, USA – the film tells the story of a similar organism beneath the Rio de Janeiro region in Brazil, which is exploited by a religious cult to create a collective consciousness (Figure 15.2). According to Stratil, a Brazilian co-producer had already been secured for the live-action scenes of this planned hybrid film. However, despite plans for a 2017 release, the project was derailed due to various challenges, including the political situation in Brazil at the time. Reflecting on the project, Stratil remarked: "Perhaps it's time to try again" (interview with the author on February 9, 2024).

Benjamin Swiczinsky has long been driven by the ambition to create an animated feature film, aiming to achieve Austria's first in this category with the now-defunct studio *NÖT* (2011–2022).[8] As early as 2012, shortly after the studio's founding, his vision was clear: "To adapt original stories and create a full-length animated film" (Benjamin Swiczinsky, as cited in *Forschen & Entdecken* 2012: 25). The film project, titled *Der Papierene* (The Paper Man),[9] was set to tell the story of Austrian footballer Matthias Sindelar (1903–1939) and his 'Wonder Team,' which won the 1932 European Cup, reclaiming national pride during a politically tumultuous period.

FIGURE 15.2 Storyboard drafts for *Bionet* by Stefan Stratil, not indicative of the final visual style planned for the film. (Courtesy of Stefan Stratil.)

While these projects are still awaiting realization, several promising endeavors were abandoned in the early 2000s. Shortly after the turn of the millennium, the Vienna-based studio *CINE Cartoon*, known for its animated series, began exploring animated feature film production. With funding secured in late 2002, the studio set out to adapt Richard Strauss's (1864–1949) opera *Till Eulenspiegel* (1895) into a "hyper-modern animated spectacle" (Der Standard, September 1, 2003: 12) for IMAX cinemas.[10] However, by 2004, the project had been scaled down to a roughly 30-minute TV special, with only a brief test sequence having been produced and surviving today.

Another ill-fated feature film project was *WinneToons*, inspired by the stories of Karl May (1842–1912). This international collaboration, involving seven partners from five countries, including *CINE Cartoon*, ultimately collapsed due to financial difficulties. A similar fate befell the *TomTom* feature film project, based on the cartoon character created by Austrian Thomas Kostron, which was particularly popular in Asia. Announced by *CINE Cartoon* at the end of 2003, the project reached the final script and animated design stage and was presented at *Cartoon Forum Kolding* (Denmark) in 2005. However, the project's funding application was rejected in 2006. In a bid to find new partners, *TomTom* was later presented as a planned TV series at *Cartoon Forum Ludwigsburg* (Germany) in 2008.[11]

While the German-Polish-Austrian co-production *Winzig, der Elefant* (Tiny the Elephant, 2007/2008), which involved the Vienna-based *CINE Cartoon*, failed due to funding issues,[12] the 2010s saw the emergence of several minority co-productions between Austrian and predominantly German international partners.[13] In these collaborations, Austrian film companies served as co-producers, gaining access to local expertise and funding. For instance, the German-Austrian animated feature *Der kleine Ritter Trenk* (Trenk the Little Knight, 2015), traditionally hand-drawn between 2013 and 2014, was co-produced with Vienna-based *Dor Film*. This company also co-produced a series of partially animated feature films centered around Hexe Lilli (Lilly the Witch, 2009, 2011, and 2017).[14]

In 2015, production for the German-Austrian film *Teheran Tabu* (Tehran Taboo, 2017) took place in Vienna. The actors, including Morteza Tavakoli (b. 1982), who had moved to Austria from Iran at the age of 5, performed their scenes in front of a green screen. The footage was later animated using a blend of motion capture and predominantly rotoscoping technique: "Animation proves to be a clever choice for this film because it provides the audience with just enough distance to digest the sexually and politically charged topic more easily" (Flossmann 2017: 23). The Austrian production company *Coop99* co-produced the film and was also involved in producing the German-Austrian animated feature *Peterchens Mondfahrt* (Moonbound, 2021) from 2019 to 2021, with music recorded at *Synchron Stage Vienna* by the *Vienna Radio Symphony Orchestra*. Additional minority co-productions included *Die Häschenschule: Der große Eierklau* (Rabbit Academy: Mission Eggpossible, 2022) and the hybrid film *Johnny & Me* (2023), as noted in Chapter 14.[15] This continues the tradition of German-Austrian co-productions, which began nearly a century earlier with Berthold Bartosch's (1893–1968) collaboration on Germany's first animated feature, *Die Abenteuer des Prinzen Achmed* (The Adventures of Prince Achmed, 1926).[16]

NORON – AN ALMOST INVISIBLE FILM

The production of *Noron: Der Kampf um Ampoa* (Noron: The Battle for Ampoa, 2015) is reminiscent of the small, defiant village in *Asterix & Obelix*: quietly and almost unnoticed by the rest of Austria, the country's first animated feature film was crafted over a decade of home-based work by the "Vorarlberg artist family" (Rauch 2015) Zwiener in Dornbirn (Vorarlberg). The story follows three chosen heroes on a mission to install a protective shield around their home planet, Ampoa, to ward off an invading fleet of Erroks. These invaders seek to steal Noron, a life-giving elixir that grows on the planet's trees, imbuing the inhabitants of Ampoa with life.

Even more remarkable than the film's storyline and imaginative character designs is its unique production history. Walter Zwiener began his career as a commercial illustrator in the early 1980s, initially employing 'analog' techniques like airbrush, ink, and watercolor. In the 1990s, he expanded his skills to include computer graphics and technical 3D illustrations, producing short, primarily technical 3D animations for advertising clients. Much like Maria Lassnig (1919–2014) viewed traditional animation as an extension of her painting, Zwiener saw computer animation as a natural evolution of his digital graphic work. By 2004, he was self-teaching the creation of short film sequences, such as animating a dragonfly. Yet, Zwiener harbored ambitions for something much larger and more complex.

His wife, Erika Zwiener (b. 1954), a primary school teacher, wrote the initial script. Meanwhile, their daughter Anne Zwiener (b. 1982), then a student at the Academy of

FIGURE 15.3 Character design of a guard for the film *Noron* (2015), created by Anne Zwiener. (Courtesy of Anne Zwiener.)

Fine Arts Vienna, designed the characters (Figure 15.3):[17] "They inspired me tremendously, but I couldn't quite bring them to life as she envisioned,"[18] Walter Zwiener recalled, admitting that his computers had struggled with the intricate details of the designs. As the project evolved, so did the concept of the film. Anne noted: "Yes, it evolved constantly. Actually, it was done in a way you're not supposed to do. I mean, you just don't make a film like that. He [Walter] did it backward: he sort of made the film first, and then we built the story around it. [...] The script was essentially completed when the film was done." Walter acknowledged this unconventional process: "I'd do it differently now, but that's how it went." Although Erika was primarily responsible for the script, she integrated creative ideas from both Walter and Anne: "The challenge was to refine and expand the story, to adapt it to the world we had created, and to make it engaging" (Erika Zwiener, as cited in Gasperi 2015: 68). Even during sound recording at a Vienna studio, Walter remained open to suggestions from the voice actors, incorporating their feedback into the film.

The Battle Commences

After several attempts and preliminary work, the actual film production began in 2006. For 7 years, two Power Macs operated continuously, day and night. Walter Zwiener attributed the lengthy production time not only to his perfectionism but also to constant technological advancements, which led him to repeatedly revise already completed scenes. He spent up to 10 hours a day working on the computer, adjusting

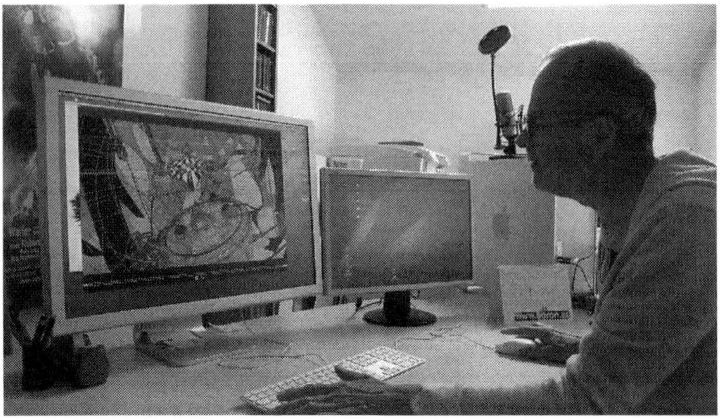

FIGURE 15.4 Walter Zwiener working on his film *Noron* (2015) on his home computer. (Courtesy of Russmedia Digital GmbH, Schwarzach (Matthias Rauch).)

scenes rendered overnight the following day: "And the whole thing was rendered in HD, which back then was a huge challenge – to render it in HD with the available computers and storage options," he explained (Figure 15.4). Even during leisure activities, such as hiking, Walter would leave the computers rendering, eager to check and adjust the results as soon as he returned. His primary job as an illustrator became secondary, often completed in just a few hours so he could return to the film project: "But the film became the main work. I got so absorbed in it that I couldn't focus on anything else," he said. In total, Walter spent more than 14,000 hours on the project, ultimately leading to physical exhaustion and a collapse that required him to take several weeks off.

Around this time, *Avatar: Aufbruch nach Pandora* (Avatar, 2009) premiered in Austrian cinemas, leaving a profound impact on Walter Zwiener and reigniting his passion for the project: "That was the point where I threw myself back into it with full force." The influence of *Avatar* (2009) is apparent not only in the film's title resemblance but also in its core message: "The adversaries of the 'Ampoans' are greedy creatures seeking to plunder the Noron reserves without regard for the planet's balance. It's a story about careful resource management" (Erika Zwiener, as cited in Gasperi 2015: 68). While Walter acknowledged the influence of 30 years of television and film, as well as his love for fantasy and science fiction movies like *Star Wars* (1977 onward), he aimed to create and animate his own unique imaginary world. Despite the presence of some action scenes, he was committed to telling a story with minimal violence: "I didn't want to make a film focused on violence; I wanted to create something as non-violent as possible." As a result, the plot centered more on defense than conflict.

As Walter Zwiener emphasized, the film could not have been completed without his daughter's increasing involvement at that time: "When my daughter Anne joined the project, she took over various aspects, such as character animation and modeling" (Walter Zwiener, as cited in Gasperi 2015: 70). For Anne Zwiener, who has since created successful animated shorts like the award-winning *Fragmented* (2017), this period became a crucial and formative experience.

FIGURE 15.5 Sound recording session in May 2013 for *Noron* (2015) at *Penzing Records* studio in Vienna. (Courtesy of Anne Zwiener.)

No Mon, No Fun?

Walter Zwiener estimated the film's total cost to be between €40,000 and €50,000, with €8,000–€10,000 allocated solely for the music. The voice actors were paid a modest fee of around €500 each, as Anne Zwiener recalled. Initially, the film was dubbed in Vorarlberg using theater actors, but the outcome was unsatisfactory. In response, Anne organized a casting session at *Penzing Records* in Vienna, where the entire film was re-recorded (Figure 15.5). The narrator of the fantastical tale was singer and composer George Nussbaumer (b. 1963), often described as 'Austria's darkest voice.'

Like *Rotzbub* (Snotty Boy, 2021), *Noron* (2015) faced skepticism from film funding authorities, who questioned the feasibility of producing an animated feature film in Austria. While the involvement of Oscar-winning producer Josef Aichholzer (b. 1950) helped secure funding for *Rotzbub*, Walter Zwiener, a relative unknown in the film industry, faced resistance. Ultimately, Walter received only a €3,000 grant from the state of Vorarlberg, with the remaining funding coming from his own savings and professional income. Despite the significant financial strain for Walter, his investment was a mere fraction of *Rotzbub*'s approximately €6 million budget. As he aptly noted, "a lot was achieved with very little money."

Noron Conquers Vienna

In the fall of 2013, *Noron*'s rough cut was finished, marking the start of post-production, which included sound design. A year later, the score was composed by Robert Bernhard, whom Walter Zwiener described as a "phenomenon." By January 2015, the film was officially completed. However, it took another 6 months for the world premiere, which took place on June 3, 2015, at the *Kulturhaus Dornbirn* (Arts Centre Dornbirn) in Vorarlberg. The venue was transformed into a cinema for the event, with a large screen set up. Despite the summer heat, the hall was filled with several hundred attendees, all engrossed by the screening. The press shared positive feedback from both young and old viewers:

"I really enjoyed the film. The landscapes are crafted with meticulous attention to detail, which must have taken a lot of work. It's not until the end that 'Noron' truly picks up excitement" (Franziska, 14, as cited in Begle 2015: 74).

"The film is very futuristic and beautifully animated. It's an impressive achievement for such a small team – hats off to them! I would recommend 'Noron' for children aged seven or eight and up" (Bernd, 34, as cited in Begle 2015: 74).

The press was equally enthusiastic: while noting that viewers "would need to warm up to the strange creatures," the film was praised as "exciting and visually stunning." It was said that the family had "created a thrilling and powerful film, unlike anything seen before" (Begle 2015: 74). On June 12, 2015, *Noron* had its cinema premiere at *Kinothek Lustenau* in Vorarlberg, but despite favorable reviews, attendance was low. Like in the case of *Rotzbub* (Snotty Boy, 2021) – originally slated for a Christmas release but instead premiering in summer – the hot weather kept audiences away. A lack of PR likely contributed to the film's poor box-office performance as well. Nevertheless, *Noron* reached the capital later that year, with a premiere at Vienna's *Top Kino* on November 27, 2015. A few months later, on April 21, 2016, the film became available online via an Austrian streaming platform.[19]

Post-producer Kurt Gehring described the film, as Walter Zwiener recalled, as "an extraordinary, unique project" that didn't fit into any conventional category. Initially, Walter anticipated a wave of festival invitations after the film's release, but instead, he faced indifference: "It was a real slap in the face." Some festival organizers considered the film too long, while others felt it lacked artistic merit. Even the local *Alpinale* film festival in Vorarlberg declined to feature it, and the ORF ignored the project despite being invited to screenings.[20] The lack of funds for effective marketing also played a role: "I was completely drained; I had put all my money into the project." Moreover, Walter lacked the network needed to break into the animation scene and promote the film within that community.

Even a decade after completing the project, Walter Zwiener remains confident in the quality of his film, which continues to captivate his grandchildren – even though it wasn't originally intended as a children's film. In hindsight, he would shorten the film to 30 or 40 minutes. This wouldn't be the first cut; the version released on streaming platforms was already reduced from 84 to 66 minutes to streamline the story. Walter had aimed for a roughly 90-minute film, which led to some scenes feeling too slow and lacking quick cuts, as he later acknowledged. "It's actually much better for children this way," his daughter Anne Zwiener defended the current version.

From the outset, Walter Zwiener was well aware that he was working on Austria's first animated feature film: "I was ambitious. You have to be ambitious to pull something like this off, especially when you're working on it for 10 years, day and night." Still, he could envision adapting *Noron* (2015) into a series format – perhaps then television networks might take an interest. The battle for Ampoa isn't over yet.

Animated Art

Walter Zwiener, who has exhibited as an artist and participated in an art group, views the film as more of an artistic endeavor that aligns with Austria's long-standing avant-garde tradition in animated cinema: "It somehow fits in." In this context, he finds the idea of having the film reimagined by artificial intelligence intriguing, especially because "it contains truly unique and unconventional patterns of thought." However, Walter considers *Noron* (2015) a one-time project, something he wouldn't repeat despite the joy it brought him: "No, it's not possible anymore. I'm 70 now and have found other hobbies. I'm always seeking new challenges, and my interests have completely changed." Still, he has no regrets about the decade-long commitment: "It was incredibly exciting. If I were back at that time, I would do it again in a heartbeat. It was a lot of fun, a truly wonderful experience – a reward in itself."

Despite all the setbacks – the lengthy production, high costs, and lack of support from film funding bodies and the media – Walter Zwiener passionately reflected on his dedication to the project: "It was incredibly fun. For me, it was number one! It was fantastic. I always enjoyed it." Today, *Noron* (2015) is almost forgotten. Initially hosted on the now-defunct Austrian streaming platform Flimmit, which was funded to promote European content, the film eventually found its way to a small commercial platform through various detours. Even a decade after its release, the film still hasn't had its TV premiere, and as of 2023, its official website is offline. Yet, with English subtitles now available, the film has garnered nearly 38,000 views on YouTube as of 2023. To put this into perspective, the fourth most successful Austrian film in theaters in 2015 attracted just under 40,000 viewers. "There's still a bit of interest," Walter summed up. And who knows – perhaps this small production, created by only 15 people, will one day surprise the world, much like Asterix did when he conquered America in his animated adventures.[21]

AN ANIMATED CHILDHOOD: AUSTRIA'S FIRST COMMERCIAL ANIMATED FEATURE

Cartoonist Manfred Deix (1949–2016) is regarded as one of Austria's most critical and influential artists. His profound impact on Austrian culture is evidenced not only by the inclusion of the term 'Deixfigur' (Deix character) in the Austrian dictionary but also by the *Karikaturmuseum Krems* (Caricature Museum Krems) in Lower Austria, often referred to as the 'Deix Museum' due to its permanent exhibition of his work. From an early age, Deix explored the complexities of the Austrian psyche, sharply criticizing hypocrisy, xenophobia, and societal norms. His characters, typically rendered in watercolor and often depicted as corpulent, have been described as "repulsive, disgusting, and damn funny" (as cited in 'Manfred Deix: Cartoonist und Maler' 2005, 00:02:14). Deix wryly responded to this characterization: "Perfect. Nothing to add" ('Manfred Deix: Cartoonist und Maler' 2005, 00:02:18).

Oscar-winning producer Josef Aichholzer (b. 1950), whose generation grew up with Manfred Deix's cartoons, had long recognized their potential: "Deix's characters have tremendous power and are practically begging to be brought to life."[22]

In 2013, while the artist was still alive, Aichholzer convinced him of this idea. When the animated film *Rotzbub* (Welcome to Siegheilkirchen, *aka* Snotty Boy) premiered in June 2021, it was celebrated as "the first feature-length animated film predominantly produced in Austria" (Schiefer 2021c: para. 1). Although Deix did not live to witness the film's success – it became the highest-grossing Austrian film of 2022 – he made history posthumously.

"This was the most challenging project of my life," recalled Josef Aichholzer. His satisfaction with the final product is even greater, and now, as an "experienced animated film producer," he has clear plans for future projects of this kind. Could there be a second 'Deix film'? Aichholzer doesn't rule out the possibility but insists on collaborating with the same team, which is currently engaged in other ventures.

Good Things Come in Threes: From Idea to Screenplay

Josef Aichholzer, best known for producing documentaries and live-action films like the Oscar-winning *Die Fälscher* (The Counterfeiters, 2007),[23] was convinced from the very beginning that a 'Deix film' could only succeed as an animated feature. In 2013, he set out to convince the cartoonist of this idea: "When we approached him, along with my co-partner from Munich, we told him that we believed his characters were begging to be animated. He looked at us and asked, 'Can I see that?'"[24] To illustrate their concept, they produced a brief 10-second test animation featuring one of Manfred Deix's characters. Pleased with the outcome, Deix agreed to collaborate.

However, this was just the beginning of a challenging journey to find the right story. The 'Deix-Universum' (Deix universe) consists of stand-alone cartoons without fleshed-out narratives. About 6 months later, the first script – created in consultation with Manfred Deix – was presented to Deix, but he felt it didn't align with his work. A second attempt met a similar fate. Despite these setbacks, Josef Aichholzer remained resolute. He didn't want to pressure Deix into accepting something he wasn't comfortable with, yet the project was too important for him to give up.[25]

Eventually, Manfred Deix himself proposed the idea of a partially autobiographical coming-of-age story. Screenwriter Martin Ambrosch (b. 1964) skillfully crafted a narrative that worked on multiple levels. On one hand, the exaggerated portrayal of rural life struck a chord with many, reflecting their own experiences. On the other, the film transcended the individual story of a young boy, capturing the coming-of-age of Austria as a nation, grappling with its post-fascist legacy: "A daring animated film about the puberty of the republic" (Tragner 2022: 37).

Heading to the Studio: How Falling Figures Learn to Walk

Once Manfred Deix approved the script, the focus shifted to character development. Josef Aichholzer brought in Marcus Salzmann (b. 1972) and his studio, *Digital Light Factory* (DLF), a Salzburg-based company specializing in visual effects and animation. Salzmann, who had honed his animation skills in Los Angeles, had returned to Austria for family reasons and initially worked on commercial animations before transitioning to visual effects for feature films like *Silentium* (2004). Aichholzer was

FIGURE 15.6 The characters of the artist Neidhardt and the mayor's wife were brought to life through a multi-stage process. (Courtesy of Aichholzer Filmproduktion, Vienna.)

confident he had found the ideal team – not only for their technical expertise but also for their cultural insight, which was essential for authentically bringing Deix's world to life (Figure 15.6).

As is typical for a project of this scale, Josef Aichholzer assembled an international team, acknowledging that "Austria still lacks the depth of experience, and the wide range of artists and craftsmen needed."[26] In addition to Austrian talents, the team included Greeks, Norwegians, Spaniards, Italians, and Germans. A core group of 25 specialists dedicated several years to the project. Aichholzer specifically sought out animation artists from "artistic collectives" that operated outside of traditional studios, deliberately avoiding those focused on children's films and bound by conventional standards. Such methods, he noted, wouldn't work for Manfred Deix's unique characters, like Marek: "The character is so corpulent that, if animated in the usual way, he wouldn't be able to walk – he'd just topple over."

Creating the necessary structural framework and capturing the "subtle details" – movement, facial expressions, and emotions – demanded meticulous artistic craftsmanship. According to Josef Aichholzer, it took 6 weeks to "build" one of the roughly 20 characters. Due to budget constraints, motion and performance capture were not viable options. However, as Marcus Salzmann explained: "The animators performed the scenes themselves in front of a camera, using those movements as a reference to animate the puppets" (as cited in *salzburg.ORF* 2022, under 'Animateure spielen die Bewegungen vor') (Figure 15.7).

Another major challenge was preserving the distinctive watercolor aesthetic of Manfred Deix's drawings, as "cinema demands bold emotions, while watercolor tends to be quite flat." To create a convincing artistic concept, the team enlisted the assistance of scientific institutes. Some critics argued that the characters should have been done in 2D, but Josef Aichholzer firmly disagrees. For him, the "Deixfigur" – a

FIGURE 15.7 Another example of character development, this time featuring Marek and Poldi, from the initial storyboard sketches to the final rendering on the computer. (Courtesy of Aichholzer Filmproduktion, Vienna.)

term so iconic it made its way into the Austrian dictionary – embodies more than just a visual style: "It's not just about the surface appearance; it's about capturing that mix of dim-wittedness and charm. And that requires a physicality you simply can't achieve in 2D. [...] Only then does Deix's vision fully come to life."

Josef Aichholzer believed that a northern German animation director wouldn't fully grasp the essence of the project as deeply as someone from eastern Austria or Bavaria (southern Germany). Since there was no Austrian animation director available, he turned to Marcus H. Rosenmüller (b. 1973) from Bavaria. With the live-action feature *Wer früher stirbt ist länger tot* (Grave Decisions, 2006), Rosenmüller had already crafted a rascal story that aligned with the spirit of the 'Deix-Universum' (Deix universe). However, after completing the film, Rosenmüller admitted: "I'd never have been able to do it by myself. That's why a few years ago Santiago López Jover came on board as co-director, bringing with him considerable know-how and a huge amount of feeling for the characterization" (Marcus Rosenmüller, as cited in Schiefer, May 2021a: para. 4).

For Santiago López Jover (b. 1980), a Spanish animation director based in Vienna at the time, his first exposure to Manfred Deix's work was a culture clash: "My first impression was definitely a shock" (Santiago López Jover, as cited in Schiefer 2021b: para. 2). To help Jover and his team immerse themselves in Deix's unique world, Josef Aichholzer brought them to the *Karikaturmuseum Krems* (Caricature Museum Krems) in Lower Austria, colloquially known as the 'Deix Museum' due to its permanent Deix exhibition. He also sent about 20 of Deix's books to their studio: "That's when the love for Manfred Deix really took hold [...] because once you dive into it, the power and brilliance of his art become undeniable."

Peanuts for the Snotty Boy

Convincing the funding bodies proved to be another challenge. For both Josef Aichholzer and the film funding authorities, an animated feature film was uncharted territory: "It was, of course, a leap into the unknown for the funders. [...] The funding structures have since evolved – particularly the application process. Back then, there wasn't even a dedicated application form for animation projects." However, due to Aichholzer's reputation as the producer of Austria's first Oscar-winning film, his company enjoyed a certain level of built-in trust.[27]

The film was initially budgeted at €8 million, with about €4 million raised in Austria. Securing foreign funding, however, proved challenging – while Austrian arthouse films are recognized and appreciated internationally, an Austrian animated feature film was still a novelty. Financially, the project was essentially dead, as Josef Aichholzer admitted, but his partners urged him on: "I was told, 'You can't *not* make a Deix film, so find a way.'" Ultimately, with some of his own resources, he managed to secure nearly €6 million for the project.

The COVID-19 pandemic (which officially lasted from March 2020 to June 2023 in Austria) not only delayed production but also increased costs. By the time the animation was almost complete, with only final tasks like compositing and lighting remaining, the team had to transition to remote work. Tasks that used to take a day now required two. To offset these additional pandemic-related expenses, a crowdfunding campaign was launched in September 2020. Within days, over a third of the €30,000 goal was met, and by the end, nearly €44,000 had been raised. For the film's distributor, the crowdfunding effort was both a crucial marketing move and a test of public interest: "And we [...] felt that people love it."

From the Hinterland to the World

The film was completed in 2020 and originally scheduled for a Christmas release. However, the onset of the COVID-19 pandemic in March 2020 led to multiple lockdowns and restrictions, making a theatrical release impossible at the time. A year later, the distributor initiated a marketing campaign, but cinema closures again delayed the release. Finally, on March 24, 2022, *Rotzbub* (Snotty Boy) premiered in Austrian theaters. Even then, the lingering effects of the pandemic – officially declared over in Austria in July 2023 – were still felt.

Despite these challenges, the film became the highest-grossing Austrian film of 2022, drawing over 107,000 viewers.[28] Josef Aichholzer received widespread praise from audiences, as the film "touched people's hearts." Even those previously uninterested in Manfred Deix's art were won over by the movie, expressing newfound enthusiasm for his work. Aichholzer attributed this success to maintaining a clear focus: "It was crucial that we told the story in a way that [...] resonated with a broader audience" (Figure 15.8).

However, the film had its world premiere in June 2021 as part of the competition at the prestigious *Annecy International Animation Film Festival* in France, Europe's most significant event for animated films. Its international appeal was

FIGURE 15.8 Production design of Marek and Poldi, described by the production company as one of its favorite motifs. (Courtesy of Aichholzer Filmproduktion, Vienna.)

further underscored a month later when it was showcased at the *Giffoni Film Festival* in Italy. While the official festival version featured the original Austrian audio with English subtitles, Italian subtitles were added for local audiences. Due to COVID-19 travel restrictions, only Italian children attended the screening in person, but the film was streamed simultaneously to cinemas in other countries, allowing a global audience to join a post-screening discussion via split-screen.

Even 2 years later, Josef Aichholzer was deeply moved by the experience: "I was speechless at how effortlessly they spoke so wonderfully about the film." The young audience not only grasped the coming-of-age story but connected it to their own lives, seeing themselves in several scenes. As Aichholzer explained: "Everyone knows that core emotion – feeling out of place in a conservative environment where you don't fit in. You know what you want, but you have to stand up for it and live it." Despite the challenges, Aichholzer and his team remained true to their vision, delivering not only a cinematic tribute to the late artist Manfred Deix but also a landmark achievement for Austrian animation.

NOTES

1 Tradition holds that the quote originated from the newspaper *Sport Kurier*, likely referencing a skiing result in which two Austrian athletes shared a ranking (cf. Dirk Stermann in Temel 2011, under "Fernseh-Fuzzys' als Autoren').

2 On the other hand, the 12-part British military animated film *Handling Ships* (1945) is also classified as feature-length, even though it was likely not used in this format for military purposes and was presented as a short film in the *Official Selection* at the 1946 *Cannes Film Festival* (France). Since the film cycle *Menschheit* (Humanity, 1919) is considered lost, it's impossible to verify whether it met the requirement of having at least 75% animation, as some segments reportedly included live-action footage, according to press descriptions.

3 The *Academy of Motion Picture Arts and Sciences*, the *American Film Institute* (AFI), and the *British Film Institute* (BFI) define a feature film as having a minimum runtime of 40 minutes. In contrast, the *Annecy International Animation Film Festival* in France sets the threshold at 60 minutes.

4 Refer to the film program *Kurz und gut* (Short and Good) from November 6, 2016 (https://www.esel.at/termin/87368). Unlike *1x1 des glücklichen Lebens* (The ABC of a Happy Life, 1987), where scenes by various artists are only loosely connected, *Life Show* (1990) qualifies as a narrative film due to its cohesive storyline. The reported runtime of *Life Show* (1990) varies between 40 and 45 minutes, with the ORF archive copy running 42.5 minutes.
5 The films can be viewed online at: https://www.kindermuseum.at/zoom_programmangebot/zoom_sammlung/lab_club_kinofilme
6 As of 2023, the Austrian cinema and film database Film.at remains the only platform to refer to *Noron* (2015) as "Austria's first animated feature film" (https://www.film.at/noron).
7 The sci-fi setting has since transformed into a love story in the vein of *Romeo and Juliet*, revolving around the forbidden romance between a bacterium named Micromeo and an antibody girl, Globia.
8 Interview with the author on July 5, 2023.
9 Austrian footballer Matthias Sindelar (1903–1939) was nicknamed 'Der Papierene' (The Paper Man) because of his delicate, slender build.
10 At MIPTV, the annual international television market held each spring, the planned film length was reported as 60 minutes in 2003.
11 In 2007, the *Filmfonds Wien* (Vienna Film Fund) approved funding for the series, while the Asian studio *Peach Blossom Media* (Singapore) joined as a production partner. Today, only a 3-minute trailer of the project remains.
12 See the section on *CINE Cartoon* in Chapter 14.
13 Minority co-production refers to the "production of a feature film where the producers of national origin provide less than the largest share of financing" (UNESCO Institute for Statistics, available online at https://uis.unesco.org/en/glossary).
14 *Dor Film* additionally co-produced the third season of the animated series *Hexe Lilli* (Lilly the Witch, 2014).
15 As of 2023, several additional minority co-productions were in the works, including *Die Heinzels: Neue Mützen, neue Mission* (The Super Elfkins, released at Christmas 2024), *Monster Mia* (Monstrous Mia, expected in 2025), and *Seeräuberin Moses* (Pirate Mo), which remained in development. For further details, refer to Chapter 14.
16 In addition to the previously mentioned minority co-productions, several animated feature films involved Austrian studios without receiving Austrian film funding. These include *Der kleine Rabe Socke: Suche nach dem verlorenen Schatz* (Raven the Little Rascal: Hunt for the Lost Treasure, 2019), *Die Heinzels: Rückkehr der Heinzelmännchen* (The Elfkins: Baking a Difference, 2019), and *Fritzi: Eine Wendewundergeschichte* (Fritzi: A Revolutionary Tale, 2019). For more information, see Chapter 14.
17 The name of the film production company, *WEA*, was derived from the initials of the family members' first names.
18 Unless otherwise indicated, all quotations in this subchapter are taken from the author's interview with Walter and Anne Zwiener, conducted via online conference on September 26, 2023.
19 Email from the now-defunct streaming provider Flimmit to the author, dated October 2, 2023.
20 The film was not selected for the *Alpinale* because of its length, as the festival focuses on short films.
21 *Asterix Conquers America* (1994).
22 Unless otherwise indicated, all quotations in this subchapter are taken from the author's interview with Josef Aichholzer, conducted on June 20, 2023, in Vienna.
23 In 2008, the film became the first Austrian entry to ever win an Oscar in the category *Best Foreign Language Film of the Year*, now known as *Best International Feature Film* since 2020.

24 The co-partner on the project was Munich-based film producer Ernst Geyer (b. 1945).

25 Josef Aichholzer learned from his conversations with Manfred Deix that several film-makers had previously attempted to adapt Deix's artistic work. However, for reasons unknown to him, those projects never came to fruition.

26 According to Benjamin Swiczinsky, discussions also took place with the now-defunct Studio *NÖT* (2011–2021), where Santiago López Jover (b. 1980), who was involved in the project, frequently collaborated (interview with the author on July 5, 2023). At *NÖT*, Jover contributed as an animator to various projects, including the animated sequences for the documentary *Auf Ediths Spuren* (Tracking Edith, 2016), the animated intro for *A Hologram for the King* (2016), and the music video *Dance Away* (2016).

27 Thomas Bogner (b. 1958), former head of the *CINE Cartoon* studio, noted that by 2011, one of the film funding authorities "had concluded that animation was not considered film and therefore no longer eligible for film funding" (email to the author, dated January 22, 2024). According to Josef Aichholzer, there were lively debates within the film funding institutions about how animated films should be supported and to what extent.

28 Despite this success, Austrian films simply can't compete with American blockbusters. For example, *Disney*'s *Avatar: The Way of Water* (2022) drew over 112,000 viewers to Austrian cinemas during its opening weekend (December 16–18, 2022). The film not only capitalized on the holiday season but also benefited from the post-pandemic period. Based on the feedback he received, Josef Aichholzer is convinced that *Rotzbub* (Snotty Boy) would have performed much better without the limitations caused by the pandemic.

16 Animation Becoming Tricky Realities

Austrian Film Festivals

While neighboring Germany saw the emergence of its first film festivals as early as the 1950s, it took until 1960 for Austria to follow suit. Another 25 years would pass before Austria saw its first film festival dedicated specifically to short films with the founding of *Alpinale* in Vorarlberg.[1] By 1982, Germany had already established the *Internationales Trickfilm-Festival Stuttgart* (ITFS, Stuttgart International Festival of Animated Film), but in Austria, animated films remained largely overlooked at festivals and were not featured in specialized programs. This might have been due to the difficulty in drawing a clear distinction between live-action and animated films within the avant-garde film scene. It wasn't until the turn of the millennium that Austria began to host film festivals dedicated specifically to animation. Festivals like *Tricky Women/Tricky Realities* (Figure 16.1), held annually around International Women's Day and recognized as the world's first festival focused exclusively on animated films by women and genderqueer people, or the *Ars Electronica Animation Festival*, where 'the Oscar of digital art' is awarded, highlight Austria's growing importance in this field.

Beyond the six film festivals outlined here, animation has increasingly become a central focus at many other festivals in Austria. For instance, at the Vienna Open Air Short Film Festival *dotdotdot*, described as "the first barrier-free short-film festival" (Lang 2019: 97), the summer of 2023 featured five animation programs under the banner of *Animated Nights*. "Some people in Austria have already started to complain that 'too many small events' are taking place each year, fearing that they will begin to cannibalize each other and compete for the few available funds" (Lang 2019: 97). Despite these concerns, the growing number of events underscores that animation has firmly established itself as a key part of Austria's film landscape. Moreover, through public film screenings and exhibitions that blend visual art with animation, *Die Kunst des Einzelbilds* (The Art of the Single Frame), as an anthology on Austrian animation once called it, has become a distinctive feature of Vienna's cultural scene.[2]

TRICKY WOMEN/TRICKY REALITIES

In 1992, Waltraud Grausgruber, along with fellow students, organized one of the first festivals dedicated to films by women. When Birgitt Wagner joined the team in 1997,[3] they came across the three-part video compilation *Wayward Girls & Wicked Women* (1992): "In the 90s we discovered all these video tapes with amazing animated films

DOI: 10.1201/9781003415442-19

FIGURE 16.1 Festival opening on March 8, 2023, at the *Gartenbaukino* in Vienna. (Photographed by the author.)

published by the BFI and Jayne Pilling – the woman responsible for kick-starting the British Animation Awards" (Waltraud Grausgruber, as cited in Whelan 2010: para. 4). They were instantly captivated by "the quality, the power, the energy of animation" ('Waltraud Grausgruber Interview' 2022, 00:00:11). In 2001, together with Antonia Cicero (b. 1964), they launched the first edition of the *Tricky Women* animation film festival. At that time, animation in Austria, outside of academic settings, still struggled for recognition, often being dismissed as merely children's entertainment. However, for Grausgruber, animation was a powerful tool for empowerment: "We saw that animation was incredibly effective at creating the tools of expression to discuss what struggles to be reduced to words" (Waltraud Grausgruber, as translated in *Vox feminae* 2021, under 'Interview with Waltraud Grausgruber by Vox feminae').

As the world's first animation film festival dedicated to works by women and genderqueer creators,[4] *Tricky Women* launched in 2001 with a program curated by Jayne Pilling, showcasing classic female animations from the 1970s to the present. Simultaneously, *Animation Austria* highlighted iconic works by Austrian women from the same era, while a special focus on Eastern Europe featured films from Yugoslavia, Romania, and Croatia. The international competition attracted 117 submissions from 20 countries, with female filmmakers vying for a prize sponsored by the City of Vienna. Beyond screenings, the festival offered discussions and lectures that provided opportunities for theoretical exploration of animation. Workshops organized in collaboration with *ASIFA Austria* allowed participants of all ages – children, teenagers, and adults – to learn and practice the art of animation themselves.

The festival's resounding success led to its continuation as a biennial event starting in 2003. That year, the spotlight was on films from the Czech Republic, Japan, and South Korea, with many South Korean films making their European debuts. The *Young Austrian Animation* program showcased the dynamic evolution of Austrian animation, and part of the film lineup was once again curated by Jayne Pilling. The program was enriched with lectures and workshops, and for the first time, a 3-month Artist-in-Residence scholarship was awarded, allowing selected female animation artists to live and work in Vienna. In 2005, the festival focused on the United Kingdom and Croatia, while paying tribute to Maria Lassnig (1919–2014), the "grande dame" (*Tricky Women* 2005: 3) of Austrian animation, with a dedicated retrospective. Following the *Global Gender Gap Report 2006*, where Sweden – alongside Norway, Finland, and Iceland – topped the rankings (with Austria placing 27th), *Tricky Women* in 2007 focused on the Nordic countries to explore whether this achievement was reflected in their animated films. In stark contrast, the festival also highlighted films from Russia and Ukraine. To foster international networking among women animation experts and female filmmakers, the festival introduced the *Connecting Animation* forum, featuring keynote speeches and discussions. Initially, the forum served as a bridge between theory and practice, featuring presentations by national and international female scholars.[5] In 2012, it was rebranded as *Best Practice*, shifting its focus to sharing practical insights and experiences.

The *Austrian Panorama*, held since 2007, "reflects the rich potential of animated filmmaking in this country" (*Tricky Women* 2008: 2). It now includes the *Hubert-Sielecki-Award for Austrian Animation*,[6] introduced in 2009, as well as the *Austrian Audience Award*. Starting in 2008, *Tricky Women* became an annual event. In the same year, the festival featured a renewed focus on Russia and highlighted international film schools, ranging from Jerusalem (Israel) and Lucerne (Switzerland) to California (USA). In 2009, the programs *Japanese Animation Today* and *From New York with Love* were showcased, the latter offering a "selection of new work and old favorites in a variety of styles from tradition cel and hand-drawn to 3D and digital painting" (*Tricky Women* 2009: 22). The festival also featured a retrospective of works by pioneering animator Mary Ellen Bute (1906–1983) and continued its focus on international film schools. Enthralled by the growing impact of documentary animation, the festival introduced a dedicated program for *Animated Documentaries* in 2010. Additionally, the spotlight was placed for the first time on award-winning animations by young girls in the U19 category of the *Prix Ars Electronica* with *U19 – Freestyle Computing Young Animations*, showcasing the full creativity and experimental spirit of Austria's emerging talent. Alongside numerous other program strands, international film schools once again received special attention.

A decade after its founding, *Tricky Women* remained the only international animation film festival dedicated to women's animation in 2011. The anniversary was celebrated with a film showcase in which ten women artists, who had significantly shaped the festival over the years, each presented three of their favorite films from 1933 to 2010. The celebration also included the publication of a book that aimed to address a gap in the theoretical exploration of feminist animation.[7] Additionally, the festival's logo was modernized. In the following years, the festival continued to impress with its diverse program, featuring themes such as *Women at Work* and *Young Russian Talents* (both in 2012), as well as *Spot on Iran* and *Spot on Spain & Mexico* (both in 2013). In 2013, the festival moved to a larger cinema, and in 2014, it showcased three animated features from Europe and the USA. The festival remained committed to presenting a comprehensive cross-section of international animation: in 2015, the focus was on the Czech Republic, Slovakia, and Australia; in 2016, Canada and its *National Film Board* (NFB) were highlighted; and in 2017, Japan took center stage.

Thanks to a collaboration with the Austrian Federal Ministry of European & International Affairs and its embassies abroad, a curated selection of Austrian animated films was made available to international audiences for the first time in 2016, reaching viewers from Australia to the United States.[8] A century after the end of World War I (1914–1918) and the introduction of women's suffrage in Austria, the 2018 festival centered on social and political upheavals, highlighting empowerment through animation.

In 2019, the festival was renamed *Tricky Women/Tricky Realities*: "Our new name is designed to add emphasis to a central aim of our festival: to explore and discuss different realities of life and take an active role in processes of social change" (*Tricky Women* 2019: 2). That year, the festival featured a country focus on China and launched a unique initiative where 20 women artists were invited to collaborate in ten production teams to create films envisioning the future of the world. Additionally, to commemorate the 30th anniversary of the fall of the Berlin Wall, the festival spotlighted nearly forgotten animated films by female filmmakers from the former East Germany (GDR). A year later, the country focus shifted to France, with the festival highlighting persistent gender inequality in the industry as reported in the *Film Gender Report*, emphasizing "that the big money still goes to the guys" (*Tricky Women* 2020: 2). The COVID-19 pandemic, which spanned from March 2020 to June 2023 in Austria, transformed the 20th-anniversary celebration in 2021 into an online event, turning the challenge into an opportunity for a global celebration, with the films streamed worldwide. The pandemic continued to affect the country the following year, resulting in a hybrid festival format that combined online and on-site events. Two prominent Austrian figures played a significant role in shaping the festival that year. The *Intergenerational Trauma* program, presented in collaboration with the *Sigmund Freud Museum*, was based on the idea that psychoanalysis and animation can speak the same language. Additionally, the festival celebrated the inaugural *Maria Lassnig Golden Film Reel Award* for outstanding animation with a retrospective of Maria Lassnig's films, paying tribute to her enduring influence on the art of animation.

The 2023 festival, once again held in a hybrid format, underscored the continued relevance of *Tricky Women/Tricky Realities*. Ukrainian artist Alexandra

FIGURE 16.2 Photo of Sarah Braid used as a reference for a character's facial expression in *Holladio hods gsogt* (Holladio She Said, 2022). (Courtesy of Sarah Braid.)

Dzhiganskaya, who fled the war, processed the conflict in her deeply personal film *Under the Endless Sky* (2022). Two other films, *Die Wand vor Augen* (The Wall in Front, 2022) by Yujin Cho and *Issues with My Other Half* (2022) by Anna Vasof (b. 1985), offered stylistically distinct reflections on the impact of the pandemic. *Holladio hods gsogt* (Holladio She Said, 2022), which won the *Hubert-Sielecki-Award for Austrian Animation*, saw Sarah Braid (b. 1993) transform a sexist pop song from a flea market record into an empowering music video (Figure 16.2).[9] In an interview, when asked about the numerous films she submitted, Braid remarked that she could compete with multiple films each year because there is still so much to address.[10] *Tricky Women/Tricky Realities* will continue to challenge social injustices and carve out a path for feminist animation:[11]

"Tricky Women/Tricky Realities is a statement! From gender equality to digitalization, from human rights to the working world, to social, economic, and ecological questions – the festival has been exploring social and political issues from a feminist and artistic perspective and offering new ways of highlighting social inequalities" (Waltraud Grausgruber, as translated in *Vox feminae* 2021, under 'Interview with Waltraud Grausgruber by Vox feminae').

BEST AUSTRIAN ANIMATION FESTIVAL

On the occasion of *International Animation Day* (IAD) on October 28, *ASIFA Austria* organized an animation retrospective in October 2004, curated by Thomas Renoldner (b. 1960). The event showcased international animated films from the previous 20 years that deviated from the artistic mainstream. Inspired by this, the idea for a film festival emerged, aligned with IAD, and in 2005, the *One Day Animation Festival* (ODAF) was launched under the auspices of *ASIFA Austria*. The festival was designed to showcase the full spectrum of Austrian animation alongside international works, spanning everything from art to commerce, abstraction to realism, and experimentation to narrative. The inaugural 2005 festival, themed *NYC meets VIENNA*, highlighted animated films from both cities, including works by American animators such as Bill Plympton (b. 1946). In 2011, the festival expanded to include the *ASIFA Austria Award* in the *Best Austrian Animation* competition. This new addition showcased films from all branches of animation, including avant-garde, puppet, and traditional animation, as well as narrative 3D computer animation. The festival's success led to its expansion and renaming in 2017 as the *2 Days Animation Festival*. That same year, in collaboration with the *Ars Electronica Animation Festival*, a program was curated featuring all the winning films from 2011 to 2017. While the 2018 festival showcased 50 films, by 2023, the number had nearly doubled to almost 100.

The COVID-19 pandemic forced a radical reimagining of the festival. Originally scheduled for November 2020, the event was postponed to January 2021 and transformed from the *2 Days Animation Festival* into a 2-week online event – effectively becoming a *2 Week Animation Festival*. This new format not only opened an international window for Austrian animation but also allowed for a broader program. In previous years, many compelling films had to be excluded due to time constraints. To address the growing number of high-quality student submissions, a new competition, *Best Austrian Student Animation*, was introduced. A special program also spotlighted the collaborative project *#FlattenTheCurve* (2020) by Austrian Kathrin Steinbacher (b. 1989) and Briton Emily Downe. This initiative invited animators worldwide to contribute short, positive reflections on the pandemic, with over 90 participants responding. The online shift also enabled the festival to achieve a long-held goal: replacing the printed film catalog with the *Best Austrian Animation Database*, where all participating films are now permanently archived.[12]

The 17th edition of the festival, originally scheduled for November 2021, was also postponed due to the pandemic, eventually taking place in April 2022. Along with this rescheduling, the festival was rebranded as the *Best Austrian Animation Festival* (BAAF!). While the festival's primary aim was to serve as a hub for the Austrian animation community, the pandemic-driven shift to an online format opened new avenues, allowing for international access. This change enabled audiences worldwide to explore the richness of Austrian animated filmmaking. In 2022, the festival also introduced a third major award for the *Best Animated Commissioned Work*.

What began as the *One Day Animation Festival* has now expanded into a 6-day event, offering equal visibility to students alongside established artists, and showcasing both independent and commissioned works. A practical symposium facilitates the exchange of ideas between students and professionals while accompanying exhibitions and multimedia performances highlight how animation can transcend cinema and influence various other art forms.

ARS ELECTRONICA ANIMATION FESTIVAL

The *Ars Electronica Festival*, held in Linz (Upper Austria) since 1979, is recognized as one of the pioneering events to explore digital art and the societal impact of digital technology. Since 1987, the festival has awarded the *Golden Nica* through its media arts competition, *Prix Ars Electronica*, emphasizing the importance of computers and digital technology as tools for artists and creatives. Often referred to as 'the

Oscar of digital art,' the *Golden Nica* is one of the most prestigious honors in the realm of electronic art and culture. From its inception, the award has included a category for *Computer Animation*, with *Pixar*'s debut film *Luxo Jr.* (1986) as its first recipient. Notably, *Luxo Jr.* (1986) was also the first fully computer-animated film to receive an Oscar nomination:

"And with respect to the Prix Ars Electronica, you can go back to the very first winner Luxo Jr, this highly complicated work of keyframe animation that six people worked on almost day and night for six months, and that cost $2.5 million, which was an exorbitant amount at the time. And you can compare that with the way a group of young artists or even an individual artist working alone can do such perfect animation today, the likes of which major Hollywood studios weren't even capable of a few years ago. An incredible amount of research has gone into making these works possible" (Christine Schöpf, as cited in Knoll 2013: para. 15).

Initially, the award aimed to recognize pioneering achievements in computer graphics (CG) and animation, but by the 1990s, the artistic dimension increasingly came to the forefront. While tech demos highlighted the capabilities of cutting-edge animation software and hardware, prestigious studios were also honored for developing groundbreaking visual effects (VFX). Reflecting this evolution, the category was renamed *Computer Animation/Visual Effects* in 1998. To acknowledge both artistic and professional achievements, the award was, for the first time, presented in two separate instances that year.

As the boundaries between animation and live-action film began to blur, driven by increasingly sophisticated VFX, the category was renamed again in 2007 to *Computer Animation/Film/VFX*. However, in 2018, in response to a renewed emphasis on the artistic aspect, the category reverted to *Computer Animation*, dropping the additional descriptors. This change also acknowledged the influence of new technologies that had shaped the category over the past decade – from art games and virtual reality (VR) projects to projection mappings.

In 2023, the category was rebranded as *New Animation Art* to further refine and sharpen its focus. This change was driven by a paradigm shift in image creation and interpretation – not only through artificial intelligence and machine learning but also through advancements in scientific visualization, such as those from the James Webb Space Telescope, and the latest trends in real-time graphics, including virtual realities and the Metaverse. The renaming aimed to better recognize works at the intersection of animation, technology, and art, ensuring the category remains a barometer for future trends in animation art.

Animation has become a prominent feature at *Ars Electronica*, well beyond the scope of the *Prix Ars Electronica* alone. In 2005, the festival launched its inaugural *Computer Animation Festival*, which not only showcased a representative selection of over 450 submitted works but also featured special programs. For instance, in collaboration with the *Japan Media Arts Festival*, a curated selection of Japanese animations was presented, while the Berlin-based media artist duo *Flashkino* brought internet-discovered Flash animations to the big screen. In 2006, the event was rebranded as the *Ars Electronica Animation Festival* and expanded to include 11 hour-long program segments. By 2007, the festival curated ten programs from nearly 1,500 films (including over 500 submissions to the *Prix Ars Electronica*) from

63 countries. For the first time, the festival's program was simultaneously screened in Linz, Vienna, and the partner city of Kyiv, Ukraine.

Even in 2008, the films remained challenging to categorize due to their varied stylistic, thematic, and technological approaches. However, a notable trend emerged among the submissions for the *Prix Ars Electronica*, with a clear preference for the classic stop-motion animation technique. A standout example was the Canadian film *Madame Tutli-Putli* (2007), which took 4 years to produce and was also Oscar-nominated, earning the 2008 *Golden Nica*. In 2010, the festival sought to embody the perspective offered by jury member Chris Bregler from New York University's Courant Institute, as reflected in the film program:

"Over its 24-year history, the Prix Ars Animation, Film and Visual Effects jury has seen many revolutions, evolutions, and historic milestones in the fields of CG, animation and VFX that have contributed to film making and storytelling. And this year, 2010, we are again witnessing the birth of some new forms, the maturing of others, and some being completely re-invented. For high-end Hollywood, 2010 is the year of Avatar, a technological breakthrough in many dimensions. For CG animation, 2010 is the continuation of the goal of 'content and concept over technique' film making. The 3D tools have matured to such a level that film makers take the technology for granted. Which is good, because now everybody can focus on what really matters: the art of animation and storytelling" (Chris Bregler, as cited in Schöpf and Hagler 2010: 428).

In 2011, the *Ars Electronica Animation Festival on Tour* was launched. In collaboration with the Austrian Federal Ministry of European & International Affairs, approximately 120 films, organized into 12 thematic programs, were distributed to Austrian cultural forums and embassies worldwide. These films were then screened by educational institutions, film festivals, and cultural organizations in countries ranging from South Korea to Mexico, Israel to Russia, and Greece to the United Kingdom.

Two years later, ahead of *Ars Electronica*, the *LENTOS Art Museum Linz*, in partnership with the Department of Digital Media at the University of Applied Sciences Upper Austria, Campus Hagenberg, hosted the *Expanded Digital Animation: Mapping an Unlimited Landscape* conference.[13] This event, featuring speakers such as Oscar-nominated Austrian filmmaker Virgil Widrich (b. 1967), was designed to offer students a specialized program on digital animation within an interdisciplinary context. Jürgen Hagler, who had been a curator for the *Ars Electronica Animation Festival* since 2009, played a key role in organizing the event. In 2014, the conference was renamed *Expanded Animation* and became a dedicated program track within the *Animation Festival*. The following year, the *Prix Forum – Computer Animation/Film/VFX*, which invited category winners to a panel discussion, was integrated into the *Expanded Animation* conference. The event now spanned 2 days and featured an additional workshop. By the time the fifth conference was held in 2017, it had already hosted 45 speakers, including media artists, theorists, curators, animation filmmakers, and executives from design and animation studios. In 2019, the book *Expanded Animation: Mapping an Unlimited Landscape* was presented following the *Prix Forum*. This publication included contributions from past speakers and artistic insights from the previous 6 years, along with an overview of the *Prix Ars Electronica* winners in the *Computer Animation* category since 2011.

The 2020 conference, ironically subtitled *The Appeal of Analog*, was held entirely online due to COVID-19 restrictions. It became the largest conference to date, with 38 speakers from 12 countries, nearly equaling the total number of speakers from the first 4 years combined. Consequently, the live streams were spread over 3 days. The pandemic continued to disrupt plans in 2021, necessitating a hybrid format for the conference. Since then, the lectures, panel discussions, and workshops have been routinely streamed online.

The expansion of the *Prix Ars Electronica* to include a dedicated *Ars Electronica Animation Festival* and the now 3-day *Expanded Animation* symposium, which delves into the evolution of digital animation's outer edges, underscores the growing importance of animation in both the artistic and scientific discourse in Austria.

PIXELVIENNA

To provide a platform for networking and collaboration among Austrian CG artists, Christoph 'Kris' Staber (b. 1979), co-founder of the animation studio *arx anima*, established the online forum *CGforum.at* in 2004.[14] The lively discussions on the platform quickly sparked a desire for in-person interactions, which regularly took place as the *CGForum Stammtisch* (CGForum Regulars' Table), often hosted at Vienna's *7Stern* cultural center. These gatherings sparked the idea of organizing a more structured event with keynote presentations, ultimately leading to the *PIXEL* Conference at the Vienna University of Technology in 2006. The conference aimed to emphasize the growing importance of the CG industry in Austria and to strengthen the country's position as an educational hub in this field.

The official festival series kicked off in the spring of 2007 with *PIXEL 1.0*, offering a diverse range of expert talks across the gaming, animation, and VFX industries. The team behind these early *PIXEL* events included Christoph Staber (co-founder of *arx anima*), Thomas Mahler (co-founder of *Moon Studios*), Ralf Habel (core developer at *Disney's Hyperion Renderer*), and Wolfram Neuer (lead artist at *Rabcat Game Art*). By fall 2007, *PIXEL 2.0* had already taken place, solidifying the festival as an annual autumn event. Interest in *PIXEL* continued to grow, and by 2009, the now 3-day *PIXEL 4.0* was relocated to the Austrian Academy of Sciences to accommodate nearly three times the previous number of attendees. This edition featured presentations by Oscar-nominated animation and VFX artists, prominent gaming industry leaders, and top international experts in CG academic research. Among the notable guest speakers was Austrian character designer Florian Satzinger (b. 1970), who created an artwork live on stage.[15] The conference also introduced an animation short film festival, featuring the *SIGGRAPH Animation Festival* reel, which showcased a curated selection of the best international works from the previous year.

In 2010, approximately 400 international experts and enthusiasts from the film, advertising, digital media, and video game industries gathered at *PIXEL 5*[16] for industry talks and knowledge exchange. Notably, representatives from *PIXAR Animation Studios* were among the distinguished guests. By the time *PIXEL 6* took place in the fall of 2011, the conference had become the largest so far, with around 500 attendees. It was also the first edition to specifically welcome students. That year marked an expansion of the film festival, which began showcasing the winning films from the *Prix Ars Electronica* in the category of *Computer Animation/Film/VFX*.

At *PIXEL 7* in the fall of 2012, the *Austrian Computer Graphics Award* (ACGA) was introduced, with submissions open in areas such as 3D and 2D animation, 3D visualization, compositing, game development, and concept art. An international jury evaluated these works through online voting.[17] Christoph Staber, one of the event's organizers, emphasized the importance of traditional skills, stating: "The fundamental tools of visual language remain pencil and paper. If you want to discuss ideas, you need to be able to draw." He highlighted that "mastering graphic tools alone is not enough for success; artistic intuition and talent are essential" (Christoph Staber, as cited in Die Presse, September 30, 2012: 13). This philosophy was showcased during the *PIXEL Battles*, where two artists competed live for 30 minutes on a given topic, using either paper and pencil or a computer, with their designs projected live for the audience. Despite – or perhaps because of – *PIXEL*'s significant international success, there was a growing desire within the community to recapture the informal spirit of the early years. This led to the creation of smaller spin-offs called *KRIXEL*, which embraced the concept of "someone prepares something and shares what they do" (Christoph Staber in an email to the author, dated March 5, 2024). These projector-based presentations were followed by informal Q&A sessions over drinks.

PIXEL 8 in 2013 featured a noteworthy premiere during the animation film festival, with *Disney*'s Oscar-winning short film *Get a Horse!* (2013) making its debut in the German-speaking world. Animator Eric Goldberg (b. 1955) provided an in-depth behind-the-scenes look at the production process as a guest speaker. To reduce confusion with similar conferences and to incorporate the event's location into its identity, a rebranding took place in 2014, resulting in *PIXELvienna*.

PIXELvienna celebrated its 10th edition in 2015 with a special exhibition documenting the festival's history through photos and memorabilia. Attendees were also treated to "insights into current major game productions, new technical developments from leading animation studios, and the opportunity to view award-winning short films" (as cited in *Der Standard* 2015: para. 2). Embracing the motto 'bigger is better,' VFX specialist Tobias Mannewitz discussed the challenges of expanding King's Landing castle with each season of the TV series *Game of Thrones* (2011–2019). At *PIXELvienna 11* in 2016, now under new leadership, the ACGA was awarded for the fifth and final time. Plans to transition the award to a biennial format were made, but the cancellation of *PIXELvienna* in 2018 prevented these from being realized.

After the festival was put on hold in 2018, a reorganization process began in the summer of 2019, during which the core team faced the challenge of finding a new location, among other tasks. The much-anticipated comeback occurred in the fall of 2020, though, ironically, during the COVID-19 pandemic, which necessitated holding the conference online, as it did the following year. However, this shift also created new opportunities, such as launching a dedicated YouTube channel in the spring of 2021. This platform proved especially beneficial for representatives of Austrian studios, including Barbara Mitterer from *Studio Citron*, Andreas Niedermayer from *Polarfux*, and Benjamin Swiczinsky (b. 1982) alongside Conrad Tambour (b. 1984) from *NÖT*. The animation festival was also revamped and expanded, introducing a new competition format. At *PIXELvienna 14* (2021), the competition was divided into separate categories for student and professional films, and by *PIXELvienna 15* (2022), further distinctions were made between national and international entries.

PIXELvienna, now firmly established as Austria's premier industry event, has returned to its former glory. The lineup of participants reads like a who's who of the computer animation world: notable speakers included Robbie Blalack (1948–2022), the Oscar-winning VFX artist for *Star Wars* (1977), and Albert Hastings, CG Supervisor for *Avatar* (2009). The conference also featured presentations by representatives from major studios such as *DreamWorks Animation*, *Walt Disney Animation Studios*, *Warner Studios*, *Blizzard Entertainment*, *Pixar Animation Studios*, *Lucasfilm*, and *Sony Pictures Imageworks*. Michael Shantzis of *Pixar Animation Studios* praised the conference's "intimate setting" ('PIXELvienna 2012' 2021, 00:01:50). In 2010, co-organizer Christoph Staber articulated the conference's mission: "The PIXEL gives an impulse to strengthen a young and prospering industry and shows that the Austrian tradition of art meeting technology, has not only a strong past but an even brighter future."[18]

ANIMATION AVANTGARDE @ VIENNA SHORTS

In 2003, several student-led initiatives focused on short film distribution came together to establish a short film festival. The first edition of this festival, named *Vienna Independent Shorts* (VIS), took place in Vienna during the summer of 2004. Each participating institution organized a day of programming, resulting in a diverse lineup of 125 short films. By the following year, the organizers formalized their efforts by founding the *Independent Cinema* Association, which became the festival's official legal entity. This milestone also marked the introduction of an international competition featuring 64 films, alongside a showcase of student works from the University of Applied Arts. Additionally, a partnership with the Academy of Fine Arts' animation studio laid the groundwork for what would later evolve into the festival's animation competition.

VIS's dedication to animated avant-garde cinema was underscored in 2006 with a special program spotlighting Mara Mattuschka (b. 1959). That year, the festival expanded beyond Vienna, with the opening program also screened in the federal states of Vorarlberg (Dornbirn), Tyrol (Innsbruck), and Styria (Graz), complemented by a television program broadcast on the Okto channel. By 2007, VIS had established itself as Austria's largest international short film festival, now featuring dedicated programs for animation and experimental films. Highlights included a tribute to Austrian experimental filmmaker Virgil Widrich and a special guest appearance by British animator Paul Bush (1956–2023), who presented several of his works.

Celebrating its fifth anniversary in 2008, VIS showcased a special focus on Swiss animation, featuring a guest program from the Swiss animation festival *Fantoche*, and a spotlight on Austrian animator Hubert Sielecki (b. 1946). Sielecki also established a new award,[19] which in 2009 was presented to Adnan Popovic (b. 1979) for his stop-motion music video *Walzerkönig* (Waltz King, 2009), created for the *Laokoongruppe*.

In its seventh year, the festival further expanded its offerings in collaboration with *ASIFA Austria*, introducing an international competition for animation, experimental film, and digital media. Curated by Thomas Renoldner and Wiktoria Pelzer (b. 1985),[20] this new section was named *Animation Avantgarde* (AA), with the *ASIFA Austria Award/Animation Avantgarde* established as its prize. However, in 2011, the festival faced the threat of closure due to the loss of its main sponsor and insufficient public funding. Aside from these challenges, the festival sought to view the internet not as a threat, but as an opportunity for expansion within its programming. VIS celebrated its tenth anniversary in 2013 by expanding the *Animation Avantgarde* competition to include an artist-in-residence scholarship. The festival also honored the work of Irish animator David O'Reilly (b. 1985), who is based in the USA, with a special program at the Austrian Film Museum. The festival's success reached new heights in 2014, with over 3,000 international submissions and more than 300 films screened over 7 days. The program also included a segment where German media artist Robert Seidel explored the boundaries of digital animation. In 2015, VIS drew nearly 10,000 visitors to more than 70 events, including a retrospective of Oscar-nominated American animator Don Hertzfeldt (b. 1976), organized in collaboration with the Austrian Film Museum.

In 2016, VIS fully embraced Hollywood by spotlighting legendary American animator Bill Plympton and becoming Austria's first and only *Oscar Qualifying Festival*. This milestone allows Austrian animated short films to qualify directly for the Oscars. In 2017, the festival's name was shortened to *Vienna Shorts*, and since 2019, its selected films have also been eligible for the *European Film Awards*. The COVID-19 pandemic in 2020 necessitated a shift to an online format, providing an opportunity to revamp the festival's visual identity with a new logo, a redesigned website, and a streaming platform tailored to the needs of digital festivals. While part of the program remained online in 2021, VIS successfully returned to its traditional cinemas in 2022. The festival's streaming portal continued to operate and was enhanced with a new festival app to enrich the experience further.

For its 20th edition in 2023, VIS awarded nearly €30,000 in prize money and introduced an innovative trophy concept: winners now receive the dedication of a freshly planted tree from the Vienna City Gardens instead of traditional trophies. Each tree features a QR plaque, allowing visitors to stream the winning film on their smartphones near the tree. This initiative has enabled audiences to enjoy animated films like *Amok* (HU/RO 2022) by Balázs Turai and *Sjeti se kako sam jahala bijelog konja* (Remember How I Used to Ride a White Horse, HR 2022) by Ivana Bošnjak Volda (b. 1983) and Thomas Johnson Volda (b. 1984) amid Vienna's greenery. Today, Vienna Shorts has become Austria's largest and most prestigious festival for short films, animation, and music videos. The international competition *Animation Avantgarde* highlights works that push the boundaries of experimental and animated films, exploring innovative content and technological diversity.

UNDER_THE_RADAR

Another animation film festival began exactly as its name implied: *UNDER_the_RADAR*. On February 27, 2011, a small group of enthusiasts 'crashed' a gallery exhibition in downtown Vienna, seizing the opportunity to connect and network during what they called an *IN-TER-MISSION*. Following this informal gathering, the official event featured a film program titled *in-567-under-radar-ter-mission*, showcasing films no longer than 567 seconds that defied conventional categorization – films that 'flew under the radar.' The small but highly engaged audience was encouraged to give impromptu short presentations.

By 2012, the festival-conference hybrid was officially renamed *UNDER_the_RADAR* and expanded into a 2-day event organized in collaboration with *ASIFA Austria* and *Webster Vienna Private University*. The event featured international guest speakers, including filmmakers from the UK, Taiwan, and the USA, who either hadn't yet made their mark in the mainstream or were intentionally working within the underground scene. The film program, *in567-liquids*, once again showcased works capped at 567 seconds, contributed by students, *ASIFA Austria* members, and independent filmmakers. The festival embraced a broad concept of animation under the banner of 'animation-and-more,' encompassing everything from experimental cinema to music videos and interdisciplinary media art: "If you don't know where exactly your work might fit in you are probably in exactly the right place."[21]

The focus on student filmmaking was significantly strengthened in 2013 through a partnership with the Institute for Theater, Film, and Media Studies at the University of Vienna. Building on this success, the festival was extended to 3 days in 2015. To mark the 30th anniversary of *ASIFA Austria*, the film program *Contemporary Austrian Animated Experiments* was introduced, aiming to "provide a focused view on the current development of animation art in Austria" (*ASIFA Austria* 2016, under 'Contemporary Austrian Animated Experiments 2016').[22]

In 2016, the University of Applied Arts Vienna joined the festival, establishing the *Radar Award*, inviting students from Austrian universities to submit films in the fields of animation and new media. That same year, the *Radar Audience Award* was also presented for the first time. By 2017, the festival had grown to 4 days and included an international film program. The following year, with the festival now spanning 5 days, Hubert Sielecki (founder of *ASIFA Austria*) introduced the *Radar Sielecki Award*. Additionally, *Tricky Women goes Radar* showcased a selection of the best films from the *Tricky Women* festival. Another noteworthy addition was the *Radar Pitch*, a unique feature in Austria: "A pitching competition preceded by a multi-day workshop led by an international expert, where participants hone their skills in professionally presenting a short film project. The best pitch is then awarded in the final competition" (email from Stefan Stratil to the author, dated February 8, 2024).

Further international expansion occurred in 2019 with the introduction of the *Radar International Award*, which included a 2-month paid artist residency in Vienna.[23]

However, due to the COVID-19 pandemic and its accompanying restrictions, the 2020 award ceremony had to be postponed. It wasn't until March 2022 that *UNDER_the_RADAR 2021/22* could return to its regular format. Over time, what began as an afternoon event has evolved into a week-long *Festival and Conference for Artistic Film, Animation, and Experimental Sequential Media.*

NOTES

1 The Super 8 boom of the 1980s sparked a wave of short-lived film festivals and screenings, including the *Filmfestival tropisch* (Film Festival Tropical), which took place from January 11–22, 1983, in Innsbruck (Tyrol).

2 For example, during *Tricky Women* 2023, a total of six venues in Vienna were utilized. Free film screenings were hosted in art spaces at two street markets in Vienna, while the gallery *Bildraum 07* featured exhibitions of artworks by female animators, inspired by their animated films. At ASIFAKEIL, a wedge-shaped exhibition space of *ASIFA Austria* in Vienna's *MuseumsQuartier* (MQ) that has been freely accessible since 2007, new exhibitions exploring the intersection of animation and visual art are presented every 6–8 weeks. These exhibitions, often accompanied by film programs from both Austrian and international artists, are curated by Stefan Stratil (initially in collaboration with Renate Kordon until 2013). Stratil, along with Holger Lang, also co-edited the catalog *Animating Art: 130 Exhibitions of Contemporary Animated Installation* (2024), published by *ASIFA Austria* (email to the author, dated February 7 and March 6, 2024).

3 Birgitt Wagner remained a steadfast part of the festival until 2020.

4 While the festival is dedicated to spotlighting women and genderqueer individuals, male viewers are equally welcome: "We are a festival of inclusion, not exclusion; our audience is diverse: All genders welcome, naturally" (Waltraud Grausgruber in 'Tricky Women/Tricky Realities 2021' 2021, 00:14:40).

5 The presenters included notable figures such as Gabriele Jutz, Maureen Furniss, Ruth Lingford, Esther Leslie, Annegret Richter, and Birgitta Hosea.

6 The *Hubert-Sielecki-Award for Austrian Animation* has been awarded to several notable artists, including Veronika Schubert (*Tintenkiller/Ink Eraser*, 2010), Mirjam Baker (*The Back Room*, 2012), Gudrun Krebitz (*Achill*, 2013), Anna Vasof (*Machine*, 2016), Nikki Schuster (*Mexico Recyclers*, 2017), Evelyn Kreinecker (*Wegstücke/Lanes*, 2018), and Claudia Larcher (*collapsing MIES*, 2021).

7 The book *Tricky Women: Animationsfilmkunst von Frauen* (Women in Animation), edited by Birgitt Wagner and Waltraud Grausgruber, features contributions in both German and English, covering the history of women in animation, contemporary developments, and media theory. A standout contribution is Franziska Bruckner's essay *Tricky Women Today*, which explores the emerging generation of Austrian female animation filmmakers.

8 By 2023, a total of five such program compilations had been created. Additionally, there were other collaborations, such as a *Tricky Women/Tricky Realities* film program featured at the Vienna Open Air Short Film Festival *dotdotdot* in the summer of 2023.

9 The film had already claimed the *Audience Award* at the *Best Austrian Animation Festival* in 2022.

10 The *Austrian Panorama* program section, which included discussions with the creators, took place on March 11, 2023.

11 The festival has expanded beyond traditional cinema venues, now showcasing various film selections in public art spaces. Past locations have included Vienna street markets such as *Brunnenpassage* at Brunnenmarkt and *Stand 129* at Viktor-Adler-Markt, as

well as *Bildraum Bodensee* in Bregenz (Vorarlberg). Additionally, works by contemporary Austrian and international female artists, examined through a feminist perspective, have been displayed in galleries like *Bildraum 07* and *Kro Art Contemporary*, both in Vienna.

12 The database is available at: https://best-austrian-animation.at/

13 The conference was held on the morning of September 5, 2013, followed by the official festival opening that evening.

14 The first member registrations occurred in April 2004, but it wasn't until 2005 that the initial discussions began.

15 Due to technical difficulties, Florian Satzinger had to complete the artwork later in his studio. Satzinger became a regular contributor to *PIXEL* in the following years, designing the festival poster in 2011 and developing the corporate design in 2013.

16 From this year onward, the '.0' was dropped from the name.

17 In this context, Christoph Staber praised the jury's exceptional composition, stating: "It was exactly as one would hope for an award – international, impartial, and highly experienced. I found it to be exceptionally well-executed" (email to the author, dated March 5, 2024).

18 Statement from the 2010 homepage (now unavailable): https://www.pixelvienna.com/5

19 The award was officially established in 2007 to commemorate the 25th anniversary of the *Studio for Experimental Animation* at the University of Applied Arts and was first presented in 2008. Today, it is awarded at various film festivals. For more details, visit: https://www.hubert-sielecki-preis.org/

20 In 2023, Louise Linsenbolz succeeded Wiktoria Pelzer in her role.

21 Statement from the 2012 info page (now unavailable): https://www.under-radar.com/symposium/info-2012.html

22 The film program was reprised at the *Vienna Shorts* (VIS) festival in late May 2015.

23 The artist-in-residence program has now been shortened to 1 month.

17 How Duckburg Became Austrian

Character Designer Florian Satzinger

In the heart of Graz, the capital of the Austrian state of Styria, stands a hill crowned by the city's iconic landmark – the Graz Clock Tower. With its square base and 28-m height, featuring clock faces over 5-m wide, the tower bears a striking resemblance to another famous structure: Scrooge McDuck's Money Bin, perched on a hill above Duckburg. Just a few beak lengths away, internationally acclaimed character designer Florian Satzinger (b. 1970) works on his craft. Satzinger has brought countless beloved cartoon characters to life, from *Disney*'s Mickey Mouse to Bugs Bunny and Daffy Duck of *Looney Tunes* fame. One of his first major assignments came in the 1990s, long before he became an established name in the industry. He was commissioned by the German publisher *Dino-Entertainment* to draw the *Looney Tunes*: "The paper smelled a bit like Hollywood" (as cited in 'Grazer Grün' 2021, 00:42:40).

"ANYTHING IS POSSIBLE IN THE DRAWING"[1]

Florian Satzinger was recognized as a gifted artist even during his school years in art class. Growing up in a time without the Internet and when video recorders were scarce, his only way to preserve his favorite TV characters was by sketching them from memory. His father, an architect, taught him the fundamentals of perspective drawing, while his mother, a journalist, instilled in him the art of storytelling. During his art history studies, Satzinger stumbled upon an advertisement for *Vancouver Institute of Media Arts* (VanArts, Canada) – a discovery that would change his career trajectory. At VanArts, he was mentored by some of the biggest names in American animation, industry veterans with decades of experience at top studios. One of Satzinger's most influential mentors was the British animator Ken Southworth (1918–2007), who began his career as a draftsman at *Disney* in 1944 and went on to work for nearly every major US animation studio during his 60-year career, including *Hanna-Barbera*, *Warner Bros.*, *MGM*, and *Walter Lantz*.

As dynamic as one of his cartoon characters, Florian Satzinger continued his education at Middlesex University in London. Soon, he began receiving his first commissions, including designing mascots for advertising agencies. During this period, he also made key connections – his early website, launched in the fledgling days of the Internet, attracted the attention of Lenora Hume, who was then Vice President of *Disney Worldwide*. Although a collaboration didn't materialize at that time, the

DOI: 10.1201/9781003415442-20

beak was pointing in the right direction. Over the years, Satzinger built an extensive network, eventually landing commissions from major studios like *Disney*, *Warner Bros.*, *Reel FX*, and *The Zanuck Company*.

As a character designer, Florian Satzinger plays a crucial role in pre-production – long before the first frame is animated, he acts as the 'midwife' of the characters. Collaborating closely with the production designer, art director, and director, he creates the blueprint for animated characters, whether modernizing existing ones or adapting static characters from comics. For example, on behalf of *The Zanuck Company*, Satzinger is helping bring a character named *A.J. Hogg*, previously only a sketch, to life on the big screen. Satzinger's portfolio boasts an impressive range of successful projects: he designed merchandise for the popular animated series *Pinky and the Brain* (1995–1998) and created several characters for *Disney*'s *Planes* (2013), helping them take flight just as the Austrian-born Fleischer brothers made Superman soar in their animated films.

In 2015, Florian Satzinger began preliminary work on the 3D animated film *Scoob!* (2020), produced by *Warner Animation Group* and *Reel FX*. Almost clichéd, the Austrian Satzinger was responsible for portraying the villains, much like Austrian actors Klaus Maria Brandauer (b. 1943) and Christoph Waltz (b. 1956) in the *James Bond* films. Satzinger attributed this to the steampunk aesthetic in many of his designs, which lent itself perfectly to the film's antagonists. His meticulous attention to detail had a direct influence on the film's production. For instance, he recalled unsolicitedly sketching an "absurd machine" for a villain, which inspired the director to incorporate it into the film.

As Florian Satzinger later learned from a *Disney* art director, he was considered for the reboot of *DuckTales* (2017–2021), though his design approach didn't align with the edgier style they sought. However, his skills were in high demand during the pre-production of an animated series based on Donald Duck's alter ego, *Phantomias* (Superduck or Duck Avenger), for which several test films were created. For the trading card game *Disney Lorcana*, launched by the German game manufacturer *Ravensburger* in 2023, Satzinger contributed initial concepts and rough sketches, as the creators wanted his distinctive take on Mickey Mouse and Donald Duck to influence the project. French comic author Denis-Pierre Filippi (b. 1972) is also a fan of Satzinger's character designs, and they are planning a Donald Duck comic together.

Florian Satzinger demonstrates the importance of networking through his weblog, *Paperwalker*, where he regularly shares insights into his work. Since its launch in October 2012, it has garnered over 100 million content views (as of 2023). This platform not only allowed him to emerge from the anonymity of the illustration profession but also helped him build an international fan base. Professionally, he connected through the Los Angeles-based *Creative Talent Network*. Today, Satzinger teaches analog animation, animation history, and media analysis at the Salzburg University of Applied Sciences and frequently serves as a guest lecturer at institutions such as VIA University College (Viborg, Denmark), Babelsberg Film University in Potsdam, and the Film Academy in Ludwigsburg (both in Germany). His design studies earned him the prestigious Nemoland Award in Florence (Italy) in 2009, and in 2023, he was also recognized in Austria with the Erich-Sokol-Prize for Digital Caricature.

"CARL BARKS ON STEROIDS"

Florian Satzinger is often called the 'duck artist.' During an interview in Vienna, even a prominent Austrian animation filmmaker instantly recognized him, exclaiming, "Ah, the guy with the ducks!" (Benjamin Swiczinsky, interview with the author, July 5, 2023). But while Satzinger is known for his numerous Donald Duck drawings, this is less about a personal love for ducks and more about fulfilling demand. "I don't mind it," he said, "but I enjoy drawing other things just as much. It's not just ducks; I find any anthropomorphic animal fascinating." Satzinger delights in playing with contrasts, like portraying a delicate watchmaker as an elephant. "I'm less interested in the knight battling the dragon, and more in what they did before or after the fight. [...] There's so much power in silence, in a hero's reflective moments. [...] I'd be intrigued by Batman sitting on a couch, mending his suit." Satzinger focuses on visualizing what captivates him, seeking out unseen moments with well-known characters – like Donald Duck as an art lover, admiring great masterpieces in a gallery.

For Florian Satzinger, Donald Duck is a far more dynamic character than Mickey Mouse. While the deliberately blank Mickey has essentially become the corporate logo of a media empire, Donald feels like a familiar companion: "He's so deeply connected to a life story. We know so little about Mickey Mouse – maybe just that he enjoys being a detective in some comic stories – but Donald Duck is profoundly understood in terms of his emotional depth. We know him; we understand how he reacts and how disappointed he becomes." For Satzinger, Donald is "one of the most well-known characters in the world, the one you feel you truly understand. Many people around the world are familiar with the character, not necessarily with his story, but with his essence. [...] When you look at the bigger picture, Donald Duck is fully recognizable in all his complexity, while Mickey Mouse remains an enigma. [...] It's surprising that a character as mainstream as Donald possesses such remarkable diversity" (Figure 17.1).

But Florian Satzinger is more than just a character designer – he's been called a "character destroyer" by a TV journalist and in a positive sense.[2] It's a label he can identify with: "When you work with established characters, 'renewal' might not be the right word. It's really about finding aspects within a character that can be developed or enhanced. In a way, that's a form of positive destruction. [...] This is what intrigues me when reworking iconic cartoon characters like Mickey Mouse or Donald Duck." However, for Satzinger, true destruction – like giving these characters inappropriate accessories such as drugs or weapons – feels too simplistic: "I don't want to show Mickey Mouse holding a bloodstained knife just to shock or get attention. I'm more interested in finding subtler ways to break through the character, without relying on cheap shock value." Instead, his focus is on reinterpretation or reinvention – such as modernizing Donald Duck's house. Yet, this always raises the question of how the character changes as a result, because a sleek new home would contradict Donald's perpetually cash-strapped persona. Altering the setting creates a strong contrast, which in the worst case could feel unbelievable. But it's precisely this delicate balance that Satzinger finds so compelling: "I'm drawn to the challenge of testing the vitality and credibility of a fictional character." Because even though Donald Duck is just a cartoon character, he appears lifelike to the audience.

FIGURE 17.1 A series of character designs titled *Donald Duckling* by Florian Satzinger from 2020. (Courtesy of Florian Satzinger.)

Florian Satzinger doesn't just draw characters; he also poses them. However, he's less interested in classic hero stances and more intrigued by everyday challenges that make a character feel distinctly human – like Donald Duck mowing the lawn, or better yet, lounging in a hammock while a robot lawnmower does the work for him: "It's all about identification and believability. That's why I think he's become such a famous character – because he's so 'ordinary.'" Donald, in essence, 'stumbles' into his fantastic adventures.

Besides Florian Satzinger, other Austrian artists are also captivated by Donald Duck. Salzburg native Michael Ferner (b. 1969) has included the duck in his portfolio, as have Viennese artist Gottfried Helnwein (b. 1948) and caricaturist Manfred Deix (1949–2016). The latter two were so enamored with the character that they curated a Donald Duck exhibition in 2007 at the *Karikaturmuseum Krems* (Caricature Museum Krems, Lower Austria). When Deix remarked, "Barks brought Donald to his peak. Everything after him is trash!" (as cited in Kromp 2007: 127), he likely hadn't seen Satzinger's work. In the comic scene, Satzinger has been regarded as "Carl Barks on steroids" (as cited in Schögler 2021: 43), an "amazing influence" (as cited in Gusenbauer (ed.) 2022: 95) for Marvel artist Jay Fosgitt (b. 1974), and simply "the Master of the ducks" (as cited in Schögler 2021: 43) according to French cartoonist Achdé (né Hervé Darmenton, b. 1961). *Warner Bros. Animation* character designer Genevieve Tsai (b. 1980) praised him by saying, "You have THE MOST creative and clever ways to design ducks. I want to visit a whole gallery full of your amazing and charming work" (as cited in Gusenbauer (ed.) 2022: 81).

This wish became a reality multiple times starting in 2021. When concerts were banned during the COVID-19 pandemic (which lasted from March 2020 to June 2023 in Austria), the *Schloßbergbühne Kasematten* in Graz was swiftly transformed into an exhibition space in the spring of 2021. Here, Florian Satzinger's *DUCKLAND* came to life – a unique cartoon exhibition featuring numerous standees and large hand-drawn banners. While Austrians were getting vaccinated against COVID, Satzinger 'vaccinated' his characters: for him, they were "stylistically anchored in the tradition of classic, hand-drawn American animation, injected with a hefty dose of contemporary art and European cartoon and comic influences" (as cited in Bacher 2021, under 'Corona-Regeln'). The exhibition was so successful that it was restaged from October 2021 to January 2022, briefly transforming Graz into Duckburg, thanks to Satzinger. Collaborating with curator Gottfried Gusenbauer (b. 1968) from the *Karikaturmuseum Krems* (Caricature Museum Krems) in Lower Austria, Satzinger organized his first museum exhibition in 2022, themed *Donald Made in Austria!* (Figure 17.2). The exhibition later toured across Europe through a partnership with the Federal Ministry for European and International Affairs.

"WHAT YOU'VE DESIGNED RARELY STAYS THE SAME"

Thomas Fluharty (b. 1962), illustrator and caricaturist for *MAD* magazine and *The New York Times*, once remarked about Florian Satzinger: "You own the

FIGURE 17.2 Florian Satzinger, 2022, featured in the exhibition *Donald Made in Austria!* at the Caricature Museum Krems alongside his character design, *Boat Hat* (2021). (Photographer: Christian Redtenbacher. Courtesy of Kunstmeile Krems.)

duck world. No one should ever attempt to draw another duck. End of story" (as cited in Gusenbauer (ed.) 2022: 147). This sentiment was echoed by German animator Harald Siepermann (1962–2013), the character designer of the titular duck from the Japanese-produced animated series *Alfred J. Kwak* (1989/1990), which was widely popular in German-speaking countries. After Siepermann's passing, his widow informed Satzinger that Siepermann had hoped for a continuation or reboot of the series under Satzinger's direction – a vision that has not yet come to fruition. A similar fate befell a project commissioned by the German children's channel KiKA, which planned an animated film centered around *Bernd das Brot* (Bernd the Bread or Bernie Bread), a children's TV character also beloved by adults. Satzinger was tasked with designing the character, a talking loaf of white bread with comically short arms and a perpetually sour mood. Satzinger envisioned contrasting the character's minimalist look by placing it within elaborate, almost baroque backgrounds presented in CinemaScope. However, the project was eventually abandoned.

In the late 2000s, Florian Satzinger came close to producing his first series based on an original creation, again in collaboration with KiKA. *Toby Skybuckle*, an 11-year-old boy, essentially reenacted Satzinger's childhood experiences – albeit with a significant dose of fiction, as Satzinger was quick to point out. Although 26 episodes were scripted, the project was shelved once more. Satzinger still harbors hope of "bringing it to life in animation." Around the same time, Satzinger worked on *The Recalibrated Fantastic Adventures of Huck Finn*, reimagining the iconic character in a style akin to Lewis Carroll's (1832–1898) *Alice in Wonderland* (1865). In 2013, the French animation studio *Tigobo Animation* began animating the wild space adventures of Satzinger's creation, *John Starduck*, a New York duck (Figure 17.3). Though Satzinger's personal work is often sidelined by his heavy workload, he remains optimistic: "But I'm not worried. As long as the famous brick doesn't fall on my head tomorrow, I hope I'll eventually have the time to focus on my own production."

When asked the common question of whether he ever runs out of ideas, Florian Satzinger replied, "There's far too much – thankfully – that needs to be drawn." He views his film work as a kind of laboratory, where he experiments without knowing the outcome in advance. Despite the humor in his creations, he approaches his work with seriousness and dedication, drawing inspiration from other art forms such as photography and painting. While world politics or contemporary public figures have little influence on Satzinger, the era he lives in does: "I'd say that my personal life – without meaning it autobiographically – inevitably shapes how I draw, influenced by the things around me." Although he doesn't consciously design his characters to reflect his own life, he certainly infuses his personal preferences, especially when it comes to genre:

"I've loved films like *King Kong* and *Godzilla* since I was a kid – not so much for the monsters, but for the way modern, urban spaces are suddenly confronted with something almost prehistoric: a giant creature that stomps the orderly city into the ground. That's exactly what I'd like to do with Duckburg, because to me, Duckburg is like San Francisco or New York, and I'd love to introduce something into it that completely doesn't belong."

Florian Satzinger's preferences also influence his choices in color and drawing style: "I tend to draw things and characters much more elongated and elastic than the

FIGURE 17.3 Test subject for *John Starduck* by Florian Satzinger. (Courtesy of Florian Satzinger.)

classic model sheets suggest, because it creates a more dynamic, interesting quality in the drawing. You can do a lot more with the limbs when they're longer, which I find really intriguing."

Florian Satzinger's constant companion is his sketchbook, which he always carries with him. Ideas come and go, and when he needs to create 50 or 60 versions of the same concept for his film work, it's invaluable to have "sketched ideas that are so universal they can be applied to any character." For Satzinger, constant observation is one of a designer's most essential tools. However, he doesn't just observe how things or creatures look but focuses on what they do. His ducks, for example, are essentially humans with beaks, but as he put it, "I don't actually see anyone with a duck bill, because that would feel pathological" (as cited in 'Grazer Grün' 2021, 00:10:32).

Although Florian Satzinger works with international clients, his studio is nestled in the heart of Austria's own Duckburg, in Graz. He values the city's balance between peace and activity – it's the perfect place to retreat and concentrate on his work before re-engaging with the (hectic) world. Here, a provincial atmosphere (in the best sense) blends seamlessly with modern art. And when Satzinger sits in the city park, sketching and observing both people and ducks, it feels as though Konrad Lorenz (1903–1989)[3] is meeting Carl Barks (1901–2000).

NOTES

1 Unless otherwise indicated, all quotations in this chapter are taken from the author's interview with Florian Satzinger, conducted on June 9, 2023, in Graz.

2 Based on a viewing of the raw material for a TV documentary for ServusTV on April 28, 2023 (with the kind support of Christian Bachmann and Melisa Krasniqi from *wega film vienna*).

3 Austrian scientist Konrad Lorenz is widely recognized as one of the key figures in classical behavioral research. In his experiments, the Nobel Prize winner imprinted ducklings on himself, earning the nickname "foster mother of ducks" (Vicedo 2009: 263).

18 Very British? Very Austrian!

Animation on Stage

Animation and theater were closely intertwined during Austria's 'pre-cinema' era. In 1847, Viennese showman and conjurer Ludwig Döbler (1801–1864) introduced projected drawings for the first time using the *Phantaskop*, a device he had developed. This event took place at the Theater an der Josefstadt in Vienna. Fast-forwarding 175 years, the Austrian theater scene faced a severe crisis during the COVID-19 pandemic, which lasted from March 2020 to June 2023 in Austria. However, the British theater group *1927* achieved unexpected success with a play that once again combined animation and theater.

Paul Barritt, animator and co-founder of *1927*, reflected on the ensemble's strong ties with Austria, which began after their breakthrough in 2012: "Yes, it's interesting how it ended up working a lot in Austria. And I don't think it was an intended thing or anything like that; it just happened that way."[1] There were additional historical connections between Austria and Britain in the world of animated film beyond the success of *1927*. John Halas (1912–1995), co-founder of the influential British animation studio *Halas & Batchelor*, was born in the Hungarian part of Austria-Hungary. His mother was Austrian, and an early viewing of *Disney*'s animation in a Viennese cinema left a lasting impact on him. Decades later, on the fringes of the 1984 *Annecy International Animation Film Festival*, he had a conversation with Austrian animator Hubert Sielecki (b. 1946), which led to the founding of *ASIFA Austria*.

Austrian Otto Neurath (1882–1945) introduced his Isotype system, the precursor of modern pictograms, to Britain in the 1940s, significantly influencing British animated educational films. Additionally, during the 1940s, Austrian filmmaker George Hoellering (1897–1980) directed propaganda animated films for the British *Ministry of Information* (MoI). *Tricky Women/Tricky Realities*, one of Austria's most important animation film festivals, was founded after Waltraud Grausgruber and Birgitt Wagner (b. 1972) fell in love with animated films from a video compilation of British works. In 2023, the festival awarded its top prize in the international competition to *Beware of Trains* (2022), directed by British animator Emma Calder (1959–2024). That same year, renowned British artist Gerald Scarfe (b. 1936), famous for his animated music videos for *Pink Floyd*, was honored with the SOKOL award for lifetime achievement in Linz, Austria.

1927 – BACK TO THE FUTURE

With the release of the first sound film, *The Jazz Singer* in 1927, the live elements of cinema – such as live orchestras and film storytellers – became obsolete.

DOI: 10.1201/9781003415442-21

When animator Paul Barritt and writer Suzanne Andrade founded their theater company in 2005, they aimed to merge the worlds of animated film and live performance on stage. This vision inspired the name of their group, *1927.* Andrade recited poetry at the Whitechapel Art Gallery while Barritt's animated films played in the background. Esme Appleton, a student friend of Andrade, saw untapped potential in this combination, believing that the two forms needed to interact and merge. After numerous experiments and setbacks, the stage show *Between the Devil and the Deep Blue Sea* premiered in 2007, featuring actors interacting with animated films and characters. Three years later, they released *The Animals and Children Took to the Streets* (2010).

Following the success of their first two shows, *1927* was commissioned by the Komische Oper Berlin to create a new interpretation of *Die Zauberflöte* (The Magic Flute), one of the most famous compositions by Austrian composer Wolfgang Amadeus Mozart (1756–1791). Paul Barritt recalled, "At the time when we first got asked to do 'Magic Flute,' we didn't even know what the 'Magic Flute' was, we didn't even know who it was by." Their 2012 production marked the ensemble's breakthrough: "It was the show that really pushed us onto a large stage." Their modern interpretation also captivated younger audiences, as Barritt remembered one young viewer's remark: "I didn't even know an opera can be like that, [...] I thought opera was boring." Eleven years later, the team collaborated on another opera reinterpretation in Graz (Austria), reflecting on over a decade of Austrian influences.[2]

In 2013, the group made its first guest appearance in Austria at the Salzburg Festival as part of the *Young Directors Project* (YDP)[3] competition with *The Animals and Children Took to the Streets* (2010). The press called it "[t]he most impressive theater production of the 2013 Salzburg Festival to date" (Schuchter 2013: introd.). Although the group did not win the prize money, they secured funding for their next play from the Salzburg Festival. Unknowingly, the group drew inspiration from the literary work of an Austrian, *Der Golem* (The Golem, 1913/1914) by Viennese author Gustav Meyrink (1868–1932): "But is he Austrian? Oh, I didn't know that; I thought he was Czech!" The group, having planned the project for some time, unintentionally created a profoundly Austrian play: when it premiered in Salzburg in 2014, it coincided with the centenary of the start of the First World War (1914–1918), which was triggered by Austria. Meyrink's serialized novel, *Der Golem*, is considered a classic of fantastic literature. In it, he explores the legend of the Prague Golem, a humanoid figure created from clay. Published at the onset of the First World War – the first fully industrialized conflict – it is often interpreted as a commentary on the potential dangers of uncontrolled technology. Cleverly, *1927* adapted this story to the modern era, transforming it into a critique of the digital age and the dangers of the modern computer world. Paul Barritt's time in Salzburg directly influenced the play's visuals. He explained that while walking through Salzburg's old town, he envisioned it as the setting for *Golem*. However, his animations also reflected the influence of Britain's long tradition of *Public Information Films* (PIFs).

After the premiere of the comedic yet pessimistic play, the team feared the harsh criticism that Salzburg is known for. However, the reviews were positive, with the play being hailed as "the most successful" (Tartarotti 2014: 26) acting premiere of the 2013 Salzburg Festival. Paul Barritt's animations received especially enthusiastic praise: "Aesthetically and thematically somewhat old-fashioned, this technically brilliant animation evokes the works of Max Ernst, films like 'Yellow Submarine,' and even the atmospheric qualities of 'Metropolis'" (Kleine Zeitung, August 24, 2014: 72).

ON THE WAY TO THE 'MOTHER SHIP'

In Vienna, the *1927* phenomenon went unnoticed for quite some time. After the Austrian premiere of *The Animals and Children Took to the Streets*, the Salzburg press expressed surprise that "this highly acclaimed production seems to have escaped the attention of the Wiener Festwochen scouts until now" (Schuchter 2013: para. 1). Following the success of *Golem*, the Viennese theater scene could no longer ignore the opportunity to collaborate. Through mediation from Salzburg, the Vienna Burgtheater, one of the oldest and most prestigious theaters in Europe (often referred to by Austrian actors as the 'mother ship' due to its importance), reached out to the group.[4] They hoped to bring the ensemble to the main stage and anticipated an adaptation of a classic play, such as Johann Wolfgang von Goethe's (1749–1832) *Faust* (1808). However, *1927* was already working on another project at the time. The Burgtheater agreed to stage the play *Please Right Back* under the title *Mehr als alles auf der Welt* (More Than Anything in the World). Although the production presented some challenges, especially with the translation, the team enjoyed full creative freedom. The Burgtheater had only one request: a hopeful ending. The team had considered more pessimistic outcomes, such as the father breaking down from imprisonment and abandoning the family or the son being crushed by the school system.

And yet, the Burgtheater was somewhat unfamiliar with the concept of a play designed for audiences aged 8–108: "It's not in their grammar. […] They just thought it was 'Kindertheater,' really… The show itself is actually the most family-oriented show we've ever made for sure." After 2 years of work, even the theater critics were irritated when the play premiered at the Akademietheater, a side stage typically known for contemporary plays. Since children's productions were usually staged at the Kasino on Vienna's Schwarzenbergplatz, another Burgtheater venue, one critic wrote: "Akademietheater as children's theater" (Wurmitzer 2022: headline). However, during the performance, the audience – who knew what to expect – was enthusiastic. By the end of the play, the little boy, the only family member to be fully animated on stage, received particularly thunderous applause.

The premiere of *Mehr als alles auf der Welt* (Please Right Back) in October 2022 coincided with the COVID-19 pandemic, which officially lasted from March 2020 to June 2023 in Austria. Although work on the piece had begun before the pandemic, Suzanne Andrade wrote most of the text during the various lockdowns that were implemented across Europe to control the spread of the virus. The story of a father who writes letters to his children, pretending to be a secret agent on a fantastical mission to disguise his imprisonment, seemed to capture the mood of the times – despite this not being the theater group's original intention.

In fact, the pandemic had a direct impact on the production. While preparing the show in Vienna, the team was unexpectedly sent into a 2-week lockdown. The play premiered during a challenging time for Austrian theaters: "Half-full is the new sold-out" (Ziegler 2022: 18) became a common phrase in the industry. The fact that the audience's favor could be regained with a play that cleverly integrated comics, animation, and acting demonstrates significant potential: "The [...] British theater group '1927' [...] appears to have scored a success with this co-production at the Burgtheater – a much-needed win for the theater" (*Puls 24* 2022: introd.).

GLANCE BEHIND THE CURTAIN

On stage, animation and acting begin to merge, but Paul Barritt's work as an animator remains entirely distinct from that of the actors. Not every actor can immediately master performing in a virtual setting, and keeping up with the precisely timed sequences can be challenging. According to Barritt, trained dancers or circus artists, who can integrate cartoon-like movements and rhythm into their acting, tend to excel in this environment. Barritt highlighted Markus Meyer (b. 1971) of the Viennese ensemble, who had always wanted to be part of a *1927* play (Figure 18.1). "The other thing they have to understand is that they really are small parts of a bigger picture, with them not used to that."

According to Paul Barritt, *Mehr als alles auf der Welt* (Please Right Back, 2022) was a script-heavy play. While an animated film has a single timeline throughout, the play required over 500 individual animations that could be triggered at the push of a button. Hundreds of timelines were combined into a long, intricate cue list: "And there were moments in Vienna last year I was just like... I actually have forgotten what I was doing." Most of the animations had been completed by that point. Barritt used hand painting and the cutout technique popular in 1920s Austria before scanning and digitizing everything. Time and again, he had to return to the studio to make adjustments.

FIGURE 18.1 A look behind the scenes of *Please Right Back* (2022) shows how the animations were projected with computer support. On stage, Markus Meyer and Isabella Knöll (b. 1990). (Photographer: Susanne Hassler-Smith.)

Although Paul Barritt creates award-winning animated films outside the theater, he considers the theater the perfect arena for his work: "I think it's a developing field of animation, I think it's a great place for animation, it's brilliant. It's a good place to see animation." The ability to gather audience feedback and continuously integrate it is a "collaborative moment" for him. This presentation style enriches both the animator and the audience: "They became passive, much more passive than they were before. The theater audience is less passive than the cinema audience. You know, it's more active, it's a more active form of viewing." For Barritt, the magic of the play truly unfolds when it's performed live in front of an audience.

VERY BRITISH, ISN'T IT?

There was criticism from the press, particularly regarding the setting of the play *Mehr als alles auf der Welt* (Please Right Back, 2022): "Why does the world premiere, created for Vienna, need to be set in England with English names instead of somewhere in Austria?" (Wurmitzer 2022, under 'Zauber für Jung und Alt'). Paul Barritt acknowledged that the play, initially "made for an Austrian audience, was totally British. [...] It's a slightly different show to other ones we've made because, I mean, in some ways, it's more British than anything we've made." It started with a subtle portrayal of post-Brexit Britain, wove in autobiographical elements – such as Suzanne Andrade's father being imprisoned during her childhood – and built up to a sharp critique of the English school system.

Yet, there was something familiar to historically savvy Austrian viewers in the gray-on-gray imagery, which depicted the conformity of schoolchildren in a setting reminiscent of Charlie Chaplin's (1889–1977) *Modern Times* (1936). When asked if Paul Barritt had drawn inspiration for this scene from the imagery of Isotype by Austrian Otto Neurath – who gained recognition in Britain in the 1930s and 1940s – he replied, "Yes, definitely. I mean, I actually love Otto Neurath. [...] You're probably the only person in the audience that actually thought: 'This is Otto Neurath here!'" (Figure 18.2).

Otto Neurath has largely faded from public memory outside academic circles in Austria, and his vision of democratizing information through simplification has receded into the background: "His idea was that you would show important information to everybody and so people could understand exactly – his idea was about transparency of information rather than an objectification of information, and that has been lost." The theater group *1927* not only revived Neurath's visual language in animated form in Austria (Figure 18.3) but also created visual masterpieces that are both understood and beloved worldwide. More than a million people across all inhabited continents have already experienced *1927*s Austria-inspired productions.

In October 2023, the *STELLA*23*, "Austria's award for exceptional achievements in performing arts for young audiences,"[5] was presented at a grand gala in Linz, Upper Austria. The jury reviewed 137 productions, and *Mehr als alles auf der Welt* (Please Right Back, 2022) received nominations in the categories of *Herausragendes Kinderstück* (Outstanding Production for Children) and *Herausragende Ausstattung* (Outstanding Scenography). Ultimately, Paul Barritt's stage design was recognized as the best. The jury's statement read:

FIGURE 18.2 Two artworks by Paul Barritt for *Please Right Back* (2022); Otto Neurath inspired the right one. (Courtesy of Paul Barritt.)

FIGURE 18.3 The artwork by Paul Barritt, inspired by Otto Neurath, is brought to life in front of an audience on the stage of the Vienna Akademietheater. (Photographer: Susanne Hassler-Smith.)

"The outstanding aspect for us is [...] the fully animated digital stage design by Paul Barritt, which blends associations, color, and movement with great poetry and precision. It is intricately detailed, elaborate, and lovingly composed in a comic style. It works seamlessly with five wonderful actors, creating a visually stunning, original performance filled with surprising moments. [...] Circus lions, pirates, ticking clocks, and an animated little boy who interacts as an equal partner with the actors and even takes a bow at the end – this well-executed, fast-paced, and constantly shifting stage design makes the theatrical experience truly special."[6]

Another production by the Vienna Volkstheater, one of the largest theaters in the German-speaking world, demonstrated that animation has firmly established itself in the Austrian theater scene. In December 2023, a "Live Animation Cinema" was created based on the best-selling novel *Die Inkommensurablen* (The Incommensurables, 2023) by Viennese writer Raphaela Edelbauer (b. 1990). Set in Vienna on the eve of the First World War (1914–1918), the production was made possible with the assistance of the German artists' collective *sputnic*. The collective defines its work as a "new performance genre, combining film, acting, and animation: a feature-length animation film is created live, right in front of the audience's eyes" (*Sputnic Künstlerkollektiv* n.d., under 'Live Animation Cinema'). For the media, "[t]he technique of the theatrical performance, which closely followed the original narrative, [was] impressive" (Hadler 2023: 63). The 180 images projected onto slatted screens were partly generated using the artificial intelligence (AI) tool *Midjourney*, potentially paving the way for the future of animation in Austria.[7]

NOTES

1 Unless otherwise indicated, all quotations in this chapter are taken from the author's interview with Paul Barritt, conducted on June 8, 2023, in Graz.

2 Ulrich Lenz (b. 1970) was the artistic director of the Graz Opera in 2023. Previously, he served as the chief dramaturge at the Komische Oper Berlin in 2012. His original plan was to replicate the success of the *1927* production of *Die Zauberflöte* (The Magic Flute) with *Hoffmanns Erzählungen* (The Tales of Hoffmann, 1851), but the theater company didn't have enough time for a full opera production. As a result, the three main acts of the opera were divided among three artists or artistic collectives. *1927* took over the act featuring Olympia, transforming her into an "animated robot lady." The opera premiered on September 30, 2023.

3 The competition, which ran from 2002 to 2014, served as a platform dedicated to fostering innovation and promoting the work of emerging directors and theater companies.

4 The Vienna Burgtheater is considered one of the most significant theaters in Europe. It is not only the second-oldest theater in Europe but also the largest German-language theater.

5 Self-definition of the award, translated from https://www.assitej.at/ (as of 2023).

6 Jury's decision, translated from https://www.assitej.at/stella/stella23/

7 Austrian animators are also currently experimenting with AI. For instance, Birgit Scholin (b. 1984) used the AI tool *Midjourney* to create an animation for a poem by Austrian poet Hertha Kräftner (1928–1951).

Epilogue

"Animation Can Save the World"

Austrian animated film, like animation in general, is undergoing a transformation. Digitalization has made it affordable to "set up your own studio at home" (Nikolaus Jantsch, interview with the author in collaboration with Franziska Proksa on April 10, 2024) at a relatively low cost. This shift also opens new possibilities for production and distribution, as demonstrated by *Le Grand Content* (2007), created by Clemens Kogler (b. 1980) and Karolina 'Karo' Szmit (b. 1978). Inspired by the ubiquitous PowerPoint culture of the time, this innovative diagrammatic film explored its philosophical potential, addressing virtually all of life's questions – from emotions and mortality to cable TV and hamsters.

In January 2007, a blogger from Graz (Styria) uploaded the film to YouTube without permission, where it quickly accumulated 200,000 views within days. By May 2007, the view count exceeded half a million. Film critic Stefan Grissemann (b. 1964) remarked in 2007 that it was likely "one of the most-watched Austrian films of the past few decades" (as cited in *film:riss* 2007, under 'Clemens Kogler: Le Grand Content'). Since then, *Le Grand Content* (2007) has been screened at over a hundred international film festivals.

Artificial intelligence (AI) is making significant strides in Austria as well. Inspired by similar projects in Germany and the USA, digital product designer Johannes Ecker created *Austrian Chancellors as Pixar Characters* in February 2023. Using the AI tool *Midjourney*, Ecker transformed photos of all Austrian chancellors of the Second Republic (from 1945 to the present) into Pixar-style characters. The remarkably convincing results quickly spread through Austrian media, with one outlet commenting: "The result is both astonishing and amusing" (*Der Standard* 2023: para. 1).

When asked whether AI would impact animation, Nikolaus 'Niki' Jantsch (b. 1978), artistic director of the Studio for Experimental Animation at the University of Applied Arts Vienna, responded: "Certainly. I believe that's beyond doubt. For now, I still view the possibilities as somewhat limited. The results we're seeing so far aren't impressive enough for me to feel concerned" (interview with the author in collaboration with Franziska Proksa on April 10, 2024).

Austrian animator Benjamin Swiczinsky (b. 1982) echoed a similar sentiment, expressing no fear of losing his job to AI but instead seeing its potential: "It's going to change a lot. [...] It could be an opportunity for new kinds of projects, or even allow amazing films to be made on smaller budgets. [...] Perhaps it'll weed out uninspired design and push people to be more creative" (interview with the author on July 5, 2023).

This creativity was exemplified by Birgit Scholin's (b. 1984) experiments in animating poems by Austrian poet Hertha Kräftner (1928–1951) using AI-generated imagery. Instead of striving to create fully AI-driven films, Scholin focused on exploring the potential of AI in animation. Meanwhile, AI has already made its way into the commercial mainstream; ahead of the 2024 Austrian parliamentary elections, a furniture store ran an ad that reimagined the leading political candidates as kindergarten children, brought to life through AI technology.

Creativity in animation also thrives on nurturing new talent. Vienna's *ZOOM Kindermuseum* (ZOOM Children's Museum), established in 1994 as Austria's first museum of its kind, has operated its own Animated Film Studio since 2001. By 2023, over 10,000 animated films had been created there, involving children and teenagers from around the world. Animation is also finding its way into schools, with one of the most successful programs being the workshops run by the *MuKaTo* collective. Founded in 2008 by media artists Muzak (né Peter Musek), Karoline Riha (b. 1977), and Thomas Renoldner (b. 1960), the initiative has received numerous accolades, including the Austrian 2015 *Prämie für Innovative Kulturarbeit* (Prize for Innovative Cultural Practice). Known for its international scope, *MuKaTo* has led projects in Austria, Slovakia, Germany, and Cyprus, collaborating with established artists from Europe and the United States to guide children in filmmaking. These collaborative films have been featured in exhibitions and festivals across Europe, garnering multiple awards.

Children's films often tackle fundamental issues like environmental protection. An online media outlet captured this sentiment with the headline: "Children Save the World… in Their Own Films" (*KiJuKu* 2021), while covering the 25th *Wiener Video & Filmtage* (Vienna Video & Film Days), where many child-produced films had focused on environmental themes. One such film, *Wir retten die Welt* (We Save the World, 2020), produced during a *MuKaTo* project, told the story of a polar bear cub separated from its family as an ice floe broke apart. "Suddenly, human hands intervene in the animated narrative to provide rescue – a reminder that climate change is not a natural law but a human-made problem and can – hopefully – still be reversed" (*KiJuKu* 2021: para. 4).

British animator Paul Barritt shared this hope: "Animation can be good, you know, it can save the world" (interview with the author on June 8, 2023). While Austrian animated films may not literally save the world, they act as cultural ambassadors through international collaboration, fostering global unity in addressing humanity's most pressing challenges and continuing Austria's long tradition of animation as a medium for bridge building.

Bibliography

MONOGRAPHS

Alt, D. (2013) *'Der Farbfilm marschiert!': Frühe Farbfilmverfahren und NS-Propaganda 1933–1945*. München: Belleville Verlag.

Amsler, A. (1997) *‚Wer dem Werbefilm verfällt, ist verloren für die Welt': Das Werk von Julius Pinschewer 1883–1961*. Zürich: Chronos Verlag.

Annett, S. (2014) *Anime Fan Communities: Transcultural Flows and Frictions*. New York: Palgrave Macmillan.

Ballhausen, T. (2015) 'Exposed: A Short History of Austrian Science Fiction Film', in J. Blankenship and T. Nagl (eds.) *European Visions: Small Cinemas in Transition*. Bielefeld: Transcript Verlag, pp. 249–257.

Ballhausen, T. and Caneppele, P. (eds.) (2009) *Entscheidungen der Wiener Filmzensur: 1934–1938*. (Materialien zur österreichischen Filmgeschichte, Vol. 11). Wien: Filmarchiv Austria.

Barsam, R.M. (1992) *Nonfiction Film: A Critical History*, Revised and Expanded. Bloomington, IN: Indiana University Press.

Baumann, M. and Gold, H. (eds.) (2007) 'Ruf doch mal an, aber fasse dich kurz: Fernsprecher und Telefon', in *Image und Information: Post und Telekommunikation im Film*. Heidelberg: Edition Braus, pp. 139–149.

Bendazzi, G. (ed.) (2016a) *Animation: A World History, Volume 1: Foundations – The Golden Age*. Boca Raton, FL: CRC Press.

Bendazzi, G. (ed.) (2016b) Animation: *A World History: Volume 2: The Birth of a Style – The Three Markets*. Boca Raton, FL: CRC Press.

Bertschik, J. (2005) *Mode und Moderne: Kleidung als Spiegel des Zeitgeistes in der deutschsprachigen Literatur (1770–1945)*. Köln: Böhlau Verlag

Bohmann, R. and Taylor, S.S. (eds.) (1972) *Who's Who in Austria*. 8th edn. Vienna: Bohmann Verlag.

Bormann, B. von (2021) 'Maria Lassnig's Anti-War Film', in E. Kondoi et al. (eds.) *Maria Lassnig: Film Works*. (FilmmuseumSynemaPublications). Wien: SYNEMA, pp. 72–75.

Brdečka, J. (2015) 'On the Beginnings of Animated Film and on Jiří Trnka', in J. Šulc (ed.), D. Lukeš and M. Stehlík (trans.) *Jiří Brdečka: Life * Animation * Magic*. Praha: Limonádový Joe, pp. 109–126.

Bruckner, F. (2011) *Malerei in Bewegung: Studio für experimentellen Animationsfilm an der Universität für angewandte Kunst Wien*. (Edition Angewandte). Wien: Springer.

Buchloh, S. (2002) *'Pervers, jugendgefährdend, staatsfeindlich': Zensur in der Ära Adenauer als Spiegel des gesellschaftlichen Klimas*. Frankfurt am Main: Campus Verlag.

Bundespressedienst (ed.) (1967) *Österreichisches Jahrbuch 1966: Nach amtlichen Quellen*. (Vol. 38). Wien: Verlag der österr. Staatsdruckerei.

Caneppele, P. (ed.) (2002) *Entscheidungen der Wiener Filmzensur: 1922–1925*. (Materialien zur österreichischen Filmgeschichte, Vol. 8). Wien: Filmarchiv Austria.

Canyon Cinema (ed.) (1992) *Film/Video Catalog 7: 25th Anniversary Issue*. San Francisco, CA: Canyon Cinema.

Coulter-Smith, E. (2005) 'Halas and Batchelor: Animation, Propaganda and Animal Farm (1954)', in J. Hill and K. Rockett (eds.) *Film History and National Cinema*. (Studies in Irish Film, Vol. 2). Dublin: Four Courts Press, pp. 90–96.

Culhane, J. (1983) *Walt Disney's Fantasia*. New York City, NY: H.N. Abrams.

Cürlis, H. (1924) 'Bildende Kunst im Film', in E. Beyfuss and A. Kossowsky (eds.) *Das Kulturfilmhandbuch*. Berlin: Carl P. Chryselius'scher Verlag, pp. 210–216.

Dewald, C., Mayr, B. and Omasta, M. (2007) 'Proletarisches Kino in Österreich: Eine Filmschau zur linken Filmkultur der Ersten Republik', in M. Pekler (ed.) *Viennale: Vienna International Film Festival, 19.–31. Oktober 2007*. Wien: Viennale, pp. 279–303.

Die ersten 50 Jahre des österreichischen Zeichentrickfilms (1987). Wien: Self-Published.

Dobson, N. (2020) *Historical Dictionary of Animation and Cartoons*. 2nd edn. Lanham, MD: Rowman & Littlefield.

Du, D.Y. (2019) *Animated Encounters: Transnational Movements of Chinese Animation, 1940s–1970s*. (Asia Pop!) Honolulu, HI: University of Hawai'i Press.

Dziemballa, M. et al. (eds.) (1983) *Filmfestival tropisch: Werkschau Super 8 vom 11.1.–22.1.1983 Innsbruck*. Innsbruck: Innsbrucker Film.

Ehrsam, T. and Wyss, R. (eds.) (2002) *Thea Sternheim Tagebücher 1903–1971, Band V: Kommentar.* Göttingen: Wallstein Verlag.

Eichenauer, R. (1937) *Musik und Rasse: Mit 43 Abbildungen und 90 Notenbeispielen*. 2nd ed. München: J.F. Lehmanns Verlag.

Eigner, C. (2013) *Neue Tendenzen im österreichischen Animationsfilmschaffen*. Diploma Thesis, University of Vienna.

Fähnders, W. (2020) "Es wäre jammerschade, wenn man nicht auch in Wien von dieser Bewegung Kunde hätte': Dada und Dada-Rezeption in Österreich', in E. Faul (ed.) *Hugo Ball Almanach: Neue Folge 11, 2020*. München: edition text + kritik, pp. 11–36.

Fawcett, L. (1928) *Die Welt des Films*. Edited by C. Zell and S.W. Fischer. Zürich: Amalthea-Verlag.

Field, R. (1940) *Ave Maria: An Interpretation from Walt Disney's 'Fantasia'*. New York City, NY: Random House.

Floimair, R. (1998) 'Ein Salzburger erster Zeichentrickfilmer', in R. Floimair (ed.) *Simon Stampfer 1790–1864: Von der Zauberscheibe zum Film*. Salzburg: Land Salzburg, Landespressebüro, pp. 5–6.

Freud, S. and Haughton, H. (2003) *The Uncanny*. Translated by D. McLintock. New York City, NY: Penguin Group.

Garncarz, J. (2015) "Europas alter Märchenzauber und Hollywoods neues Zaubermärchen': Walt Disneys Snow White and the Seven Dwarfs in Deutschland', in T. Bräutigam and N.D. Peiler (eds.) *Film im Transferprozess: Transdisziplinäre Studien zur Filmsynchronisation*. (Marburger Schriften zur Medienforschung, Vol. 58). Marburg: Schüren Verlag, pp. 226–259.

Gierczynski, S. (2005) *Egbert Lammers (1908–1996): Glasmaler zwischen Historismus und Moderne*. (Kunstwissenschaftliche Studien, Vol. 123). München: Deutscher Kunstverlag.

Giesen, R. (2003) *Lexikon des Trick- und Animationsfilms*. Berlin: Schwarzkopf & Schwarzkopf.

Giesen, R. (2020) *Bienenstich und Hakenkreuz: Zeichentrick aus Dachau – die Deutsche Zeichenfilm GmbH*. Frankenthal: Mühlbeyer Filmbuchverlag.

Giesen, R. (2023) *Animation in Europe*. Boca Raton, FL: CRC Press.

Giesen, R. and Khan, A. (2018) *Acting and Character Animation: The Art of Animated Films, Acting and Visualising*. Boca Raton, FL: CRC Press.

Giesen, R. and Storm, J.P. (2012) *Animation under the Swastika: A History of Trickfilm in Nazi Germany, 1933–1945*. Jefferson, NC: McFarland & Company.

Gusenbauer, G. (ed.) (2022) *Donald Made in Austria! Der Character Designer Florian Satzinger = Character Design by Florian Satzinger.* Krems: Karikaturmuseum.

Häfele, M.S. (2015) *Martin Arnold Found Footage: Film als Palimpsest*. Diploma Thesis, University of Vienna.

Halas, V. (2006) 'My Family and Other Animators', in V. Halas and P. Wells (eds.) *Halas & Batchelor Cartoons: An Animated History*. London: Southbank Publishing, pp. 73–107.

Happ, A. (2004) *Lotte Reiniger 1899–1981: Schöpferin einer neuen Silhouettenkunst.* (Tübinger Kataloge, Vol. 67). Tübingen: Kulturamt.

Havas, H. (2012) 'Peter Eng – das Bindeglied?', in E. Sackmann (ed.) *Deutsche Comicforschung 2012*. Hildesheim: Comicplus+, pp. 28–35.

Hazeu, W. (2012) *Marten Toonder: Biografie*. 3rd ed. Amsterdam: De Bezige Bij.

Horwath, A. (2005) 'Singing in the Rain: Supercinematography by *Peter Tscherkassky*', in A. Horwath and M. Loebenstein (eds.) Peter Tscherkassky. (Filmmuseum Synema Publications, Vol. 2). Wien: SYNEMA, pp. 10–48.

Ihara, H. (2022) 'From Pictorial Statistics to Pictographic Animation: Philip Ragan's Investigation of Pictographic Animation to Dramatize Facts (1934–1946)', in G. Bruyns and H. Wei (eds.) *[ ] With Design: Reinventing Design Modes (IASDR 2021)*. Singapore: Springer Nature, pp. 2851–2873.

Jennings, M.W., Eiland, H. and Smith, G. (eds.) (1999) *Walter Benjamin: Selected Writings, Vol. 2, Part 2, 1931–1934*. Translated by R. Livingstone. Cambridge, MA: Belknap Press of Harvard University Press.

Jerrendorf, M. (1985) *Grimms Märchen in Medien: Aspekte verschiedener Erscheinungsformen in Hörfunk, Fernsehen und Theater*. Doctoral Thesis, University of Tübingen.

Kaiser, B. (2014) 'Zoom Animated Film Studio: The Media Lab for Children and Teenagers', in E. Menasse-Wiesbauer (ed.) *20 Years of ZOOM Children's Museum*. Wien: Verein ZOOM Kindermuseum, pp. 184–185.

Kaluza, L. (2015) *Once Upon a Time There Was a War*. Hoosick Falls, NY: Merriam Press Memoir.

Kieninger, E. (1999) 'Einleitung', in F. Bono, P. Caneppele and G. Krenn (eds.) *Elektrische Schatten: Beiträge zur Österreichischen Stummfilmgeschichte*. Wien: Filmarchiv Austria, pp. 7–8.

Klein, N.M. (1993) *Seven Minutes: The Life and Death of the American Animated Cartoon*. London: Verso.

Kondor, E. et al. (eds.) (2021) *Maria Lassnig: Film Works*. (Filmmuseum Synema Publications). Wien: SYNEMA.

Kuc, K. (2016) *Visions of Avant-Garde Film: Polish Cinematic Experiments from Expressionism to Constructivism*. Bloomington, IN: Indiana University Press.

Kunz, M. (ed.) (1989) *Maria Lassnig: Mit dem Kopf durch die Wand*, Klagenfurt: Ritter Verlag.

La Speranza, M. (2003) *Bomben auf Wien: Zeitzeugen berichten*. Wien: Ibera Verlag.

Lang, H. (2019) 'Austria Unlimited – Chances, Spirits and Limitations of a Small Production Environment', in F. Bruckner et al. (eds.) *Global Animation Theory: International Perspectives at Animafest Zagreb*. New York City, NY: Bloomsbury Academic, pp. 83–98.

Laqua, C. (1992) *Wie Micky unter die Nazis fiel: Walt Disney und Deutschland*. Reinbek bei Hamburg: Rowohlt Taschenbuch Verlag.

Lettner, N. (2022) *Maria Lassnig: The Biography*. Translated by J. Crowder. Zürich et al.: Hauser & Wirth Publishers, Maria Lassnig Foundation, Petzel.

Low, R. (1979) *The History of the British Film 1929–1939: Documentary and Educational Films of the 1930s*. (The History of British Film, Vol. 5). London: George Allen & Unwin.

MacDonald, S. (1995) 'Sp… Sp… Spaces of Inscription: Scott MacDonald im Gespräch mit Martin Arnold', in A. Horwath, L. Ponger, and G. Schlemmer (eds.) *Avantgardefilm: Österreich, 1950 bis heute*. (Wespennest–Film). Wien: Wespennest, pp. 285–300.

Mader, V. (2007) 'List of Works in the Sammlung Verbund', in G. Schor (ed.) *Held Together with Water: Art from the Sammlung Verbund*. Ostfildern: Hatje Cantz Verlag, pp. 377–391.

Mattuschka, M. and Groschup, S. (2010) 'Gott spielen mit dem Film, Göttin sein! Gespräch mit Bady Minck und Virgil Widrich', in C. Dewald, S. Groschup and T. Renoldner (eds.) *Die Kunst des Einzelbilds: Animation in Österreich – 1832 bis heute*. ASIFA Austria. Wien: Verlag Filmarchiv Austria, pp. 341–360.

Mekas, J. (1970) 'Interview with Peter Kubelka', in P.A. Sitney (ed.) *Film Culture Reader*. New York City, NY: Praeger Publishers, pp. 285–299.

Miessgang, T. (2002) 'Beyond the Words', in G. Matt and T. Miessgang (eds.), T. Appleton (tran.) *Martin Arnold: Deanimated*. Wien: Springer Verlag, pp. 15–19.

Moritz, W. (1997) 'Bartosch's The Idea', in J. Pilling (ed.) *A Reader in Animation Studies*. London: John Libbey Publishing, pp. 93–103.

Moser, K. (2019) *Der österreichische Werbefilm: Die Genese eines Genres von seinen Anfängen bis 1938*. Berlin: De Gruyter Oldenbourg.

Moser, K. (2020) 'Begrenzte Grenzenlosigkeit: Inhaltliche Konzeption und filmische Strategien der Werbefilme der Austria Tabak 1948–2000', in K. Moser, M. Keller, and F.X. Eder (eds.) *Grenzenlose Werbung: Zwischen Konsum und Audiovision*. (Werbung – Konsum – Geschichte, Vol. 2). Berlin: De Gruyter Oldenbourg, pp. 109–144.

Neupert, R. (2014) *French Animation History*. Malden, MA: Wiley-Blackwell.

Orosz, M. (2011) *Vissza a szülőföldre! = Back to the Homeland!* Translated by J. Balai. Kecskemét: KAFF.

Orosz, M. (2014) *(Film) Experiments Brought to Life: The First Cinema of the Avant-Garde*. Edited by J. Borus. Budapest: Hungarian National Gallery.

Remes, J. (2020) *Absence in Cinema: The Art of Showing Nothing*. (Film and Culture Series). New York City, NY: Columbia University Press.

Renoldner, T. (2010) 'Animation in Österreich – 1832 bis heute', in C. Dewald, S. Groschup and T. Renoldner (eds.) *Die Kunst des Einzelbilds: Animation in Österreich – 1832 bis heute*. ASIFA Austria. Wien: Verlag Filmarchiv Austria, pp. 41–152.

Renoldner, T. and Frischengruber, L. (1998) *Animated Films in Austria, Part 1: 1920–1970*. Translated by A. Curtis. Wien: ASIFA Austria.

Roy, A. (2020) 'Communication and Propaganda', in R.B. McFarland, G. Spitaler, and I. Zechner (eds.) *The Red Vienna Sourcebook*. Rochester, NY: Camden House, pp. 689–706.

Schätz, J. (2016) 'Parsing the Archive of Rudolf Mayer Film, Vienna, 1937–9', in B. Florin, N. de Klerk, and P. Vonderau (eds.) *Films That Sell: Moving Pictures and Advertising*. (Cultural Histories of Cinema). London: British Film Institute, pp. 257–265.

Schauer, P.A. (1997) *Beiträge zur Geschichte des österreichischen Zeichentrickfilms*. Reprint. Wien: Self-Published.

Schauer, P.A. (1999) *Johann Weichberger und der Zeichentrickfilm*. (Schriftenreihe des Öst. Filmarchivar-Verbandes). Wien: Self-Published.

Schmidlechner, F. (2011) ''Der Jude mit der roten Badehose': Jüdische Helden, Stereotypen und Antisemitismus im Trickfilm bis 1945', in B. Eder, E. Klar, and R. Reichert (eds.) *Theorien des Comics: Ein Reader*. Bielefeld: Transcript Verlag, pp. 303–320.

Schmidt, E. Jr. (1982) 'Kommerz und Avantgarde: Zur Situation des österreichischen Films', in O. Breicha and R. Urbach (eds.) *Österreich zum Beispiel: Literatur, bildende Kunst, Film und Musik seit 1968*. Salzburg: Residenz Verlag, pp. 395–409.

Schöpf, C. and Hagler, J. (2010) 'Ars Electronica Animation Festival 2010', in H. Leopoldseder, C. Schöpf, and G.S. Stocker (eds.) *Ars Electronica 2010: Repair*. Ostfildern: Hatje Cantz, p. 428.

Schumann, R. (1838) 'Franz Schubert's letzte Compositionen', republished in *Gesammelte Schriften über Musik und Musiker*, Vol. 2 (1854). Leipzig: Georg Wigand's Verlag, pp. 234–240.

Schwartz, J.A. (2021) *Radiation Sounds: Marshallese Music and Nuclear Silences*. Durham, NC: Duke University Press.

Sielecki, H. (1990) 'Der neue österreichische Animationsfilm aus dem Studio an der Hochschule für angewandte Kunst in Wien', in F. Aspetsberger, H. Lengauer, and R. Schwendter (eds.) *Marginalisierung: Die Literatur und die neuen Medien*. (Schriften des Instituts für Österreichkunde, Vol. 54). Wien: Österreichischer Bundesverlag, pp. 95–99.

Sperner, W. (1976) *Linz: Porträt einer Stadt*. 3rd edn. Linz: Oberösterreichischer Landesverlag.
Spira, B. (1997) *Die Legende vom Zeichner. Wien – Vernet – Gross-Rosen – Paris.* (Antifaschistische Literatur und Exilliteratur, Vol. 17). Edited by K. Kaiser with V. Vertlib. Wien: Döcker Verlag.
Spottiswoode, R. (1951) *Film and Its Techniques*. Berkeley, CA: University of California Press.
Starr, C. (ed.) (1951) *Ideas on Film: A Handbook for the 16mm. Film User*. New York: Funk & Wagnalls.
Steinlechner, G. (2013) 'Riten der Selbstauflösung = Rites of Self-Dissolution', in G. Bast (ed.) *Renate Kordon: Lebenslinien = Lifelines*. Wien: Ambra, p. 146.
Stewart, J. (2021) *The Story of British Animation*. (British Screen Stories). London: British Film Institute.
Strasser, C. (1998) 'Simon Stampfer in Salzburg (1790–1825)', in R. Floimair (ed.) *Simon Stampfer 1790–1864: Von der Zauberscheibe zum Film*. Salzburg: Land Salzburg, Landespressebüro, pp. 7–113.
Tolentino, R.B. (2001) 'Animating the Nation: Animation and Development in the Philippines', in J.A. Lent (ed.) *Animation in Asia and the Pacific*. Bloomington: Indiana University Press, pp. 167–180.
Tscherkassky, P. (1995) 'Die rekonstruierte Kinematografie: Zur Filmavantgarde in Österreich', in A. Horwath, L. Ponger, and G. Schlemmer (eds.) *Avantgardefilm: Österreich, 1950 bis heute*. (Wespennest–Film). Wien: Wespennest, pp. 9–92.
Tscherkassky, P. (2005a) 'Epilogue, Prologue: Autobiographical Notes along the Lines of a Filmography', in A. Horwath and M. Loebenstein (eds.) *Peter Tscherkassky*. (FilmmuseumSynemaPublications, Vol. 2). Wien: SYNEMA, pp. 102–160.
Ulrich, R. (2004) *Österreicher in Hollywood*. Wien: Verlag Filmarchiv Austria.
Vansant, J. (2019) *Austria Made in Hollywood*. Rochester, NY: Camden House.
Wells, P. and Hardstaff, J. (2008) *Re-Imagining Animation: The Changing Face of the Moving Image*. Lausanne: AVA Publishing.
Widrich, V., Reiter, S. and Unger, S. (eds.) (2012) *Inszenierung und Neue Medien = Presentation and New Media*. Wien: Springer.
Winkelmayer, S. (2004) *Der österreichische Zeichentrickfilm in der Stummfilmzeit*. Diploma Thesis, University of Vienna.
Zglinicki, F. von (1979) *Der Weg des Films. Textband*. Hildesheim: Olms Presse.

PRINTED PERIODICALS

Agde, G. (1998) 'Goebbels-Gründung und DEFA-Erbe. Beinahe vergessen: Die Deutsche Zeichenfilm GmbH und ihr Nachlaß (1942 bis 1947) mit einem Nachtrag 1950', in *Film und Fernsehen*, 26 (3–4), pp. 36–42.
Arbeiter-Zeitung (1923) 'Der Wahlkampf: Das Kino der Zehntausend', October 5, p. 8.
Arbeiter-Zeitung (1931) 'Tagesneuigkeiten: Der neue Feind', June 26, p. 4.
Arbeiter-Zeitung (1945) 'Ein Wiedergefundener: Otto Neuraths 'Wiener Bildstatistik'', December 1, p. 3.
Begle, M. (2015) 'Weltpremiere in Dornbirn!', in *Wann & Wo*, June 7, p. 74.
Bekker, P. (1934) 'Musik und Rasse', in *Pariser Tageblatt*, February 19, p. 4.
Berichte und Informationen (1959) 'Werbung mit Firmennamen oder Gebrauchsanweisung. Wie man die Reklame auf den Kinobesucher losläßt', 14 (666), pp. 11–12.
Bieler Tagblatt (1938) 'Bieler Kino-Rundschau: Tonfilmtheater Apollo, 'Schneewittchen'', October 12, p. [2].
Bíró, G.I. (2020) 'Michael Polanyi's Neutral Keynesianism and the First Economics Film, 1933 to 1945', in *Journal of the History of Economic Thought*, 42 (3), pp. 335–356.
Böhm, G. (1962) 'Wiener Maler bereitet einen Marionetten-Farbfilm vor', in *Die Presse*, January 28. Vienna Künstlerhaus Archives.

Business Screen Magazine (1947) 'Let the Public Know', 8 (8), p. 34.
Das Kino-Journal (1923) 'Notizen: Union-Film', March 10, p. 3.
Der Filmbote (1920) "Die Jagd nach dem Kopfe.' Trickfilmgroteske von Strix', July 3, p. 15.
Der Filmbote (1922) 'Kalif Storch', June 3, p. 19.
Der Filmbote (1924) 'Gullivers Reisen im Film', March 1, p. 15.
Der Morgen (1936) 'Film-Morgen: Film-Diskussion', March 23, p. 10.
Der neue Tag (1919) "Menschheit': Politik und Wissenschaft im Film', May 22, p. 6.
Der Spiegel (1968) 'Lenica: Adam 2', December 22, p. 151.
Der Standard (2003b) 'Eulenspiegel mit Hightech-Kern: Die innovativen Ideen der Zeichentrickfabrik Cine Cartoon', September 1, p. 12.
Der Tag (1923) 'Film Reporter: Trickfilm', October 19, p. 8.
Der Wiener Tag (1937) 'Recht des Autors auf Namensnennung', March 26, p. 9.
Die Filmwelt (1921a) 'Filmwelt-Telegramme', (6), p. 13.
Die Filmwelt (1921b) 'Von der Sascha Filmindustrie A.-G.', (11), p. 6.
Die Filmwelt (1923a) 'Die neue Winterwoche', (5), p. 6.
Die Filmwelt (1923b) 'Filmwelt-Telegramme', (6), pp. 14–15.
Die Filmwelt (1923c) 'Filmwelt-Telegramme', (7), pp. 14–15.
Die Presse (2001) 'Von Rittern, Zauberern und Ameisenbären: Zeichentrick aus Österreich', October 23, p. 30.
Die Presse (2012) 'Pixel Vienna: Computer, Bleistift und Papier', September 30, p. 13.
Die Stunde (1923) 'Film: Peter Eng', April 25, p. 5.
Die Stunde (1934) 'Peter Eng', October 4, p. 2.
Die Stunde (1935) 'Wiener Groteskfilm', August 8, p. 9.
Die Wiener Bühne (1938) 'Ein Löwensprung = 24 Kunstwerke', (475), pp. 28–29.
Documentary News Letter (1941) 'New Documentary Films: A Few Ounces a Day', 2 (11), p. 207.
Documentary News Letter (1942) 'New Documentary Films: Filling the Gap', 3 (4), p. 55.
Documentary News Letter (1945) 'A New Visual Education Unit: Unifilm Ltd', 5 (50), p. 100.
Dörfler, G. (1966) 'Das 'Studio A' in Linz', in *Filmkunst*, (47), p. 17–18.
Dugan, J.E. (1944) 'The Film and International Understanding: Film Technique Gives Life and Meaning to Abstract Ideas and Mass Statistics', in *The Educational Screen*, 23 (8), pp. 350–351.
Eng, P. (1920) 'Der Trickfilm', in *Die Filmwelt*, (35), pp. 5–8.
Eng, P. (1925) 'Trickfilmkarriere', in *Die Bühne*, (18), pp. 44–45.
Eng, P. (1936) '18 Jahre Trickfilm – unbedingt', in *Tonfilm Theater Tanz*, 4 (5), pp. 1–2.
Erde (1919) 'Das Filmwerk Menschheit', May 20, p. 1–2.
Filmkunst (1950) 'Unterrichtsfilm: Filme für und über Kinder', (5), p. 256.
Filmkunst (1991) 'The Austrian Documentary and Television Productions 1990', (131), pp. 24–52.
Filmpresse (2011) 'Beim 'Trickfilm-Altmeister': Ein 'Interview' mit Rudolf Enter', 47 (1), pp. 16–17.
Fischer, M. (2022) 'Erstmals sind wir unser eigener Kunde', in *Kleine Zeitung*, March 11, p. 64.
Flossmann, G. (2017) 'Eine tiefschwarze Abrechnung', in *Kurier*, June 7, p. 23.
Flossmann, G. (2019) 'Eine Webserie entsteht im Wiener Biedermeierhaus', in *Kurier*, September 17, p. 24.
Forschen & Entdecken (2012) 'Animierend', (2), p. 25.
Fränkel, L. (1930) 'Der Tonfilmamateur', in *FunkMagazin*, 3 (6), pp. 583–592.
Freiheit*!* (1929) 'Die ewige Verkehrschweinerei: Statt einer Untergrundbahn – Karikaturen', May 17, p. 4.
Füringk, M. (1947) 'Marienkäfer Siebenpunkt und sein Schöpfer Gustl Peuker', in *Mein Film*, 17 (18), May 2, p. [6].
Gasperi, W. (2015) "Es gab keine Grenzen, was Story, Charaktere oder Animation betrifft", in *Zeitschrift für Kultur und Gesellschaft*, (6), pp. 68–70.

Gasteiger, A. (2004) 'Besuch bei Tomtom, Till und Talis', in *Kurier*, July 29, p. 27.

Gesek, L. (1987) 'Die dreißiger Jahre: Ein Schlüsseljahrzehnt der Filmgeschichte', in *Filmkunst*, (113), pp. 1–2.

Giesinger, G. (2015) 'Von Wien in die weite Welt – und zurück', in *Horizont*, (39), September 25, p. 19.

Gloger, J. (1993) 'Der 'österreichische Walt Disney': Begegnung mit Franz Bresnikar', in *Filmkunst*, 45 (139), pp. 19–25.

Greuling, M. (2003) 'Grippekranke Giraffe', in *Die Furche*, October 2, p. 17.

Hadler, D. (2023) 'Effektreich in den Krieg gezogen', in *Kleine Zeitung*, December 9, p. 63.

Hagler, J. and Rauscher, R. (2022) 'Chained Animation: Collaborative Forms of Filmmaking in Education', in *Animation*, 17 (2), pp. 178–194.

Hirsch, L.E. (2007) 'The Berlin Jüdischer Kulturbund and the 'After-Life' of Franz Schubert: Musical Appropriation and Identity Politics in Nazi Germany', in *The Musical Quarterly*, 90 (3–4), pp. 469–507.

Illustrierter Film-Kurier (1935) 'Micky spielt auf', (1273).

Irzykowski, K. and Coates, P. (1987) 'The Tenth Muse (Excerpts)', in *New German Critique*, (42), pp. 116–127.

Irzykowski, K. and Helbig-Mischewski, B. (2013) 'Der Zeichenfilm', in *Montage AV*, 22 (2), pp. 51–57.

Jacobson, J. (1997) 'Franz Schubert and the Vienna Synagogue', in *Choral Journal*, 38 (1), pp. 9–15.

Jenewein, P. (1978) 'Computerfilme und Video-Synthesis', in *Filmkunst*, (79), pp. 3–5.

Kinematographische Rundschau (1911) 'Der Werdegang der Kinematographie in Österreich', December 31, pp. 2–11.

Kinematographische Rundschau (1914) 'Zensurergebnisse', November 22, pp. 57–58.

Kinematographische Rundschau (1915a) 'Die Vorführungen der Woche', October 31, pp. 55–60.

Kinematographische Rundschau (1915b) 'Vom dieswöchentlichen Filmmarkte', January 3, pp. 38, 40–41.

Kinematographische Rundschau (1915c) 'Vom dieswöchentlichen Filmmarke', February 28, pp. 8, 63–64.

Kinematographische Rundschau (1916) 'Neueste Nachrichten von Philipp & Pressburger', November 12, pp. 13–14.

Kleine Volks-Zeitung (1938) 'Strom für alles: Die E-Werke gehen mit der Zeit', November 5, p. 5

Kleine Zeitung (2014) 'Zwischen skurrilem Slapstick und apokalyptischem Horror', August 24, p. 72.

Klocker, E.M. (2019) 'Different Faces: Mara Mattuschka', in *WUK Info Intern*, (2), pp. 3–6.

Kromp, R. (2007) 'Donald regiert die Welt: Duck-Invasion in Krems', in *News*, 07 (10), March 8, pp. 126–130.

Kuplent, F. (1934) 'Zeichenfilme – eine Beschäftigung für die langen Winterabende', in *Photo- und Kinosport*, (1), pp. 15–17.

Kurier (2003) 'Premiere für 'Spirello': Neuer Zeichentrick', September 25, p. 31.

Lauterstein, H. (1923) 'Zum Geleite', in *Die Filmwelt*, (Breitbart-Sonderheft), p. 2.

Lehmann, H. (1911) 'Kinematographische Tricks', in *Allgemeiner Tiroler Anzeiger*, November 8, pp. 1–2.

Linzer Tages-Post (1910) 'Bläsers Kinematograph', October 9, p. 6.

Littmann, H. (1920) 'Kino und Jugend', in *Neue Kino-Rundschau*, October 30, pp. 6–7.

Maier, W. (1993) 'Vor 47 Jahren …', in *Filmkunst*, 45 (139), p. 26.

Mailler, H. (1925) 'Abenteuer mit dem Autobus', in *Reichspost*, April 19, p. 7.

McIlvaine, J.S. (1949) 'Facts Can Be Interesting: The Disney of the Scientist Teaches by Animated Cartoons', in *The Philadelphia Inquirer Magazine*, December 18, pp. 6–7.

Mein Film (1927) 'Die lebende Trickfigur', (58), p. 7.
Mein Film (1929) 'Ein interessanter neuer Trickfilm', (162), p. B.
Mein Film (1936) 'Architekt Stefan Wessely gestorben', (523), p. I.
Mein Film (1946) 'Das fröhliche Lachen', 16 (51–52), December 20, p. [14].
Mittagausgabe (1937) 'An der Geburtsstätte des Zeichenfilms: Stars mit Rundköpfen', June 28, p. 2.
Moderne Welt (1935) 'Carmen in zehn Minuten: Ein Wiener Trickfilm wird gezeichnet', 16 (6), p. 10, 39.
Neue Freie Presse (1914) 'Wirklichkeit und Trick im Kino', March 8, p. 28.
Neue Kino-Rundschau (1918) 'Vorführung der Firma 'Danubia': Gretls Filmtraum', November 23, p. 10.
Neue Kino-Rundschau (1919) 'Wissenschaftliche Films', August 9, pp. 3–4.
Neue Kino-Rundschau (1920a) 'Die Astoria-Film-Gesellschaft', July 3, pp. 13–14.
Neue Kino-Rundschau (1920b) 'Die Filmneuheiten der Woche: Apollo', November 6, p. 19.
Neue Kino-Rundschau (1920c) 'Die Jagd nach dem Kopfe', November 20, p. 21.
Neue Kino-Rundschau (1920d) 'Neuestes aus Deutschland: Das Arbeitsfeld des Lehrfilms', May 1, p. 12.
Neue Zeit (1950) 'Kunst und Wissen: Russische Kulturfilme', December 19, p. 3.
Neues Volksblatt (2001) 'Knappe und Ameisenbär', October 25, p. 37.
Neues Wiener Journal (1919) 'Wissenschaft im Film: Ein Werk des Instituts für Kulturforschung', May 28, pp. 6–7.
Neues Wiener Tagblatt (1911) 'Die 'Wunder' der Kinoschauspiele', February 12, pp. 13–14.
Neues Wiener Tagblatt (1914) 'Theater, Kunst und Literatur', April 16, pp. 13–14.
Neuigkeits-Welt-Blatt (1929) 'Die Gemeinde Wien ist wohltätig auf Kosten der Straßenbahnfahrgäste', June 28, p. 5.
New York Times (1982) 'Obituaries: Hugh Harman, 79, Creator of 'Looney Tunes' Cartoons', November 30, p. 12.
Oertel, R. (1955) 'Organisationsformen der Filmwirtschaft', in *Filmkunst*, (16), pp. 19–23.
Österr. Film-Zeitung (1938) ''Schneewittchen' – ein Sensationserfolg in Los Angeles', January 7, p. 2.
Österreichische Volksstimme (1947) 'Stars, die keine Gagen verlangen', July 11, p. 3.
Österreichische Volksstimme (1950) 'Die Tschechoslowakische Filmfestwoche', November 10, p. 6.
Österreichische Zeitung (1947) 'Ein neuer Schubert-Film', July 25, p. 5.
Österreichische Zeitung (1950) ''Achtung, Aufnahme!' Ein Gigli-Film im Tabor-Kino', July 30, p. 7.
Paimann's Filmlisten (1959) 'Erstaufführungen: Fantasia', January 28, p. 10.
Pavlik, R. (2004) 'Trickfilm: Strichmännchen Made in A', in *Celluloid*, (2), pp. 28–29.
Payer, P. (2000) 'Brigittenauer Lichtspiele: Kino und Film im 20. *Wiener Gemeindebezirk* (1908–1986)', in Wiener Geschichtsblätter, 55 (3), pp. 161–196.
Photo-Sport (1928) 'Ergebnisse des Pathé-Baby-Filmpreisausschreibens', (11), p. 4.
Polanyi, M. (1940) 'Economics by Motion Symbols', in *The Review of Economic Studies*, 8 (1), pp. 1–19.
Porges, F. (1930) 'Die tanzenden Männchen', in *Wiener Magazin*, 4 (4), pp. 10–13.
Priesching, D. (2024) 'Bizarres Serien-Schönbrunn', in *Der Standard*, March 13, p. 18.
Profil (1983) 'Der Kamera-Akrobat: Mister Fantasy', (12), March 21, p. 66.
Putz, P. (1988) 'Starke Tricks: Ein Streifzug durch die Animation im Film', in *Die Brücke*, (1), pp. 28–32.
Rathaus-Korrespondenz (1971) ''Unbequeme Zeitgenossen': Viennale 1971 eröffnet', March 25, p. 869.
Reichspost (1916) 'Der Trickfilm', March 25, p. 22.

Salzburger Nachrichten (2018) 'Zeichentrick-Affe bringt Industrie auf die Palme', November 17, p. 21.

Salzburger Nachrichten (2021) 'Atombombe auf Wien: Empörung über ein Video', January 25, p. 12.

Salzburger Volksblatt (1910) 'Der Kinematograph und seine Auswüchse', April 16, pp. 17–18.

Sandner, G. (2019) 'Isotype: Visuelle Erziehung und Politik', in *JUNI-Magazin für Literatur und Kultur*, (55–56), pp. 223–239.

Sandner, G. (2021) 'Rudolf Modley and the Americanization of Isotype', in *Journal of Austrian-American History*, 5 (1), pp. 32–61.

Schmid, M.A. (2002) ''Talis und die tausend Aufgaben': Eine österreichische Erfolgsstory', in *Wiener Zeitung*, July 11, p. 14.

Schmidt, E. Jr. (1985) 'Die synthetische Wirklichkeit: Der neue österreichische Animationsfilm', in *blimp*, (Heft Grün), Summer, pp. 34–39.

Schneider, U. (2011) 'Neues von Peter Engelmann (Ps. Peter Eng) und Anny Engelmann (Ps. Suska): Die Geschwister von Paul Engelmann, Figuren einer verschwundenen europäischen Moderne', in *Mitteilungen aus dem Brenner-Archiv*, 30 (2011), pp. 119–144.

Schögler, V. (2021) *Fazitbegegnung: Von Enten und Monstern*, in *Fazit*, (171), April, pp. 42–43.

Scott, H. (1947) 'Atomic Energy Visualized', in *Everybody's Weekly, The Philadelphia Inquirer*, April 20, pp. 2, 14.

Sport im Bild (1934) 'Stimmen zur Mode: Richard Dillenz', 40 (6), March 20, p. 258.

Tages-Post (1920) 'Der Film im Dienste des politischen Lebens', October 2, p. 8.

Tartarotti, G. (2014) ''Golem': Die Maschine ist an der Macht', in *Kurier*, August 2014, p. 26.

Taylor, F.J. (1943) 'Pal of the Puppets', in *Collier's*, January 16, p. 15, 61.

Tonfilm Theater Tanz (1938) 'Peter Engs Kleinkunst', 6 (3), p. 8.

Tragner, C. (2022) 'Braune Flecken übermalen', in *Kronen Zeitung*, February 27, p. 37.

Trenczak, H. and Kehldorfer, R. (1985): 'Achtzig Prozent der Filmarbeit sind Geldbeschaffung. Ein Gespräch mit Elfriede Jelinek', in *Blimp*, (2), pp. 12–17.

Vicedo, M. (2009) 'The Father of Ethology and the Foster Mother of Ducks: Konrad Lorenz as Expert on Motherhood', in *Isis*, 100 (2), pp. 263–291.

Völkischer Beobachter (1935) 'Ein neuer Filmkobold', June 22, p. 6.

Wallnöfer, P.A. (2001) 'Quirliger Trickheld', in *Salzburger Nachrichten*, October 25, p. 30.

Welt am Abend (1947) 'Was sagt die Kirche zum Film?', October 2, p. 3.

Wiener Allgemeine Zeitung (1915) 'Fräulein Wildleders Liebesroman', December 1, p. 3.

Wiener Allgemeine Zeitung (1920) 'Die Filmredoute', February 6, p. 2.

Wiener Kronen Zeitung (1943) 'Eine Künstlerhand, vom Herzen und vom Humor geleitet: Abschied von Ladislaus Tuszynski/'Tusch', der Zeichner des Wienertums', September 29, p. 4.

Wiener Zeitung (1857) 'Amtlicher Theil', December 25, pp. 3671–3672.

Zentralblatt Handelsregister (1952) '3451. Wien, Herold Zeichenfilm Gesellschaft m. b. H.', 51 (20), May 14, p. 241.

Ziegler, M. (2022) 'Halbvoll ist das neue Ausverkauft', in *Wiener Zeitung*, September 16, p. 18.

ONLINE SOURCES

Agar, T.K. (2015) *Getting to Know Moon Studios*, in *Refined Geekery*, March 16. Available at: https://refinedgeekery.com/2015/03/16/getting-to-know-moon-studios/

Amidi, A. (2016) *The Tom Hanks Film 'A Hologram for the King' Had an Inventive Cartoon Sequence That Was Cut*, in *Cartoon Brew*, September 14. Available at: https://www.cartoonbrew.com/feature-film/tom-hanks-film-hologram-king-inventive-cartoon-sequence-cut-143058.html

André, E. (2018) *Animals, Tamers, and Clowns: Martin Arnold*, in *Mousse Magazine*, February 12. Available at: https://www.moussemagazine.it/magazine/martin-arnold-emmanuelle-andre-2018/

ASIFA Austria (2016) 'Under the Radar: Screenings', in *ASIFA Austria*. Available at: https://www.asifa.at/under-the-radar-2016-screenings/

Bacher, J. (2021) *Duckland: Cartoon-Ausstellung in den Kasematten am Schloßberg*, in Graz, March 30. Available at: https://www.graz.net/duckland-ausstellung-kasematten-schlossberg-13224/

Beck, J. (2017) *Cartoons Considered for an Academy Award 1973*, in *Cartoon Research*, October 30. Available at: https://cartoonresearch.com/index.php/cartoons-considered-for-an-academy-award-1973/

Betty Boop in Japan (no date) in *Fleischer Studios*. Available at: https://www.fleischerstudios.com/betty-in-japan.html

BFI Collections Search (no date) 'Unemployment and Money', in *British Film Institute*. Available at: https://collections-search.bfi.org.uk/web/Details/ChoiceFilmWorks/150021048

Blumesberger, S. (2008) *Aufarbeitung des Nachlasses und der Biografie der Grafikerin und Illustratorin Susi Weigel, Endbericht Teil I*. Research Report, Wien. Available at: https://phaidra.univie.ac.at/o:73

Bonn, A. (2023) *Kreation des Tages: Jung von Matt macht mit diesem Cartoon Lust aufs Sanieren,* in Werben & Verkaufen, July 18. Available at: https://www.wuv.de/Themen/Kreation-Design/Jung-von-Matt-macht-mit-diesem-Cartoon-Lust-aufs-Sanieren

Burger-Utzer, B. and Arnold, M. (2010) *Shadow Cuts*, in *Stadtkino Wien*. Available at: https://stadtkinowien.at/film/shadow-cuts/

Constantin Film (ed.) (2021) *Hinterland Presseheft*, in Österreichisches Filminstitut. Available at: https://filminstitut.at/wp-content/uploads/2021/09/HinterlandPresseheftAT.pdf

Der Standard (2003a) "Krieg und Kino' im Filmarchiv Austria', January 17. Available at: https://www.derstandard.at/story/1185306/krieg-und-kino-im-filmarchiv-austria

Der Standard (2003c) 'Streaming & TV: 'Spirello'', September 30. Available at: https://www.derstandard.at/story/1429118/spirello

Der Standard (2015) 'Games: Pixel-Konferenz holt Designer von 'Mirror's Edge' und 'Game of Thrones' nach Wien', October 21. Available at: https://www.derstandard.at/story/2000024263660/pixel-konferenz-bringt-designer-von-wow-mirrors-edge-und-game

Der Standard (2023) 'Designer lässt KI-Software österreichische Bundeskanzler als Pixar-Figuren darstellen', March 2. Available at: https://www.derstandard.at/story/2000144048829/grafiker-laesst-ki-software-oesterreichische-bundeskanzler-als-pixar-figuren-darstellen

Dinkla, L. (2021) *There Is Exactely Enough Time*, in *DOK Leipzig*. Available at: https://www.dok-leipzig.de/en/film/es-ist-genau-genug-zeit/archive

Festré, A. (2020) *Michael Polanyi's Vision of Government and Economics: Spanning Hayek and Keynes*, in *GREDEG Working Papers Series*, (No. 2019-41). Available at: https://shs.hal.science/halshs-03036824/document

film:riss (2007) 'Ausstellung: film:riss:präsentationen Marlies Pöschl & Clemens Kogler'. Available at: https://www.filmriss.at/07/?page_id=29

Filmverband Sachsen (2017) 'Trickfilm Made in Austria: Die neue Ausstellung des DIAF stellt Animationsfilmkollektive aus', in *film.land.sachsen*, August 2. Available at: https://www.filmverband-sachsen.de/trickfilm-made-in-austria/

Forster, R., Giesen, R., Goergen, J. and Petzold, V. (no date) *Chronologie zum Animationsfilm in Deutschland 1940–49*, in DIAF. Edited by R. Giesen and V. Petzold. Available at: https://www.diaf.de/forschung/chronologie-zum-animationsfilm-in-deutschland/chronologie-zum-animationsfilm-in-deutschland-1940-49/

Frenkel, D. (2005) *Frenkel Animated Cartoons*. Brooklyn, NY: Historical Society of Jews from Egypt. Available at: https://www.hsje.org/Arts/MishMish/mishmish.pdf

Fuchs, M. (2021) *Bei Festival in Annecy: Deix-Film 'Rotzbub' feiert im Juni Weltpremiere*, in *Kronen Zeitung*, May 22. Available at: https://www.krone.at/2420279

Gasser, F. (2012) *Erotik-Spiele: Scharfe Megabits*, in *ZEIT Online*, March 22. Available at: https://www.zeit.de/2012/13/A-Pornospiele

Geremus, F. (no date) *The Arctic: Our Last Great Wilderness*, in *Kaiserlicht*. Available at: https://kaiserlicht.at/portfolio/the-arctic/

Giesen, R. and Goergen, J. (no date) *Chronologie zum Animationsfilm in Deutschland 1910–19*, in DIAF. Edited by R. Giesen and V. Petzold. Available at: https://www.diaf.de/forschung/chronologie-zum-animationsfilm-in-deutschland/chronologie-zum-animationsfilm-in-deutschland-1910-19/

Greuling, M. (2021) *Film: Ruzowitzkys 'Hinterland' feiert Premiere in Locarno*, in *Wiener Zeitung*, August 7. Available at: https://www.tagblatt-wienerzeitung.at/nachrichten/kultur/film/2115615-Ruzowitzkys-Hinterland-feiert-Premiere-in-Locarno.html

Hairapetian, M. (2022) *Paths to Glory 2022: Marc Hairapetian on Five Special JETS Winners*, in *WEP Films*, March 9. Available at: https://wepfilms.com/2022/03/paths-to-glory-2022-marc-hairapetian-on-five-special-jets-winners/

Heller, E. (1986) *'Papageno': Lotte Reiniger und Mozarts Zauberflöte*, republished in *Kinder- und Jugendfilm Korrespondenz*. Available at: http://www.kjk-muenchen.de/archiv/index.php?id=768

Huber, C. (2020a) *Jubiläumsveranstaltung: Leben in Bildern*, in *ray Filmmagazin*, October. Available at: https://ray-magazin.at/leben-in-bildern/

Huber, C. (2020b) *Retrospective: Shot-Countershot*, in *Viennale*. Available at: https://www.viennale.at/en/film/shot-countershot

Karl, J. (2021) *Tip und Top Werbefilm Österreich: Archivale des Monats Juli 2021*, in Österreichisches Staatsarchiv (ÖSta), July 1. Available at: https://www.oesta.gv.at/veroeffentlichungen/archivale-des-monats/Archivale-des-Monats-Juli-2021.html

Kato, K. (2017) *Rare Japanese Anime Goes Online to Mark 100th Anniversary*, in *Asia Times*, May 19. Available at: https://asiatimes.com/2017/05/rare-japanese-anime-goes-online-mark-100th-anniversary/

KiJuKu (2021) 'Kinder retten – in eigenen Filmen – die Welt…', October 10. Available at: https://kijuku.at/buehne/kinder-retten-in-eigenen-filmen-die-welt/

Knoll, M. (2013) *Computer Animation/Film/VFX: Origin and Development*, in *Ars Electronica*, February 6. Available at: https://ars.electronica.art/aeblog/en/2013/02/06/computer-animation-film-vfx-entstehung-und-entwicklung/

Marboe, I. (2018) *Architekt aus Leidenschaft: Graphic Novel über Karl Schwanzer*, in *architektur.aktuell*, December 9. Available at: https://www.architektur-aktuell.at/news/graphic-novel-ueber-karl-schwanzer

Mayerson, M. (1997) *Tulips Shall Grow*. Washington, DC: Library of Congress National Film Registry. Available at: https://www.loc.gov/static/programs/national-film-preservation-board/documents/tulips.pdf

Mayorga, E. (2021) *'Tadeo' Producer Lightbox, Austria's Arx Anima Team to Create Arxlight*, in *Variety*, June 17. Available at: https://variety.com/2021/film/festivals/the-joint-venture-feature-monstrous-mia-1234999392/

Müller, R. (2002) *Einige österreichische Flüchtlinge in Großbritannien*. Research Project, University of Salzburg. Available at: https://www.literaturepochen.at/exil/multimedia/pdf/exilantenlistereinhard.pdf

Neurath, M. (1946) *Isotype in Films*, republished in *Isotype Revisited*. Available at: https://isotyperevisited.org/1946/06/isotype-in-films.php

NFA (ed.) (2010) *AFIT 1941–1944 (1948): Inventář*, in *Národní filmový archiv* (NFA, Czech Film Archive). Available at: https://nfa.cz/dokumenty-ke-stazeni/badatelske-pomucky/instituce-a-spolecnosti/afit.pdf

Pavido, M. (2019) *Austrian Animation Cinema: The Invisible Art*, in *Cinema Austriaco*, June 10. Available at: https://cinema-austriaco.org/en/2019/06/10/austrian-animation-cinema-the-invisible-art/

Pavido, M. (2022) *Copy Shop (2001) by Virgil Widrich: Review*, in *Cinema Austriaco*, September 19. Available at: https://cinema-austriaco.org/en/2022/09/19/copy-shop-2/

Pavlik, R. (2016) *NÖT: Der Adler ist gelandet!*, in *HomeMovieCorner*, July 8. Available at: https://homemoviecorner.wordpress.com/2016/07/08/noet-der-adler-ist-gelandet/

Perraudin, R. (no date) *Rückblick: Zweiter Weltkrieg*, in *Wilfrid Perraudin*. Available at: https://www.perraudin.eu/zweiter-weltkrieg.html

Pezold, A. (2012) *Erste Kluser kurzFilmnacht begeisterte die Zuschauer*, in *VOL*, November 4. Available at: https://www.vol.at/erste-kluser-kurzfilmnacht-begeisterte-die-zuschauer

Puls 24 (2022) 'Familienstück: Animierende Animation im Akademietheater', October 9. Available at: https://www.puls24.at/news/entertainment/familienstueck-animierende-animation-im-akademietheater/277809

Rathauskorrespondenz (2016) 'Kurzfilmwettbewerb 'The Rhythm of Vienna': 'Morbide, schön und ziemlich skurril'', September 21. Available at: https://presse.wien.gv.at/2016/09/21/kurzfilmwettbewerb-the-rhythm-of-vienna

Rathauskorrespondenz (2020) 'Corona-Erklärvideo für Kinder: Großes Interesse auch außerhalb Österreichs', March 21. Available at: https://presse.wien.gv.at/presse/2020/03/21/corona-erklaervideo-fuer-kinder-grosses-interesse-auch-ausserhalb-oesterreichs

Rauch, M. (2015) *'Noron': Vorarlberger Künstlerfamilie schafft Animationsfilm in Heimarbeit*, in *VOL*, May 30. Available at: https://www.vol.at/noron-vorarlberger-kuenstlerfamilie-schafft-animationsfilm-in-heimarbeit/4342851

Röder, M., Mayer, G. and Kohler, F. (2018) *Herrscher hört die Signale: Habsburgs Untergang vor 100 Jahren*, in *Luzerner Zeitung*, November 11. Available at: https://www.luzerner-zeitung.ch/leben/uber-nacht-wurde-die-650-jahre-alte-habsburger-dynastie-zur-geschichte-ld.1325685

Romney, J. (2001) *OK, Kids – Shoot! Jonathan Romney on the Rotterdam Film Festival*, in *The Guardian*, February 3. Available at: https://www.theguardian.com/film/2001/feb/03/rotterdamfilmfestival.festivals

Rudle, D. (2016) *Paul Wenninger: Nicht dem Wohlgefühl dienen*, in *Tanzschrift*, October 20. Available at: https://www.tanzschrift.at/buehne/nah-besehen/413-paul-wenninger-dem-wohlgefuehl-dient-meine-arbeit-nicht

salzburg.ORF (2022) 'Kultur: Salzburger animieren Figuren in Deix-Film', April 11. Available at: https://salzburg.orf.at/stories/3151569/

Schiefer, K. (2021a) *Interview: 'My First Impression Was Definitely a Shock.'*, in *Austrian Films*, June. Available at: https://www.austrianfilms.com/interview/santiago_lopez_jover/snotty_boy_EN

Schiefer, K. (2021b) *Interview: 'Poetic, Cheeky, Bawdy and Surprising.'*, in *Austrian Films*, May. Available at: https://www.austrianfilms.com/interview/marcus_h_rosenmueller/snotty_boy_EN

Schiefer, K. (2021c) *Interview: 'Schau, ein Deix.'*, in *Austrian Films*, May. Available at: https://www.austrianfilms.com/interview/josef_aichholzer/rotzbub_produktion_DE

Schuchter, N. (2013) *Salzburger Festspiele: Straßenunruhen in Stummfilmästhetik beim YDP*, in *Salzburg24*, July 31. Available at: https://www.salzburg24.at/themen/salzburger-festspiele/salzburger-festspiele-strassenunruhen-in-stummfilmaesthetik-beim-ydp-43582636

Sputnic Künstlerkollektiv (no date) 'Stage, Space & Video: A Magic Mix of Narrative and Technology', in *sputnic visual arts*. Available at: https://sputnic.tv/en/buehne/

Staber, C. and Weiss, T. (2012) *Walt Disney Records & Outfit 7 engagieren Animationsstudio mit Regisseur aus Wien für neues Disney Animations-Kurzfilmprojekt*, in APA-OTS, July 6. Available at: https://www.ots.at/presseaussendung/OTS_20120706_OTS0028/

Steinschaden, J. (2011) *ThriXXX: Tiroler Pixel-Sex erobert die Welt*, in *Futurezone*, March 10. Available at: https://futurezone.at/digital-life/thrixxx-tiroler-pixel-sex-erobert-die-welt/24.563.233

Swiczinsky, B. (2022) *Birne, Schädel & Haupt: Web Series*, in *SWICZ*. Available at: https://swicz.com/birne-schadel-haupt/

Taanila, M. (2001) *Interview with Martin Arnold*, in *Avanto Festival 2001*. Available at: https://www.avantofestival.com/avanto2001/2001_screenings/fv_arnold_interview.html

Temel, P. (2011) *Stermann: 'Bin hauptberuflich Deutscher'*, in *Kurier*, December 5. Available at: https://kurier.at/kultur/stermann-bin-hauptberuflich-deutscher/714.355

Tricky Women (2005) 'Programmheft Tricky Women 2005'. Available at: https://www.trickywomen.at/sites/default/files/field/file-upload/programmheft_tricky_women_2005.pdf

Tricky Women (2008) 'Tricky Women Programmheft 2008'. Available at: https://www.trickywomen.at/sites/default/files/field/file-upload/programmheft-08-1ralf_layout_1red.pdf

Tricky Women (2009) 'Tricky Women Programmheft 2009'. Available at: https://www.trickywomen.at/sites/default/files/field/file-upload/tw-programmheft-09-download-150.pdf

Tricky Women (2019) 'Tricky Women 2019 Programmübersicht'. Available at: https://www.trickywomen.at/sites/default/files/field/file-upload/trickywomen19_programneu.pdf

Tricky Women (2020) 'Tricky Women 2020 Program Overview'. Available at: https://www.trickywomen.at/sites/default/files/field/file-upload/twtr-20-programm-mail_0.pdf

Tscherkassky, P. (2005b) *Shorts: Instructions for a Light and Sound Machine*, in *Viennale*. Available at: https://www.viennale.at/de/film/instructions-light-and-sound-machine

Tscherkassky, P. and Grissemann, S. (2018) *Now Available: Peter Tscherkassky's The Exquisite Corpus*, in *Canyon Cinema*, September 19. Available at: https://canyoncinema.com/2018/09/19/now-available-peter-tscherkasskys-the-exquisite-corpus/

Tschütscher, D. (2021) *Neuer Österreichischer Trickfilm: 'Die Situation ist deutlich besser als vor zehn Jahren'*, in *Cinema Next*, December. Available at: https://www.cinemanext.at/portraets/neuer-oesterreichischer-trickfilm

U.S. Mission Austria (ed.) (2022) *70 Years Marshall Plan in Austria*, in *U.S. Embassy in Austria*. Available at: https://at.usembassy.gov/70-years-marshall-plan in-austria/

VdFS (2023) Distribution Rules. Available at: https://www.vdfs.at/media/vdfs_distribution_rules_01-2023.pdf

Vogel, S.B. (2002) *Martin Arnold*, in *Artforum*. Translated by S. Ogger. Available at: https://www.artforum.com/events/martin-arnold-178682/

Voß, K.W. (2014) *Ave Maria* (Film Description), in *YouTube*, June 23. Available at: https://youtu.be/zIvuLzIV97M

Vox feminae (2021) 'Interview with Waltraud Grausgruber by Vox feminae', in *Calliope*, September 21. Available at: https://www.calliope.at/waltraud-grausgruber

Vrecer, M. (no date - a) *Lebenslauf: English*, in *Max Vrecer, willkommen!* Available at: https://www.maxvrecer.at/bio_english.html

Vrecer, M. (no date - b) *Presse*, in *Max Vrecer, willkommen!* Available at: https://www.maxvrecer.at/Presse.html

Wagner, H. (2019) *Teil des Storyboards und Set-Designs kommen aus Österreich*, in *Kurier*, October 1. Available at: https://kurier.at/kiku/teil-des-storyboards-und-set-designs-kommen-aus-oesterreich/400634960

Walker, M. (2018) *How We Made the Most Successful Christmas Ad Ever*, in *About Iceland*, December 14. Available at: https://about.iceland.co.uk/2018/12/14/how-we-made-the-most-successful-christmas-ad-ever/

Whelan, S. (2010) *Tricky Women Pushing Boundaries*, in Dazed, March 5. Available at: https://www.dazeddigital.com/artsandculture/article/6977/1/tricky-women-pushing-boundaries

Widrich, V. (2021) *There Is Exactly Enough Time*, in *Widrichfilm*. Available at: https://www.widrichfilm.com/en/projekte/there_is_exactly_enough_time

Wiener Jugendzentren (2021) 'Corona Party (Trickfilm)', in *Verein Wiener Jugendzentren*, April 7. Available at: https://www.jugendzentren.at/wer-wir-sind-was-wir-tun/newsarchiv/corona-party-trickfilm/

Wurmitzer, M. (2022) *Premiere: Akademietheater als Kindertheater*, in *Der Standard*, October 9. Available at: https://www.derstandard.at/story/2000139812088/akademietheater-als-kindertheater

Wurz, O. (2016) *Seit drei Generationen hinter der Filmkamera*, in *MeinBezirk*, August 17. Available at: https://www.meinbezirk.at/linz-land/c-wirtschaft/seit-drei-generationen-hinter-der-filmkamera_a1824394

Zan, M. (2012) *Rezension: Deutsche Comicforschung 2012*, in *ComFor*. Available at: https://www.comicgesellschaft.de/wp-content/uploads/2012/07/Rezension011.pdf

Zryd, M. (2004) *Alone: Life Wastes Andy Hardy*, in *Senses of Cinema*. (32). Available at: https://www.sensesofcinema.com/2004/cteq/alone_life_wastes_andy_hardy/

AUDIO & AUDIOVISUAL SOURCES

'2 Days Animation Festival' (2017) *Oktoskop*. Benjamin Swiczinsky and Martin Lorenz interviewed by Robert Buchschwenter. [TV Programme]. OKTO: November 19, 2017.

'Arnold: Stadtkino' (1993) *Kulturjournal*. Directed by C. Teissig. [TV Programme]. ORF: March 3, 1993.

'Auf-gerollt' (1990) *Seitenblicke*. (745). [TV Programme]. ORF: October 17, 1990.

'Die Nacht der Avantgarde: Filme anders sehen' (2012) *Kulturmontag*. Directed by B. Thalberg and E. Semrad. [TV Programme]. ORF: October 22, 2012.

'Grazer Grün' (2021) *Aufgetischt*. (99). Directed by K. Heigl. [TV Programme]. ORF: August 15, 2021.

'Hans O. Sindelar' (2011) *Heute in Österreich*. Directed by T. Arico. [TV Programme]. ORF: January 14, 2011.

'Krieg der Zeichner' (2015) *ZDF-History*. Directed and written by R. Schlosshan. [TV Programme]. ZDF: June 14, 2015.

'Manfred Deix: Cartoonist und Maler' (2005) *Alpha Forum*. Interviewed by K. Kastan. [TV Programme]. ARD-alpha: May 27, 2005.

'Nachruf Max Vrecer' (2010) *Steiermark heute*. Directed by R. Rosbaud. [TV Programme]. ORF: December 12, 2010.

'Österreicher in den USA: Los Angeles' (1985) *Auf rot-weiß-roten Spuren*. (5). [TV Programme]. Directed and written by F. von Thun. ORF: July 5, 1985.

'Österreicher in Venedig' (2010) *Kulturmontag*. Directed by C. Konrad. [TV Programme]. ORF: September 6, 2010.

'Österreichische Avantgarde' (1995) *ZIB 19.30-Kultur*. Directed by D. Pirker. [TV Programme]. ORF: June 19, 1995.

'PIXELvienna 2012' (2021) *PIXELvienna*. [Online Video]. Available at: https://youtu.be/UWJuqlkCoEM

'Rudolf Enter: Film-Animateur' (2020) *Home Movie Day 2020*. With an introduction by Vrääth Öhner. [Online Video]. Austrian Film Museum. Available at: https://youtu.be/I8Wd-s6GvWA

'Rudolf Enter: Puppen-Trick-Film-Leidenschaft' (2013) *Uni Wien Broadcast*. Directed by G. Mokesch. [TV Programme]. OKTO: January 2, 2014.

'Schwerpunkt Wien und die Welt der Animation' (2016) *Kurzschluss*. [TV Programme]. Arte: June 10, 2016.

'Tricky Women/Tricky Realities 2021' (2021) *#wienLEBT*. [TV Programme]. OKTO: March 22, 2021.

'Videostatement Benjamin Swiczinsky 'Coming Home'' (2020) *OnlineFestival.ITFS.de.* [Online Video]. Available at: https://youtu.be/867_cdgrZps

'Waltraud Grausgruber Interview' (2022) *CINANIMA 2022.* [Online Video]. Available at: https://youtu.be/TR-kobKgj4U

'Werkschau Paul Wenninger' (2021) *Oktoskop.* Interviewed by L. Maurer. [TV Programme]. OKTO: May 23, 2021.

'Zeichentrickfilm 'Der kleine schwarze Fisch'' (1976) Österreich-Bild. [TV Programme]. ORF: August 27, 1976.

Confetti Clubbing (1999) [TV Programme]. ORF: November 21, 1999

Eventyret om dansk tegnefilm (2008) Directed and written by L. Jakobsen. [Video: DVD]. Forlaget Fabel.

Kurzschluss (2005) [TV Programme]. Arte: December 30, 2005.

Kurzschluss (2006) [TV Programme]. Arte: May 26, 2006.

Kurzschluss (2011) [TV Programme]. Arte: July 1, 2011.

Making of Es ist genau genug Zeit (2021) Directed by V. Widrich. [Online Video]. Available at: https://vimeo.com/559105311

Neues vom österreichischen Film (2002) Directed by G. Flossmann and H. Bergmann. [TV Programme]. ORF: November 11, 2002.

Österreichische Film-Tage Wels 1989 (1989) Directed and written by W. Wippersberg. [TV Programme]. ORF: November 20, 1989.

Sindelar, H.O. (2011a) 'Oral History Interview mit Hans Sindelar – 7. Teil'. Interviewed by M. Maier in Unterolberndorf, August 10. *Österreichische Mediathek.* Available at: https://www.mediathek.at/atom/14D4EB66-066-000EE-00000E84-14D435B8

Sindelar, H.O. (2011b) 'Oral History Interview mit Hans Sindelar – 8. Teil'. Interviewed by M. Maier in Unterolberndorf, August 10. *Österreichische Mediathek.* Available at: https://www.mediathek.at/atom/14D4EB84-2E7-000F0-00000E84-14D435B8

The Fantasy Film Worlds of George Pal (1985) Directed and written by A. Leibovit. [Video: DVD]. Image Entertainment.

The Roots of Japanese Anime until the End of WWII (2008) [Video: DVD]. Zakka Films.

ARCHIVAL DOCUMENTS

Abgangszeugnis Richard Dillenz (1919) Vienna: Art Collection and Archive, University of Applied Arts

Application from Mr Henryk Henenfeld for Nationalization (1946) PR_000003016847, HOME_POLITICAL_E_1946_NA_F-32-376. New Delhi: National Archives of India.

Arbeitsbuch Herta Cmyral (1940–45) Private Collection Matthias Markl.

Nationale Bruno Wozak (1918) Vienna: Art Collection and Archive, University of Applied Arts.

Nationale Johann Thomas (1918) Vienna: Art Collection and Archive, University of Applied Arts.

Zulassungskarte Prüf-Nr. 49012 der Film-Prüfstelle Berlin (1938) 'Laßt Farben sprechen', August 31. Berlin: Bundesarchiv (BArch).

Name Index

Note: *Italic* page numbers refer to figures and page numbers followed by "n" denote endnotes.

Title Index

Note: *Italic* page numbers refer to figures and page numbers followed by "n" denote endnotes.

Made in the USA
Las Vegas, NV
05 June 2025

566f913d-f0eb-4b24-bce9-bc39b2471827R01